To Know Wisdom
Meditations on Proverbs

by D. Marion Clark

Marion Clark

*The Lord's blessings
be with you
4/23/17*

ISBN-13:978-1540437945
ISBN-10: 1540437949

Printed in the United States of America

To Ginger

He who finds a wife finds a good thing
and obtains favor from the Lord.

(Proverb 18:22)

The Limit of Proverbs

Proverbs 1:1

The proverbs of Solomon, son of David, king of Israel:

This first verse is instructive. These proverbs are the results of Solomon's writings and his collection of ancient sayings. Consider this description of Solomon in 1 Kings 10:23: "Thus King Solomon excelled all the kings of the earth in riches and in wisdom. And the whole earth sought the presence of Solomon to hear his wisdom, which God had put into his mind." We know this is the result of God answering his prayer for wisdom to govern his people. Because Solomon asked for wisdom, God granted wisdom and riches and fame.

Solomon became a success, but like many who do achieve it, success becomes its own seductress. He became famous not only for wisdom but for his lavished lifestyle. Though he will warn young men in his proverbs of the danger of the forbidden woman, he will fall in love and marry "many foreign women...from the nations concerning which the Lord has said...You shall not enter into marriage with them..." He built and maintained grand building projects but at the expense of reducing his people to slave-like labor, so that their hardship became the grounds for a rebellion that split the kingdom. Finally, his foreign wives "turned away his heart after other gods, and his heart was not wholly true to the Lord his God, as was the heart of David his father" (1 Kings 11:4).

Let our first lesson in Proverbs be that it is not enough to hear wise sayings and to discipline ourselves to follow them, for we do not have the power to change our hearts, much less to remove them from the bondage of sin. That is the work of the Holy Spirit. Let us cling to Christ; let us go daily to the mercy throne of God; let us pray for the Spirit to daily strengthen us and sanctify us. These proverbs give us direction; they reveal the wisdom of the path of life. But no self-effort can suffice to follow that path. It is Christ who must be our Entrance to the path and our constant Pillar of Cloud and Fire to lead us. And it is the Spirit who must enable us to walk obediently. Pray even now that, as you learn wisdom, God's Spirit will enable you to live what you learn.

To Know Wisdom

Proverbs 1:2-4

To know wisdom and instruction,
  to understand words of insight,
to receive instruction in wise dealing,
  in righteousness, justice, and equity;
to give prudence to the simple,
  knowledge and discretion to the youth—

It is not enough to know your goal, be it to obtain financial security or to win the world for Christ. Knowing the goal is essential, but one must also be wise to attain it. We must have wisdom to understand the goal and its value. We must engage in wise dealing, knowing what pitfalls to avoid, how to speak in a way that wins our hearers. It is well enough to desire righteousness, justice, and equity – but to achieve such things in a world of sin takes shrewdness, for there are shrewd enemies.

Most of all we have to deal with the great obstacle of our own sinful nature. We may think we are for righteousness, justice, and equity, but it takes wisdom to recognize our selfishness and prejudices so that we can actually make progress. We need prudence and knowledge to protect ourselves from our own desires, desires that are fanned by the temptations of the world. Many an idealist has fallen because he failed to use prudence.

Many a Christian falls because he thinks being a Christian automatically makes him wise. Because he is a Christian surely his motives are in order, he thinks. He is baffled by how others get so easily offended and keep misinterpreting his words and behavior. He is even baffled by God allowing bad things to happen to him when he is living for the Lord!

Turning to Christ is but the beginning of turning to wisdom; following Christ is committing oneself to a lifetime of studying wisdom. Proverbs is a good instruction book for meditating on the wisdom needed to follow Christ and to be a useful servant.

Increase in Learning

Proverbs 1:5-6

Let the wise hear and increase in learning,
*   and the one who understands obtain guidance,*
to understand a proverb and a saying,
*   the words of the wise and their riddles.*

Note the supposition of Solomon. The wise can always increase in learning. They do not reach a stage of knowing all they need to know. Furthermore, it requires wisdom to learn. Two individuals may have the same mental faculties, but one is able to benefit from knowledge in a way the other does not. Why? One possesses the wisdom to know that he needs to learn more and the wisdom to discern what is worth learning. The other is foolish, thinking he already knows more than enough or else uses knowledge for foolish purposes. Thus, "let the wise hear and increase in learning."

Take these verses as a call to you to prepare your mind for learning and obtaining guidance. You want to know how to better communicate with your neighbors, how to deal wisely with the daily challenges of life, how to use your money properly, and so on. These proverbs will give you practical counsel in these things, but they will require of you thoughtful attention. You will have to think through what they are saying (some in riddles), discern their practical implications, and (the hardest work of all) examine your heart and life in light of them. You will have to ask yourself how you have played the fool and even the role of the wicked as described in these proverbs.

For as a person who grows in righteousness through sanctification

3

sees more clearly the depth of his sinfulness, so the person who grows in wisdom sees more clearly his foolishness.

The Fear of the Lord

Proverbs 1:7

The fear of the LORD is the beginning of knowledge;
  fools despise wisdom and instruction.

To have right knowledge, one must have a right perspective on reality. The skills of a mountain climber avail him nothing if the climber is ascending the wrong mountain. Indeed, they take him further away from the goal. Reality is grounded in God. Thus, knowledge begins with a right understanding of God. And yet, knowledge about God is not enough, as Satan has demonstrated. There are scholars who know more about Christian doctrine than most true believers, and yet they do not believe. And there are those who "sort of" believe, even have convinced themselves they do believe, but do not *fear* the Lord – the essence of belief.

One cannot know God and do not fear him; for even that small part that we can know should move us to acknowledge him as our Sovereign Ruler whom we exist to serve. To know God is to grasp that we live for his glory. To know God is to grasp that all creation exists for his glory. To fear God is not a mere matter of being a bit frightened by him as we would a supernatural being. Surely to be in the presence of God would be an unnerving experience as demonstrated by Isaiah and John. Surely we should tremble to be in the presence of Holiness. But the essence of biblical fear is about right relationship – the relationship of the Creator and his creatures.

It is this matter of relationship which accounts for the latter half of the proverb – that fools despise wisdom and instruction. They despise true wisdom and instruction because such things require that they know and accept a right relationship with their Maker. They must acknowledge God as Lord over them, and that is exactly what they refuse to do. Thus, however they may grow in mastering

4

information, they are in the same dilemma as the misguided mountain climber.

Keep this in mind as you study and meditate on these proverbs. For if you begin on any other path than the fear of the Lord, they will only help you move more easily along the wrong path. And how do we know the right path? By passing through the right Gate, Jesus Christ. In him alone will these proverbs take you along the path of true knowledge and righteousness.

Teach Your Children Well

Proverbs 1:8-9

Hear, my son, your father's instruction,
and forsake not your mother's teaching,
for they are a graceful garland for your head
and pendants for your neck.

This is a good lesson for parents and children. First to children: what you may regard as chains around your neck burdening and holding you down are really garlands and pendants to adorn you. Their instructions and rules are for your protection and your growing in maturity and wisdom – and wisdom is the finest of jewels. Their teachings which may appear to be outdated are based on principles that have stood the test of time, and much of what they have to teach they have learned from experience. Understand further that they have been entrusted by God with raising you according to his ways. It is a great responsibility and all the more reason then for you to listen to them *regardless of how well you think they follow their own rules*. You will be held accountable by God for how well you listened and obeyed godly instruction, regardless of your parents' ability to obey. You will be accountable for your own behavior.

Then to parents: see the great responsibility laid upon you. Are you indeed giving instruction that is graceful and valuable? Are you teaching the ways of the Lord? Are you teaching what it is to be just, to be godly, to be merciful? Or do you lay heavy burdens on the necks of your children that you yourself would not bear? And are you

5

living before your children the very principles that you teach them to observe? You must teach your children; you must give instruction. You cannot evade that responsibility. All the more then, study the Word of God, seek after wisdom, and follow what you teach.

And always point your children to the Word – Jesus Christ. Do not let them think that life is about following the right rules. Teach them the salvation found only in our Lord, and teach them to live by his grace and mercy.

True Victims of Crime

Proverbs 1:10-19

My son, if sinners entice you,
do not consent.
If they say, "Come with us, let us lie in wait for blood;
let us ambush the innocent without reason;
like Sheol let us swallow them alive,
and whole, like those who go down to the pit;
we shall find all precious goods,
we shall fill our houses with plunder;
throw in your lot among us;
we will all have one purse"—
my son, do not walk in the way with them;
hold back your foot from their paths,
for their feet run to evil,
and they make haste to shed blood.
For in vain is a net spread
in the sight of any bird,
but these men lie in wait for their own blood;
they set an ambush for their own lives.
Such are the ways of everyone who is greedy for unjust gain;
it takes away the life of its possessors.

The simple moral here is that crime does not pay. It is wrong to do evil even if it should pay, but it doesn't, especially for young men like those in this illustration who join in gangs and commit violence. It is only a matter of brief time that they will be thrown in jail or be beat up or killed. They do not realize that they are setting up their own violent trap.

But so is the way for any who are "greedy for unjust gain." Being greedy will hurt you. If your focus is on getting as much money as you can, you will take risks and make foolish decisions that will harm you. But being greedy for unjust gain, that is, by taking advantage of others, will all the more make your downfall certain as you create enemies (both of the wicked and the righteous) who become intent on revenge or justice.

Don't let making money be your ultimate goal. Don't choose careers because they will make you rich. If being rich becomes your goal, it will corrupt you, however moral you may start off. Greed will hurt you. It will take away your life.

And consider this: all who seek to gain heaven without the imputed righteousness of Christ are guilty of pursuing unjust gain. For heaven cannot be bought; it cannot be stolen; it cannot be earned; it cannot be acquired by one's own means. It must be received by Christ's work and as his gift.

Lady Wisdom

Proverbs 1:20-21

Wisdom cries aloud in the street,
  in the markets she raises her voice;
at the head of the noisy streets she cries out;
  at the entrance of the city gates she speaks:

Wisdom is cast as a woman contrasted with the forbidden woman who leads men astray. Men are attracted to the latter, but it is Wisdom who will prove to be of lasting value and delight.

Wisdom unabashedly goes out into the streets and public places trying to attract men. But instead of using "smooth words" like the forbidden woman and painting herself to appeal to lust, she proclaims truth. She "cries aloud," "raises her voice," and "cries out."

7

Note her earnestness, her zeal and sincerity as she tries to reason with the masses. Wisdom does not keep to herself. She is not reserved for intellectual speculation. She is meant to take part in the daily lives of common men and women.

Do you allow Wisdom to be manifest in your life on the streets and in the marketplace? Or do you keep her reserved for your religious life and worldly wisdom for daily life? Do you make the excuse that godly Wisdom will not work in the world? Will you today, as you walk along the street and go into the markets and through the city gates, heed the voice of Wisdom crying out to you to listen, to follow her, and to live out what she has to teach?

Where will the voice of Wisdom come from? From the Word of God, the Scriptures, which point to the Word made flesh. You will hear many voices claiming to be of God, but it is the voice of Wisdom that goes forth from God's Word that will be truly of God.

Refusing to Listen

Proverbs 1:22-25

"How long, O simple ones, will you love being simple?
How long will scoffers delight in their scoffing
   and fools hate knowledge?
If you turn at my reproof,
behold, I will pour out my spirit to you;
   I will make my words known to you.
Because I have called and you refused to listen,
   have stretched out my hand and no one has heeded,
because you have ignored all my counsel
   and would have none of my reproof,"

Why do fools fall? Because they love foolishness. The simple love playing the role. They find wisdom difficult to attain, and so they'd rather play the part of a simpleton than work at wisdom and fail. Scoffers delight in scoffing. They like to appear that they see through the surface of things and expose the falseness and silliness of others. But it is not truth they are after; they are in love with hearing themselves and being thought witty. Fools hate knowledge; or rather, they hate knowledge that is inconvenient, that would make them change the way they perceive reality and the way they live. Thus the truth about the simple, the scoffer, and the fool is not that they do not hear but that they refuse to listen.

They are like the fools of Paul Simon's song, "The Sound of Silence":
> "Fools," said I, "you do not know.
> "Silence like a cancer grows.
> "Hear my words that I might teach you.
> "Take my arms that I might reach you."
> But my words like silent raindrops fell
> And echoed in the well
> Of silence.

Pray for the Holy Spirit to change hearts so that ears may be willing to listen. Pray for your neighbors and family and colleagues. For they cannot, will not, hear the gospel without the work of the Holy Spirit. Wisdom can present truth; only the Spirit can make it heard.

The Disaster of the Fool

Proverbs 1:26-33

"I also will laugh at your calamity;
*   I will mock when terror strikes you,*
when terror strikes you like a storm
*   and your calamity comes like a whirlwind,*
*   when distress and anguish come upon you.*
Then they will call upon me, but I will not answer;
*   they will seek me diligently but will not find me.*
Because they hated knowledge
*   and did not choose the fear of the LORD,*
would have none of my counsel
*   and despised all my reproof,*
therefore they shall eat the fruit of their way,
*   and have their fill of their own devices.*
For the simple are killed by their turning away,
*   and the complacency of fools destroys them;*

but whoever listens to me will dwell secure
  and will be at ease, without dread of disaster."

The time will come for all fools when disaster strikes, and then it will be too late to turn to wisdom. The consequences of their folly cannot be avoided nor turned back. Wisdom, who had appealed to them almost shamelessly, will now mock them as they mocked her. They shall "eat the fruit of their way and have their fill of their own devices."

Why such a heartless response from Wisdom? Shouldn't she always be available to anyone who would turn to her? Shouldn't foolishness be pardonable when a fool comes to his senses? Three thoughts to note here. One, there must eventually be a point of no return. Disaster can be avoided only so many times. The day of Final Disaster (the Day of Judgment) will come. Folly must reap its consequences. The fools are given many times to repent. Wisdom goes daily into the streets calling out to fools to turn to her. Fools many times reap smaller consequences of their behavior that should have caused them to listen up. Fools will earn what they have ingrained in themselves.

Two, fools are in their position not because of mental deficiency but because of a willful attitude. They hate knowledge; they despise counsel and reproof. Teachers understand this. They know that what marks the achieving student from the failing student has little to do with ability and everything to do with motivation. Thus, the disaster coming upon fools is what they have brought upon themselves.

Three, fools choose not "the fear of the Lord." God does take folly personally because it is ultimately a rejection of him. The fool does not acknowledge God, or if he does so, he acknowledges God through conscious rebellion. This is what marks him a fool. The fool and the wicked are synonymous. A fool is wicked because he is rebelling against God; the wicked is a fool because it is foolish to rebel against the One who sees all things and will carry out justice.

Is it not ironic that we who do turn to God through Christ are counted as fools? But which would you rather have – to be counted a fool by the world or a fool by God? Pray for the foolish of the world

10

who are no different from us before the Spirit intervened. Pray for the Holy Spirit to make fools of the world into fools for Christ.

What You Value

Proverbs 2:1-4

My son, if you receive my words
and treasure up my commandments with you,
making your ear attentive to wisdom
and inclining your heart to understanding;
yes, if you call out for insight
and raise your voice for understanding,
if you seek it like silver
and search for it as for hidden treasures,

The precondition for wisdom is that you must desire it. You learn what you want to learn. A mechanic is baffled by how much knowledge a physician has about the body and is able to diagnose his problem. That same physician is baffled by the knowledge and ability of the mechanic to diagnose and fix his car's engine. The truth is that each is able to learn what he enjoys learning.

Even so, this illustration falls short of what the passage is fully conveying. It does not matter that one person does not take the same interest as another in regard to specialized knowledge. Indeed, that is the value of having different interests and mental capacity. We complement and help one another. But wisdom is not specialized knowledge, nor is it a mental process that one can do without. It is not dependent on advanced degrees.

What is needed is a desire for it. If you will pray for wisdom; if you will seek after wisdom through study and observation and through learning from others who are wise, then you will attain that wisdom necessary for well-being. For again, wisdom is not related to the amount of information you possess, but to being a keen observer, to having a prudent approach to situations that arise, to controlling your tongue, and so on. Wisdom is related to attitude. Do you want to act wisely?

And do you? When you look back over a day, can you conclude that your words and behavior were the result of wanting to act wisely or wanting to get your own way? What you want will determine what wisdom you will find.

The Source of Wisdom

Proverbs 2:5-8

then you will understand the fear of the LORD
*   and find the knowledge of God.*
For the LORD gives wisdom;
*   from his mouth come knowledge and understanding;*
he stores up sound wisdom for the upright;
*   he is a shield to those who walk in integrity,*
guarding the paths of justice
*   and watching over the way of his saints.*

If you truly seek wisdom, you will end up before the presence of God. That is where the path to wisdom leads you, for the Lord is the source of wisdom. If you are truly seeking wisdom, it is because God is leading you to do so and leading you along the path to himself. All the more, then, pray to him for wisdom; pray to him to lead you along the path of wisdom.

Once you come to God, know that he will then give to you from his storehouse of wisdom. He will furthermore protect you and watch over you. For just as wisdom is connected to a desire to live rightly, so it is connected with a desire to glorify God. Wisdom is not reduced to a body of information to master nor even to principles to observe. Wisdom is about glorifying God. The desire to glorify God is the essence of wisdom; it is the magnet that draws forth more wisdom because God gives wisdom to those who strive to glorify him. To "understand the fear of the Lord and find the knowledge of God" is to desire and know how to glorify God who then "gives wisdom" and "knowledge and understanding."

But key to all of this is coming to God through Christ, who is the

12

Truth, the Way, and the Life, who is the only door leading to God. There are many who appear to be wise; many who have much understanding and even appear to have wisdom about God. Nevertheless, they have not humbled themselves in Christ, recognizing their utter dependence upon the work of Christ. Until then, their "wisdom" only leads them astray from the Truth. In Christ alone will you find the knowledge of God and receive from the Lord true wisdom.

The Blessings of Wisdom

Proverbs 2:9-12

Then you will understand righteousness and justice
*   and equity, every good path;*
for wisdom will come into your heart,
*   and knowledge will be pleasant to your soul;*
discretion will watch over you,
*   understanding will guard you,*
delivering you from the way of evil,
*   from men of perverted speech,*

Far from being burdens, wisdom and its companions make great guests in your heart. Knowledge is pleasant to your soul. It enriches your life; it helps you to rise above the petty grievances and jealousies that make others miserable. It frees you from the anxiety that those who do not know God and his goodness cannot have. Discretion and understanding protect you from the evil purposes of the wicked. They keep you from stepping into danger that others blindly walk into, and they deliver you when you are in danger.

Again and again the proverbs show the fundamental fallacy of the foolish and wicked who forsake wisdom because they want to enjoy life. They look upon the wise and the righteous as those who choose being good over having pleasure. But the wise and the righteous are able to have both the good and the pleasurable, while the foolish and wicked lose whatever fleeting pleasure they grab after.

The good (righteous) path is the good (pleasurable) life, for it avoids

13

the pitfalls of the wicked and finds deeper, lasting pleasure that the wicked cannot begin to know. And that deeper, lasting pleasure is found in Jesus Christ, the very source of wisdom and knowledge.

Evil Men

Proverbs 2:12-15

delivering you from the way of evil,
  from men of perverted speech,
who forsake the paths of uprightness
  to walk in the ways of darkness,
who rejoice in doing evil
  and delight in the perverseness of evil,
men whose paths are crooked,
  and who are devious in their ways.

Yes, there are men out there who want to harm you and take advantage of you. They enjoy doing evil. They take pleasure in planning mischief; they are excited by the wicked deed; they look back with fond memory over their escapades. Perversion is fun. While we are fuming, "How could they...," they are congratulating one another and themselves over mischief well done.

This pleasure motivates them to use their skill and ingenuity to plot and carry out their mischief. The same individuals who drop out of school with failing grades will show a high level of creativity and complex thinking to do evil. The more motivated criminal mind will grow in knowledge for the purpose of stealing, destroying, and murdering. Con men make a living out of devising ways to part you from your money.

And as a predator who looks for the weak to pounce upon, so these wicked men look for the person who appears naive and unwilling to use discretion and wisdom for protection. The best way to protect yourself is not to live in the fear of man, but in the fear of the Lord (2:5). By such an approach to life, you will then find the wisdom of the Lord which he will give to you; and that wisdom will protect you. Your mind will become sharper; you will become more observant,

14

more discerning. Discretion will lead you away from much danger, and understanding will deliver you when danger is upon you.

Living in the fear of the Lord is not to live naively, "trusting" the Lord to take care of you regardless of you walking about blindly and without thought. Trusting the Lord is to avail yourself of the wisdom he reveals through his Word and through the Holy Spirit. Remember Jesus' words, "Be wise as serpents and innocent as doves" (Matt. 10:16).

The Forbidden Woman

Proverbs 2:16-19

So you will be delivered from the forbidden woman,
  from the adulteress with her smooth words,
who forsakes the companion of her youth
  and forgets the covenant of her God;
for her house sinks down to death,
  and her paths to the departed;
none who go to her come back,
  nor do they regain the paths of life.

This is the first mention of the "forbidden woman." It is significant that she is described here as one who forsakes and forgets. This is not a woman raised outside the faith but rather one raised as a covenant child, had confessed faith in the Lord, and married in the faith. What a tragic story. What led her astray? We are not told, but she is all the more dangerous for she has tasted the way of life and rejected it. She is all the more set against the righteous life, desirous to lead the righteous astray, and knowledgeable on how to do it with her smooth words. And those who fall into her trap are likely to end up like her, unable to regain the paths of life.

Whether or not the "forbidden woman" who is tempting you has the same history, she does have the same consequences. Therefore avail yourself of God-given wisdom and discretion and *stay away!* You are not given wisdom to win her over; you are given wisdom to protect yourself. Christian men and women are standing on the edge of adultery, rationalizing that they can keep from falling off. You can't! If you are standing on the edge now, avail yourself of discretion now and back off. Do what you must. Get help from others. Seek the prayer of others.

Proverbs will say this again. Sexual temptation is not a game; it is not a minor temptation; it is a primary weapon of Satan to entrap God's people and render them useless for the kingdom, even to shame God's kingdom. "Her house sinks down to death." *Back off now!*

The Path of the Good

Proverbs 2:20-22

So you will walk in the way of the good
and keep to the paths of the righteous.
For the upright will inhabit the land,
and those with integrity will remain in it,
but the wicked will be cut off from the land,
and the treacherous will be rooted out of it.

What do you gain by walking the path of the good? You gain the eternal inheritance of God's kingdom. The upright will inhabit the land of God's kingdom. He who is wise understands this inheritance. He who is wise looks to the heavenly city, not the earthly city, for his hope. He who is wise knows that the blessings and the curses of this life are a momentary joy or momentary sorrow compared to the "weight of glory" that is his in Jesus Christ (cf. 2 Cor. 4:17). That is why he is not racked with anxiety or with anger when confronted with the troubles of life. That is why he can walk along the path of the good. The wicked see only this life; their hope is only in what can be found in this life. That is why they are lured to the forbidden woman and steal and murder. And so when this life is ended for them, they are cut off from the eternal land of God's kingdom.

Do you seek the heavenly city, the eternal reward? Then walk along the path of the good. Keep your eyes straight ahead. Put your hope in Christ who has saved you for such an end. Call upon the Spirit who gives you the power to walk that path. Rely on God who has called

16

you such a destiny. Each day, remember the path you are to walk and the land that awaits you.

Remember and Keep

Proverbs 3:1-2

My son, do not forget my teaching,
    but let your heart keep my commandments,
for length of days and years of life
    and peace they will add to you.

How to live longer and healthier is vitally important in our society, especially to those entering retirement years. When we reach middle-age we begin to measure our life-span. We are at the halfway mark to death if we remain healthy. Now is the time to watch what we eat. We make some lifestyle changes that lessen stress. We read the innumerable articles and books that teach diet, exercise, spirituality, relationships, and so on that will help us achieve a long, healthy life.

There is nothing new under the sun. Proverbs is the ancient book on how to live such a life. Its secret formula is somewhat different from the modern approaches, for its "secret formula" is to live a morally good life, which is defined by righteousness, which is defined by keeping the commandments of God as revealed in Scripture, which are summed up as "the fear of the Lord."

Remember and keep. Many people forget the good principles and commandments taught them in their early years and so are led astray. Many remember these lessons but reject them in rebellion or like to think of themselves as outgrowing such childish beliefs. Remember and keep, or as the epistle of James says, hear and do (cf. Jas. 1:22-25). If we are not doers of the Word, we become forgetters of the Word. We may remember what we are taught, but we forget the power and the blessing of obedience. Like a former athlete, we remember what we performed but we forget the feeling of the performance – we forget how healthy we felt.

Remember and keep. Remember the commands of your Lord – of

your Lord Jesus Christ – and keep them. Remember his command to believe in him whom God the Father sent (John 6:29). Remember his instruction that if we love him, we will keep his commandments (John 14:15). Remember his own example, for he remembered all the commandments of his Father and kept them, that he might win our salvation. All the more then, we should remember and keep.

Love and Faithfulness

Proverbs 3:3-4

Let not steadfast love and faithfulness forsake you;
*   bind them around your neck;*
*   write them on the tablet of your heart.*
So you will find favor and good success
*   in the sight of God and man.*

These are new words in the Proverbs – steadfast love and faithfulness. Note the overall focus on steadiness. We are to have a love that is steadfast. This same term for love is repeated over and over again in the Psalms for the love of God. His love is a steadfast love based on his covenant promise which he will not break. Faithfulness – keeping one's promise to keep a relationship and commitment – is also used often for God. Indeed, God's steadfast love and faithfulness form the basis for hope and confidence for God's covenant people. They can count on God to come through with his promises even though they stumble and fail to keep their promises.

But this proverb is not teaching that it is okay to fail to keep steadfast love and faithfulness. It makes the point that as much as one is able to keep these attributes, then he can expect to find favor and good success in the sight of God and man. For people respect a person who keeps steady, especially who loves with a steady love; a person who can be counted on to keep his word and does not change with the direction of the wind.

Such attributes are to be bound around the neck and written in the heart. How do you do this? By meditation on God's Word that teaches what love is and to what we are to be faithful; by daily prayer for love and faithfulness; and by conscious obedience. Like any habit, it is repetition that ingrains an attribute in us. Practice love and faithfulness. Make such qualities priorities in your life. Just as you make time for what is truly important to you, so it is with these attributes. You will work at loving and being faithful if they matter to you.

How important are they? Important enough that they identify God's relationship to us in Christ. For Christ was obedient to his Father so that steadfast love might be shown to us.

Trust in the Lord

Proverbs 3:5-6

Trust in the LORD with all your heart,
and do not lean on your own understanding.
In all your ways acknowledge him,
and he will make straight your paths.

Here is the guide to life for the Christian: *Trust in the Lord with all your heart.* Trust God in all circumstances to know what he is doing, to keep his promises, to bring all things to a conclusion that serves our good and glorifies him. Trust his commandments; trust his written Word; trust his Redeemer Jesus Christ for your salvation. Trust the Holy Spirit to complete the "good work" of sanctification begun in you and to keep you till the day of Christ's return.

Do not lean on your own understanding. Seek the wisdom of God laid out in his Word. Meditate on and study diligently the Scriptures, which will make you wise unto salvation.

In all your ways acknowledge him. Acknowledge God at work in your life, especially through the trials of life. Acknowledge that all your ways are to be the ways of the Lord, following along the path of righteousness. You live for God not for yourself. Every decision is to be made with the thought of serving him and glorifying him.

And he will make straight your paths. You cannot make your own paths straight. It is only by turning your life over to him – by daily turning it over to him – that you will keep along God's path. The path may be difficult at times to walk, but it will not lead you astray as the paths you create inevitably will.

Trust in the Lord Jesus Christ with all of your heart, and he will lead you along the path of righteousness by the power of the Holy Spirit to your heavenly Father.

Healing and Refreshment

Proverbs 3:7-8

Be not wise in your own eyes;
    fear the LORD, and turn away from evil.
It will be healing to your flesh
    and refreshment to your bones.

Verse 7 presents a good definition of humility. First, be not wise in your own eyes. This is not false humility but recognition of your limits. The essence of wisdom is recognizing how little you know. There are many scholars and persons of high intellect who nevertheless are fools because they overestimate their knowledge and their ability to use that knowledge wisely.

Second, fear the Lord. Acknowledge the one who is all-wise, who knows all things, and who does accomplish his will. Acknowledge him and obey him. Third, turn away from evil. The humble person knows that if he does not turn away from evil, it will draw him in and lead to his undoing. He does not trust his ability to withstand temptation.

This humble attitude leads to well-being by keeping you out of trouble, by leading you along a peaceful path often outwardly and especially inwardly. The way of the Lord is the way of healing and refreshment.

Firstfruits

Proverbs 3:9-10

Honor the LORD with your wealth
*   and with the firstfruits of all your produce;*
then your barns will be filled with plenty,
*   and your vats will be bursting with wine.*

This proverb is referring to tithing the firstfruits of all your produce. We talk about giving all of ourselves to the Lord and yet somehow find it difficult to part with ten percent of our income. Surely it matters how we spend all of our money, and we give to the Lord by being financially responsible, taking care of our families, and so on. But it requires faith and discipline to let go of a portion of our money as we earn it. We must trust the Lord to provide. We must give attention to how we spend the remainder. We must acknowledge that we owe to the Lord everything, that he has a right to us and what we have.

Will we then be blessed with plenty? It is more likely to happen than if we hoard what we have. Time and again the proverbs link earthly reward with righteousness and the fear of God. The blessing of the Lord is not measured by earthly prosperity; nevertheless, prosperity often comes as a byproduct. As we focus on honoring the Lord, he blesses his people. It may not always be through physical prosperity, but do not be surprised if it does come. All the more then do not let that prosperity lead you astray, but honor the Lord giving him the firstfruits of your produce.

God's Discipline

Proverbs 3:11-12

My son, do not despise the LORD's discipline
*   or be weary of his reproof,*
for the LORD reproves him whom he loves,
*   as a father the son in whom he delights.*

Are you experiencing trials at this time? Do you feel like you are going through a specially difficult time? Then consider the "devotional" written by the writer of Hebrews on this proverb.

> *It is for discipline that you have to endure. God is treating you as sons. For what son is there whom his father does not discipline? If you are left without discipline, in which all have participated, then you are illegitimate children and not sons. Besides this, we have had earthly fathers who disciplined us and we respected them. Shall we not much more be subject to the Father of spirits and live? For they disciplined us for a short time as it seemed best to them, but he disciplines us for our good, that we may share his holiness. For the moment all discipline seems painful rather than pleasant, but later it yields the peaceful fruit of righteousness to those who have been trained by it* (12:7-11).

We are disciplined for a reason. God is correcting us. We are not merely to get through our trial; we are to come out of it having learned a lesson and stronger for it. Do not make the mistake of thinking that the lesson is seeing more clearly the sins of others. Discipline is for the purpose of correcting our own sins. What is it that God would have you see about yourself? Do the difficult work of examining yourself. It is that difficult work which yields the peaceful fruit of righteousness.

Value of Wisdom

Proverbs 3:13-15

Blessed is the one who finds wisdom,
and the one who gets understanding,
for the gain from her is better than gain from silver
and her profit better than gold.
She is more precious than jewels,
and nothing you desire can compare with her.

Essential for a meaningful life is knowing what to value. The cause of much unhappiness is prizing things that are either of little value or even harmful. To set great value on objects will lead to distress. You can experience the pain of losing an object, or the anxiety of holding on to it, or the restlessness of finding that it does not satisfy your pleasure. To value specific achievements causes trouble. You sacrifice and work hard to achieve your goal; then you get injured or sick and your long anticipated achievement is lost. You work hard only to find a competitor who still beats you because you are not quite good enough. Or you fail because you were cheated or fate just didn't go your way. Or you reach your goal only to find new pressure to stay at the top, to keep your fortune.

The value of wisdom is that, first, she is of true value. Her value has nothing to do with how much others desire her; she is not subjected to fashion and ratings. She does not have to be kept locked up. Insurance is not needed to protect her as an investment. She resides easily in the possession of the poor as well as of the wealthy. There is no competition to fight against to obtain her. She resides easily in the possession of the under-educated as well as the highly-educated. The very possession of her increases peace and security rather than heightens worry about losing her. And the more that wisdom is spent, all the more then that wisdom increases.

How odd then that wisdom is so little valued, and when she is valued, it is only as a means to attain something trivial or of great risk. To gain wisdom first understand her value. Treat her with respect and know the blessing that she brings.

Tree of Life

Proverbs 3:16-18

Long life is in her right hand;
in her left hand are riches and honor.
Her ways are ways of pleasantness,
and all her paths are peace.
She is a tree of life to those who lay hold of her;
those who hold her fast are called blessed.

Wisdom proves her value. She provides long life. She keeps the possessor out of danger and provides discernment for knowing how to live a healthy life. She provides riches and honor. Through her the possessor makes wise decisions on the use of his money and teaches him not to waste his money on things that do not satisfy. By wisdom he receives recognition and respect from his neighbors.

Wisdom leads the possessor along the ways of pleasantness. He values and experiences those things that are good for the soul, uplifting for the spirit, and helpful to the body and mind. He walks along wisdom's path of peace. Guided by her he finds inner peace and learns to live peacefully with his neighbors. She provides an abundant, blessed life full of rich memories.

But understand the true value of wisdom. She leads the possessor to God who provides eternal life. Through wisdom the possessor has the eyes to see who Jesus Christ truly is and to embrace him. Through wisdom he finds pleasantness and peace in Christ who has reconciled him to God.

Wisdom is the tree of life, because wisdom is the Holy Spirit granting eternal life in Christ. The Spirit reveals to us the mysteries of God that he chooses to reveal in Christ and in his written Word. It is the Spirit who makes us wise to comprehend the Gospel and the Scriptures. It is the Spirit who convicts us of sin and gives us faith. It is the Spirit who applies the blessing of God.

Creative Wisdom

Proverbs 3:19-20

The LORD by wisdom founded the earth;
by understanding he established the heavens;
by his knowledge the deeps broke open,
and the clouds drop down the dew.

Consider this proverb from two perspectives. For one, we are to understand that creation is not a cosmic happen-chance. It is the work of God, the intentional work of God. He founded the earth; he established the heavens, and brought forth the seas, rivers, and lakes. We are not here by chance. The universe may be immense and the earth by comparison nothing but a speck; but it was created by the Lord of the universe for his good purposes.

Creation also gives us a perspective about God. Its beauty, complexity, even its terror reveals a God of wisdom, understanding, and knowledge that go far beyond man's ability to attain. God's act of creating and sustaining the earth (and the universe) should impress upon us not to question his deeds and purposes. "Who has measured the waters in the hollow of his hand and marked off the heavens with a span, enclosed the dust of the earth in a measure and weighted the mountains in scales and the hills in a balance?" asks Isaiah (Isa. 40:12). Who then proposes to counsel God? "Where were you when I laid the foundation of the earth? Tell me, if you have understanding," God asks of Job (Job 38:4). We actually do know more than Job or Isaiah about the world. But the deeper we delve into knowledge, the deeper we find the sea of complexity to be and the more marvelous creation is.

It is interesting that the proverb says nothing about God's power. Surely creation testifies to the power of God, but let us take away one more lesson. Without wisdom power is nothing more than brute force. Without knowledge the deeps break open and destroy. We so often strive for power to overcome our obstacles, when what we really need is the wisdom and knowledge to understand those obstacles. We want power to do good oftentimes before we understand what is good. Seek wisdom; seek knowledge. You will then learn how to use the power God gives.

Wisdom and Discretion

Proverbs 3:21-24

My son, do not lose sight of these—
keep sound wisdom and discretion,
and they will be life for your soul
and adornment for your neck.
Then you will walk on your way securely,

and your foot will not stumble.
If you lie down, you will not be afraid;
  when you lie down, your sleep will be sweet.

To lie down and not be afraid – now that is a blessing indeed. To lie down and not worry about who is out to get you; not to worry about how the bills will be paid; not to worry about what will happen tomorrow – that is a blessing we would be happy to pay for.

And we do try. We work hard to get money to buy security through a solid bank account and a nice home. We buy contentment through a nice sound system and through exotic travel destinations. We invest heavily in security and peace through clinging desperately to relationships. We even try to buy sweet sleep through pills to dull our senses.

But sweet, peaceful sleep comes not through earnest effort but from wisdom and discretion. For security rests not in building defense systems and accumulating objects or even people; security comes from knowing what matters; it comes from knowing the One who created us, who holds us in his hands. Peace comes from knowing the peace of our Redeemer who did the hard work on our behalf. Security and peace comes from knowing to whom we belong, who he is, and what he intends for us.

Pray for such wisdom and discretion to know what is of eternal value and what really does not matter. As you attain such knowledge, as you adorn wisdom and discretion around your neck, then you walk on your way securely and lie down without fear.

Confidence in the Lord

Proverbs 3:25-26

Do not be afraid of sudden terror
  or of the ruin of the wicked, when it comes,
for the LORD will be your confidence
  and will keep your foot from being caught.

It is the suddenness of destruction that strikes fear in us. One moment all is well; another moment and terror comes. And so will be the Day of Judgment. It will come suddenly, but it will come upon the wicked. And though we may feel its impact, yet we will be safe because the Lord who brings the judgment is also our protector.

Let us not be afraid as though we were not followers of Christ. We have a Redeemer who has saved us from the guilt of our sins. We have a Savior who has clothed us in his righteousness. We have a High Priest who intercedes for us. He will keep our feet from being caught in the same net as the wicked.

Can sudden trouble come upon us? Yes, but we cannot be caught in the net that drags us to destruction. What matters most – the eternal security of our souls – is what lies most secure. Upon that basis we do not fear. We can be harmed, but we cannot be destroyed. Whatever sudden troubles may come upon us, know that there is a greater sudden phenomenon that will take place: the sudden appearing of our Lord who will bring us into eternal glory.

Doing Good

Proverbs 3:27

Do not withhold good from those to whom it is due,
    when it is in your power to do it.

Break this into three parts. First, we are told not to withhold good. We tend the think that as long as we are not doing evil, then we are being good. But here we are commanded not to withhold good. Apparently, we are guilty of transgression simply by letting an opportunity to do good go by. We kill by not coming to someone's aid. We steal by withholding a good deed.

Secondly, we are to do good to those for whom it is due. To whom do we owe good deeds? Sounds like a question once asked of Jesus: Who is my neighbor? If we follow Jesus' answer to this question given in the parable of the Good Samaritan, we have to conclude that the person to whom it is due is whatever person God places along our path. As soon as we try to determine who is worthy of receiving good, we get into trouble. For to judge anyone as unworthy of receiving good from us is to place ourselves in a position of higher value than a fellow human being.

Finally, there is the condition of knowing when it is in your power to do good. When is good in our power? This takes discernment. Doing good is always in our power, and it is always in our power to act in a good manner. Yet, where Christians get into trouble is not discerning what the good is that the other person needs and sometimes not discerning one's own ability to meet those needs. We can enable others to maintain sinful patterns through our good intentions. We can also harm ourselves or our families in our unwise actions. Be ready to do good to anyone but use wisdom so that you are truly helping the person in need without bringing harm to others (such as your family members).

Give Today

Proverbs 3:28

Do not say to your neighbor, "Go, and come again,
tomorrow I will give it"—when you have it with you.

The previous proverb instructs us not to put off doing good. This proverb tells us not to delay doing what we can. The most effective means to avoid doing good for our neighbor is to procrastinate. Tomorrow usually ends up being never. But even if we do intend to help the next day, we should not delay what we can do today. Why?

First, when God gives us opportunity to serve him, we should not delay. Remember, whatever good we do for another we are doing it as to the Lord. Why, then, would we hold off serving our Lord for another day?

Another reason is that we do not know what the next day will bring. We do not control our future. Anything can happen to us and to our neighbor to prevent the opportunity from coming again.

Related to this, we are to do good today while we have it with us. The "it" may be money or some object that our neighbor needs. We have the possession now; we may not have it tomorrow. The "it" can also be our ability. Now we have the sharpness of mind to be of real help; tomorrow we may not. Now we have the physical energy and strength necessary for the task; tomorrow we may not. Give now when you have it with you because you don't know when you will lose what you have.

Finally, do good and give help now because that is what you would want. Nothing is more disheartening than to ask for help and to be put off when we know our neighbor has the means to help us. When we ask for help we want it now, and to be told to come back the next day not only inconveniences us, it discourages our spirits.

Today, if your neighbor asks for help, will you give? Will you do good today while you have it within you?

Being a Good Neighbor

Proverbs 3:29

Do not plan evil against your neighbor,
  who dwells trustingly beside you.

This is certainly a heinous act. It is terrible to do wrong to anyone, but especially against your neighbor who dwells trustingly beside you. Aren't we glad we are not like that!

Have we never desired for our neighbors, when they have offended us, to get their just desserts? Are we guilty of imposing motivations and intentions on our neighbors for actions that bother us? "He slammed that door on purpose." "She knows I hate hearing her dog bark." "They love to disturb us with their parties."

We may not plan evil, but then we are guilty of not planning good, which may be the same thing in God's eyes. We don't invite them into our homes. We don't bring over food to encourage them. We don't do unto them as we want done for ourselves. Instead, we plan to avoid them, plan to complain to them or about them, maybe even to sue them. We plan not to lift a hand to help them. Is this not evil – to withhold good when it is in our power to give it?

And our reasoning is that we are only seeking what is fair. Give thanks to God that he sought not what was fair in regard to us but what was merciful.

The Contenders

Proverbs 3:30

Do not contend with a man for no reason,
  when he has done you no harm.

Do not pick a fight. It seems an easy enough rule to follow, and yet we transgress it more than we may think. We don't consciously say to ourselves that we want to start a fight, but then our actions may reveal more than we care to admit. Just trying to have a little fun, we tease someone and are "surprised" that he would take it so seriously.

Some of us take pride in speaking our mind, letting people know where we stand. Or to say it another way, we are ready to take anyone on. We contend for no reason when we speak or act rudely. We make unnecessary remarks about a person's appearance or cut in front of another car or a person standing in line. We are contending, riling up another person unnecessarily.

This proverb does not forbid contending; it forbids contending against someone who is not doing us harm. There are enough times when we are to contend for the sake of justice, to have truth be heard, and in proper self-defense. All the more then we are not to contend when it is uncalled for. Otherwise, the appropriate times to contend lose their effectiveness because we are regarded as contentious persons anyhow. "That's the way _____ is. Just ignore him."

Christians should be known as those slow to anger and slow to cause anger. It is laid upon us to contend for the sake of the gospel. Thus,

to be known as people who contend for the sake of trivial matters –
and especially to contend without cause – embarrasses our witness
for the gospel of Christ. As much as is possible, let us today be at
peace for the sake of the gospel.

Envy

Proverbs 3:31

Do not envy a man of violence
  and do not choose any of his ways,

Do not envy a person who violates the law of God. Our society
exalts violence. TV shows are as popular according to the amount of
violence, promiscuity, and rancor that can be displayed. Reality shows
are only as interesting as the producers are able to manipulate conflict
among the contestants. Shows awarded for being cutting edge are
shows that glamorize the mob, other forms of violence, and
promiscuity. Notoriety is the preferred form of fame and the easiest
path to take to popularity. Those who are notorious are hailed for
their independence and their boldness. Radio and TV talk show hosts
reach success by being rancorous.

Do not envy such persons. Do not exalt them. And definitely do not
copy them. Envy the man of peace, the person who strives to serve
God, the individual who is marked by humility. Envy the person who
possesses wisdom, the one who follows God's royal command to
love his neighbor as himself. Envy the person who is content.

Envy the person who loves Jesus Christ because he knows the peace
of Christ.

Our Status before God

Proverbs 3:32

for the devious person is an abomination to the LORD,
  but the upright are in his confidence.

Do not choose the ways of a devious person because in so doing you put yourself at odds with the Lord. The sinner forgets this all important factor. The person who loves to "stir things up," who finds it amusing to take advantage of others must stand before the Almighty God who will not be mocked, who will act in justice. He sees all of our schemes, and as Psalm 2:4 explains, "He who sits in the heavens laughs; the Lord holds them in derision." No one gets away with anything.

Note how our offenses are described. They are an abomination to the Lord. He does not find sin amusing, though he laughs in derision at our arrogance. Violence and devious scheming are an abomination to him. He takes sin personally as an affront to his righteousness and holiness. Pray for the wicked; pray they will come to their senses and repent. For judgment that they cannot escape awaits them.

But the upright, take heart that you are in God's confidence. You are looked upon with affection; you are considered God's friend.

And yet you say, "But I too sin and am as guilty as the most notorious sinner." You would be guilty if not for the grace bestowed upon you through Jesus Christ who bore your sin and gave to you his righteousness. Through Christ, God remains "just and the justifier of the one who has faith in Jesus" (Rom. 3:26). In Christ you are counted as upright.

Incredible? Are you unworthy? Yes! Yes! Give humble praise to your God now who has shown and continues to show his steadfast love through Jesus Christ our Lord.

True Blessing

Proverbs 3:33

The LORD's curse is on the house of the wicked,
but he blesses the dwelling of the righteous.

Rewards and trials fall on us throughout our lives. Consider then by what manner you most want to receive them and from whom.

What is the blessing that God gives to the righteous? He may or may not give physical health and prosperity. The proverbs teach that the righteous typically can expect better health, longer life, and greater prosperity; even so, those are the natural results of godly living. The righteous, along with the wicked, do suffer illness, die early deaths, and struggle to pay bills. What then is the blessing they can expect that the wicked cannot have?

There is eternal salvation – eternal bliss living in the presence of God and his favor, eternal worship in the midst of multitudes of his saints, the freedom from all suffering, the freedom from ever committing, even contemplating, a sin.

There is the present blessing of this assured hope; the blessing of God's revealed Word which fills us with knowledge of our God, of his salvation, and of his instruction for life; the blessing of possessing the Holy Spirit who gives us the ability to please God and to resist sin; the blessing of the gospel of Christ which assures us of forgiveness when we do sin; the blessing of Christian fellowship and of ministering in the name of Christ; the blessing of knowing what is true, what is good; the blessing of seeing the beauty of creation and knowing the Creator.

The list can go on. The point is to know what is true blessing and from whom you want to receive it. Jesus spoke of the Pharisees who displayed their religiosity in public so as to receive acclaim. He said that they have received the reward they will get. Seek not after temporal blessing that ends in judgment. Seek the blessing of God that enters into the dwelling of your heart now and lasts through eternity.

Scorn and Favor

Proverbs 3:34

Toward the scorners he is scornful,
but to the humble he gives favor.

The difference between God's scorn and that of the scorners is that God's is just and directed towards those who deserve it. The scorners in this proverb are those who scorn what is good. We see this everywhere in the world where the righteous and the moral are mocked. The Ten Commandments are ridiculed. The biblical standards for sexual relations and for marriage are belittled. Students and business people laugh at those who will not cheat. But God is not bemused by their humor and he will hold them accountable.

Those who do follow God's laws do so out of humility. They understand that there is a law above themselves. And like children who trust their father to know what is best, they humbly obey him. Thus God bestows his favor upon them.

From whom would you rather receive favor, and from whom are you more willing to receive scorn?

Honor

Proverbs 3:35

The wise will inherit honor,
but fools get disgrace.

The wise inherit the honor often received for showing good judgment, rendering fair decisions, and coming up with good solutions. It is one thing to be famous, yet another to be liked, and another to be honored. Fools can be popular and liked (as can foolish activities such as TV programs) even as they are recognized as fools.

But the true honor, which the wise inherit and for which they strive, is the honor received from the Lord. Is there any greater honor than to hear the words, "Well done, good and faithful servant"? Is there any greater glory than that bestowed by the King of Glory?

Fools see only what their eyes can see, only what is temporary. The wise see what is unseen, what is permanent. Thus they look to an inheritance that is eternal, that cannot be destroyed or stolen, and for which they are guarded, because in the wisdom granted them they

34

have become not mere servants, but the sons of God who inherit eternal life. He will guard them so that they will receive that inheritance.

A Father's Counsel

Proverbs 4:1-9

Hear, O sons, a father's instruction,
and be attentive, that you may gain insight,
for I give you good precepts;
do not forsake my teaching.
When I was a son with my father,
tender, the only one in the sight of my mother,
he taught me and said to me,
"Let your heart hold fast my words;
keep my commandments, and live.
Get wisdom; get insight;
do not forget, and do not turn away from the words of my mouth.
Do not forsake her, and she will keep you;
love her, and she will guard you.
The beginning of wisdom is this: Get wisdom,
and whatever you get, get insight.
Prize her highly, and she will exalt you;
she will honor you if you embrace her.
She will place on your head a graceful garland;
she will bestow on you a beautiful crown."

Ah, a father passing on to his son the words passed to him by his father on the subject of how to handle a woman! If only fathers would be so diligent to speak about this woman. They would surely pass on a lasting legacy that would bless their sons. For Wisdom is truly to be treasured. She cannot be prized too highly; she cannot be given too much attention. For the more she is embraced, the more blessed is our friendship with others. The more we love her, the more we will love God and our neighbor, including our closest loved ones. Honoring her leads to honor.

Today and every day, pray to get Wisdom. Contemplate her beauty;

strive after her. Study the Word that you might know her more deeply. Observe your circumstances, looking for her in your experiences. Above all, fear and love the Lord, which is the beginning of Wisdom.

Hold On

Proverbs 4:10-13

Hear, my son, and accept my words,
that the years of your life may be many.
I have taught you the way of wisdom;
I have led you in the paths of uprightness.
When you walk, your step will not be hampered,
and if you run, you will not stumble.
Keep hold of instruction; do not let go;
guard her, for she is your life.

All that the father here can do is instruct, admonish, and exhort. He can provide words. But the son must accept those words. The son must walk in the wisdom and knowledge taught him. He must keep hold of instruction and guard her.

As a high school principal and teacher, I discovered that the biggest barrier to learning is the student's own attitude toward learning. The student not motivated to learn will do poorly regardless of ability; conversely, the motivated student will rise to the occasion. Profiting from instruction is a heart issue. That is why God will not accept ignorance as an excuse for sin and for unbelief. If you desire God; if you seek true wisdom, then you will hold on to the instruction in God's Word.

The result of such motivation is life. To let go of instruction – be it out of rebellion or laziness – is to end up with death. Hold on to instruction; hold on to the Truth that is Jesus Christ.

Get Away!

Proverbs 4:14-15

Do not enter the path of the wicked,
  and do not walk in the way of the evil.
Avoid it; do not go on it;
  turn away from it and pass on.

Can the instruction from Scripture be any clearer regarding our attitude toward wickedness? Why then do we delight in entertainment that glorifies violence and immorality? Why do we put ourselves in compromising situations? Why do we flirt with danger? We excuse ourselves claiming we know what boundaries not to cross or that we hope to be good witnesses or to understand the world better.

Scripture is clear – don't go there! As sinners, we will stray into the way of the evil if we take a look. We are weaker than we appear to ourselves; our heart is more corrupt than we take it for. Even if we are called to minister to those caught up in wickedness, all the more precaution we are to take in protecting ourselves from getting entangled. Many a Christian has yielded to the very sin he has tried to rescue others from. Don't trust in your own willpower.

Flee from sin and flee to Christ!

The Happy Wicked

Proverbs 4:16-17

For they cannot sleep unless they have done wrong;
  they are robbed of sleep unless they have made someone stumble.
For they eat the bread of wickedness
  and drink the wine of violence.

Here we are given insight into the psyche of the wicked. When we come across crime, especially something like vandalism, we ask how someone could do such a thing, as though the perpetrators' conscience should be troubling them. Not only are they not troubled; they are delighted by their mischief. They feel powerful; their self-esteem is strengthened as they accomplish a goal through their ingenuity and skill.

They delight in taking advantage of others. Violence is one means; deception and theft are others. Cheating is honored. For the wicked, these things are achievements. All the more reason to avoid the wicked, both in terms of being victims and in associating with them.

Can the wicked change? God can change anyone. But don't be foolish enough to think that if you hang around in a wicked crowd, you will be the good influence that changes them. More likely they will change you before you realize what is happening, or you get caught in a compromising situation, or you become their victim.

Righteous Light

Proverbs 4:18-19

But the path of the righteous is like the light of dawn,
*   which shines brighter and brighter until full day.*
The way of the wicked is like deep darkness;
*   they do not know over what they stumble.*

Consider in two ways how the light of dawn comes. The path of the righteous is lighted for them as they walk in obedience. Isaiah 58:6-8 says:

> Is not this the fast that I choose:
>   to loose the bonds of wickedness,
>   to undo the straps of the yoke,
> to let the oppressed go free,
>   and to break every yoke?
> Is it not to share your bread with the hungry
>   and bring the homeless poor into your house;
> when you see the naked, to cover him,
>   and not to hide yourself from your own flesh?
> Then shall your light break forth like the dawn,
>   and your healing shall spring up speedily;
> your righteousness shall go before you;
>   the glory of the LORD shall be your rear guard.

As the righteous practice justice and righteousness, so the Lord promises to be their guide: "And the Lord will guide you continually" (Is. 58:11). But the very obedience of the righteous becomes itself light which shine brighter and brighter. It breaks through the darkness of injustice and wickedness, exposing what is unjust and revealing what is good, right, and true.

It is such light by which Christians are to walk and which we are to display, as instructed in Ephesians 5:8-14:

> ...for at one time you were darkness, but now you are light in the Lord. Walk as children of light (for the fruit of light is found in all that is good and right and true), and try to discern what is pleasing to the Lord. Take no part in the unfruitful works of darkness, but instead expose them. For it is shameful even to speak of the things that they do in secret. But when anything is exposed by the light, it becomes visible, for anything that becomes visible is light. Therefore it says,
> "Awake, O sleeper,
> and arise from the dead,
> and Christ will shine on you."

That last line reveals where our light comes from. We were the people characterized in Matthew 4:16 (which translates Isaiah 9:2):

> ...the people dwelling in darkness
>   have seen a great light,
> and for those dwelling in the region and shadow of death,
>   on them a light has dawned.

The light of Christ has dawned on us. Now we are to shine forth his light through our obedience to him. Will you shine forth Christ's light in the darkness of this world at your workplace or school?

Springs of Life

Proverbs 4:20-23

My son, be attentive to my words;
  incline your ear to my sayings.
Let them not escape from your sight;
  keep them within your heart.
For they are life to those who find them,
  and healing to all their flesh.
Keep your heart with all vigilance,
  for from it flow the springs of life.

"Where did that come from?" we will ask when we have surprised ourselves with an inappropriate remark or action. It came from the heart where it was lurking deep within. Jesus taught as much when he said, "What comes out of a person is what defiles him" (Mark 7:20). In like manner, we may be surprised how we have risen to the occasion and spoken or acted in some generous manner. Our proverbs explain that we are to take care of the heart through diligence in studying the wisdom of God's Word. Just as our body is impacted by the flow of blood pumped through the heart, and thus we are to care for the physical heart, so our lives are impacted by what flows out of the spiritual heart, and we need to provide good care for it.

Thus we need to daily read and meditate upon God's Word. We need to continually be instructing our heart by that Word. But instruction also includes Word-informed teaching. And so we should be reading sound Christian books, listening to biblical preachers and teachers, and listening to solid Christian music. By being attentive to such words and keeping them within our heart, we shall not only find life and healing for ourselves, but become a source for springs of life for others.

Just Don't Do It

Proverbs 4:24-27

Put away from you crooked speech,
  and put devious talk far from you.
Let your eyes look directly forward,

and your gaze be straight before you.
Ponder the path of your feet;
  then all your ways will be sure.
Do not swerve to the right or to the left;
  turn your foot away from evil.

Just don't do it. Don't try to fit in with the speech of the unrighteous. Don't talk behind the backs of others under pretense of seeking justice or their good. Don't visit places of temptation in order to understand the needs of sinners. Don't try to fit in with the unrighteous by telling their jokes, speaking their language, and living by their morals.

Keep your eyes on Christ – on his sacrifice for you, on his love for you, on his commands to follow him, on the hope of his return and reward. Follow the example of the Apostle Paul:

> Not that I have already obtained this or am already perfect, but I press on to make it my own, because Christ Jesus has made me his own. Brothers, I do not consider that I have made it my own. But one thing I do: forgetting what lies behind and straining forward to what lies ahead, I press on toward the goal for the prize of the upward call of God in Christ Jesus (Phil. 3:12-14).

The Forbidden Woman

Proverbs 5:1-6

My son, be attentive to my wisdom;
  incline your ear to my understanding,
that you may keep discretion,
  and your lips may guard knowledge.
For the lips of a forbidden woman drip honey,
  and her speech is smoother than oil,
but in the end she is bitter as wormwood,
  sharp as a two-edged sword.
Her feet go down to death;
  her steps follow the path to Sheol;

she does not ponder the path of life;
   her ways wander, and she does not know it.

Interestingly enough the first characteristic of the forbidden woman is the way she communicates. This happens in each section where she is brought up: 2:16, she is the adulteress with her smooth words; 6:24, the smooth tongue of the adulteress; 7:5, the adulteress with her smooth words. We can see then the contrast being set up. It is between vying ways of life – that offered by wisdom and the other offered by sensuality, or rather, folly. What seems to be a choice between stoicism and sensual pleasure is really between deeper, lasting pleasure and bitter delusion. The forbidden woman's speech seems sweet and smooth, and for a while she may seem to deliver on her promises; but in the end her taste is bitter and even deadly. Why? Because she herself is a fool, and as Proverbs 10:10 notes, a babbling fool will come to ruin. Unlike the wise and the righteous, she does not ponder the path of life. She does not contemplate what truth is and what does bring real life. Indeed, she is oblivious to where her life choices are taking her. And as Proverbs 13:20 warns, the companion of fools will suffer harm. Join up with the forbidden woman, and you will join in with her destruction.

Who is the forbidden woman? She may well be a woman tempting you to adultery. She is also the sex industry trying to draw you in so your money will be taken. She is the secular society trying to lure you into her world. She lures both men and women. And she is effective because of her smooth words.

Do not underestimate her persuasiveness, nor overestimate your willpower to resist. Seek the wisdom of Scripture; appeal to the Holy Spirit for understanding and strength to obey God's commands. Follow your Lord Jesus Christ.

Keep Away

Proverbs 5:7-11

And now, O sons, listen to me,
   and do not depart from the words of my mouth.

42

Keep your way far from her,
  and do not go near the door of her house,
lest you give your honor to others
  and your years to the merciless,
lest strangers take their fill of your strength,
  and your labors go to the house of a foreigner,
and at the end of your life you groan,
  when your flesh and body are consumed,

Keep away from the "forbidden woman"! If she is in your travel route, take a detour – a wide detour. Instead of matching your wisdom against her folly, just stay away. She will not listen to you. As Proverbs 18:2 explains, "A fool takes no pleasure in understanding." And 15:14 adds that "the mouths of fools feed on folly." The more likely scenario is that she will lead you astray and to your ruin.

What happens when you yield to the forbidden woman? You lose your honor, your good name. Perhaps you are young and earning a good name. You are accomplishing much good. Perhaps you are effectively ministering for God's kingdom, but you yield to the enticements of the forbidden woman and become publicly shamed and thus disqualified for your work. You lose your years of a fruitful life.

The years of a meaningful, productive life are taken away as you waste them indulging in folly or suffering the consequences of your folly. Many good, talented men and women have had their talent wasted because of going near the door of her house.

You lose your possessions. Strangers those who have no interest in you reap your possessions. The lovers of money take from you your money. Understand that our society is saturated with sexual temptations, not because of mere sensual impulse, but because sex is a lucrative business. Like casinos, the sex industry is all about becoming wealthy off of you giving in to temptation. And of all the temptations, illicit sex is the easiest to exploit because sexual impulses makes fools of us all.

And you lose more than money. You may lose your spouse. You may lose your family and your friends. You may lose your job. What was dear to you ends up with someone else.

And you lose your health. It is impossible not to connect rampant venereal disease with rampant sexual promiscuity. But there are other tolls on your health: anxiety, depression, the dangers connected with linking up with fools, to name a few.

Keep away and embrace the Wisdom who will strengthen you with the gospel of Christ.

The Life of Regret

Proverbs 5:12-14

A scoffer does not like to be reproved;
   he will not go to the wise.
A glad heart makes a cheerful face,
   but by sorrow of heart the spirit is crushed.
The heart of him who has understanding seeks knowledge,
   but the mouths of fools feed on folly.

These verses are echoed in the song, "Yesterday, When I Was Young" (lyrics by Charles Aznavour; English translation by Herbert Kretzmer):

   So many wayward pleasures lay in store for me,
   And so much pain my dazzled eyes refused to see.
   I ran so fast that time and youth, at last, ran out,
   I never stopped to think what life was all about;
   And ev'ry conversation I can now recall
   Concerned itself with me, and nothing else at all.
   I used my magic age as if it were a wand,
   And never saw the waste and emptiness beyond.
   The game of love I played with arrogance and pride,
   And ev'ry flame I lit too quickly, quickly died;
   The friends I made all seemed somehow to drift away
   And only I am left on stage to end the play.
   There are so many songs in me that won't be sung,

I feel the bitter taste of tears upon my tongue;
The time has come for me to pay for yesterday
When I was young.

The tragedy of the words spoken in these Proverbs verses and in the song is that they speak of regret that knows no hope. It is shocking to wake up to a ruined life which is the result of foolish living; it is bitter to know only regret and no redemption. Pity the blind fool who someday must face his folly. Pray that he will come to his senses while there is time to repent. Pray that he will repent and turn to the Lord who alone can redeem his soul and turn his ruin into a foundation for a meaningful life...while there is time.

If you are one now who has awaken to your folly, the time is not too late for redemption. Whether you are "at the brink of utter ruin" or the only one "left on stage to end the play," now is not too late to turn to your Savior. You cannot go back in time to recoup what you have lost, but you can do what is even better, you can go to the Savior who will redeem what you have squandered and will turn your present and your future into true treasure. He is, after all, the Lord of yesterday, today, and tomorrow.

Good Delight

Proverbs 5:18-19

Let your fountain be blessed,
and rejoice in the wife of your youth,
a lovely deer, a graceful doe.
Let her breasts fill you at all times with delight;
be intoxicated always in her love.

The answer to illicit pleasure is legitimate pleasure, that which rightfully and delightfully belongs to the one who is married. I find this embarrassing to read publicly because it is so uninhibited in expressing the passion of legitimate, marital, sexual pleasure. Passion, even sexual passion, is not only not bad; it is greatly to be desired within the appropriate boundaries.

This instruction is calling you to devote yourself to your spouse, family, whatever is good. Do some of you think, if only you knew my wife (or husband)? You would like to rejoice in your spouse if only he or she were desirable or would cooperate. First note the reality that the proverb recognizes here. Even the husbands and wives of desirable and cooperative spouses will yield to sexual temptations. Many a newly married person has been startled to learn that the same temptations that plagued him or her as a single remain in the marriage. It is true that the temptations grow stronger if the marriage is not pleasurable, but the answer is not in wishing that your spouse would get with the program. Rather it is in you being attentive to loving your wife or husband. Turn your attention to blessing your marriage.

If you are single, take the same principle and focus on taking delight in good, legitimate pleasures. Contrary to the foolish propaganda of the world, sex is not the only pleasure and passion of life; it does not even rank first. What does? Here are a few things. Better than having sex is making a real difference in someone else's life for the good. Do you want to feel good about yourself and have happy memories that build up your self-worth? Then do good deeds. The world will say that such good deeds are substitutes for missing out on sexual passion. We say the world turns to sex as a poor substitute for missing out on a meaningful life. C.S. Lewis would say that turning to sex is a cheap alternative to having the passion for God which is placed in us as his creatures. The point is that we are created to desire after something. We do need to have passion for something, and the foolish world says it is sex. Say what anyone will about love, the world means sexual love at best or the mere animal act. But we know that we were created to have a passion for God.

But even here be careful. God has made us physical beings and created us to live in a physical world. Our goal should not be to become spiritual beings who take no interest in physical pleasures; rather we delight in God through delighting in the legitimate physical pleasures he has given. Thus, the godly spouse will delight in physical intimacy with his or her spouse. The godly married person and the single will delight in the beauties of the created world, in doing good, in the joy of meaningful relationships. The answer to sexual sin is not mere restraint but pouring ones desires and passions into whatever is true, honorable, just, pure, lovely, and commendable (cf. Phil. 4:8).

The Eyes of the Lord

Proverbs 5:20-23

Why should you be intoxicated, my son, with a forbidden woman
and embrace the bosom of an adulteress?
For a man's ways are before the eyes of the LORD,
and he ponders all his paths.
The iniquities of the wicked ensnare him,
and he is held fast in the cords of his sin.
He dies for lack of discipline,
and because of his great folly he is led astray.

Think what you are doing in adultery. If fear of what you may lose does not deter you, if the pleasure of your wife does not entice you, at least understand that you live before the eyes of the Lord. You get away with nothing. The Lord ponders all your paths. He sees everything, even into your heart. You will get caught, and when you do you will have no one to blame but yourself for your lack of discipline and your folly.

Live consciously under the watch of God. You are living under his watch whether you wish to acknowledge it or not. Anytime you are tempted, understand that your Lord is watching you at that moment.

In the midst of such sober warning, heed this counsel. When you are tempted, and when you give in to temptation, yes, you should be convicted and repentant for your sin. But also give thanks and praise to God. For is it not wondrous that when we come before God we find him sitting on the throne of grace? For our Lord Jesus Christ is our sympathetic High Priest interceding for us and covering us with his righteousness. His righteousness! Nothing will give you greater strength to battle against the temptations of illicit sex than to revel in the grace and mercy of our God that comes to us through Christ Jesus our Lord. Nothing will give you greater resolve to live for the glory of God than to enjoy the pleasures of his grace. There is no passion greater than the passion that springs from redemption. And what we need is not so much daily determination to be good, as it is to daily re-awake to the goodness of God shown to us through Jesus Christ. He is the Door not only to go near, but to pass through to the abundant and truly passionate life.

Insecure Security

Proverbs 6:1-5

My son, if you have put up security for your neighbor,
*   have given your pledge for a stranger,*
if you are snared in the words of your mouth,
*   caught in the words of your mouth,*
then do this, my son, and save yourself,
*   for you have come into the hand of your neighbor:*
*   go, hasten, and plead urgently with your neighbor.*
Give your eyes no sleep
*   and your eyelids no slumber;*
save yourself like a gazelle from the hand of the hunter,
*   like a bird from the hand of the fowler.*

This counsel is not forbidding generosity but rather risk-taking. A friend or family member approaches you to co-sign for a large loan. He appeals to your relationship; he promises that he can be trusted even though the venture is risky and he has not proven himself to carry through on his commitments. Indeed, that is why the co-signing is necessary. He has not shown the discipline necessary to build his own credit.

Understand that you are not doing him good to co-sign. You are enabling him to get into yet another bind, only this time you will have to make good for his promises. Where before you pitied him, now you will despise him for getting you into financial trouble.

Do not act against a hesitant instinct. You may be worried that you are not trusting enough or caring enough. It is worthwhile to pray about the matter and seek counsel, but be sure to take these steps before committing yourself, especially if others depend on you. A married person with children does not have the freedom to make financially risky commitments, and as stewards of God's money we all have an obligation to use money wisely.

Whatever you do loan, do so as though you are giving money generously with no expectation of return. But give to what is helpful, not what enables dependency. Should you be more willing to give to family? Yes, but still with an eye on what is for the other person's good and not simply to get him off your back. The generous giver is still to be a wise giver.

A Little Sleep

Proverbs 6:6-11

Go to the ant, O sluggard;
  consider her ways, and be wise.
Without having any chief,
  officer, or ruler,
she prepares her bread in summer
  and gathers her food in harvest.
How long will you lie there, O sluggard?
  When will you arise from your sleep?
A little sleep, a little slumber,
  a little folding of the hands to rest,
and poverty will come upon you like a robber,
  and want like an armed man.

A little watching of TV, a little more time playing computer games, a little extra time... you add to the list your own time-wasting activity. We all need breaks from work, and the best worker knows how to pace himself. But he paces himself in order to accomplish more. The sluggard works as little as possible, always seeking (and always finding) an excuse to avoid work.

Where are you in this description? When your alarm clock goes off in the morning, do you get up or catch a few more minutes of rest? Do you need that rest because necessity kept you up late or because your TV show kept you up? Do you need naps in the day because you fail to eat right and exercise? Do you not have time for exercise because you will not keep a schedule? Do you fail to keep a schedule because your goals are aimless and you prefer rest and entertainment to productive labor?

Learn to use your time wisely. There is more time for rest and relaxation than you may realize if you learn to work efficiently and productively. But then you must find value in work. If you do not, is it because you are not employed in the right endeavor or you do not like being employed? It is easy to choose the former reason, but examine yourself honestly regarding the latter. Most good workers work productively in whatever endeavor they are given.

Worthless Persons

Proverbs 6:12-15

A worthless person, a wicked man,
  goes about with crooked speech,
winks with his eyes, signals with his feet,
  points with his finger,
with perverted heart devises evil,
  continually sowing discord;
therefore calamity will come upon him suddenly;
  in a moment he will be broken beyond healing.

The worthless man considers himself cunning, able to get away with mischief, and yet, all he is doing is setting himself up for a great fall. But before we dismiss this proverb as applying to "those" worthless people, compare this description with the Apostle Paul's list in Romans 3:10-18:
> "None is righteous, no, not one;
>   no one understands;
>   no one seeks for God.
> All have turned aside; together they have become worthless;
>   no one does good,
>   not even one."
> "Their throat is an open grave;
>   they use their tongues to deceive."

"The venom of asps is under their lips."
  "Their mouth is full of curses and bitterness."
"Their feet are swift to shed blood;
  in their paths are ruin and misery,
and the way of peace they have not known."
  "There is no fear of God before their eyes."

The scary thing about Paul's words is that he is applying them to all mankind. We are all under sin and are worthless under God's penetrating eye. We must all repent before we are broken beyond healing, regardless of how we seem in the eyes of others. Thanks be to God that he has provided us with the righteousness of Jesus Christ whom we receive by faith. Let us strive to have a good reputation among men, but let us find our confidence of how we stand before God only in Christ.

Abomination

Proverbs 6:16-19

There are six things that the LORD hates,
  seven that are an abomination to him:
haughty eyes, a lying tongue,
  and hands that shed innocent blood,
a heart that devises wicked plans,
  feet that make haste to run to evil,
a false witness who breathes out lies,
  and one who sows discord among brothers.

What God hates, so should we; and yet, we may be more tolerant than we suppose. Because we value people who agree with us on issues – be they theological, political, or socially; because we are loyal to our fraternity or denomination or family, we will tolerate and excuse in them what we denounce in others. We will chuckle at misleading comments of those on "our side" and pounce on the same types of comments on the other side. We admire the haughty eyes on our side as representing jealousy for truth, while we condemn the arrogance on the other side. We excuse sowing discord by those on our side by claiming the other side cannot handle truth; yet we are quick to expose the slander on the other side.

These seven wicked traits are an abomination to God regardless of who exhibits them, although it is likely he despises them more when found in someone who claims to represent him. Jesus' harshest words were reserved for the men who claimed closest allegiance to God. Note further that these traits are found together. That is why they are a single abomination. Whoever is guilty of one of these traits will be guilty of all the others.

Note more deeply that all of these traits can be found in every one of us. We have all lied; we have all looked down on someone else. We may not have literally shed blood, but we have harmed others emotionally; we have all desired some kind of harm to come. We have all said something, done something that caused discord. Do not fool yourself as the Pharisee who could not think of anything to confess before God. Because you are human, even though you are redeemed by the blood of Christ, your heart is far from being fully sanctified. Do not excuse what God so easily sees. Go each day to the mercy throne to find the forgiveness that is in Christ and to receive the daily grace needed to grow in sanctification. Give thanks to God that, though your heart expresses too often what is an abomination, he sees you clothed in the righteousness of Christ.

The Teachings of Parents

Proverbs 6:20-24

My son, keep your father's commandment,
and forsake not your mother's teaching.
Bind them on your heart always;
tie them around your neck.
When you walk, they will lead you;
when you lie down, they will watch over you;
and when you awake, they will talk with you.
For the commandment is a lamp and the teaching a light,
and the reproofs of discipline are the way of life,
to preserve you from the evil woman,
from the smooth tongue of the adulteress.

Listen, keep, and remember the lessons of your parents. They will guide you and protect you throughout your life. If you keep them, they will protect you from the most pervasive of temptations in our society – that of sexual sin.

Of course, the premise here is that the teachings of your parents are instruction in the commandments of God. Parents are to teach what those commandments are; they are to teach the reasons for following the commandments and the wisdom of these laws. They are to model obedience. They are to teach from their own experience the blessings of obeying the commands and the pain of disobeying them. Parents are to discipline and reprove their children upon disobedience, and they are to encourage and praise their children when they obey.

The result is that as the children mature, they recognize the wisdom of their parents' teaching and will obey out of that trust. They also are taught how to discern and use discretion; thus, they gain the ability to spot sin and avoid it. They learn from their parents not merely to obey the law, but to love God's commands, so that they do not think they are choosing between pleasure and obedience. They know the greater pleasure lies in obedience.

Parents, are you teaching your children commands and teachings that are worthy of binding them on your children's hearts and around their necks? Are your teachings a lamp leading along the way of life? The "evil woman" will be using all her wiles to lead them astray. What are you giving them now to preserve them?

Give them the righteous commands of the law. But give them the gospel day after day after day. The law alone will only set up their fall. It is the gospel that will be the shining lamp leading them through life's perils. Show them Christ and how to keep their eyes upon him.

Lacking Sense

Proverbs 6:25-35

Do not desire her beauty in your heart,

and do not let her capture you with her eyelashes;
for the price of a prostitute is only a loaf of bread,
but a married woman hunts down a precious life.
Can a man carry fire next to his chest
and his clothes not be burned?
Or can one walk on hot coals
and his feet not be scorched?
So is he who goes in to his neighbor's wife;
none who touches her will go unpunished.
People do not despise a thief if he steals
to satisfy his appetite when he is hungry,
but if he is caught, he will pay sevenfold;
he will give all the goods of his house.
He who commits adultery lacks sense;
he who does it destroys himself.
He will get wounds and dishonor,
and his disgrace will not be wiped away.
For jealousy makes a man furious,
and he will not spare when he takes revenge.
He will accept no compensation;
he will refuse though you multiply gifts.

The key verse is 32 – "He who commits adultery lacks sense; he who does it destroys himself." Sex makes fools of us, and illicit sex sends us to our destruction. How else can we explain the actions of both men and women who sacrifice marriages – good marriages – and families, and who ruin their reputations and careers because of the wink of eyelashes and a few words spoken?

There is some logic to the actions of a thief, even of a liar, but to commit adultery with a married woman or with a married man? Again, there is some empathy for a person yielding to sexual impulses, but what is the instinct for adultery with a married person? Why do women latch on to married men who either will not make a commitment to them or must destroy their marriages to do so? Do these women believe they can then trust these men to be faithful to them? Why do men yield to the charms of a married woman? If she is willing to make a fool of her husband, is she not willing to make fools of them?

54

Adultery may be fun material for TV, but its topic is devastating in the real world. People's hearts are broken; their lives are ruined; children suffer and all because someone cannot control his or her sexual impulses. Why do you suppose so much space is given in Proverbs on this subject of illicit sex? Is it not because the temptation is so strong and the consequences so devastating? All the more, then, stay away. Be faithful to your spouse. If you are single, be chaste. However difficult you may think your situation is or your desires so strong, you will rue the day you yield. Do not carry fire next to your chest.

The Best Intimate Friend

Proverbs 7:1-5

My son, keep my words
and treasure up my commandments with you;
keep my commandments and live;
keep my teaching as the apple of your eye;
bind them on your fingers;
write them on the tablet of your heart.
Say to wisdom, "You are my sister,"
and call insight your intimate friend,
to keep you from the forbidden woman,
from the adulteress with her smooth words.

How do we expect to withstand the enticements of the "forbidden woman," if we treat her and her companions as our kin and regard the values of the world as our intimate friend? How do we do so? We turn to the secular entertainment world for our nurture. We depend on TV sitcoms and reality shows to present the priority issues and the values we are to hold. Do you disagree with this analysis? How much time, then, do you spend exposed to secular entertainment as opposed to godly and biblical influences?

How much now is the Christian community immune to hearing profanity, viewing illicit sex and gratuitous violence, and associating in activities that oppose the gospel? To make wisdom and insight

55

your "intimate friend," means more than giving passing attention to a sermon. It means more than reading the Bible. One must study the Scriptures and meditate upon them. One must study the teachings of wise and godly teachers. One must develop the skill to think Christianly. It does not come naturally, even to the redeemed believer. We have been too much tainted with sin to take to the gospel truths easily.

Keep the commandments and the promises of God's Word ever before you and within you. Do you find reading the Word difficult and studying theology boring? Would you rather be watching a show that, though it espouses worldly values, makes you laugh and entertains you? Then repent and all the more discipline yourself to embrace what is true and good and God-honoring. Life is not a TV show. The stakes are real and they are high. Satan wants your soul, and if he cannot get it, he at least wants to render you ineffective for God. All the more, then, embrace the wisdom of God's Word.

The Road Wrongly Traveled

Proverbs 7:6-15

For at the window of my house
  I have looked out through my lattice,
and I have seen among the simple,
  I have perceived among the youths,
  a young man lacking sense,
passing along the street near her corner,
  taking the road to her house
in the twilight, in the evening,
  at the time of night and darkness.

And behold, the woman meets him,
  dressed as a prostitute, wily of heart.
She is loud and wayward;
  her feet do not stay at home;
now in the street, now in the market,
  and at every corner she lies in wait.
She seizes him and kisses him,

and with bold face she says to him,
"I had to offer sacrifices,
and today I have paid my vows;
so now I have come out to meet you,
to seek you eagerly, and I have found you.

The simple man is about to fall prey to a woman wanting his money and to use him for her own purposes. He falls prey because he knowingly puts himself in the position to be lured. He walks to her house and at a time he knows she will be looking for a "customer" and in the night where his own actions can be hidden. The forbidden woman uses her wiles to lure him, but then he is already desirous of her.

Consider her ways. She is bold, upfront with her intentions, flaunting her body and her desires.

How pathetic they both are – a senseless young man who looks to a prostituting wife for happiness. That is the motive for them both. They want to be happy through sex and money. The adventure of forbidden sex; the rush of power for the woman in dominating yet another man – these are the cheap thrills that will cost them their lives and rob them of meaningful living.

It is good to seek happiness, but seek it where it truly lies – in the gospel of Christ, in the glory of the Lord. Understand that you will not find power to withstand worldly and illicit sexual pleasure until you grasp that your choice is not giving up pleasure for duty, but of giving up illusory pleasure that harms you and turning to the One who seeks you as the Good Shepherd and carries you in his arms.

Smooth Talk

Proverbs 7:16-27

I have spread my couch with coverings,
colored linens from Egyptian linen;
I have perfumed my bed with myrrh,
aloes, and cinnamon.

Come, let us take our fill of love till morning;
*   let us delight ourselves with love.*
For my husband is not at home;
*   he has gone on a long journey;*
he took a bag of money with him;
*   at full moon he will come home."*

With much seductive speech she persuades him;
*   with her smooth talk she compels him.*
All at once he follows her,
*   as an ox goes to the slaughter,*
or as a stag is caught fast
*   till an arrow pierces its liver;*
as a bird rushes into a snare;
*   he does not know that it will cost him his life.*

And now, O sons, listen to me,
*   and be attentive to the words of my mouth.*
Let not your heart turn aside to her ways;
*   do not stray into her paths,*
for many a victim has she laid low,
*   and all her slain are a mighty throng.*
Her house is the way to Sheol,
*   going down to the chambers of death.*

The smooth talker lures her victim in with promises of exotic and erotic adventure (16-17), of love (18), and of safety (19-20). However exciting the adventure may be to the fool, love certainly has nothing to do with her designs. It is a momentary illusion that leads to devastation.

The assurance that the husband is away is not only a comforting thought for one's safety, but adds to the pleasure of the fool, thinking that he is making a fool of another man. At no other instance is a fool's folly so evident as when he thinks he is outwitting another person. As 21-23 make clear, he is merely setting himself up for his own entrapment.

The answer for us all is not to become wise enough to outwit the forbidden woman. The teacher does not counsel his sons how to debate the woman nor how to instruct her. He tells them to turn away from her altogether. The simpleton in this chapter walked into his own trap by knowingly walking to where the forbidden women lived. Walk away from smooth talk. Do not answer it; do not try to reason with it. Walk away.

Wisdom Calling

Proverbs 8:1-11

Does not wisdom call?
Does not understanding raise her voice?
On the heights beside the way,
at the crossroads she takes her stand;
beside the gates in front of the town,
at the entrance of the portals she cries aloud:
"To you, O men, I call,
and my cry is to the children of man.
O simple ones, learn prudence;
O fools, learn sense.
Hear, for I will speak noble things,
and from my lips will come what is right,
for my mouth will utter truth;
wickedness is an abomination to my lips.
All the words of my mouth are righteous;
there is nothing twisted or crooked in them.
They are all straight to him who understands,
and right to those who find knowledge.
Take my instruction instead of silver,
and knowledge rather than choice gold,
for wisdom is better than jewels,
and all that you may desire cannot compare with her.

Compare Wisdom to the Forbidden Woman. Both go out into the public places (8:2-3, 7:12); both speak out (8:1, 7:11); both make offers to men (8:4-11, 7:14-20). Now contrast the two women. Whereas the Forbidden Woman entices the simple to commit sin and join her in wickedness, Wisdom offers what is noble, true, and righteous (7:18-20, 8:5-8). The Forbidden Woman views the simple and foolish as prey; Wisdom views them as those needing help (7:21-23, 8:4-5). The Forbidden Woman entraps men; Wisdom makes their way straight (7:22-23, 8:9). The Forbidden Woman's enticements lead to destruction; Wisdom's gifts lead to possessions greater than physical riches (8:10-11, 7:21-27).

It seems an easy choice to make, and, yet, more choose the Forbidden Woman than Wisdom. Why? Verse 9 – "to him who understands" – suggests the reason. To choose Wisdom, one must already have some understanding as to what is wise and good; one must be a seeker of knowledge. Most people are seekers of easy pleasure, of what satisfies the ego. Thus, what Wisdom regards as crooked, most people regard as straight paths to their pleasure. What Wisdom regards as wickedness, fools regard as releasing restraints.

The heart must already be prepared to receive Wisdom. All the more, then, pray for that work which belongs to the Holy Spirit – to prepare the heart to receive the Wisdom of the gospel. Pray for the Spirit to awaken them from the dead, giving them ears to hear, and turning their hearts of stone to hearts of flesh that will be convicted and will turn to the truth of the gospel. Pray for your neighbors to have their ears and minds open to her. Pray for yourself, as well, for you also are dependent upon the sanctifying work of the Holy Spirit to open your ears and minds.

The Reward of Wisdom

Proverbs 8:12-21

"I, wisdom, dwell with prudence,
and I find knowledge and discretion.
The fear of the LORD is hatred of evil.
Pride and arrogance and the way of evil
and perverted speech I hate.
I have counsel and sound wisdom;
I have insight; I have strength.
By me kings reign,
and rulers decree what is just;
by me princes rule,

and nobles, all who govern justly.
I love those who love me,
and those who seek me diligently find me.
Riches and honor are with me,
enduring wealth and righteousness.
My fruit is better than gold, even fine gold,
and my yield than choice silver.
I walk in the way of righteousness,
in the paths of justice,
granting an inheritance to those who love me,
and filling their treasuries."

Persons may rise to power through lucky circumstances or even through deceitful and wicked behavior. Individuals may obtain wealth through the same means. But their rise sets up their downfall, for they mistake power and wealth for what only Wisdom can provide – prudence, knowledge, discretion, counsel, sound wisdom, insight, and inner strength. It is the ruler who decrees what is just and who governs justly that is able to withstand his enemies and carry out his rule with riches and honor.

Whether as a government ruler or in any other position of authority, the one who rules with pride, arrogance, and the way of evil and perverted speech can at best hold on to his position through intimidation. That is a precarious position. He continually creates enemies, and his sin must increase in order to keep his semblance of security. It is only a semblance of security, because his greatest enemy is Wisdom. She hates such traits. She withholds from the wicked her virtues that bring lasting joy and security, and she gladly bestows these gifts on those who diligently seek her.

Why then envy the wicked? Why bemoan your circumstances which seem to be worse than that of the arrogant? As easily as they may seem to rise to position and wealth, as easily they will fall. And pray that they will fall in this lifetime so that they may repent and diligently seek Wisdom; otherwise, their destruction is inevitable. You, if you have found the Wisdom of the gospel, have been given the assurance of an eternal inheritance that cannot be destroyed. Your trials can only result in praise and glory and honor at the revelation of Jesus Christ (cf. 1 Pet. 1:3-9).

61

Ancient Wisdom

Proverbs 8:22-31

"The LORD possessed me at the beginning of his work,
the first of his acts of old.
Ages ago I was set up,
at the first, before the beginning of the earth.
When there were no depths I was brought forth,
when there were no springs abounding with water.
Before the mountains had been shaped,
before the hills, I was brought forth,
before he had made the earth with its fields,
or the first of the dust of the world.
When he established the heavens, I was there;
when he drew a circle on the face of the deep,
when he made firm the skies above,
when he established the fountains of the deep,
when he assigned to the sea its limit,
so that the waters might not transgress his command,
when he marked out the foundations of the earth,
then I was beside him, like a master workman,
and I was daily his delight,
rejoicing before him always,
rejoicing in his inhabited world
and delighting in the children of man."

What a wonderful expression of creation and the joy of that creation! And what an awesome revelation of Wisdom's place! She is ancient; she is intimate with God; she was used in creating; she knows the foundations of the earth; she delights in this creation, in its creatures, in mankind.

Wisdom is not only beautiful, not only valuable like gold and jewels; she is sacred and profound and steeped in the pure joy of God the Maker. That is the Wisdom offered to you as your companion. Seek after her; she is worthy to be found.

W.H.O.

Proverbs 8:32-36

"And now, O sons, listen to me:
  blessed are those who keep my ways.
Hear instruction and be wise,
  and do not neglect it.
Blessed is the one who listens to me,
  watching daily at my gates,
  waiting beside my doors.
For whoever finds me finds life
  and obtains favor from the LORD,
but he who fails to find me injures himself;
  all who hate me love death."

Note how easy Wisdom is to obtain. It is simply a matter of hearing her instruction and then following through on it. There is no mountain to climb; one must simply sit by her door waiting for her to step out. She is not hidden. Finding her is merely an act of waiting patiently for her. So the simple steps are Wait, Hear, Obey. And yet these steps are apparently difficult for us. Consider them.

Wait: But we don't have time! There is much to do and deadlines to meet. We are growing older and the time seems to be going faster.

Hear: How do we hear when there is so much noise we are also listening to? If in the car, we have the radio on; if walking we have our iPods on; if at home the TV is home. Perhaps we can slip in a few minutes of Bible reading, but there is too much to do in a day!

Obey: We will obey when we can afford the luxury to obey. Meanwhile, we have pressing demands; we have many troubles. When we get our lives in order, then we can think about obeying.

It always comes back to the heart. We will make time to W.H.O. (Wait, Hear, Obey) for what matters to us. And God will not be as sympathetic to our supposed motives as we are. Those who will not

W.H.O. will be regarded as those who hate Wisdom and love death. For that is their destiny.

Wisdom's Call

Proverbs 9:1-6

Wisdom has built her house;
  she has hewn her seven pillars.
She has slaughtered her beasts; she has mixed her wine;
  she has also set her table.
She has sent out her young women to call
  from the highest places in the town,
"Whoever is simple, let him turn in here!"
  To him who lacks sense she says,
"Come, eat of my bread
  and drink of the wine I have mixed.
Leave your simple ways, and live,
  and walk in the way of insight."

We will see later the contrast that is being set up in this chapter between Wisdom and Folly. For now, note again the attempt of Wisdom to draw the foolish away from their folly. She has a well-built house to invite others to. She has prepared a sumptuous feast. She has sent out her messengers who use the most public means possible to send out her invitation. She offers blessing to those who turn to her.

What she calls them to do, she calls of us all:

Leave: leave our simple ways. That is, leave the paths we travel out of mindless following. These are the ways of fashion, of popularity, of whatever is the latest fad. They are ways that we follow because we will not be thoughtful about how we live.

Live: really live rather than merely stay alive. Live a life that is productive, that is fruitful, that is meaningful. Don't live the life of the fool who, if he works, does so merely to make a living and who in his spare time merely looks for stimulation.

Walk: walk in the way of insight, not in mindless following. Go through a day, through a life using your brain and not merely "following the heart" which the world insists that you do. Instruct your heart, so that it moves you to do what is right; instruct your heart so that it discerns between what is loving and what is harmful.

Think of this in light of Christ's calling to you. Leave the world for Christ, live abiding in Christ, and walk in the way that he has instructed you and prepared for you.

If You Scoff

Proverbs 9:7-12

Whoever corrects a scoffer gets himself abuse,
  and he who reproves a wicked man incurs injury.
Do not reprove a scoffer, or he will hate you;
  reprove a wise man, and he will love you.
Give instruction to a wise man, and he will be still wiser;
  teach a righteous man, and he will increase in learning.
The fear of the LORD is the beginning of wisdom,
  and the knowledge of the Holy One is insight.
For by me your days will be multiplied,
  and years will be added to your life.
If you are wise, you are wise for yourself;
  if you scoff, you alone will bear it.

Why does Wisdom's effort to instruct the foolish so often fail? Because the foolish are foolish. They are not foolish because no one gave them right instruction. They are foolish because they love what is folly and hate what is good. The scoffer likes to scoff. Wisdom may scoff at the foolish, but that is because she hates folly and desires what is good for the fool. The scoffer merely likes to belittle others. It makes him feel important and gives him a false sense of being wise. To learn from Wisdom, he would have to take on the humble position of receiving knowledge that he does not have. He would have to admit that others know more. He hates such a position and thus will hate anyone who tries to teach him.

Because the wise person possesses the fear of the Lord, humility is a natural and desirable position to take. Because he has some insight into the character of God, because he knows the Lord, he will love receiving knowledge and growing in wisdom. Thus, he gladly receives instruction from whoever may give it.

Pray, then, for the foolish. For they have no hope except that the Holy Spirit works in them to change their nature and give them love for what is good and hatred for what is wicked. It is pride that turns all men and women away from God, just as it was pride that led Satan to rebellion. Remember, the fear of the Lord is the beginning of wisdom. Humility is the key, but not alone. It is a humility that delights in the Lord – that delights in the fear of the Lord – that will lead a person not only to walk in righteousness but to walk that path in devotion and joy.

The Call

Proverbs 9:13-18

The woman Folly is loud;
she is seductive and knows nothing.
She sits at the door of her house;
she takes a seat on the highest places of the town,
calling to those who pass by,
who are going straight on their way,
"Whoever is simple, let him turn in here!"
And to him who lacks sense she says,
"Stolen water is sweet,
and bread eaten in secret is pleasant."
But he does not know that the dead are there,
that her guests are in the depths of Sheol.

Folly is presented in comparison and contrast to Wisdom. Both have a house; both call out from high places; both call to the simple. Yet unlike Wisdom, Folly is merely loud, not wise. She knows nothing. Wisdom possesses ancient knowledge from her close relation to God the Maker. Folly's sitting at the high places displays her impudence; she sits where she has no right. Whereas Wisdom calls to the simple in order to deliver them from their foolish ways, Folly calls out to the simple precisely because they are so easily led into such ways. Wisdom appeals to the simple to eat of her bread and drink of her wine, which nourish and refreshes the mind and soul; Folly presents what is stolen as sweet. It may well taste sweet for the moment, but Folly is leading her simple followers to their death. Wisdom offers life.

Who will be chosen by the fool? Verses 7-12 observe it will be Folly. We shake our heads at such foolishness, but we need to ask ourselves how often we have chosen Folly as well. We choose what will give us a rush. When our lives become routine, we look for some kind of adventure that stirs us, some kind of escape from our troubles and boredom. Folly understands that. That's the basis of her appeal about stolen water and bread eaten in secret.

How do we resist her? Self-control helps to a degree, but it gives in after time. What we need to do is grasp the adventure that belongs to any who would follow Wisdom. Remember, Wisdom is a companion of God who created the world with all its mysteries and awe-inspiring beauty. Wisdom leads to life, which is not mere avoidance of death; it is life abundant; it is life that has meaning, that produces what is of real value. It is a life that leads unto glory.

When we turn to Christ, we enter into the kingdom of God which moves forward in mysterious ways, winning converts and battling against the forces of evil such as Folly and the Forbidden Woman. Souls are at stake, and God gives to us the privilege to join in the battle. He gives to us the privilege to be builders of the kingdom. He gives us the joy to be explorers of his nature and of his grace; to search far and wide his ways and how his counsels are being carried out. The one who is able to withstand Folly as she calls out is the one too excited, too busy, too devoted for Christ and for his kingdom.

The Wise Son

Proverbs 10:1

A wise son makes a glad father,

but a foolish son is a sorrow to his mother.

A foolish son or daughter is a sorrow to parents, for whatever else they may achieve in life, it is in their children that they take greatest pleasure and pride. It is their children whom they love most and through whom they hope to leave a loving and honorable legacy.

How great then must be the joy and pride of God the Father in his wise son. How joyful was the day of his son's baptism when he declared, "This is my beloved son, with whom I am well pleased." How joyful it was to see his son live a life of perfect obedience, always doing his father's will. Whatever the pain of the cross when his wrath must come down upon his son, yet great was his gladness that his son would bear it willingly and victoriously, so that we prodigals could be restored as sons and daughters. Give thanks this day for this Wise Son, who is not ashamed to call us his brothers and sisters (cf. Heb. 2:11).

Profitable Treasure

Proverbs 10:2

Treasures gained by wickedness do not profit,
but righteousness delivers from death.

Crime does not pay. Most likely the treasure itself will be the downfall of the wicked, as they are caught in their crime sooner or later. Perhaps they are not caught; nevertheless, they must hide their deeds and live in guarded fear either from the law or from others who are wicked. Perhaps they live without fear, confident in their invincibility; even so their names are tarnished, their friends are bought, and their curse lies on their family. Perhaps they die in peace, but what awaits them is an everlasting nightmare. What profit is it to gain the temporary treasures of the world, only to lose the eternal treasure of one's soul?

But righteousness truly delivers from death. By his righteousness, Christ was able to die the death that would bring complete deliverance over sin and death. And because his righteousness has been imputed to us, we are truly delivered from death. What greater motivation do we need to earn our living through righteous means? Do not give in to the temptation to compromise righteousness for the sake of temporary gain.

Good Hunger

Proverbs 10:3

The Lord does not let the righteous go hungry,
but he thwarts the craving of the wicked.

Perhaps Jesus had in mind this proverb when he taught, "Blessed are those who hunger and thirst for righteousness, for they shall be satisfied" (Matt. 5:6). It is for righteousness that the righteous hunger, and surely God will not fail to feed such fine food to his people. The wicked crave what is unjust and immoral, thinking that by such things they will be satisfied. But they remain hungry, never satisfied with what they have, either wanting more or something else.

The meal of the wicked does not satisfy, either because the meal is bad or the means of getting it taints the food. But whatever comes from the Lord is rich and satisfying. What will you eat today? Will it be what is good and honorable and wise, or will it be the scraps of superficial entertainment and worldly fare? Hunger for righteousness; hunger for holiness; hunger for the heart of God, and you will find a bountiful meal indeed.

How to Get Rich

Proverbs 10:4

A slack hand causes poverty,
but the hand of the diligent makes rich.

Commenting on the bad luck of an individual who kept having trouble holding down jobs, it was noted, "Sometimes you have to make your own luck." That is the point of this proverb. We cannot control all of our circumstances, but more often than not our success or lack of success reflects personal discipline and attitude.

The hard worker usually will fare better than the lax worker. The worker aspiring to improve himself and his circumstance will normally do better than the one merely hoping that life will get better. One of my observations as a high school principal was that a person's rank academically was more closely tied in with the work ethic of the student than with the student's natural ability. In most years, the valedictorian was not the most academically gifted, but almost always the hardest and smartest worker.

Apply this principle spiritually. In truth, our growth spiritually is the result of the Holy Spirit working in us to sanctify us. But typically, that work can be seen in the attention we give to growing spiritually – our attentiveness to studying and being taught Scripture; our attention to prayer; our desire to be active in the church body and to serve in God's kingdom; our consciousness of being a witness for Christ in the workplace, school, and home by the good work that we do and the love we demonstrate. How diligent are you in becoming rich spiritually?

Sleeping Disorder

Proverbs 10:5

He who gathers in summer is a prudent son,
 but he who sleeps in harvest is a son who brings shame.

It is prudent to think ahead and "gather" while one can in preparation for the future. One of my more prudent decisions in college was to get the reading list for the fall course on American novels. As a slow reader, I knew I didn't stand a chance trying to read a novel every week for the class. By reading half the books, I was able to keep up the work load in the fall. In contrast to the prudent son is the lazy son who not only fails to prepare for the fall harvest, but sleeps when the harvesting time comes. Undoubtedly he had rational excuses for his failure. Perhaps he had been busy during the summer and needed to catch up on his rest. The time seemed to fly by before he could be ready. The lazy person is lazy because...well, he is lazy. And his laziness brings not only shame upon himself, but harms his family who were depending on his help. But then, the lazy person fails to take into account how his behavior affects those around him.

Spiritually, take Jesus' admonition to be praying for harvesters (and being harvesters) in the fields for the gospel harvest. Be gathering now, serving his kingdom faithfully and zealously. Do not be found sleeping when the Lord returns for his harvest.

Commentary on the Righteous and the Wicked

Proverbs 10:6

Blessings are on the head of the righteous,
but the mouth of the wicked conceals violence.

Psalm 1 presents the best commentary on this proverb:
Blessed is the man
who walks not in the counsel of the wicked,
nor stands in the way of sinners,
nor sits in the seat of scoffers;
but his delight is in the law of the LORD,
and on his law he meditates day and night.

He is like a tree
planted by streams of water
that yields its fruit in its season,
and its leaf does not wither.
In all that he does, he prospers.

The wicked are not so,
but are like chaff that the wind drives away.
Therefore the wicked will not stand in the judgment,
nor sinners in the congregation of the righteous;
for the LORD knows the way of the righteous,
but the way of the wicked will perish.

Remember, the Lord knows. He knows the way of the righteous and of the wicked, and he brings each to his just reward.

Blessed Memory

Proverbs 10:7

The memory of the righteous is a blessing,
  but the name of the wicked will rot.

Philadelphia has many historic sites made famous because of great national leaders. The names of Benjamin Franklin, Thomas Jefferson, and, of course, George Washington have been evoked in veneration time and again for their contributions to America. Their memory is a blessing to American citizens. Contrast their names with Benedict Arnold, whose name has become a byword for traitor.

But God gives memory of the righteous such as the biblical and church saints who stir us on to live in their example. He gives memory of good friends and relatives who have blessed us, whose very memory make us blessed. And how thankful we are for such memory! Think now of the good memory someone has left you with, and thank God that he would so bless you with such a memory. And then, pray to God that through you, he will bless someone else with good memories. Someone will give thanks for the memory of a kindness you showed, of the example you modeled. Perhaps the greatest gift we can give anyone is a good memory.

And do not forget the words of our Lord, who told us to remember him. The sacrament of the Lord's Supper is the sacrament of memory, of remembering the death, the atonement of our Lord and Savior Jesus Christ. And because God will never forget that death, we shall forever be known before our God.

Wise of Heart

Proverbs 10:8

The wise of heart will receive commandments,
  but a babbling fool will come to ruin.

This is a recurring theme in Proverbs and the basis upon which the proverbs are offered. Solomon wrote in chapter 1:5ff, "Let the wise hear and increase in learning, and the one who understands obtain guidance, to understand a proverb and a saying, the words of the wise and their riddles...fools despise wisdom and instruction."

Are you looking for someone with wisdom from whom you can learn and in whom you can trust? Then find someone who easily receives instruction himself, indeed, someone who is eager to keep learning. Find someone who takes seriously learning and obeying God's commandments. It is the fool who delights in his own words, who desires not so much to pass on knowledge but to appear knowledgeable. The fool listens to no one; the wise are always receptive to what is true, good, and useful. The best teacher is the best student; the wisest counselor is the humblest of learners; the strongest leader is the most willing to receive good direction.

True Security

Proverbs 10:9

Whoever walks in integrity walks securely,
  but he who makes his ways crooked will be found out.

Crooked ways will be found out, if only because the sinful impulses that take us along such ways blind us to the greatest danger of all – our own inadequacies. Always on the lookout for the dangers in our path, we neglect to look inside to see the dangers being fomented in our own hearts – pride, anger, greed.

To walk in integrity, by definition, is to focus on the heart. A businessman of integrity may desire to be successful, but because he knows the dangers of the heart, he acts with greater wisdom and thus walks securely.

That is the proverb from the perspective of human experience. The deeper and simpler truth is that the Lord protects the person of integrity and brings down the crooked person. The righteous Judge will see that justice prevails. We cannot hide our sins from God, but also know that our obedience to his commands are also seen and commended. And understand the greatest security that we have: we "by God's power are being guarded through faith for a salvation ready to be revealed in the last time" (1 Pet. 1:5).

Fools and Fool Makers

Proverbs 10:10

Whoever winks the eye causes trouble,
  but a babbling fool will come to ruin.

"Winks the eye" refers to one who plans mischief. He deceives his neighbor, perhaps in collusion with another. Even if harm is not intended, the winker may be making someone else the butt of a joke. The babbling fool appears again with the same result of verse 8 – he comes to ruin. The babbler thinks he is spouting wisdom, winning respect for himself, when all he is really doing is exposing his foolishness. He cannot see himself as others see him. But the fool, and the one who likes to make fools of others, are in the same pit of destruction. The trouble caused will come around and bring down the trouble maker. One may be able to deceive for a while, but he will sooner or later be revealed for the kind of person he is and become more avoided than the babbling fool. The fool is recognized for what he is and can be tolerated. No one tolerates the winker who delights in making fools of others.

Satan is the great winker, seeking to make fools of God's people. Take heed of Peter's admonition to be watchful for this lion who seeks to devour us (cf. 1 Pet. 5:8).

Fountain of Life

Proverbs 10:11

The mouth of the righteous is a fountain of life,
  but the mouth of the wicked conceals violence.

The words spoken by the righteous give life, as a river gives life to the land it flows through. For the words that come out of a person who is Christ-like are words of truth, love, and grace. The words spoken are true, not false; frank, not deceptive; faithful to God's Word, not adding or twisting his meaning. The words are loving, not violent; intended to build up, not tear down or win a score. The words are gracious, spoken with kindness and generosity. But the words of the wicked harm and destroy life. They break the spirits of others; they are deceptive; they are harsh; they are spoken by a person desiring his own advantage over others.

Whatever the words are, they neither make the speaker righteous nor wicked. Jesus said as much in Mark 7:14ff and in Matthew 7:15ff. What comes out of the heart defiles and reveals a person. This is also the perspective of Proverbs. Out of a righteous heart life giving words will come; out of a wicked heart, harmful words will come. To our shame and confusion, we speak both kinds of words. As James notes in 3:10, "From the same mouth come blessing and cursing." Be reminded that though Christ has saved us and imputed his righteousness to us, we nevertheless have the old sinful nature clinging to us. The work of sanctification will always be necessary in us.

All the more, then, pray for words that are a fountain of life to come out of us. Think of it this way: we have the fountain of life in us – the life-giving Holy Spirit. Nevertheless, the plumbing through which the water passes through and out of us is still tainted with sin-germs. Diligent filtering still needs to take place to prevent harmful words from coming out. The best filtering monitoring device is still conscious, consistent, honest prayer.

To Hate or to Love

Proverbs 10:12

Hatred stirs up strife,
but love covers all offenses.

Will you commit this day to prayer that your words and actions will promote peace? There is a likely chance that someone will say or do something offensive either to you or in your company. Will you cover over the offense? There will be opportunity for you to stir up strife through a careless remark. Most likely you will stir up trouble in someone's spirit if you do not consciously pray for Christ's love to work in you. We are sinners. Without the Spirit's work in us, we will sin like a car out of alignment that will veer from the road if our hands are removed from the steering wheel.

Don't read this proverb thinking that you do not hate anyone, thus you are not guilty of stirring up strife. If by love you are not covering offenses made against you, you are endangering yourself to stir up strife. There is a good chance that at work, school, the store, the neighborhood, and the home there is opportunity to stir up trouble or further trouble by making the careless remark or response to someone else's stirring the pot. The truth of the matter is that our words and actions reveal either hatred or love. There is no in-between. To be indifferent to another person is to hate. To show the smallest of concern is to love. Every person we meet today is an opportunity to hate or to love. Which will it be for you?

Good Wisdom Hunting

Proverbs 10:13

On the lips of him who has understanding, wisdom is found,
but a rod is for the back of him who lacks sense.

As a high school principal I had students who could not figure out why teachers were hard on them. They concluded that the teachers had it in for them for no particular reason, unless it was because they did not try to be favorites like those students who were clearly the teachers' pets. These "oppressed" students lacked sense. They could not make the connection between their poor behavior and lazy work habits and the way their teachers regarded them. I would try to explain how the teachers probably were harder on them than the others because of their (the students') attitude and behavior. But no, they couldn't believe that would be the real reason.

How refreshing is the person with understanding. Instead of the nonsensical thought pattern of the fool, clear commonsense wisdom comes forth. It is such a delight to be around the person who is able to cut through ambiguity and faulty reasoning and to speak wisdom. How refreshing then was Jesus in cutting through the stilted, foggy reasoning of the scribes and Pharisees and getting to the real truth of biblical principles and commands. Why don't you turn to the gospels and read a passage of his teaching? Delight in the pure wisdom and the one man with perfect understanding.

Laying Up Knowledge

Proverbs 10:14

The wise lay up knowledge,
but the mouth of a fool brings ruin near.

The wise build up storehouses of knowledge. Go to a wise person and he always seems to have a good answer, even if it is to lead you to where the right answer is. A wise person lays up knowledge through all of life's experiences. He lays up knowledge from his mistakes as well as from his successes. Every incident becomes a learning experience. On the other hand, the fool loses the value of his experience as fast as it passes out of memory. Furthermore, his experiences make him more dangerous. The older, more experienced he becomes the more false confidence rises in him so that he thinks he is spouting wisdom, while in reality he is spouting foolishness and arrogance.

What are you going to learn today from your experiences? Whether your experiences are pleasant or distasteful, will you grow in wisdom, using them to grow in knowledge and maturity? What is God teaching you about himself? What are you learning about grace and the gospel? How is God's Word being tested for its truthfulness through your experiences? Lay up knowledge today.

True Wealth

Proverbs 10:15

A rich man's wealth is his strong city;
  the poverty of the poor is their ruin.

Consider this proverb as an observation. The rich man uses wealth to build financial security, and if used wisely, to build a stable, productive life. The poverty of the poor can, and often does, break the spirit and well-being of the poor. They become entrapped in a cycle of poverty.

Now, consider this proverb spiritually. The spiritual riches of the Christian – "the riches of God's glorious inheritance in the saints" (Eph. 1:18) – is his strong city. He is able to withstand the struggles of life because he knows his inheritance. When we know who we are, what we possess, and what is our destiny, then we can endure whatever troubles may come our way. The riches of God form the strong city walls.

But for the one spiritually poor, who does not possess the gospel and its blessings, then such poverty truly is their ruin. Just look around at the hardness, the pain, the myriad of troubles that beset those who do not know the love of Christ, who have no hope of an eternal inheritance.

A woman came to me for counsel on how to deal with her mother and sister who, according to her, mistreated her. She was a Christian and they were not. I counseled her not to resent them, but all the more to pity them and pray for them. She was wealthy; they were poor. Let us have compassion on the poor – yes, those who are financially poor, but all the more for those poor in the gospel. Instead of resenting your colleagues who try you, pray with compassion for them; pray that God would use you to show the riches they might have in Christ.

78

Earning a Good Wage

Proverbs 10:16

The wage of the righteous leads to life,
the gain of the wicked to sin.

Both the righteous and the wicked earn wages from their respective labors, but those wages lead to different ends. The contrast of the ends is not quite what we would expect. If the wage of the righteous leads to life, then shouldn't the gain of the wicked lead to death? Isn't it redundant to speak of the wicked being led to sin?

Perhaps the proverb has the same concept in mind as that written in Romans 1:18ff. Verse 18 notes: "For the wrath of God is revealed from heaven against all ungodliness and unrighteousness of men, who by their unrighteousness suppress the truth." How is that wrath revealed? Note the following: "Therefore God gave them up in the lusts of their hearts to impurity" (v. 24); "For this reason God gave them up to dishonorable passions" (v.26); "God gave them up to a debased mind to do what ought not to be done" (v.28).

All, then, that the wicked gain by their sin is to be given up to committing further sin, which leads them further into judgment. As much as children may dislike discipline, every child knows that it is worse to be given up on, especially by one's parents. It seems fun to get away with sin for a while, but when the father or the mother gives up in exasperation, and you are left with the feeling of having no one to care, particularly with no one to have hope in you, such wages are bitter indeed. Such wages lead to a living death.

As restrictive as the righteous life may seem for the time, is it not much better to live a life that leads to life? A life that is full of life? It was the way Christ followed and the life he offers now to those who believe and follow.

Dangerous Leading

Proverbs 10:17

Whoever heeds instruction is on the path to life,
but he who rejects reproof leads others astray.

This proverb is similar to the previous one. A contrast is made between the one who heeds instruction and the one who rejects reproof. The obedient one is on the path to life, but again, where we expect the contrast to be the path to death, it is about sin. This time, the observation goes further than noting that the disobedient is led to further sin; rather, his disobedience leads others to sin.

In "A Hymn to God the Father," a meditation on sin, John Donne writes:

> Wilt Thou forgive that sin which I have won
> Others to sin, and made my sin their door?

It is a heavy burden to be responsible for others going astray. Parents, keep this proverb in mind when you speak in front of your children against the authorities over you. Christian, keep this in mind when you publicly reject the teaching and reproof of the elders and ministers in your church. You may be bold enough to speak your mind or go your own way, but are you prepared to set such an example for others to follow? What will you say to your Lord who asks you to give an account, not only for your rejection of godly reproof, but for leading others to do the same?

Take care to listen to instruction. Be not quick to reject reproof. Even if you think the reproof is unjust, trust God to be using that reproof for your good. Take the time to consider it carefully. For more than your welfare may be at stake.

Lying Hatred

Proverbs 10:18

The one who conceals hatred has lying lips,
and whoever utters slander is a fool.

The hater conceals his hatred through false flattery and false kind words. He will slander the very person he flatters. Hatred cannot be concealed completely. It will reveal itself in subtle ways, if we are alert.

We should be wary of the person who speaks well of another but then will whisper to us a denigrating remark. The slanderer acts as though he is taking us into his confidence, when his real intent is to harm the reputation of the other person. He is trying to make us a vessel to carry on the slander.

We should also be wary of the person who only speaks flattery to us, especially when he speaks ill of others, and especially when you have heard him flatter the person he speaks ill of. Be attentive. Don't let flattery go to your head keeping you from observing the subtle signs of a hating, deceiving spirit.

We do not need to be suspicious of everyone who speaks in a flattering manner. But if we have already a proper humble regard for ourselves, we will not let flattery cloud our thinking and power of observation. Again, hatred can be observed if we keep our heads about us. Lying lips cannot hide hatred fully if we do not allow those lips to divert our focus on honoring Christ.

Many Words

Proverbs 10:19

When words are many, transgression is not lacking,
but whoever restrains his lips is prudent.

We have a similar saying: Give a man enough rope and he will hang himself. The more verbose we are the more likely we will say something to get ourselves in trouble or cause trouble.

The reason is simple. We are sinners. Sin is always looking for an outlet and the mouth provides a wide open one. We speak inappropriate words. We speak words that in themselves are fine, but our tone of voice is inappropriate. We speak at inappropriate times.

Thus, the prudent person is the one who literally speaks fewer words. He waits for others to speak before throwing out his opinion. He gives thought to what he says, and that very exercise of thinking before speaking leads to fewer words.

Better to regret not speaking than to regret what was said. Better to leave others wishing you had spoken than wishing you had not.

Valuable Speech

Proverbs 10:20

The tongue of the righteous is choice silver;
  the heart of the wicked is of little worth.

The tongue of the righteous is choice silver, for the words he speaks convey beauty and truth. From the heart of the wicked comes vulgarity and lies, worthless words.

What is the value of your tongue? Are you known for building up others through your words? Do they bring healing for hurting spirits, peace for troubled souls? Do they shed light on perplexing problems and moral dilemmas? Do they convey the gospel and apply truth and grace? Or do people seem oversensitive to your words? It seems that you are often misunderstood. They don't like hearing the truth you speak. They don't listen to what you say.

It is important to examine yourself in this. Don't write off the proverb because it speaks of the wicked and therefore not to you. Even we who are born again in Christ have remnants of the old wicked man inside of us. We are justified but not fully sanctified, and the tongue is the most common means of giving vent to the wickedness still remaining.

Use the reaction of others as the weighing balance to determine if your tongue is of choice silver or of little worth. It is possible that poor reaction to your words reveal the wickedness in the hearers' hearts. Jesus can attest to that. But he can also attest to how those with ears to hear recognized the value of his words. Perhaps that is a good measuring tool as well. How much value do you give to his words, all of his words? How convicted are you by his words intended to penetrate your heart? How comforted are you by his words intended to assure you of his grace?

Feeding

Proverb 10:21

The lips of the righteous feed many,
  but fools die for lack of sense.

The lips of the righteous feed the souls of many. They feed truth to those hungry for righteousness and for wisdom. They feed life to those starving for words to nourish their spirits. They feed conviction to those straying off the path of life, and they feed comfort to those needing yet again to hear the grace of the gospel.

But fools neither feed others nor themselves. They have nothing of true nourishment to give. They are like the sham doctors and experts who hawk worthless "nutritional" pills and foods, except that fools actually believe their worthless products are valuable. That is why they are fools. They hear what the righteous have to say and dismiss such richly laden words as though worthless. That is why they die from spiritual malnutrition. It is not that they live where there is famine but that they will not receive what is true nourishment.

Thus, God will not excuse the many who dismiss the words of life that are easily available to them. He will not excuse their objections as to why they refused to listen to his Word because of their perceptions of Christians and churches. Those with ears to hear will feed upon the gospel. They will recognize what is truly nourishing, if they are not fools.

The Blessing of the Lord

Proverbs 10:22

The blessing of the LORD makes rich,
and he adds no sorrow with it.

Perhaps the best way to understand this proverb is to contrast the blessing of the Lord with the blessing of the wicked, for they do offer blessing. The forbidden woman offers sensual blessings. If you join with them, the wicked offer the spoils from oppressing the poor, from taking advantage of the weak and the gullible, and from stealing. The worldly offer to bless you with earthly fame, money, and entertainment. They all offer to make you rich, and some of them are quite sincere, for they actually believe they live the blessed life.

But be sure that with such blessing will come sorrow. And it is not the sorrow that may come upon us because of the troubles that life throws at us. It is not the sorrow of being victim to the wickedness of others. It is the sorrow of knowing that we have lived for nothing. It is the sorrow of realizing that in the end no one cares whether we had lived or died, for we gave nothing of any value. Indeed, what we did give brought sorrow to others, for we blessed others with the empty blessing we received.

A person can weather much sorrow if he believes that he has been truly blessed. He can live in poverty if he knows that he is actually rich. Like the Apostle Paul, he can suffer much and yet attest that the grace of our Lord overflowed for him with the faith and love that are in Christ Jesus (1 Tim. 1:14).

Bad Joke

Proverb 10:23

Doing wrong is like a joke to a fool,
but wisdom is pleasure to a man of understanding.

This proverb strikes at the root of what distinguishes the wise person from the fool. It is not intellectual ability. It is not education or training. It is what gives a person pleasure.

The fool takes pleasure in doing wrong. It is a joke to him, which is the highest level of pleasure that a fool attains. The fool cannot comprehend the concept presented in Philippians 4:8: "Finally, brothers, whatever is true, whatever is honorable, whatever is just, whatever is pure, whatever is lovely, whatever is commendable, if there is any excellence, if there is anything worthy of praise, think about these things." No, the fool finds pleasure only in mocking such concepts.

But the person of understanding pursues wisdom and everything in the above list because he delights in them. He does not pursue them for the respect he will win by them, or to fit in with the culturally elite, or through them to gain riches. No, he enjoys them for their own sake.

Such pleasure may not come naturally or at least takes some effort to cultivate. Indeed, much of what is truly excellent takes some effort to recognize. The reason is due to the sin that is in us, which dulls our senses and makes it difficult to both recognize what is of value and then to enjoy it. Sin and delighting in sin come easy to us. Wisdom and righteousness do not. Take time to cultivate the latter and you will find a deeper, more satisfying pleasure.

Of Dread and Desire

Proverb 10:24

What the wicked dreads will come upon him,
but the desire of the righteous will be granted.

The wicked dreads judgment. He dreads getting caught for his wickedness and receiving his just reward. The righteous desire the reward of heaven, of being received into glory and hearing the blessing of his Lord. Each is sure to receive what is coming to him.

The wicked strives to put his fear behind him and for a while may be successful. He convinces himself that this life is all that there is. He surrounds himself with pleasurable things so that he might suppress thoughts about death. He invests in security measures to protect himself and his property and for a time feels secure. But at night, when he is alone with his thoughts, his dread returns. He cannot shake off the inner feeling that a day of reckoning must come.

The righteous strives to keep his hope of a heavenly city before him. The struggles of life, the temptations of the world, the weakness of his flesh, and the attacks of Satan all work to cast doubt and to raise fear. But he is able to carry on for he knows that the Righteous One has died for his sins and has opened the way into heaven. His Savior has gone to prepare a place for him. It is this faith that stirs his hope and gives him the peace and joy that carry him through his inner struggles.

Ultimately, the difference between the wicked and the righteous is their standing before the Righteous One. The wicked fear him; the righteous find their comfort in him. To the former, he comes as a fearsome nightmare; to the latter, he is the inspiring dream. Each will receive his due reward from him.

The Tempest

Proverb 10:25

When the tempest passes, the wicked is no more,
but the righteous is established forever.

The foundation upon which the wicked builds is nothing but sand. However deep he may dig and high he may build, the tempest will wash it away. The tempest may come in his lifetime. More often than not, the wicked is continually having to rebuild what justice or other wickedness tear down.

The righteous weathers the tempest because God who controls the very tempest is his Refuge, his Rock, his Tower, his Stronghold. He learns to regard the tempest as God's very means of making him more dependent upon his Lord.

But the tempest is that which we must all pass in death. As we enter

86

into the presence of God, what will remain after that tempest? What will remain of our works? What will be our condition after the tempest has stripped bare our foundation? What will the foundation prove to have been?

What it needs to be is the righteousness of Jesus Christ. Our works, our own efforts at morality will be washed away. Christ's righteousness is established forever. Upon that foundation we are to live and to place our security. Remember this during whatever tempest comes your way. Christ and those who place their security on him are established forever.

The Sluggard

Proverbs 10:26

Like vinegar to the teeth and smoke to the eyes,
  so is the sluggard to those who send him.

As vinegar sets teeth on edge and smoke stings the eyes, in the same way the sluggard exasperates and irritates those who depend on him. In this case, he is sent to carry out a work for another – perhaps delivering a message or an item, perhaps retrieving an item. Whatever the case, he wastes time and likely costs his employer money, maybe squandering an opportunity for his employer.

Most of the proverbs are directed towards the "wicked," "evildoer," and "fool." Even so, the sluggard can be as vexing a problem. A sluggard can be wicked and foolish, but often he appears to be a pleasant, care-free person who means no one any harm. But harm is exactly what he causes. The sluggard worker harms business – costing money, driving clients away, and fomenting resentment among his colleagues. The sluggard student is more taxing to the teacher than the disruptive student who will at least do his work. The very good natured attitude of the sluggard irritates all the more, because it reveals that he really does not care how his behavior affects others. Moreover, the sluggard is less likely to change. A wicked man is more likely to be convicted in his conscience and repent than a sluggard is to change his lazy habits.

The tendency towards laziness can be found in all of us. Examine yourself about this. You may be a hard worker at some things only to be a sluggard in other things that matter more. Do you work long hours, putting in extra time to get your work done? Good, but how much effort do you put into prayer? To reading and studying God's Word? Are you conscientious in getting a project completed? Fine, but how conscientious are you in loving your neighbor? The sluggard's problem is not that he doesn't get anything done. He accomplishes what he wants to do – sleep and eat. His problem is that he does not know what should be priorities. Our activeness and sluggardliness reveal our priorities.

How to Live Longer

Proverbs 10:27

The fear of the Lord prolongs life,
  but the years of the wicked will be short.

Is there any life insurance company that uses this criterion in evaluating life expectancy? One who fears the Lord, diligently obeying his laws, should have better odds of living longer than the one whose wicked life invites danger and violence. But the fear of the Lord entails more than an effort to not sin. One who fears the Lord delights in God; he finds peace and contentment through trusting God; he finds purpose in living. And as all medical experts know, the one who lives in contentment is more likely to live longer than the one who is anxious, always pursuing something more, and living on the edge. Living a good life promotes wellbeing, as does living a contented life.

But the proverb is more likely to be thinking of God's protection over those who fear him. We may follow the right diet, do the right exercises, and live righteous and contented lives, but have our lives cut short nevertheless by any number of causes. It is to the Lord that we look for preservation.

Even so, the full truth of this proverb lies not in how many years of this physical life that we can accumulate, but in the work of the Lord to give eternal life to his people who fear him. "I am the resurrection and the life. Whoever believes in me, though he die, yet shall he live, and everyone who lives and believes in me shall never die" (John 11:25-26). Now that is prolonged life!

Joyful Hope

Proverbs 10:28

The hope of the righteous brings joy,
  but the expectation of the wicked will perish.

Here is the Apostle Paul's commentary about the hope of the righteous: "Therefore, since we have been justified by faith, we have peace with God through our Lord Jesus Christ. Through him we have also obtained access by faith into this grace in which we stand, and we rejoice in hope of the glory of God. More than that, we rejoice in our sufferings, knowing that suffering produces endurance, and endurance produces character, and character produces hope, and hope does not put us to shame, because God's love has been poured into our hearts through the Holy Spirit who has been given to us" (Rom. 5:1-6).

Our hope is for the glory of God to be revealed in the return of Christ. We will behold our Lord in all of his glory; the glory of God will be the sun for us; and we ourselves will become glorious beings. Let this hope be your joy today.

The Way of the Lord

Proverbs 10:29

The way of the Lord is a stronghold to the blameless,
  but destruction to evildoers.

Consider this proverb from different levels. The writer most likely is thinking of the "way of the Lord" as following God's law. For the keeper of the law, such a way is a stronghold, a fortress against the wicked who seek the righteous' destruction, and from the efforts of the worldly to lead the righteous astray. Surely, the one who reads, meditates upon, and obeys the law finds strength and protection.

The evildoer, however, is brought to ruin by the law. It exposes his sin and magnifies his weakness. The law entraps the wicked, so that, as noted in many other proverbs, his life comes to an end suddenly and violently.

For the Christian, who is found blameless in Christ, the law is also a stronghold, for it reveals the life that is pleasing to God. It shows the path of obedience that brings fruitfulness and peace. The law presents the life that withstands the afflictions and temptations of the world. For the person who rejects Christ, the law reveals his selfish, wicked heart.

But moving to a higher level, Jesus makes clear that he is the way of the Lord. "I am the way, the truth, and the life" (John 14:6). The law is a stronghold for those able to keep it; Jesus is the stronghold for all who will turn to him, confessing their inability to keep the law. Only in Christ can we apply the identification of "blameless." It is Christ alone who has fulfilled the law; it is to Christ, which the law is intended to drive us. The "Way of the Lord" is our Redeemer, Jesus Christ, who delivers us and protects us.

For the evildoers who will not repent and turn to Christ as their stronghold, Christ is the revealer of their wicked hearts and will be their judge. On the last day when he returns in his glory, Christ will be the stronghold of the blameless who follow him, protecting them from punishment and delivering them into glory; yet, he will be the judge and the avenger against the wicked.

As you face the challenges and temptations of the world today, pray to your Stronghold to keep you safe and to empower you to obey God's law.

Land Dwellers

Proverbs 10:30

The righteous will never be removed,
but the wicked will not dwell in the land.

"The land" is the Israelites' inheritance in the Promised Land. No other possession was dearer to an Israelite than his land, and the whole land of Israel was identified with the kingdom of God. Thus, the righteous will never be removed from the kingdom of God, but the wicked will not dwell in that kingdom.

Peter tells believers: "According to God's great mercy, he has caused us to be born again to a living hope through the resurrection of Jesus Christ from the dead, to an inheritance that is imperishable, undefiled, and unfading, kept in heaven for you, who by God's power are being guarded through faith for a salvation ready to be revealed in the last time" (1 Pet. 1:3-5). That is a fuller way of saying, "The righteous will never be removed." Jesus puts it this way: "Let not your hearts be troubled. Believe in God; believe also in me. In my Father's house are many rooms. If it were not so, would I have told you that I go to prepare a place for you? And if I go and prepare a place for you, I will come again and will take you to myself, that where I am you may be also" (John 14:1-3).

Christ, who has clothed us in his righteousness, will keep his promise. God, who has elected us and caused us to be born again to a living hope, will not let that hope be thwarted. We will not be moved because our stronghold is Jesus Christ, the Way of the Lord.

The Mouth of Wisdom

Proverbs 10:31

The mouth of the righteous brings forth wisdom,
but the perverse tongue will be cut off.

The mouth is like a tree. The mouth of the righteous is like a strong, healthy tree: it bears (brings forth) good fruit (wisdom). But like a fruit tree which bears sickly fruit or is barren, the tongue of the perverse (those who twist what is true and good) will be cut off.

Those who twist the truth (perjury, false witness, lying, deceit) may be cut off through the justice system. Others may find themselves cut off socially, as they prove themselves untrustworthy and mean. This is especially true of those who twist what is good through gossip and jokes. And then, there are many who will be made famous and popular through their perverse speech as they ridicule biblical truth and goodness. But God will not be mocked and justice will be carried out whether on earth or at Christ's return.

Meanwhile, bear the good fruit of wisdom. Cultivate wisdom so that you may bless others through wise counsel. Make it a matter of great concern how you speak and what you say to others. Today, you will either bless or disconcert others by what comes out of your mouth. How do you cultivate wisdom? Begin now by praying daily for wisdom and that God will direct your tongue. Study Scripture and especially study Christ, who is Wisdom personified.

Instinct

Proverbs 10:32

The lips of the righteous know what is acceptable,
  but the mouth of the wicked, what is perverse.

We have the popular expression today "_____ knows _____." "Bo knows music." "Julia knows food." "Michael knows basketball." It means that the person credited doesn't merely know about a subject but that he knows it, or performs it, so well that he becomes identified with it. He is "at one with it." He doesn't have to think about what to do because it has become an instinct for him.

So with the righteous and the wicked. The righteous know what is acceptable. It is natural for them to speak what is good and right. They know the right thing to say at the time needed. The wicked know what is perverse. They naturally make a joke of what is good and sacred. They instinctively put down others, especially those who are good.

Examine yourself in this matter. In the course of a day, do you find people encouraged by your speech? Do they walk away more thoughtful? Or do you find that for various reasons they seem to be sensitive to what you say? If the latter, then something is wrong inside and you need to address it. You can read books on how to speak, but if the heart is not addressed, saying "right" words will only have the wrong effect. If your heart has resentment, disappointment, pride, vanity, and the like, such attitudes will come out. Get to the heart of the matter, which is your heart.

Pleasing God

Proverbs 11:1

A false balance is an abomination to the Lord,
  but a just weight is his delight.

God hates cheating; he delights in integrity. This is a good proverb to remember as we are tempted to cut corners on a job, to omit information on our taxes, to "get help" on a paper, or to gain an advantage over a competitor. The end does not justify the means.

Besides the outright crooked people who cheat, many of us do the same and rationalize our actions, either justifying why cheating is needed this one time or denying that cheating is happening: "The government shouldn't be taxing me for this anyhow"; "If I fail this test in the class, which I shouldn't have to take anyhow, my future will be shot"; "Everyone in my field does the same; I won't be able to compete."

Such an attitude betrays trust in God, who set the rules for right behavior. Acting righteously matters more to him than achieving the goal, which he alone has the power to grant or take away. Thus we see why he delights in integrity. He is not a mere observer. He is the true goal of us who believe in him. Whatever may be our objectives, pleasing God is to be our one goal, and we please him by obeying his righteous laws and by trusting him with the outcome.

Wise Humility

Proverbs 11:2

When pride comes, then comes disgrace,
but with the humble is wisdom..

Jesus' parable in Luke 14:7-11 provides commentary for this proverb. The person who out of pride sits himself at the head of the table is disgraced when asked to take a lower seat, while the humble person ends up honored. It is interesting that the proverb connects humility with wisdom. It makes sense.

Pride, by definition, is foolishness. Caught up in promoting himself before the eyes of others, the person with pride cannot see things as they really are. He misjudges how he appears to others; he is blind to others' virtues; he fails to comprehend what is of real value.

The humble person, on the other hand – because he is not caught up in himself – more clearly sees the real picture. If working with a team on a project, he is able to avail himself of the strengths of others, not worried about how he will be perceived. Sports provide a good example. Teams that do best are the teams that implement the best teamwork – each player unselfish, more concerned with the goal of winning than of having the best personal statistics. That is wisdom.

Humility allows us to focus on what matters. It clears our minds so as to focus with clarity on the task at hand and in discerning the truth. All the more sense, then, in understanding why humility is essential in grasping the gospel, the most profound truth of all for us.

Wise Integrity

Proverbs 11:3

The integrity of the upright guides them,

but the crookedness of the treacherous destroys them.

Like the previous proverb, this one presents the connection between virtue and wisdom, and between sin and foolishness. We are often taught that to think we can maintain integrity in the business world or academics or whatever field is to be naive. Everyone else compromises or outright cheats; we must compromise our ethics if we are to keep pace, especially such ethics as taught in Jesus' Sermon on the Mount.

Yet the sins of greed and pride lead the brightest and most gifted astray. Men begin with startling success only to crash because their sins cloud their ability to see clearly the coming disaster that they set up for themselves.

When our priority is to do what is right and not "get ahead," decision making becomes easier and the results more satisfying. After all, even if our decisions cause us to lose the promotion, the sale, or the game, all we have lost is temporal success. But what we gain in this life is more enduring – peace of mind, contentment, a good name, trust.

But we must take this proverb to its ultimate conclusion. The treacherous will be destroyed at the Judgment Day. Whatever "success" they may achieve in this life will only gall them all the more in their condemnation. But the one who in integrity remains faithful to Christ and his teachings will be guided along the path of eternal life.

Dying Well

Proverbs 11:4

Riches do not profit in the day of wrath,
but righteousness delivers from death.

In medical news a report was published that people with at least $70,000 in assets die better. Their last year of life is less painful, presumably because they can afford better healthcare and have more leverage in demanding good care.

But riches – be it $70,000 or $70 billion – will be of no avail at the final judgment. People speak of good and bad death: to die young or violently is a bad death; to die old and in one's sleep is a good death. The only good death, however, is to die in the arms of Jesus Christ, our Righteousness, who delivers us from death.

Certainly, it is wise to prepare financially for one's death, especially if you have dependents. And it is good to keep healthy. But death is inevitable, if our Lord tarries in his return, and what matters is not how pain-free our death it, but whether or not it becomes the doorway into our Savior's arms.

Walking in Balance

Proverbs 11:5

The righteousness of the blameless keeps his way straight,
but the wicked falls by his own wickedness.

How does the gymnast on the balance beam keep her balance? For one thing she keeps her head straight and eyes focused. To stay on the straight path, we must keep our head straight, following the righteous laws and commands of Scripture. Such laws steady us and keep us on the right track.

Even so, the very laws and commands of Scripture can be unnerving if we depend upon them to make us blameless. Indeed, they expose our wickedness. Whereas, we may have walked confidently in our illusion of self-righteousness, they unsettle us and tip us off the beam.

Our help, then, is found in Christ, our Righteousness. Stay focused on him. Keep your eyes upon him, upon the work he has already done for you in laying the path and placing you on it. Look to him now as he intercedes for you, as his Spirit steadies you. Look to the final destination where he will stand ready to bring you into glory. The wicked have only their own wits to help them navigate a treacherous world. The righteous have Christ, the Son of God, who is Lord over all to take them through the dangers of this world and bring them safely to glory. Keep focused.

Ethics and Wisdom

Proverbs 11:6

The righteousness of the upright delivers them,
but the treacherous are taken captive by their lust.

You should be picking up a theme by now: to be righteous is to be wise, which leads to success; to be wicked is to be foolish, which leads to failure. Because the focus of the righteous is to do what is right, God will deliver them; also, the focus on doing right gives them clarity about reality and discernment into wisdom. The wicked, on the other hand, have distorted views as to what is real – about themselves, about what is of real value, about how to achieve goals. Thus, inevitably their ways lead to failure. Even if they achieve the goal of wealth, they become poor in the things that really matter – good name, loving relationships, productive lives – and more often than not, they lose their wealth.

Let's say a colleague at work is competing with you for advancement. If "wicked," he will choose foolish means of fulfilling his lust for wealth – flattery, brown-nosing the boss, lying about you and about himself. He may work longer hours, sacrificing relations with his family. Because your concern is to follow the righteous path of Christ, focus on performing your job to the best of your ability, encouraging the performance of your colleagues, and being truthful and loving in Christ. More likely, you will advance because of the respect you have earned.

But even if the colleague advances, he is only setting himself up for a greater fall as he grows even more blind to where his conduct is leading him. You, on the other hand, though you may not advance as you desire, are developing the habits of a peaceful, productive life. Lust clouds good thinking; righteousness clears the clouds away.

Pity the Wicked

Proverbs 11:7

When the wicked dies, his hope will perish,
and the expectation of wealth perishes too.

Pity the wicked. Their hope will perish. All their dreams – what drives them to live – will vanish. If they are fortunate, their hope will perish while in their lifetime. Then they might come to their senses like the prodigal son, repent, and turn to God. But if they are not shown such mercy, their wealth and earthly success might grow, leaving them blind to their destiny. They are like the hypocrites that Jesus spoke of in Matthew 6:16, who obtain their goal of receiving earthly recognition for false spirituality. They obtain the reward they are seeking, and it is all they will obtain, for God sees all and will give the appropriate eternal reward.

Has someone taken an inheritance that should have been yours? Has someone unethically taken credit you should have received, been promoted over you? Pray for God's mercy upon him. For his earthly success only serves to blind him to his poverty. But don't let his success blind you to your riches. What may the righteous in Christ expect? "An inheritance that is imperishable, undefiled, and unfading, kept in heaven for you, who by God's power are being guarded through faith for a salvation ready to be revealed in the last time" (1 Pet. 1:4-5). That is wealth beyond measure that you cannot lose. Now that's a good deal!

Walking into Trouble

Proverbs 11:8

The righteous is delivered from trouble,
and the wicked walks into it instead.

The wicked does not read warning labels. He ignores danger signs. He doesn't look both ways when crossing the street and prefers to take shortcuts through alleys and dark parks. He does not think wisely about danger, not so much thinking that he will be safe, but not thinking about the subject at all. He just acts, doing whatever pops in his mind.

There is also the person who is attracted to trouble like a moth to a light. He does like to court danger; it is thrilling to him. He will test the limits and likes getting away with doing something forbidden or at least coming close.

And there is the person who wants to "experience" what others are doing, afraid that he is missing out on something good. So he will check out the parties, the late-night excursions "just to see" what's going on, thinking that he is wise enough, strong enough to resist temptation.

There is the person who exposes himself to temptation – the man who walks by the pornography store, the wife who keeps running into the understanding male friend, and so on. We walk near trouble, telling ourselves we know when to step back, but all along we are really walking straight into trouble.

Pray to Christ to deliver you from your temptations. Read his Word for wisdom and for the promises of deliverance. Seek the help of Christian friends. Do what you need to do for deliverance; otherwise, you are walking into trouble.

Wise Righteousness

Proverbs 11:9

With his mouth the godless man would destroy his neighbor,
but by knowledge the righteous are delivered.

Jesus is the best example of proving this proverb. He was followed by men bent on destroying his reputation and even seeking his life by either laying verbal traps before him or outright slandering him. And yet, because of his wisdom born out of righteousness, he always had a ready answer that rebutted slander and even exposed their foolishness.

Again the theme is repeated in the proverbs. Righteousness and wisdom go hand in hand. We always sin out of foolishness; wisdom never leads us to sin; sin never guides us to be wise (it is repentance, not sin, that makes us wise after a fall). Sin makes us dangerous to our neighbor – either we hate our neighbor and seek his harm, or in our sinful foolishness, we become safety hazards.

Seek wisdom that you might grow in righteousness; seek righteousness that you might grow in wisdom. Seek to be like Christ and follow his commands that you might obtain both.

Righteousness in the City

Proverbs 11:10

When it goes well with the righteous, the city rejoices,
and when the wicked perish there are shouts of gladness.

Is this proverb really true? It can seem that the city mocks the righteous and exalts the wicked. But then, what we have in mind is the city mocking our morals. Righteousness, of course, includes morality, but the focus here is on that aspect of righteousness in which the welfare of the city is being sought. A righteous mayor is one who is striving for the good of the city. He is resistant to corruption and shows justice to all, disregarding any citizen's social or financial status. The wicked mayor is one seeking his own gain, who favors the rich over the poor, and does not take care to defend the city.

The question for us as Christians is how well we display such righteousness. Do we demonstrate that we love the city? That we desire her prosperity? That we will play our role in being a blessing to the city? Do we as individual neighbors practice being good neighbors, taking personal interest in our neighborhood? Or are our speech and actions conveying disdain for having to live where we do?

Our neighbors may laugh at our morality; they may look askance at our social views; nevertheless, they ought to be able to attest to our being good neighbors who are there for them in their troubles. They should know that we care for them. They should see in us neighbors who like the city. They should rejoice when it goes well with the righteous.

Blessing the City

Proverbs 11:11

By the blessing of the upright a city is exalted,
but by the mouth of wicked it is overthrown.

The blessing of the upright may be the blessing that the upright give to the city. Thus, we bless the city when we pray for her, when we befriend our neighbors, pitch in to help the neighborhood, vote for good leaders, even run for public office. We bless the city by living upright lives and thus not contributing to delinquency, disorderly conduct, and unethical treatment of others.

The blessing may also be the blessing that God gives to the city because of the presence of the upright. God was willing to spare Sodom and Gomorrah for the sake of ten upright persons which proved to be too high of a number. How much blessing has come to your city because God's people live there, and the blessing he has poured out on them has spilled over to their neighborhoods and workplaces?

Our presence in the city is intended for blessing, whether it is through the blessing we pass on in the name of Christ or the blessing spilling over from God as he cares for his people. Pray today that you will be a blessing where God has placed you – in or out of the city. Because you live where you do, work where you do, go to school, do shopping, have fun – whatever the reason, pray that because you are present those around you will be blessed because of the Spirit of Christ flowing through you.

A Wise Neighbor

Proverbs 11:12

Whoever belittles his neighbor lacks sense,
but a man of understanding remains silent.

Why is it foolish to belittle one's neighbor? He can get even! He can play his music loud, have his dog use your yard, etc. He can make daily life miserable. A wise person understands this. He keeps his views about his neighbor's habits and tastes to himself. He does not take it upon himself to "improve" his neighbor with "helpful" comments.

Why else is it foolish to belittle one's neighbor? Because we incur our Lord's displeasure who commanded us to love our neighbor. Far from belittling our neighbor, we are to look for ways to show him respect.

Why else is it foolish to belittle one's neighbor? Because we sabotage our own intentions. If our neighbor needs Christ, we ruin whatever prayers and efforts we may make to witness because we have offended him. Perhaps what we belittle are behaviors that do need changing; nevertheless, because we have shown our neighbor disrespect, he will not listen to us and rebuff whatever help we may offer.

Even if we belittle our neighbor in private, such an attitude harms our witness. God does not honor such an attitude. And if we inwardly mock a neighbor, it will somehow come out in the way we relate to him.

Why else is it foolish to belittle our neighbor? There is so much in us to belittle. But God, instead of mocking us, showed us the highest honor by sending his Son to die for us. Such is the attitude God calls on us to have for our neighbor. Today, what regard will you show for your neighbors who live next to you?

Half-Truth Tellers

Proverbs 11:13

Whoever goes about slandering reveals secrets,

but he who is trustworthy in spirit keeps a thing covered.

"Perhaps I shouldn't say this, but Tom told me..."
"I'm not supposed to say anything, but I thought you should know..."
"I wonder why Sally was going into..."

And the beat goes on. Note that the proverb says slandering reveals secrets. The viciousness of slander lies in that it spreads half-truths – the half that puts the person in a bad light. I hear half-truths often when a spouse comes to me to share about the unjust behavior of the other spouse, or when anyone comes to present their "concerns" about someone else. But the slander here is not the half-truth spoken in a private counseling session, but that which is spread publicly (and privately when shared with someone who has no business in knowing or the slanderer has no business in telling anyone).

When a baseball pitcher was caught on camera responding badly to a cameraman, a sports writer wrote an article recalling instances when athletes had not treated him well. He named each athlete and described the confrontation. He seemed oblivious to the issue that really is at the heart of athletes' frustration with the media, which is the media's power to affect how they are perceived publicly. In this article, we were given a detailed description of the athlete's bad behavior and a sympathetic picture of the writer. His one article of these instances will color how most of the readers will always view these athletes.

We can do the same with other people's reputations. A single remark of questioning a person's actions, especially questioning his motives, will prejudice the hearers, so that, despite what the truth is or what the person does for good, the doubt remains in the hearer's minds. Slander is ruthless because it has to prove nothing, merely suggest.

The one who is trustworthy in spirit keeps secrets told him. And when he sees something which does not involve him, he is slow to reveal it. He either goes to the person who has done something questionable, or he keeps it covered, trusting God to bring to light what needs to be. He does this for several reasons. One, he knows that he can ruin a good person's reputation and for love of his neighbor he will keep silent. Two, he knows the injunction that if he

103

sees his brother in sin, he is to go to that person instead of spreading the news to others. Three, he knows that he can stir up strife, creating greater trouble than the one he supposedly sees. Four, he knows his limits. He knows that he may not know the whole story and thus will not take the chance of spreading half-truths. Five, he knows that there are limits to his responsibility. He is not to be the judge or take responsibility of everyone he sees doing something he questions. He entrusts them in God's hands and in the hands of others who do have responsibility.

Keep this proverb in mind today as you hear and see what goes on around you.

Needed: Counselors

Proverbs 11:14

Where there is no guidance, a people falls,
but in an abundance of counselors there is safety.

All of us need counselors, and the greater authority we possess the more needed are good counselors. Some persons think that the mark of true leadership is to act without counsel, at least without the counsel of those who would be under their authority. Husbands make this mistake regarding their wives; elders may miss the wise counsel of the deacons. Bosses will ignore counsel from their employees. But one of the premises of the book of Proverbs is that the mark of wisdom is knowing when wise counsel is being given. The wise leader, therefore, desires to hear the counsel of others, whatever their position may be. He asks good questions; he elicits the opinions of those under him. He, then, as a leader must make the decision and bear the responsibility. All the more, he needs counselors.

We all need, of course, the one whom Jesus called the Counselor, the Holy Spirit. The wisest counselors are the biggest fools without the inspiration of the Holy Spirit. It is the work of the Spirit within and among counselors in which a people and a church will find safety.

Givers, Not Lenders Be

Proverbs 11:15

Whoever puts up security for a stranger will surely suffer harm,
but he who hates striking hands in pledge is secure.

This is a proverb that many of us have learned the hard way as we tried to help out someone in need with a loan or signing for a loan. If you wish to help someone, then give. If you make a loan, or co-sign for a loan, then only do so with the expectation that you will not get that money back; otherwise, you set yourself up for a fall.

Friendships have been destroyed and family relations broken over the lending of money. The money owed becomes a sore-spot; the one owing the money starts to avoid you. Conversation is strained because you both know the issue is always present. Or perhaps the friend seems to show no concern. All the more then his attitude aggravates you. Doesn't he care?

Do not put others in your debt, especially when it comes to money. What you part with, do so freely and cheerfully. Know the cost of co-signing and be willing and ready to pay that cost. Scripture tells us to give liberally, but never to lend liberally.

That is the gospel. God gave freely his Son; the Son gave freely his life. Thus, we are free of the burden of having to pay a debt that we can never pay. We are free to love our Friend, our Brother, our Lord.

Contrasting Rewards

Proverbs 11:16

A gracious woman gets honor,
and violent men get riches.

An English teacher would have given this proverb poor marks for its attempt at making a contrasting parallel. It goes from singular to plural, from woman to man, and the objects do not match. One would think that violent men would get dishonor. But they get the money. And as far as they are concerned, they get the better end of the bargain.

But then, the writer would note, they are fools. Their very problem is that they get what they value, and only what they value. And, as other proverbs note, they get the wrong end of the bargain. Consider these:

> Riches do not profit in the day of wrath,
> but righteousness delivers from death (11:4).

> Whoever trusts in his riches will fall,
> but the righteous will flourish like a green leaf (11:28).

> A good name is to be chosen rather than great riches,
> and favor is better than silver or gold (22:1).

An implied contrast between the gracious woman and the violent men is that the latter obtain mere money. To be gracious, by its very nature, means that the woman's goal is to bless others. One can feign to be gracious in order to win honor, but one cannot actually be gracious with the same goal in mind. Virtue actually is its own reward or achieves its reward. For honor will come from other people but especially from God the Just Rewarder and the only rewarder who matters.

Personal Benefits

Proverbs 11:17

A man who is kind benefits himself,
but a cruel man hurts himself.

What typically happens when you do a kind deed? You hold the elevator door open instead of letting it close on the person walking to it; you let the driver pull in front of you in heavy traffic; you help your colleague complete a task; you carry the bag for your neighbor. Usually such kind deeds earn a smile and a thank you. What happens to you then? You smile and feel happy; your kindness benefits you

106

with well-being; your day becomes more enjoyable; you feel contented, and all because of being kind.

But the person who shuts the door, refuses to let anyone in front of him, and begrudges giving help, harms his well-being. His day is a chore to get through; it is filled with stress as he fights for his own advantage; he has tension with his neighbors and colleagues. His cruel acts are actually hurts against himself.

Do you want to enjoy today? Start off with acts of kindness. Do you want to mature in your faith and sanctification? Show kindness. Do you want to grow closer to God? Be kind to your neighbor. For such kindness was shown to us by God through the greatest kind act of all – sending his Son to redeem us.

A Sure Reward

Proverbs 11:18

The wicked earns deceptive wages,
  but one who sows righteousness gets a sure reward.

This proverb is a commentary on the proverb two verses ago: "A gracious woman gets honor, and violent men get riches." The "riches" that the wicked earn are deceptive. They are but the precursor to disaster and misery, be it in this lifetime or the next. The honor that the righteous receive is a sure reward because it is the honor bestowed by God.

Satan and Christ exemplify this proverb. Satan, in his attacks against Jesus, earned deceptive wages. He appeared to get what he wanted – Jesus disgraced and defeated. What he really earned was his sure downfall. Because Jesus, though tempted, did not sin, because he lived in righteousness, his sacrifice produced his reward of glory and his inheritance – us!
>   "...when his soul makes an offering for sin,
>   he shall see his offspring;
>   he shall prolong his days;
>   the will of the Lord shall prosper in his hand.

107

Out of the anguish of his soul
he shall see and be satisfied;
by his knowledge shall the righteous one, my servant,
make many to be accounted righteous..." (Isa. 53:10-11).

Keeping Steadfast

Proverbs 11:19

Whoever is steadfast in righteousness will live,
but he who pursues evil will die.

The contrast is between states of attitude. There are those who strive to do the right thing, and there are those who strive only to get ahead of others through whatever means it takes. Indeed, there are some who delight specifically in cheating and in hurting others.

Jesus weighs in on the first attitude: "Blessed are those who hunger and thirst for righteousness, for they shall be satisfied" (Matt. 5:6). They will be satisfied because their heavenly Father will protect them and reward them often in this life and especially in the life to come. He who pursues evil will die, often an untimely death in this life, but worse, he will die the second death. As Jesus said, "Rather fear him who can destroy both soul and body in hell" (Matt. 10:28).

Then there is the contrast between those who are in a state of righteousness and those in a state of sin/evil. Romans 1-3 presents these conditions and the dilemma: "all, both Jews and Greeks, are under sin" (Rom. 3:9). Scripture makes the case that no one can be steadfast in righteousness; even the person with a conscience to do good only fails (Rom. 7:15ff). Where then is our hope? "My hope is built on nothing less than Jesus' blood and righteousness," says the hymn. We are given "the righteousness of God through faith in Jesus Christ for all who believe," says Scripture (Rom. 3:22).

Remain steadfast, then, in Jesus Christ. Keep your faith in him. "Whoever believes in him is not condemned, but whoever does not believe is condemned already, because he has not believed in the name of the only Son of God" (John 3:18).

God's Delight

Proverbs 11:20

Those of crooked heart are an abomination to the Lord,
but those of blameless ways are his delight.

Meditate on what pleases God:

> His delight is not in the strength of the horse,
>   nor his pleasure in the legs of a man,
> but the LORD takes pleasure in those who fear him,
>   in those who hope in his steadfast love (Ps. 147:10-11).

> Thus says the Lord: Let not the wise man boast in his wisdom, let not the mighty man boast in his might, let not the rich man boast in his riches, but let him who boasts boast in this, that he understands and knows me, that I am the Lord who practices steadfast love, justice, and righteousness in the earth. For in these things I delight," declares the Lord (Jer. 9:23-24).

> Lying lips are an abomination to the Lord,
> but those who act faithfully are his delight (Prov. 12:22).

> "You are my beloved Son; with you I am well pleased" (Mark 1:11).

> Through him then let us continually offer up a sacrifice of praise to God, that is, the fruit of lips that acknowledge his name. Do not neglect to do good and to share what you have, for such sacrifices are pleasing to God.... Now may the God of peace who brought again from the dead our Lord Jesus, the great shepherd of the sheep, by the blood of the eternal covenant, equip you with everything good that you

109

may do his will, working in us that which is pleasing in his sight, through Jesus Christ, to whom be glory forever and ever. Amen (Heb. 13:15-16, 20-21).

Assured Justice

Proverbs 11:21

Be assured, an evil person will not go unpunished, but the offspring of the righteous will be delivered.

While watching a sporting event, such as a basketball or football game, you will notice a coach get extremely angry, sometimes for no apparent reason. He screams at the officials. His assistants may have to hold him back. Why is he so angry? He sees what he perceives to be cheating by the other team. That's bad enough, but what pushes him over the edge is that he can't get the officials to see the cheating and punish it. "They are getting away with it!"

What especially gets our anger is the perceived injustice that involves us. The driver who cuts in front of us; the co-worker getting away with being a slacker or advancing through cheating; the fellow student who gets a better grade because he cheated, and so on. "They are getting away with it!"

No, they are not. God sees all, and God will reward each person for what he has done. We might see the punishment come; we might not. Quite likely the punishment or reward will not be what we expect because we do not judge rightly. We also are sinners; we also commit the same sins in different forms. Our sense of justice is influenced more by how we are affected. That's why we can read of a murder taking place without a tinge of emotion if we know none of the parties, but we will become outraged because a company made a mistake on our bill.

Be assured. Be contented. Evil will not go unpunished. No one is getting away with anything. The righteous will not only be delivered, but their offspring as well. God is in control. What we need to do is trust God. Our concern is to be obedient to his laws and not let the

110

evil of others unduly influence us. How else could Jesus go calmly to the cross except that he entrusted himself into his Father's hands knowing that justice, not evil, would prevail?

Indiscretion

Proverbs 11:22

Like a gold ring in a pig's snout
is a beautiful woman without discretion.

A gold ring in a pig's snout is a waste of beauty and value – so is a woman who acts foolishly, especially in the area of relationships and sexuality. Such indiscretion wastes her beauty. Her very beauty ought to be an adornment that enhances her "value," and yet, through indiscretion she wastes it. A gold ring in a pig's snout is out of place. They together make a laughable picture. So, again, a beautiful woman turns herself into a mockery.

So it is when we misuse any gift we have been given by God. We all have been given gifts of one kind or another. It may be physical beauty; it may be high aptitude in a particular skill or expertise; it may be athleticism. Whatever it is, we should not let it be said of us, "There goes a waste of talent."

Why do we waste what we are given? For one thing, we have inordinate desires. We desire what is sinful, what does not belong to us, is not fitting for us. We covet the gifts of others, not satisfied with ours. Disappointments cause us to lose perspective about what really matters.

Our sin and folly then make our gifts our very weaknesses. Physical beauty is a danger for a foolish, sinful woman. Great athleticism becomes a danger for a foolish athlete who cannot handle the rewards. Pride is always lurking in our exercise of our gifts; all the more reason we must use them with wisdom.

Endings

Proverbs 11:23

The desire of the righteous ends only in good;
  the expectation of the wicked in wrath.

Note first that the desire of the righteous is righteous desire. The righteous and the wicked may desire the same job and the wicked win out. They may both desire to win the game and the wicked triumphs. But in the end, because the righteous desire righteousness above all, their desires will bring good. Thus, God causes all things to work for the good of those who love him (Rom. 8:28). For the wicked, on the other hand, temporal gains and triumphs will ultimately end in bearing God's wrath.

Pray for the wicked, that they experience defeat now so that they might then repent and turn to God. Their "triumphs" only drive them further away building up a false sense of security. Pray for those who disdain you because of your faith; pray for those who take advantage of your obedience to righteousness. What matters most is not how the story unfolds, but how it ends. Thank God that he has already shown us the ending and guaranteed it through Christ.

The Free Giver

Proverbs 11:24

One gives freely, yet grows all the richer;
another withholds what he should give, and only suffers want.

The one who gives freely already is ahead because he is free from the control of money and possessions. His security and self-esteem are not bound to possessions; rather, his joy is in blessing others and in furthering the work of God's kingdom. To put it another way, it is bearing fruit that gives him delight. The "Scrooge," however, is a slave to money and possessions, always fearful of losing them. Even if he may be compelled to give some small amount away, he loses because his focus is on his loss not on the blessing he imparts.

The irony that the proverb notes is that the generous giver typically ends up richer than the money-keeper. I'm reminded of a fundraisers' seminar I attended. The speaker noted the difference between those who inherit wealth and those who earned their wealth. The former, when considering if and how much to give, think in terms of subtracting from their wealth. (If I have 10 million and give 1 million, I will have 9 million left over.) The latter, on the other hand, believes he will be able to replace what he has given.

The proverb's point, however, is not that givers know how to earn money better than nongivers, but that God who sees all and controls all will bless the person who is like him in giving. For God is a generous giver. And he especially delights in our giving to real need, in giving cheerfully, in giving generously, and in giving to please God.

God gave his Son freely and with delight. The Son gave freely of himself. The Father and the Son give freely the Holy Spirit. Just as we have been freed from bondage of sin to live righteously, so we have been made wealthy in Christ that we may give freely. What will you give today? Will it be money? A gift? A possession? An act of friendship? The gospel? Pray that today you will give generously.

The Blessed Giver

Proverbs 11:25

Whoever brings blessing will be enriched,
and one who waters will himself be watered.

"They bless me more than I bless them."
"I get a whole lot more than what I give."

These are the kind of statements that are common to hear from those who go on mission trips, do acts of mercy, and get involved in ministry. They know the truth of another proverb that it is better to give than to receive, for giving brings a more satisfying pleasure. There is the joy of seeing the joy in others who are blessed, and there is the satisfaction of feeling useful.

Two attitudes make us depressed and feeling empty. One is to feel that we are not loved; another is to feel that we serve no purpose. To bring blessing cures both, for to perform acts of love will draw out love from others and make us useful.

Are you feeling down? Then do an act of kindness. Jesus said that even a cup of cold water will bring reward. What matters is not the cost nor degree of skill, but that you give out of love for your neighbor and for God. It is God who touches the giving and makes it a blessing, and it is God who waters the one giving water. Just as no sin slips by his watchful eyes, so no good deed. What will you do today to bring blessing? What watering will you do?

Providing a Chance

Proverbs 11:26

The people curse him who holds back grain,
but a blessing is on the head of him who sells it.

The crime here is not merely that one is a miser, but that he withholds what is needed for survival. He is not even being asked to give, but to sell. Instead he hordes the grain, perhaps to run up the price; perhaps he is fearful of not having enough for himself. His one concern is for himself, and he is willing for others to suffer. The one who sells is blessed for giving others fair opportunity to buy or earn what is needed. He is a good neighbor, a businessman who cares about his community.

We too should strive to be fair, to give others a fair chance of earning their way. Sometimes someone just needs a helping hand, sometimes a second chance to prove himself, and we have the means to help. As with the previous proverbs, we are called to be persons who do not hold back what we have to give and to bless others.

Think also of our Lord's generosity:
> "Come, everyone who thirsts,
> come to the waters;
> and he who has no money,

114

come, buy and eat!
Come, buy wine and milk
 without money and without price.
Why do you spend your money for that which is not
bread,
 and your labor for that which does not satisfy?
Listen diligently to me, and eat what is good,
 and delight yourselves in rich food. (Isa. 55:1-2).

Finding Favor

Proverbs 11:27

Whoever diligently seeks good seeks favor,
but evil comes to him who searches for it.

Do yourself a favor – try to be good. The world's proverb is wrong: good guys finish last. The bad guys may think they have moved into first place, but they will only prove Jesus' proverb: the first shall be the last.

The "good guys" who live for God, who place others before themselves will find the favor of God who gives more generously than we can even ask. For, as if the many blessings in this life are not enough, he gives us the reward of everlasting life, indeed, everlasting glory. Paul, who had a glimpse of this glory, could write about his harsh, continuous sufferings, "For this slight momentary affliction is preparing for us an eternal weight of glory beyond all comparison" (2 Cor. 4:17).

But the "bad boys" who look for evil will find it and its reward. They will find it turn on them so that they have lost control of themselves, becoming addicted to bad habits and entangled in the troubles that evil will cause for them. Worse, they will receive their eternal weight of disgrace beyond all comparison.

Apply this proverb to Christ and Satan. The Son diligently sought obedience and won the favor of the Father; as a result, he now sits in glory and reigns over God's kingdom. But evil has come to Satan, who because he sought to rebel against God and to harm his Son, is doomed forever to suffer in the lake of fire. Thanks be to God that the good of the Son has brought immeasurable good to us.

In Whom Do We Trust?

Proverbs 11:28

Whoever trusts in his riches will fall,
but the righteous will flourish like a green leaf.

In _____ we trust. In whom? In what do you trust your welfare? Is it in your bank account? Perhaps your trust is in your skill or training. Perhaps it is in your insurance policy. Perhaps your trust is in your ability to call the shots. God has a way of shaking our trust when placed in anything else other than him.

We will be shaken in something. We may have control of our jobs and find our family relations shaken. We may be secure in our relationships and lose our jobs or drop out of school. The truth of the matter is that we cannot control everything which touches us. Our "control" is an illusion, for we may lose anything and everything, except for...

Except for the righteousness given to us in Jesus Christ. The inheritance of salvation is promised to us; it is kept in heaven for us and cannot be stolen or destroyed. We are kept safe in Christ through faith. Jesus said that we are in the Father's hands and no one can snatch us out. He said that all whom the Father has given him will receive eternal life and will not perish. The result is that the one thing that we cannot lose is the one thing that is eternal.

In God may we trust, so that whatever may befall us in this life cannot shake us, because we know that in him we cannot fall.

Inheritance

Proverbs 11:29

Whoever troubles his own household will inherit the wind,
and the fool will be servant to the wise of heart.

Inheritance is the cause of many troubles in households. "Mom knew how much I always wanted the dining furniture." "You never cared about tools anyhow; I should have them." And then there is the money to quarrel over; should the home be sold? But then, it is not the inheritance that troubles a household. It is the selfish heart, the greedy heart, the spiteful heart.

James explains this well in his letter: "What causes quarrels and what causes fights among you? Is it not this, that your passions are at war within you? You desire and do not have, so you murder. You covet and cannot obtain, so you fight and quarrel" (Jas. 4:1-2). What the troubler ends up inheriting is the wind, something he cannot hold onto. Even if he gets the money, he loses it. Even though he gets the heirloom, it gives no pleasure. He ends up with nothing.

The troubler is a fool, for he foolishly places his hopes in what cannot keep its promise and in what creates trouble for himself. Thus, he ends up being a servant to the one who is wise. Note that the wise is the wise of heart. He is not merely clever, but his heart is right. There are many who are clever but wicked, but the truly wise are those whose hearts are right with God. Then they receive clarity; then they bring forth good fruit; then they are rewarded by their God who sees all things, even into their hearts.

Good Fruit

Proverbs 11:30

The fruit of the righteous is a tree of life,
and whoever captures souls is wise.

The fruit of the righteous is a tree of life because good fruit comes from good trees. Jesus noted this. You can tell the heart of a person by the fruit he bears. One can try to imitate goodness, but if his heart is not good his outward goodness will appear superficial.

There is a difference between controlling one's tongue from saying angry words and from not thinking of angry words at all. There certainly is a difference between learning to act good so as to get one's way and taking delight in blessing others. Focus on righteousness and the good fruit will come. Make Christ the model of righteousness, and trust in him to provide that righteousness. A good tree is good because its roots draw rich nourishment. Find your nourishment in God's Word, in Christ's work, and in the Spirit's indwelling.

Finally, seek to be a soul-winner. There are different ways to capture. There is the face-to-face witness, doing good deeds, being a good friend, writing, praying. One thing that stymies us is projecting activities that unnerve us and may be what we are not gifted in doing; often the result is missing out on opportunities given us. Thus, as we fret about doing street evangelism, we miss the opportunity given when our neighbor strikes up a conversation with us. We don't need to ask God to give opportunity to witness so much as to ask him to open our eyes to the many opportunities he already places before us.

Pray today that you will be a tree of life to your neighbor; pray that you may capture a soul through your love and good fruit. And thank God that he captured you!

Repaid Well

Proverbs 11:31

If the righteous is repaid on earth,
how much more the wicked and the sinner!

This proverb aptly sums up Chapter 11. "Righteousness delivers from death"; "a gracious woman gets honor"; "a man who is kind benefits himself"; "the one who sows righteousness gets a sure reward"; "whoever is steadfast in righteousness will live"; "the desire of the righteous ends only in good"; "one gives freely, yet grows all the richer"; "whoever brings blessing will be enriched"; "whoever diligently seeks good seeks favor"; "the righteous will flourish like a green leaf."

Now if the righteous is repaid with blessing, all the more the wicked will be repaid with condemnation. The wicked receive disgrace, destruction, captivity, perished hope, trouble, hurt, deceptive wages, death, punishment, want, cursing, evil, empty inheritance.

If you care about yourself, if you want what is best for you, which path, then, should you choose? Whom should you choose to follow? In whom should you place your hope? Should you be angered by the person who uses wicked ways to get ahead of you, or should you pity him? Who is richer: your unscrupulous neighbor or you? Perhaps this prayer needs to be made for you today: "That the God of our Lord Jesus Christ, the Father of glory, may give you a spirit of wisdom and of revelation in the knowledge of him, having the eyes of your hearts enlightened, that you may know what is the hope to which he has called you, what are the riches of his glorious inheritance in the saints" (Eph. 1:17-18).

Stupid Thinking

Proverbs 12:1

Whoever loves discipline loves knowledge,
  but he who hates reproof is stupid.

That is a blunt translation! It gets, however, to the essential difference between the wise and the foolish; indeed, it expresses the reason the wise are wise and the foolish are foolish. The lover of knowledge loves discipline because discipline leads him to knowledge. He wants to be corrected when his thinking is going astray because more dear to him than his ego is obtaining truth.

The fool hates reproof because more important to him than truth is his pride. It is more important to him to think that others consider him knowledgeable than to actually be knowledgeable. Opinion – opinion about himself – is what matters most.

That kind of thinking, according to the proverb, is plain stupid because it leaves the fool with a stupid mind. He is stupid about what truly matters and is stupid in relation to how much knowledge he possesses. The wise use reproof to their benefit to train their minds, to gain further knowledge, to become more self-disciplined, and thus lead to respect and usefulness.

Apply this spiritually. Remember, God disciplines us because we are his children. We are to desire discipline so that we may grow in righteousness, that we may know God rightly, that we may be useful in Christ's kingdom. We should desire to be corrected about our speech, our doctrine, our behavior so that all the more we will conform to Christ Jesus. Be alert to God's ways of correcting you today through your circumstances and the words of others however they may be said to you.

The Good Man

Proverbs 12:2

A good man obtains favor from the Lord,
  but a man of evil devices he condemns.

This proverb seems to make the case that we do earn favor from the Lord, that he will accept us into heaven according to our goodness. Those who are good obtain favor; those who are bad lose out.

That last sentence is actually true. God does not receive the unrighteous into heaven. Our problem is that no one is good. "None is righteous, no, not one" (Rom. 3:10). And as Jesus said, "A healthy tree cannot bear bad fruit nor can a diseased tree bear good fruit" (Matt. 7:18). Every person then must somehow be made good for his deeds to be truly good and thus obtain God's saving favor.

Thanks be to God for sending the one Good Man who perfectly fulfilled the law and obtained favor from the Lord that he might save his people. He has given to us his righteousness that we might be "good" before God and thus obtain his favor. Give thanks to God today for the Good Son of Man who has made you good before God. All the more determine to live in such a way, not to win, but to show your delight in God's favor.

120

Established in Christ

Proverbs 12:3

No one is established by wickedness,
  but the root of the righteous will never be moved.

No one is established by wickedness because the soil of such a heart is too poor to sustain strong roots. The soil is rocky and prevents roots from burrowing deep; it is barren of nutrients that feed the roots; it is infested with weeds and thorns that choke whatever may be lasting. Thus, though the wicked may appear to be established, though they may appear to grow quickly, they will wither or be plucked. God sees them and he will pluck them easily from the harvest.

The roots of the righteous, on the other hand, grow deep because of fertile clean soil. They are fed with the water of the Holy Spirit; they feed upon the nutrients of God's Word. They are tended by the Good Gardener who protects them from blight and pests. Thus, they grow strong and fruitful.

How is your prayer life? Your study of God's Word? Your fellowship with God's people? These things are meant to nurture your spiritual roots. Now that you are planted in Christ by Christ, all the more give attention to the means he has provided for your growth in him.

Crown or Rottenness

Proverbs 12:4

An excellent wife is the crown of her husband,
  but she who brings shame is like rottenness in his bones.

An excellent wife is her husband's glory (1 Cor. 11:7). She is the fulfillment of the original intention of being a "helper fit for him" (Gen. 2:18). She is her husband's joy, and he delights in praising her: "Many women have done excellently, but you surpass them all"

(Prov. 31:29). And likewise an excellent husband is the joy of his wife. He makes her secure in his protection and in his love, for, like Christ for the church, he gives himself up for her to present her to Christ in splendor.

All the reason then, wives and husbands, that you should strive for excellence as wives and as husbands. You have power to be great blessings; wives have the potential to be the glory of their husbands and husbands to be as Christ for their wives.

But the wife who brings shame is like rottenness to her husband's bones. She has the power to tear down his spirit through her shameful behavior. She is the one in whom he should delight; instead, she brings him shame. So does the shameful husband for his wife. The one whom she is to look up to becomes the very one who acts disgracefully, and so it shatters her spirit.

Again, all the more reason, wives and husbands, to strive for excellence. Your sins do not merely affect yourselves, but can devastate your partner who is one with you. Keep before you to glorify God through the way you honor and love your spouse. For Christ so glorified his Father by sacrificial love for the church.

Wise Counsel

Proverbs 12:5

The thoughts of the righteous are just;
the counsels of the wicked are deceitful.

To whom do you look for counsel? Where do you go for advice? You may unwittingly be using counselors who present to you a deceitful view of life. Your counselors may be TV shows through whom you are learning about relationships. They may be movies from which you are learning to accept violence and easy sex. They may be through advertisements, secular books, and magazines. All these venues are giving you counsel. Do you understand that most of such counsel is deceitful, either telling outright lies or distorting truth. Every work of fiction is doing more than telling a story; it is presenting a point of view that you may even unconsciously be taking in.

All the more reason then that you should be receiving the "thoughts of the righteous." You need to be attending worship. David says in Psalm 73:16-17 that he had a distorted view of life until he "went into the sanctuary of God." Paul says in Philippians 4:8, "whatever is true, whatever is honorable, whatever is just, whatever is pure, whatever is lovely, whatever is commendable, if there is any excellence, if there is anything worthy of praise, think about these things." Expose yourself to good counsel, whether it be that you are seeking godly counselors or that you are exposing yourself to godly influences.

Today, whom will you listen to? Who will inform your worldview? Who will set the pace for how you look at your day and respond to the circumstances in your life? Pray to God for wise counselors.

Deliverance

Proverbs 12:6

The words of the wicked lie in wait for blood,
  but the mouth of the upright delivers them.

The intent of the wicked is to harm. Out of anger they may try to ruin another's reputation, perhaps try to coax the other to anger and sin. That is what Jesus' enemies tried to do with their questions and slander. The wicked use words to draw blood. Sometimes, though, the wicked are acting out of mere desire for advancement. You happen to be a competitor for promotion, to get a sale, to earn the academic award, to buy the house. The wicked will lie, cheat, do whatever to get the advantage, not concerned about the blood that is drawn from you.

How, then, do you respond? Play by the same rules so that you are on the same playing field? Use the eye-for-an-eye principle? The best course of action is to speak and act righteously; not self-righteously with arrogance, but in biblical righteousness in which you speak and act in the spirit of Christ. You are called of God to live as a citizen of his kingdom, following the standard Jesus lay forth in his teachings and lived out for us as an example. Your true words spoken in love and in integrity will time and again deliver you.

But more to the point is that God hears the prayers of the upright who cry out to him. He is your deliverer. Put your trust in him to meet your daily needs and protect you. His guarantee is that he will always do what is good for you and allows you to glorify him. The mouth of the upright delivers them for they put their confidence, not in man, but in God.

Overthrown

Proverbs 12:7

The wicked are overthrown and are no more,
but the house of the righteous will stand.

Good guys finish. The wicked may think that such persons finish last, but what matters is that – first, second, or last – the good guys are left standing in the end. The wicked, no matter how fast and how tough they may be, will eventually be overthrown. Someone faster and stronger will come along and bring them down. Or their wicked means of achieving success will be found out, and they will be disgraced. Regardless of momentary achievement, the truth is that God will overthrow the wicked. As Jude so chillingly declares, they are "wandering stars, for whom the gloom of utter darkness has been reserved forever" (Jude 13).

Meanwhile, the house of the righteous will stand because they are built on the foundation of solid rock – the words of Christ (Matt. 7:24ff), who is himself the Rock. Do not yield to temptation to compromise your obedience to Christ in an effort to keep up with the wicked. Stay with the sure win; stay with Christ.

Good Sense

Proverbs 12:8

A man is commended according to his good sense,
  but one of twisted mind is despised.

This proverb presents a virtue that is often overlooked and underestimated but may be the most important in success. It is the difference maker for ability to manage people and to achieve any goal that involves people. It is good sense, also known as commonsense.

A man may possess tremendous knowledge and skill, but if he lacks commonsense his genius can become a curse for him, as well as for others. A person may know the right goal, but if he lacks good sense about obtaining that goal, he will not only fail to reach it but stir up greater trouble.

Good-hearted Christians often create trouble for lack of good sense. We read a command in Scripture, and in our effort to obey it we set ourselves up for failure, as well as offend others. We overestimate our abilities and those of others. We don't think through how to speak in love, so intent we may be to speak the truth (as we interpret it). We don't use commonsense. We may not have twisted minds, but we earn for ourselves the same reward – resentment.

Pray today that you will use good sense in your interactions with others and as you work to achieve your goals. Seek the counsel of others, especially those who have earned a reputation for good sense. Humbly learn from them.

Better to be Lowly

Proverbs 12:9

Better to be lowly and have a servant
  than to play the great man and lack bread.

It is better to have shown the wisdom and done the labor to provide for oneself and one's family, than to give the appearance of prosperity and yet in truth have nothing that is secure. Thus, it is better to not be able to join the fashionable crowd that spends freely because you are wisely keeping to your budget, than to run up debt in an effort to appear well-to-do.

We are tempted to play at being what we are not. We buy the clothes that make us seem more prosperous and more worldly than we are. We buy music, see movies, etc. based on the opinion of the crowd we want to fit in with. We "play" the part that others deem important.

But again, it is better to be lowly in the eyes of others and be true to ourselves, or rather, be true to God. For as we are true to God, so we are true to what we are made to be. As we are true to God, so we will prove to be wise. As we are true to God, so we will find true security in him.

Regard for Life

Proverbs 12:10

Whoever is righteous has regard for the life of his beast,
but the mercy of the wicked is cruel.

The righteous has regard for his beast because he is just, compassionate, and wise. It is a matter of justice to protect and preserve life. God is Creator of the animals, and we must have just cause to harm his creatures, especially those whom he has given to serve us. Righteousness includes compassion, as exemplified by the mercy our Righteous God has shown us. And then, it is wise to care for the beast who serves his master, thereby extending and promoting his usefulness.

Besides encouraging good care for animals, the point of the proverb is that righteousness leads us to care for everyone regardless of their status in life. The righteous have regard for the unborn, the handicapped, the terminally ill, the aged, the poor. Our regard for those who are considered the weak in society signifies our maturity in Christ.

Is there someone at work, in the neighborhood, in school who is shown little regard? By you? Take time to give him/her attention. Show regard for the life which God has made.

Good and Worthless Pursuits

Proverbs 12:11

Whoever works his land will have plenty of bread,
  but he who follows worthless pursuits lacks sense.

This proverb distinguishes between the persons who seem to have the good luck of keeping work and having enough provisions and those who keep running into the bad fortune of not finding the right job or getting the fortunate break. We all experience bad fortune one time or another. Circumstances occur beyond our control. But if we continually bounce from job to job; if we keep having the bad luck of working for the wrong boss or with the wrong colleagues; if we can't seem to find anyone to appreciate our "unique" gifts, we need to do some serious self-examination.

Whoever works his land will have plenty of bread because he is not ever looking at his neighbor's land wishing he had the good soil and the tools of his neighbor. He is not day dreaming about the career that is not his gift or calling. He may dream, but he works hard to reach that dream and works diligently now so as to prove himself when the opportunity comes. If a man is married, he must place the welfare of his family first. He can be sure that his calling includes providing for his family.

How do we know if what we are pursuing is a worthless pursuit? We ask. We ask those who know us well; we ask those whom we think have "made it"; we pray to God for wisdom; we commend our dreams to God. Whatever our pursuit may be, it must be for the glory of God and to serve God.

Bearing Good Fruit

Proverbs 12:12

127

Whoever is wicked covets the spoil of evildoers,
  but the root of the righteous bears fruit.

The wicked sees the ill-gotten gain of other wicked persons and concludes that their way is the way of success. The wicked respect successful wicked people. They want to be like them. In a perverted way, they think that obtaining "success" by evil deeds is clever, even honorable, as they desire above all to have the same success. Indeed, best of all would be to take away from the very persons they admire.

Beyond the obvious evil motives of such persons is the exposure that they are worthless fools. The wicked cannot bear fruit, that is, good fruit. They are a drain, a ravaging parasite that sucks out what is good and fills in its place what is toxic. The "spoil" of evildoers is an apt description of their possessions which may seem desirable, but in reality have been spoiled by evil ways.

But the root of the righteous, which dives deep in the nutrient-rich ground of righteousness and wisdom bears wholesome fruit. There is the fruit of good deeds, of good dispositions, of knowledge and love, of mercy and justice; there is the fruit of healthy relationships, and more often than not, the fruit of financial gain and security, the fruit of stability, of economic and social progress.

And this fruit bears the seeds that allow for the growth of more fruit. It is self-sustaining. Not so the spoil of the evildoers that cannot reproduce and will be wasted by the evildoers themselves. Do not covet the spoil of evildoers, for there is nothing of value to covet. Desire to plant yourself in righteous and wise soil. You will then bear your own good, lasting fruit.

Ensnared or Vindicated

Proverbs 12:13

An evil man is ensnared by the transgression of his lips,
  but the righteous escapes from trouble.

However he might, the evil person will ensnare himself because he cannot always keep up a false appearance. A powerful political person was caught on tape speaking threats against those who would oppose him. He apologized for a lapse of character, but in truth, the image he tried to convey publicly is a lapse of his real character. The heart, sooner or later, will reveal itself.

That is why it is essential to work on real change in our hearts. Learning etiquette and methods to influence and win friends is helpful. Many times good-hearted persons offend others because they have not learned the proper customs of good communication; nevertheless, the righteous heart (and one must have a kind heart to be righteous) will time and again vindicate its owner.

The righteous person will often be protected by others who will speak up for him. His integrity will serve him well when slandered. His righteousness gives him wisdom to know how to avoid trouble and how to escape when evil comes against him.

But the true test will come at the Day of Judgment before God, when, as Jesus says, "people will give account for every careless word they speak, for by your words you will be justified, and by your words you will be condemned" (Matt. 12:36-37). When the recordings of our lives are played, our words will either ensnare us or vindicate us as they reveal the true condition of our hearts.

Word and Work

Proverbs 12:14

From the fruit of his mouth a man is satisfied with good,
and the work of a man's hand comes back to him.

When a person learns the truth of both statements, he will find so much of the contentment and success he finds missing. "From the fruit of his mouth" – from speaking words that are wise, words that are loving, words that are wholesome – from such speech a person will reap great reward. The reason is that he will have blessed others, and when others are blessed, they will return the blessing. They will respond with praise and with kindness.

They will overlook mistakes. A man may be a hard worker, but if he speaks harshly he will be criticized for his work; he will not be given a break for his mistakes. A person who knows how to speak can change people's views, enable them to admit their faults and to be motivated to work harder. A person who speaks foolishly and harshly only reinforces stubbornness and incites resentment, making goals harder to attain. The reason that many projects are not successful have nothing to do with the inability of a team to know what to do, but everything to do with jealousy, hurt feelings, egos bruised, competition, and so on.

Others fail because they have not connected their success with their work ethic. As a high school principal, I observed the simple rule that conscientious students far excelled lazy students. I noticed that the valedictorian often was not the smartest student, but invariably proved to be hard working. Lazy students, meanwhile, attributed their failures to bad luck, teachers picking on them, and not being as smart as the successful students. They could not, or would not, attribute the problem being their own attitude.

Make the connections! If there is a pattern of offending people, examine the fruit of your mouth. If you remain stuck in your career, examine your work ethic. There are other circumstances that you may not be able to control, but you have more influence than you think. Your words are powerful if they conform to love and righteousness. Your labor is effective, if you work honestly, seeking reward from your Master, Jesus Christ. If your focus in word and work is to glorify God, to serve Christ's kingdom, you will find good fruit and reward.

Right in His Own Eyes

Proverbs 12:15

The way of a fool is right in his own eyes,
but a wise man listens to advice.

130

This is the problem of the fool. Because he has a foolish perspective about himself, he cannot learn and escape from his foolishness. He thinks he is charming when he is boorish. He believes he is knowledgeable about things of which he is ignorant. He cannot read the faces of those who see him as a fool; and when they do express their feelings, he attributes their reaction to jealousy. If he is a student and doing poorly, he attributes the problem to the teacher, thinking that he is a good student. If he does poorly at work, he blames others, unable to see his faults.

The wise man is wise precisely because he does listen to others. Because he is wise he knows whom to listen to; he even knows how to benefit from the advice of the foolish. He is attentive to others; he observes before forming his opinions; he asks perceptive questions. He is also quick to give credit where it is due. He is unashamed to change his ideas when someone presents a better point of view; he welcomes the expertise that he does not possess; he will even accept correction by someone who has less knowledge than he.

Why the different reactions? Because the wise love wisdom and the fools love being thought wise. Thus the wise gain wisdom while the fools remain stuck in their foolishness.

Of Insults

Proverbs 12:16

The vexation of a fool is known at once,
but the prudent ignores an insult.

"What did you say about me?"
"Are you laughing at me?"
"Don't ignore me!"

The vexation of a fool is known at once because his focus is on himself. He is bothered when his opinion is not highly regarded; he is attentive to the attention he receives or doesn't receive. His primary concern is not contributing, but getting "his due." Thus he is frustrated a lot. Most people are not free with compliments anyhow, and a fool will receive even less.

The prudent ignores an insult because he is not wrapped around his ego. An insult loses its power to sting when aimed at a truly humble person, that is, someone whose focus is serving and glorifying God. The prudent also recognizes the cost of paying attention to an insult. It costs emotional energy to dwell on an insult; it costs valuable time that could be used productively. The prudent ignores the insult because insults are foolishly spoken, and it is a waste of time trying to respond to foolishness. Insults are either spoken by fools with whom one cannot reason, or spoken in a foolish moment by the wise, who will recognize their own folly and repent as they come to their senses.

Thus Jesus was able to withstand the many insults hurled at him. His focus was on doing the will of his Father and carrying out the work given him. He knew the hearts of men and ignored their foolish ways. The times that he did respond, however, was not to vindicate himself, but to publicly vindicate his Father and the truth. Even then, he did not brood on the insults of the Pharisees and other enemies, but committed himself to the love and keeping of his Father.

How will you handle insults and slights that may come your way today? Keep your eyes on your Lord, and you will find yourself better able to be prudent and ignore the darts sent your way.

Honest Evidence

Proverbs 12:17

Whoever speaks the truth gives honest evidence,
  but a false witness utters deceit.

The two lines seem redundant, but the focus appears to be on the end result of each person. The truth speaker gives honest evidence. Don't you feel good by that expression honest evidence? Your inner sense of justice is aroused, even your aesthetic sense of beauty. Honest evidence – yes, this is right; this is good. That is what truth does – it brings forth rightness and goodness.

But deceit — the very sound of the word causes you to recoil. You hate lying; you hate the attempt of another person to deceive you. And that is the intent of the false witness. Whether for gain or protection, he wants to cover, to distort honest evidence for his own benefit. He takes what is right and good, and then covers it with what is repugnant and ugly.

That is what we do when we lie. We utter deceit, covering over honest evidence. That is what ministers do who use their pulpits to cover over the honest evidence of Scripture. That is what we Christians do when we speak and act like persons without the gospel in our lives. Remember, we ourselves are to be honest evidence of the gospel. Let us be those who both give honest evidence and exhibit honest evidence.

Sword Thrusts

Proverbs 12:18

There is one whose rash words are like sword thrusts,
  but the tongue of the wise brings healing.

We need to understand the consequence of our rash words which we speak without our giving consideration to the person to whom we are speaking. Rash words are the ones we speak in anger. They are the flippant remarks we make. They are the speaking-my-mind words, and the I-say-what-I-think words. Understand that whatever the intent may be, the effect is that of thrusting a sword into another person's spirit.

Saying that a person shouldn't be so sensitive with our remark is the same as saying that he ought to wear armor for his clothing. It is placing the onus on the other person to handle better our rashness. What needs to happen is for us to learn to speak thoughtfully.

That is how the wise speak, and that is why their words bring healing. They think about how their speech will actually be received. Like the doctor who checks to see what his patient may be allergic to before he prescribes medication, so the wise person observes in the other person what speech he or she is capable of receiving.

Of course, the presumption being made is that the wise person desires to heal. That, ultimately, is the difference between rash speech and wise speech. The former does not care to heal; the latter does. Once you have the right motive, you will find your rash speech declining and your wisdom growing.

Lips That Endure

Proverbs 12:19

Truthful lips endure forever,
but a lying tongue is but for a moment.

A lying tongue creates a momentary sensation. It riles the emotions as it makes the headlines. But the lie eventually is buried, along with the liar. It is not the lies that are recalled from history, but the words that are noble, that are inspiring, that spread light on truth. And so those who speak such truth are remembered for their words.

In particular, the lips that profess the gospel will endure. For the very truthful message itself is the truth that saves. The lying tongue is itself for a moment, for its very lies condemn it.

Keep your thoughts on the gospel truth. Do not get caught up in the sensation of the day's lies. The day will pass. What matters is the eternal day. Listen to and pass on gospel truth, for it is such truth that will endure forever and give you life forever.

Joy

Proverbs 12:20

Deceit is in the heart of those who devise evil,
but those who plan peace have joy.

Delve into the heart of the evil-doer and one will find a heart filled with lies. There are the lies he has in store for others – lies by which to cheat, to manipulate, to do whatever he thinks necessary to obtain joy. There are the lies the evil-doer tells to himself – lies by which to rationalize his evil, to hide his evil from himself, to convince himself that he has joy or at least deserves it. There are the lies for God – lies by which to manipulate God or to contend against God or to deny God, all for the sake of obtaining his version of joy.

And then there are those who plan peace. They desire peace with their neighbors. They desire peace for their neighbors. They are thankful for the peace of God granted to them, and they strive to see that peace manifested in their lives and in the world. Such persons have joy, for peace is joy. Peace is free from resentment and bitterness. It is free from enmity. It has no need for deceit, no one to cheat or to manipulate. Peace already obtains within itself the joy that the evil-doer bitterly strives to obtain.

The Good Life

Proverbs 12:21

No ill befalls the righteous,
but the wicked are filled with trouble.

The ill addressed by this proverb is the ill of retribution. The wicked are filled with such trouble because they continually rile up grievances. They must protect themselves from the enemies they have created by their stealing and cheating and offending. Their rash tongues invite angry words. Their acts of deceit result in distrust. Their greed and ambition incite backlash. Their promiscuity produces disease; their indulgence produces debt; their anger produces domestic strife. And there is the response of the authorities acting to bring the wicked to justice.

The righteous fear no such ills. By their love they win friends rather than enemies. By their holiness they avoid the pitfalls of the profligate life. By their integrity they win the respect of neighbor and civil authority. The man faithful to his wife does not fear sexual disease. The person honest in his dealing does not fear imprisonment. The man moderate in his drinking avoids the shame that befalls the drunken man.

The righteous life is the peaceful life. It is the healthy life. Because it seeks after what is good, it experiences goodness.

Prudent Use of Knowledge

Proverbs 12:23

A prudent man conceals knowledge,
  but the heart of fools proclaims folly.

Why would it be prudent to conceal knowledge? It would be prudent to conceal knowledge from people who will misuse that knowledge. They may publicize what ought to be kept private. They may maliciously use the knowledge to hurt others or obtain ill-gotten gain. It would be prudent to conceal knowledge from the foolish who may then harm themselves and others simply by their foolishness. It would also be prudent to conceal knowledge from those who would disdain that knowledge. And it would be prudent to withhold knowledge from those who would only be stirred up to commit blasphemy and create turmoil.

Once, someone asked my counsel about whether or not to reply to an offensive email. I counseled not to because she most likely would only receive further offense. The other person was set in her opinions and would not receive reproof well. Wisdom includes knowing when and when not to speak. Jesus himself counseled not to throw pearls before swine. A person must have the right frame of mind in order to receive knowledge.

What then do we do? We pray, for it is the work of the Spirit to give ears to hear. Pray for the Spirit to open the door for the truth to be heard (Paul's own prayer: Col. 4:3). Pray for wisdom to know when to speak and how to speak. Treat knowledge as you would treat anything that has potential for good and harm.

Defining Lying

Proverbs 12:22

Lying lips are an abomination to the Lord,
  but those who act faithfully are his delight.

Do you read such a proverb and give thanks that you are not a person who lies? Consider what the Larger Catechism has to say about breaking the ninth commandment.

Q. 144. What are the duties required in the ninth commandment?
A. The duties required in the ninth commandment are, the preserving and promoting of truth between man and man, and the good name of our neighbor, as well as our own; appearing and standing for the truth; and from the heart, sincerely, freely, clearly, and fully, speaking the truth, and only the truth, in matters of judgment and justice, and in all other things whatsoever; a charitable esteem of our neighbors; loving, desiring, and rejoicing in their good name; sorrowing for, and covering of their infirmities; freely acknowledging of their gifts and graces, defending their innocence; a ready receiving of a good report, and unwillingness to admit of an evil report concerning them; discouraging tale-bearers, flatterers, and slanderers; love and care of our own good name, and defending it when need requireth; keeping of lawful promises; studying and practicing of whatsoever things are true, honest, lovely, and of good report.

Q. 145. What are the sins forbidden in the ninth commandment?
A. The sins forbidden in the ninth commandment are, all prejudicing the truth, and the good name of our neighbors, as well as our own, especially in public judicature; giving false evidence, suborning false witnesses, wittingly appearing and pleading for an evil cause, outfacing and overbearing the truth; passing unjust sentence, calling evil good, and good evil; rewarding the wicked according to the work of the righteous, and the righteous according to the work of the wicked; forgery, concealing the truth, undue silence in a just cause, and holding our peace when iniquity calleth for either a reproof from ourselves, or complaint to others; speaking the truth unseasonably, or

maliciously to a wrong end, or perverting it to a wrong meaning, or in doubtful and equivocal expressions, to the prejudice of truth or justice; speaking untruth, lying, slandering, backbiting, detracting, tale bearing, whispering, scoffing, reviling, rash, harsh, and partial censuring; misconstructing intentions, words, and actions; flattering, vain-glorious boasting; thinking or speaking too highly or too meanly of ourselves or others; denying the gifts and graces of God; aggravating smaller faults; hiding, excusing, or extenuating of sins, when called to a free confession; unnecessary discovering of infirmities; raising false rumors, receiving and countenancing evil reports, and stopping our ears against just defense; evil suspicion; envying or grieving at the deserved credit of any, endeavoring or desiring to impair it, rejoicing in their disgrace and infamy; scornful contempt, fond admiration; breach of lawful promises; neglecting such things as are of good report, and practicing, or not avoiding ourselves, or not hindering what we can in others, such things as procure an ill name.

Act faithfully today by confessing honestly your sins.

Diligence

Proverbs 12:24

The hand of the diligent will rule,
 while the slothful will be put to forced labor.

The students who do the best work are the students who are most diligent in their labor. They are the students who excel in grades, get the awards, and win the scholarships. The employees who are most diligent find the same kind of results; so do rulers, athletes, musicians. Indeed in every field, the same pattern holds out – the diligent rise above the slothful.

The slothful never catch on. They think the diligent's success has to do with luck or with favoritism. They don't make the connection between success and diligence. They connect success with being shrewd. Even then they think shrewdness has to do with succeeding without having to work.

Jesus once told a parable about the shrewd use of talents (money) entrusted to servants. According to the diligence in which each servant used the money, he was awarded all the more. The servant who thought he was being shrewd by burying the talent given, lost everything. The simple principle is that our faithfulness in small things leads to being entrusted with greater responsibilities.

We need to examine our hearts about this. I've listened to Christians complain about being treated unfairly in school or the workplace presumably because of their Christian convictions. And yet, how often is the real case being that they were not diligent in their labors. It is a terrible witness for a vocal Christian to be a slothful worker. We should be the most diligent, knowing that it is for Christ whom we labor, whatever the job; it is God whom we are to glorify by the quality of whatever work that we do.

How diligent will you be today in the work that you have to do?

A Good Word

Proverbs 12:25

Anxiety in a man's heart weighs him down,
  but a good word makes him glad.

We can say, "Amen," to both of these statements for their verity. Anxiety weighs a person down. He feels drained; he lacks enthusiasm. He has difficulty sleeping; his attention span is short. He can even physically look weighed down as though carrying a burden on his back, which is truly what he is doing. Anxiety is a burden; not only a burden but one that is carried alone. It isolates the burden-bearer; he feels alone. Anxiety blinds the burden-bearer; he not only fails to see a solution but fails to see the help that others can and want to give.

All the more, then, is the blessing of the good word that comes to him like a ray of sunshine breaking through a dark sky, cheering him. It is the fresh water dashed on his pale face, refreshing him. And all it takes is a good word. It doesn't take skilled counseling; it doesn't require complex involvement. All it takes is a pleasant word from a kind voice.

A word has amazing power, for even a stranger can change the complexion of an anxious person with a simple pleasant, courteous remark. Today, you can make glad someone who is bearing anxiety. By your cheerful word, your kind tone of voice, by your smile – you can bring blessing. And blessing is what everyone needs. Be quick to bless; be quick to show the love and the mercy of Christ Jesus to your neighbor. For you do not know what anxiety lies in his or her heart; you do not know the power that your good word can have.

Guide and Guided

Proverbs 12:26

One who is righteous is a guide to his neighbor,
  but the way of the wicked leads them astray.

For good or ill we are all guides to our neighbors. Whether we are vocal or silent, withdrawn or sociable, we guide our neighbors and they guide us. This is called life experience. Some neighbors are consciously guided by us; some are unaware that we affect them at all. Even so, because God has placed us in their life experience, we are affecting them for good or ill. And they us: God has placed neighbors around us to impact us.

Here is the question then for us. Will our righteousness impact our neighbor for the good and also protect us from being led astray? Will our righteousness be seen for integrity or hypocrisy? We cannot, of course, control how others perceive us; even so, we must always examine our behavior because we remain sinners. We do not have the luxury to sin in front of our neighbor or against our neighbor and then shrug it off. We do not have the freedom to "sow our wild oats," to explore sin, because of this thing called "witness." We are witnesses to the life-transforming power and love of Christ; we are witnesses to his call upon our lives. What kind of witness will we be today?

And how well will we handle the influence of our neighbors on us? How many times will we react to sinful behavior with sinful response? Keep your eyes upon Christ, upon the gospel. Let his grace be the all-dominating influence on you today. If so, then your righteousness will indeed be a guide to your neighbor and your protection from the influence of the wicked.

Diligence

Proverbs 12:27

Whoever is slothful will not roast his game,
but the diligent man will get precious wealth.

Diligent people know the truth of this proverb: slothful people don't get it. They blame circumstances for their failures. Indeed, the one thing for which they are diligent is to think of ways in which they could not be expected to succeed.

The diligent man is not merely a hard worker, but a smart worker. One of my English students would present her initial paper drafts to me to discuss with her. The result was that I would correct her errors and point her in the right direction so that she invariably ended up with A papers. She was diligent in pursuing wise and clever means of achieving her goals.

And yet, how ironic that one can be diligent in matters of temporary significance, and yet be slothful about eternal matters. This phenomenon frustrated Blaise Pascal and is behind his "wager" argument that one should side with Christianity for self-protection. He was amazed that a man could diligently and passionately pursue billiards and show no interest in his eternal condition. So it is with a world filled with people pursuing their goals diligently, yet all along aiming for the wrong goals.

Be diligent in your salvation and sanctification that you may obtain the precious wealth of Jesus Christ. Be diligent to study and grasp the grace of the gospel.

The Path of Righteousness

Proverbs 12:28

In the path of righteousness is life,
and in its pathway there is no death.

The best commentary on this proverb is Jesus' statement: "I am the resurrection and the life. Whoever believes in me, though he die, yet shall he live, and everyone who lives and believes in me shall never die" (John 11:25-26). Or consider another statement: "I am the way, and the truth, and the life. No one comes to the Father except through me" (John 14:6). Jesus is the path of righteousness upon which and through which we walk into everlasting life.

Jesus is our righteousness. He has exchanged our rags of sins for his robe of righteousness. We are covered by him; he has opened the way into the holy place by his righteousness, and now we may enter clothed in his righteousness.

> While thy glorious praise is sung,
> Touch my lips, unloose my tongue,
> That my joyful soul may bless Thee,
> the Lord my Righteousness.
> ("To Thy Temple I Repair," by James Montgomery)

Meditate on this great truth today. Whatever befalls you, whatever hits you may take today, in the path of Jesus Christ is life, and in Christ there is no death.

Wise Listening

Proverbs 13:1

A wise son hears his father's instruction,
but a scoffer does not listen to rebuke.

The attention here is on the order of authority. Whereas our society exalts the maverick who rejects authoritative instruction, Scripture upholds an authority structure by which we are to live. A wise son listens to his father and his mother because of their position over him. A wise employee listens to his supervisor. A wise student listens to his teacher. And when rebuke is given by a superior, the wise person uses it to learn and improve himself.

We are to respect the position of authority and not adopt a "show-me" attitude that makes the person over us prove himself before we will listen and obey. For understand that we also are sinners and lacking in knowledge and mature wisdom. If we are quick to spot the faults of our superiors, then we will be slow and blind to our own faults, allowing ourselves to blame our superiors for our faults.

What attitude will you take into work, into school? How will you regard your government leaders and others who have some authority over you? Will you show the respect of listening? Remember, it takes wisdom to listen.

Sowing Your Desire

Proverbs 13:2

From the fruit of his mouth a man eats what is good,
  but the desire of the treacherous is for violence.

We reap what we sow, and we sow what we desire. If I desire peace with my neighbors, I will sow seeds to bless them and thus obtain peace. If I desire to gain advantage over them, or if I desire only my interests, I will sow seeds that produce conflict and aggravate troubles. If I desire to be productive, I will sow seeds that grow into fruitful plants. If I desire only to consume the produce of others, I will leave barren fields.

What do you desire? What do you desire today at work? To be productive and to help your colleague or merely to get through a day? What do you desire at home? To bless your spouse and children, or simply not to be bothered with problems? Your desire will guide what you say and how you communicate. Desire the right end, and your tongue will say the right words; desire selfish or hurtful ends, and your tongue will produce violence.

Pray for the Lord to give you right desires that you may enjoy good fruit. Pray for the Holy Spirit's sanctifying work in you that you might emulate Christ and show Christ to your neighbor.

Guarding Your Mouth

Proverbs 13:3

Whoever guards his mouth preserves his life;
  he who opens wide his lips comes to ruin.

Every time we speak we provide opportunity for trouble. We might insult someone; we might offend; we might lie; we might speak folly; we might gossip; we might ignorantly pass on wrong information; we might speak out of turn or what is inappropriate for the moment. It is perhaps easier to sin through speech than through any other means.

It takes little effort to use the tongue. One does not have to be strong. We can whisper as well as shout sinfully. We can speak out in large crowds or quietly in private conversation. We can speak in anger or even in what we think is love. And yet so often our words come back to haunt us. What was I thinking? I didn't know he would take it that way. I didn't realize she was so sensitive. Sometimes the problem is not so much with us but with the hearer. Speaking the truth, even in love, can be misinterpreted and misused.

That is why the wise guard their mouths. They understand the dangers of saying the wrong thing or having the right words misconstrued. Words are powerful and easy to be abused by both the speaker and the hearer. Therefore, be not quick to speak, but make it your way of habit to observe your hearer, to examine your own heart, and to weigh the merits of what you will say. This is difficult to do. But the quicker we are to speak, the more likely trouble will come.

Of Cravings

Proverbs 13:4

The soul of the sluggard craves and gets nothing,
  while the soul of the diligent is richly supplied.

The sluggard lacks the basics of physical provision because he does not work, whereas the diligent applies himself. But there is also a deeper craving that is not satisfied. Whatever the sluggard may claim or disclaim, because he is human made in the image of God he has a craving for more than keeping his belly full. He craves meaning, fulfillment. He craves, whether he admits it or not, to be connected with his Creator.

But he gets nothing. For even to receive the free gospel, even to receive the gracious gift of God requires effort. God calls people to come to him; if the sluggard is too lazy to come, he will not receive. Christ calls those who would come to him to follow him and to take up his own cross. Such a life takes too much effort. One may reason with him the riches are greater than the sacrifices; Christ will return treasure beyond what we give; his yoke is easy and his burden is light. But nothing works for the sluggard who cannot find it in himself to make a sustained effort.

Not so for the diligent who sees the gospel for the priceless treasure that it is, who yearns to be at peace with his Creator and to experience the blessing of his love. Eagerly he responds to the bidding of his Savior's call to come. Joyfully he serves a master whom he knows to be generous. Ultimately, the difference between the sluggard and the diligent is not that the sluggard doesn't crave and the diligent does. Rather, the diligent recognizes what, or rather who, fulfills his cravings and so already tastes the goodness of the Lord. The sluggard merely knows the feeling of emptiness; the diligent knows when he has tasted the goodness of the Lord and so makes every effort to be filled.

Hating Falsehood

Proverbs 13:5

The righteous hates falsehood,
  but the wicked brings shame and disgrace.

The righteous person hates falsehood, whether it be to hear it or to disseminate it. It is distasteful to him. The wicked person is intrigued by falsehood. He appreciates a good lie; he likes to see how he can use falsehood to his advantage. Inevitably he will bring upon himself and those connected with him shame and disgrace.

For the righteous person, to indulge in a lie immediately brings personal shame. He feels guilt regardless of whether he has been caught. It does not settle well within his soul. His inner conscience plagues him. But the wicked person considers a successful lie to be an accomplishment. Success encourages him to indulge in falsehood all the more. It takes the failure of getting caught to subdue him. Even then he is likely to be more ashamed of getting caught than for lying itself. The disgrace comes in the consequences not the pangs of a conscience.

If you identify with the righteous person, still be careful. It is easy to hate falsehood seen in others. It is easy to spot falsehood or supposed falsehood in those with whom you disagree. Make sure it really is falsehood that you hate. If it is, you will spot it in yourself and hate it as much or more than when you spot it in others. Do you recognize that falsehood lies within your own heart? If not, then your hatred of falsehood is hypocritical. Hate falsehood wherever it is found.

Righteous Guard

Proverbs 13:6

Righteousness guards him whose way is blameless,
  but sin overthrows the wicked.

Righteousness is not only a standard to meet, but armor to wear and protect us from the enemy who would destroy our souls. A garment

146

of sin not only doesn't protect us from the evils of life, but it strengthens the power of evil to harm us.

The Christian has failed already, who, thinking it necessary to survive in the world, compromises Christian ethics. God will not honor such thinking and behavior, and thus the Christian sacrifices his one true Guard. All the more likely then will he be overthrown.

Is your job threatened? Are you in danger of losing what seems necessary for living? Are you in danger of losing someone you love? Then for your sake do only what is right in the eyes of the Lord. Do what Scripture teaches is right. It certainly is simpler to follow the clear teaching of Scripture than to figure out alone what is the cleverest action to take. And what can be safer than to walk along the path of the Lord under his protection?

But always remember that it is not our righteousness that provides security; it is Christ's righteousness. Here is the proverb in the light of Christ: The righteousness of Christ guards him who follows his Lord, but to remain under the bondage of sin is our downfall.

Rich or Poor

Proverbs 13:7

One pretends to be rich, yet has nothing;
another pretends to be poor, yet has great wealth.

One can take this proverb negatively or positively. We look down on the person who pretends to be what he is not. We consider him foolish who pretends to have wealth he does not possess by spending himself in debt or going to great length to look like he has wealth. And we find the wealthy person a bore who pretends to be poor by complaining about costs and how little he has.

On the other hand, it is admirable not to let poverty get you down, but instead to live with the attitude of being rich by enjoying each day and using wisely what you have. And it is proper not to flaunt your wealth, living simply with the knowledge that wealth is fleeting.

To apply this proverb in the latter manner, what we really need is to be rich in Christ and poor in spirit. We need to own and rejoice in the riches that we have in Jesus Christ, for truly as such we are wealthy beyond all earthly means. And if we are poor in spirit; that is, if we are humble about our own personal abilities and wealth, then all the more we will more freely exercise and enjoy Christ's riches. In Christ we are indeed rich, though we may have no earthly wealth; and without Christ we are indeed impoverished, though we may have all the wealth in the world.

True Peace

Proverbs 13:8

The ransom of a man's life is his wealth,
  but a poor man hears no threat.

The wealthy person is more likely to be kidnapped for ransom. His wealth becomes both his danger and his ransom from danger. The wealth he accumulates for pleasure must also be used for protection. But the poor man hears no threat since he has nothing worth taking and no wealth for a ransom.

Wealth can be both blessing and curse. The wealthy person can pay for more expensive pleasures; his wealth can provide financial security; but he also must pay more for protection; there is more to lose. His wealth makes him a target, especially if he is also well known. He must buy an expensive home not merely for pleasure but for security – security gate, alarm system, and perhaps guards. He must keep alert for all kinds of attempts to rob and to take advantage of him. He has to hire professionals to watch over his possessions and finances; the greater the wealth, the more to lose and more opportunities to lose it. The poor person can have less anxiety. Indeed, the poor tend to be more generous precisely because they have little to lose.

And we would do well to learn from this principle. We spend too much time wishing we had wealth. "If only I had a million dollars..."

We would pay off our debt; we would put money away for security; we would take that vacation we always wanted; buy that car; get that second home; give to our favorite ministry; buy lots of gifts for others; go to the Super Bowl; move into our dream house... And the list goes on. Indeed, it easily gets out of hand.

And then we forget the taxes; we don't think of the many requests from family, friends, charitable groups, etc. The more popular we become because of our money, the more demand on our time. And again, now we must be more concerned for security.

The key to happiness is not in accumulating wealth, nor, for that matter, in making ourselves poor. The proverb is not exalting poverty; it is merely pointing out that wealth is not all that it is made out to be. The key to happiness is peace. For as great as the peace of mind we have, then will be the level of happiness. And the ultimate peace is that which Christ gives.

"Peace I leave with you; my peace I give to you. Not as the world gives do I give to you. Let not your hearts be troubled, neither let them be afraid" (John 14:27).

Joyful Light

Proverbs 13:9

The light of the righteous rejoices,
 but the lamp of the wicked will be put out.

Note the contrast between the light of the righteous and of the wicked. It is not merely that the light of the righteous will continue to shine and the wicked's will end, but that the righteous' light "burns merrily." Righteousness is not merely about living right but about living well.

The wicked don't understand this. They pursue wickedness and immorality, thinking that those things bring happiness. They scorn the righteous whom they presume must be unhappy and uptight. They consider themselves happy: see, they party and laugh; they have

149

"fun." And yet it is a desperate fun that they must manufacture each day.

True joy – true fun – is delighting in what is good and what produces blessing and peace; it is what flows out of love. And what greater joy is there than delighting in the light of Jesus Christ, who reconciles us to God, makes our lives fruitful and meaningful, and who leads us in the dance of redemption.

Let your light shine today. Let your flame burn merrily as you give thanks throughout this day for the light of Christ in your life.

Receiving Advice

Proverbs 13:10

By insolence comes nothing but strife,
but with those who take advice is wisdom.

This is insolence of pride. The insolent person rudely rebuffs help and counsel, especially from others whom he deems below himself. He believes it is beneath his dignity or a sign of weakness or a giving in of his authority. Thus the insolent professional does not need advice, especially from a nonprofessional. The person in authority will not take counsel from those under him.

Christians fall under this same spell through spiritualizing the same attitude. Church officers, citing that they are responsible to God for the use of their authority, may be resistant to seek the counsel of their flock. A husband intent on being the "head" of the family may not listen to the counsel of his wife and children.

But it is true wisdom to receive and consider good advice from whomever it comes. The wise person is wise precisely because he knows his limitations and because he desires wisdom and knowledge above reputation. The one who seeks to protect his reputation often loses it because such a goal will lead to foolish decisions. But the one who prizes wisdom will rise in the estimation of others, even those who differ with him.

Seek wisdom today. Listen to whatever advice is given. Indeed, listen more carefully to the advice of those you least respect. God may be speaking to you through them. In his wisdom, he may very well choose the foolish and the weak to deliver his wise message to us.

Accumulating Wealth

Proverbs 13:11

Wealth gained hastily will dwindle,
  but whoever gathers little by little will increase it.

This is a proverb we don't like. We all dream of being surprised by a large inheritance from an unknown relative or winning the lottery (from a ticket someone else bought for us). If only I could get rich now! But this proverb teaches that wealth gained quickly without effort is likely to dwindle easily. It is those who through diligence and wisdom build wealth, who will more likely use the same diligence and wisdom to maintain it.

Wealth is dangerous to those immature to handle it, and immaturity is normally related to lack of experience. Thus, if we have little experience handling money, a sudden rush of it into our hands can be our downfall rather than our salvation.

But are you accumulating wealth even little by little? Are you budgeting how you earn and spend your money? Your wisdom regarding money lies not in how much you earn but in how well you live with what you earn. Live prudently so that you may increase what you have, so that you may build security for yourself and your dependents, and that you may be generous in giving to others.

Fulfilled Desires

Proverbs 13:12

Hope deferred makes the heart sick,
  but a desire fulfilled is a tree of life.

151

Remember this proverb on motivation. If you desire a person to work hard towards a goal (produce more, win a competition, be nice to you), then see that desires are fulfilled along the way. Provide rewards. Positive motivation is more effective than negative motivation.

What are desires that can be fulfilled? Receiving encouragement is important. The laborer is more likely to produce twenty gadgets a day if he is praised for raising his production from five to ten. But if he receives no encouragement, then his production is likely to decline. In my counseling, I've noticed that this is a common problem in marriages. Wives will focus on what their husbands are failing to do, baffled that their husbands will not change. ("How many times do I have to remind him?") Husbands are frustrated that their wives have to keep being told that they are loved. ("Shouldn't she just know?") We all need rewards and encouragement to motivate us to press on. A fulfilled desire is life renewing and gives us the strength to move forward.

That is what God does for us. Our greatest hope – glorification at Christ's return – has remained a long-awaiting hope. But we press on for the desires that are fulfilled now – the joys of salvation, of Christian fellowship, of spiritual sanctification. We are given the Lord's Supper to give us tastes of the heavenly banquet and be comforted. We are given earthly blessings of family, friends, productive work, and so on.

God knows how weak and sinful we are, and so he grants us fulfilled desires that keep the real hope before us. Let us do the same for one another. Make it your business today to encourage your neighbor, your spouse, your family – whomever God places in your path.

Heed the Word

Proverbs 13:13

Whoever despises the word brings destruction on himself,
but he who reveres the commandment will be rewarded.

The proverb sums up Jesus' parable of "The Rich Man and Lazarus." Because the rich man did not heed "Moses and the prophets," he brought destruction upon himself in Hades. Lazarus, though he suffered in his earthly life, was rewarded with heaven, no doubt as a keeper of the commandments.

Jesus' parable makes the further point that the despiser of the Word is not to expect extra efforts made to turn him around – no visits from ghosts like Scrooge received, no extraordinary miracles. The Word of God is enough on its own, and, indeed, it serves to reveal the true state of our hearts. Those who reject Scripture feel justified now, claiming that it contains contradictions, is filled with error, etc. They may claim now that Scripture does not bring with it enough evidence to be believed. But once they have died or Christ has returned, all arguments will be seen for what they are – excuses to cover up pride and rebellion.

Now is the time to heed God's Word. Now is the time to heed his gospel. And today is the time to read God's Word, meditate upon it, and let it examine your heart so that you will live for him in obedience.

Fountain of Life

Proverbs 13:14

The teaching of the wise is a fountain of life,
   that one may turn away from the snares of death.

How well are you tuning into wise teaching? Are you reading daily the wise teaching of Scripture? Do you read the wise teaching of the Gospels, of Christ himself? Do you listen to the sermons of wise preachers, to the lessons of wise teachers? Do you read the writings of wise men and women of God?

You must go to the fountain to drink. All about you are the snares of death – the teachings of the world which bombard you daily through TV, movies, advertisements, novels, secular teachers, colleagues, neighbors. These things influence you more than you think. Indeed, the genius of good advertising is to enter into your unconscious thoughts. I like to read well written novels and watch well produced movies. Good books and movies are thought provoking and can help me see life in a way I would not have before. But they come with danger, presenting perspectives that run counter to God's truth. Thus, I must keep up a steady diet of Christian teaching, writing, and arts. Foremost, I must keep up the steady study of God's Word.

Be sure to go to the fountain of life today and drink deeply of God's wisdom.

Good Sense

Proverbs 13:15

Good sense wins favor,
  but the way of the treacherous is their ruin.

There are two reasons the "treacherous" come to ruin. The first is justice. Usually in this lifetime, always in the next life, justice punishes wrongdoing. The other reason is that wrongdoing is not wise. It can seem to be clever to lie, to plot ways to get ahead of a competitor or take advantage of a customer, but such actions lay traps for future failure. Such a person earns distrust and contempt. He must now expend energy protecting himself from his enemies. He becomes suspicious of everyone because through his own example he knows how devious others can be.

"Good" people often act without good sense. For one thing, they put too much confidence in their own goodness, thinking that others will act the same way, that others will recognize their good behavior and intentions. They become puzzled to learn that they have offended their colleagues, not realizing how their "goodness" comes across as self-righteousness, how their "goodness" has blinded them to the ways they have offended others through their speech and behavior.

Good sense means being sensible to the people around you. It means being able to judge properly the circumstances in which you find yourself and not barging into a situation with your own agenda unaware of how foolish or offensive you may appear. Use good sense today. Pray for good sense. You don't know what awaits you. All the more reason to go through the day prayerfully, asking the Spirit to grant you good sense.

With Knowledge

Proverbs 13:16

In everything the prudent acts with knowledge,
  but a fool flaunts his folly.

How will you act today at work, at school, the home? Will you speak without thinking, merely reacting to others and circumstances? Will you lose your temper because traffic is bad or a sales clerk is rude? Will you express your frustrations to whoever happens to be near? Or will you go through the day praying to God for wisdom? For God to keep you alert that you not give in to sin? For God to keep you alert to the opportunities to witness for him, to show the love of Christ?

The prudent acts with knowledge – knowledge of what is going on around him, knowledge of wise and ethical behavior, and foremost, knowledge of the gospel. The more one understands the gospel, the more prudent he will be in life's daily circumstances. The more he knows grace, the more gracious he will be. The more he knows God in Christ, the more Christ-like he will be.

Faithful Envoy

Proverbs 13:17

A wicked messenger falls into trouble,
  but a faithful envoy brings healing.

Apply this to preaching. Tremble for the preacher who uses his pulpit to preach that the Scriptures are not reliable, waters down the gospel to a formula of good works, and assures sinners and unbelievers that they have nothing to fear.

Tremble for the preacher who uses his pulpit to preach politics and push his social agenda. Tremble for the preacher who is not faithful in preaching the message of his scripture text; who wins a following for his entertaining style and not his substance; who becomes a self-help guru instead of a prophet for God's Word. Such a messenger will fall into trouble before the God who called him to be a faithful envoy of the gospel and the full counsel of God found in Scripture.

But the faithful envoy who week after week proclaims God's Word and makes it clear, such a person truly brings healing to his people who hurt from sin and sinning; who need to hear God speaking to them; who need to hear again and again the gospel. Real healing comes from God's Word working in us.

True Honor

Proverbs 13:18

Poverty and disgrace come to him who ignores instruction,
but whoever heeds reproof is honored.

The downfall of the person who ignores instruction comes about for two reasons. One, he remains an ignorant person. Those with knowledge will pass him by in competition. His ignorance will expose him to danger and traps. It will lead him along the wrong paths. Two, he loses respect before others. Only the fool ignores instruction, and foolishness is highly visible. Others will mock him and delight in his failure.

Conversely, the person who heeds instruction and reproof will be honored for the same reasons. By heeding reproof, he grows in knowledge and skill, thus gaining advantage over others who are lazy or foolish. He is also honored by others. It is the wise who prize knowledge and are humble enough to receive it; and wisdom is also visible, especially in the eyes of others who are wise.

If you want to win respect before others, then prove yourself to be a good student. And if you seek commendation from God, then humble yourself and learn from all experiences he grants you. Study his Word; learn from his servants, both those who are learned in the Scriptures and from the lowest of his servants. Seek God's wisdom. Pray for it. Gladly receive correction.

Good Desire

Proverbs 13:19

A desire fulfilled is sweet to the soul,
  but to turn away from evil is an abomination to fools.

The key to this proverb is knowing what should be our desire. John Piper's book *Desiring God* has seemed misguided, even heretical, to some because of his strong emphasis on fulfilling desire. His argument rests, however, on having right desires, namely the enjoyment of God. We are often left feeling unfulfilled, not because others have prevented us from obtaining our desires, but because we are, as C. S. Lewis notes, content with too little. We think temporal objects will fulfill us – a vacation, good food, sex, entertainment. But they cannot replace love, holy fear, peace with God, redemption. They cannot replace the invisible eternal, and they are only as satisfying as they give a taste of the eternal rest, eternal banquet, eternal joy that will someday be ours.

Fools are fools precisely because they take pleasure in what is evil. They think it is fun to act in shameful ways. Getting drunk is something to laugh about and even boast about. Illicit sex is exciting. Taking advantage of others fulfills inner desires to feel superior.

The folly of the world is that it upholds the first line of this proverb and deletes the second line. To live with passion is the fulfilled life according to the foolish world. A life worth living is a life lived with passion. That is the basic plot line of many movies in which a debauched character teaches a clean-cut character to "really" live, which always includes illicit sex and getting drunk.

The choice is not between living a life of desire or passion and that of living a dull life of good behavior. It is living a life of right desire.

Wise Companionship

Proverbs 13:20

Whoever walks with the wise becomes wise,
*   but the companion of fools will suffer harm.*

There are individuals who were foolish in their behavior and beliefs yet fell into friendships with mature, godly believers, and then came to a strong faith that turned them around. There are also individuals who professed Christ and seemed mature, yet came into the circle of unbelievers and/or foolish people, and then fell away from the faith and/or engaged in foolish behavior.

Who are the wise with whom you associate? Is there a wise person whom you look to for counsel? Are there wise persons whom you emulate? Think about that right now. Can you name companions who are godly, wise persons whose counsel and behavior are to be trusted? What of foolish companions? Do you have companions who get into trouble; who act immaturely; who have yet to exhibit mature faith? Your companions will infect you with either wisdom or folly.

Depending upon your circumstances, you may need to proactively seek out wise companions. We cannot control who all our companions will be at work, family, school, and neighborhood. But we can control whom we will look to for counsel and example. You may need to call on the telephone, email on the computer, or invite to your home wise companions. But seek them out.

Meanwhile, you always have your wise Lord, and you may share in his vast wisdom through the study of his Word and through prayer. Seek after the Lord's wisdom. Whomever you seek counsel from and emulate, let it be one who is walking in the path of God.

Disaster and Reward

Proverbs 13:21

Disaster pursues sinners,
   but the righteous are rewarded with good.

Sinners do not merely flirt with danger; they place targets on their back to make sure danger does not miss the mark. Furthermore, they do not see that disaster is already upon them. They are unaware of the seeds of destruction they have sown: a marriage destroyed before they know it; a job loss before the notice has come; friends who have unknowingly become enemies. They are strolling in the park, unaware that an army of destruction is bearing down on them.

The righteous court reward; their very behavior invites positive responses from the people around them. Their behavior naturally keeps them away from sinful activities that lead into disaster.

But the worldview of the proverb makes a strong statement about disaster and reward in the light of God serving as judge. The righteous Judge will punish the wicked and reward the righteous. This would be frightening news to us if we did not know the gospel, which reveals Christ's atoning work whereby he exchanged his righteousness with us and received our sin, thus bearing our punishment and giving us his reward.

Let us not be filled with anger towards our neighbors who offend us and engage in sin. They are getting away with nothing. All the more pray for God's mercy to awaken them to their sin and know Christ.

Inheritance

Proverbs 13:22

A good man leaves an inheritance to his children's children,
   but the sinner's wealth is laid up for the righteous.

Much could be said about what the inheritance of a good man entails.

Foremost is leaving a legacy of faith in Christ and of walking in righteousness. But we should not be quick to lay aside the subject of money. Indeed, Christians are quick to do so, somehow disconnecting a righteous life from how money is handled. There are many Christians devoted to ministry and yet leave their families in a destitute state. Christian financial consultant Ron Blue tells of a minister who only served small churches until his retirement; and yet he had a million dollars in assets. How? By spending less than he took in and saving the remainder bit by bit.

This proverb is not teaching that you must leave lots of money for your grandchildren when you die. It is, however, teaching that goodness includes handling money wisely. The sinner's wealth ends up in the hands of the righteous, not because they take it from him, but because he is foolish with his money. His pride and greed lead him to make foolish choices.

How are your finances? Are they in order? If you are struggling in debt, is the reason because you do not earn enough or because you are not wise with what you have?

Poverty and Injustice

Proverbs 13:23

The fallow ground of the poor would yield much food,
  but it is swept away through injustice.

Here is a sobering observation, not to make us cynical but to make us compassionate and zealous for justice. It is a reminder that righteousness is not merely to be about personal holiness but about how we care for others, particularly those who are poor and defenseless.

Somehow, evangelical Christianity has become known as the religion about morality and of little interest in justice. How did that happen, considering that the rise of evangelicalism corresponded with the societies formed in the 1800s to combat slavery, child and women oppression, and poverty? Jesus said that we would always have the

160

poor with us, one reason being that we always have injustice with us. Do not be quick to explain poverty away on laziness. Scripture, God's Word, observes that the poor may be kept in poverty through injustice.

As you examine your life, what do you do to support the cause of justice and to help the poor?

Wise Discipline

Proverbs 13:24

Whoever spares the rod hates his son,
but he who loves him is diligent to discipline him.

Understand the message here. It is that parents – because they love their children – will exercise appropriate discipline to correct them. They teach their children that sinful behavior brings punishment.

The message is not that parents must always use physical punishment for discipline. Wise parents will choose the appropriate means depending upon the offending behavior and depending upon the nature of the child, as well as upon the nature of the parent. A parent who struggles with anger must be all the more careful not to let anger control how he disciplines. Discipline is necessary, but it must be coupled with wisdom and love to carry out God's intentions.

Which leads to the next application: because God is wise and loves us, he disciplines us. He does not watch idly as we go astray, but will see that our sins bring correcting consequences. Many of the troubles we complain about are the results of our own sins. This does not mean that because I sin, God then causes a loved one to be ill. It means that God allows the natural consequences of sinful behavior to take place. As Proverbs points out, if I choose to hang out with wicked friends, I will get into trouble. If I choose to lie and slander, it will turn on me.

By grace, God protects me from many consequences, the most important of which is my damnation. But by his grace, he lets many

161

consequences fall on me so that I may turn from sin and to him through Christ.

Good Appetite

Proverbs 13:25

The righteous has enough to satisfy his appetite,
  but the belly of the wicked suffers want.

The righteous has enough because: 1) his lifestyle curbs immoral and unethical impulses that lead to trouble and loss; 2) he curbs his appetite so that it does not control him; 3) God blesses the righteous; 4) his appetite is for God and God satisfies such an appetite.

Like the person who craves only non-nourishing food, the wicked's belly always aches. He craves what does not satisfy. Furthermore, his appetite controls him; an uncontrolled appetite cannot be satisfied. The wicked's lifestyle causes him to waste his money, leads him into activities that harm his body and ruin relationships. His wickedness separates him from God, bringing wrath instead of blessing.

What do you want today? What will satisfy you today? Are you looking in the right direction? Is your craving for the blessing of God?

Wise Building

Proverbs 14:1

The wisest of women builds her house,
  but folly with her own hands tears it down.

Though the proverb may be contrasting two persons – one who is wise and another who is foolish – it can be describing a person who starts off wise and later turns foolish. Solomon himself is an example. By wisdom, he built Israel to its greatest height, and yet, in foolishness he prepared its downfall. By wisdom, he honored God with the temple and his own devotion; by foolishness he brought in idol worship through his many wives. By wisdom, he built cities and made Israel strong; by foolishness, he over taxed and over worked his people, leading to revolt after his death.

Many a woman and a man has achieved great deeds and built up wealth because of wise strategy and decision making. Yet, their very success led them astray to trusting too much in their ability and to wanting too much. If a person is not satisfied with God, nothing else will satisfy and eventually she will overstep her limited wisdom. Then the house she built will fall down.

Wisdom is the fear of God applied. Remove the fear of God, then wisdom becomes mere cleverness. And there is nothing like cleverness to pump one's pride, which then makes one blind. Then comes the downfall.

Good Fear

Proverbs 14:2

Whoever walks in uprightness fears the Lord,
  but he who is devious in his ways despises him.

C. S. Lewis writes of this fear phenomenon in his Narnia Chronicles in the reaction of characters when they first meet the lion Aslan, who represents Christ. The good are drawn to him. As the horse Hwin in *The Horse and His Boy* said to him, "Please, you're so beautiful. You may eat me if you like. I'd sooner be eaten by you than fed by anyone else." That is the fear of the Lord. The wicked despise him. And so the witch of *The Magician's Nephew* throws a bar at him and runs away in a fearful hatred.

And then there are the sinners who do not dread him yet are uncomfortable, for the sight of him (and hearing his voice) removes the veil by which they considered themselves. Before Aslan, excuses fall away and sin is exposed. And yet, unlike the wicked who run away in hatred, the sinners find that what follows the painful exposure of sin is the peace of forgiveness and the blessedness of welcome into Aslan's fellowship.

163

So is the experience of those made righteous in Christ. To fear the Lord is to know one's sin and the Lord's holiness. It is to be made humble. And in that humility one finds grace. Pity the devious who only devises his own misery. Give thanks to the Lord for the grace of teaching you the fear of him.

Wise and Foolish Speech

Proverbs 14:3

By the mouth of a fool comes a rod for his back,
  but the lips of the wise will preserve them.

When David was still on the run from Saul, he asked for food from a rich rancher named Nabal to feed his men. Nabal, as a fool, rebuffs the messengers sent to him. As a miserly, harsh man, Nabal does not consider the ancient custom of showing hospitality to those requesting his help, particularly, as in this case, to those who have treated his servants well and fairly. As a fool, he doesn't consider his own vulnerable position. David has a small army and can take what he wants. Nabal does not consider how much he will be offending a man renowned as a warrior. Fortunately, Nabal has a wife who is discerning, and by her wise action and words, she preserves the life of her husband and all the men. (Read the story in 1 Sam. 25.)

Are you foolish or wise with your lips? Here are some warning signals. Do these remarks characterize you?

"I pride myself in speaking my mind."
"People always know where they stand with me."
"I'm not afraid to shoot from the hip."
"I call it like I see it."

If you make such remarks, if you don't see what these remarks really convey, then you are likely in the fool's camp. What is missing in the remarks is a wise understanding of your own limitations and sin. Our minds are clouded with sin. However clear a perspective we may think we have, it is quite likely we do not see clearly. We have limited mental abilities, and even the wisest mind is nevertheless clouded with sin.

To speak wisely requires humility. It requires the right goal – to glorify God. If you simply ask yourself this question before you speak, wisdom will come to you to know the right words: Will what I am about to say glorify God? For glorifying God is ultimate wisdom.

Worthwhile Investment

Proverbs 14:4

Where there are no oxen, the manger is clean,
  but abundant crops come by the strength of the ox.

When there are no oxen, the farmer does not have the trouble of feeding them or cleaning up after them. He can keep his barn nice and neat. His one problem is that he cannot plow his fields! If he desires abundant crops, then he needs his oxen and must be willing to invest in them. The moral, then, is that if we desire to reap wealth, we must be willing to put in the labor and make the sacrifices to produce a harvest.

Risk and sacrifice are necessary for achieving worthwhile goals. The risk may be money or emotional vulnerability or pride; the sacrifice may require years of preparation or hard labor. What makes the risk and sacrifice acceptable to undergo is the greatness of the goal.

What is your goal today? To make a deal? To pass a test? Here was the Apostle Paul's goal that gave him the motivation to suffer and to achieve beyond ordinary ability: "But one thing I do: forgetting what lies behind and straining forward to what lies ahead, I press on toward the goal for the prize of the upward call of God in Christ Jesus" (Phil. 3:13-14).

A Lying Nature

Proverbs 14:5

A faithful witness does not lie,
  but a false witness breathes out lies.

For some people lying makes them uncomfortable, while for others it is second nature.

There is a movie in which a "city-wise" cop is teamed with two "do-it-by-the book" cops. All through the movie, he tries to loosen them up by telling lies whenever necessary to keep out of trouble with the police department. They are not bad cops, just officers having to break some rules so they can get the bad guys. Finally, the movie ends with the two other cops telling a lie to their superior officer, and thus, the movie ends happily.

Lying has become not only second nature, but esteemed as a virtue for achieving good ends. I remember reading a book by a successful Christian salesman, who gave example after example of techniques based on lying. The premise is that as long as the salesman truly believed in his product, then he may take liberties with his stories.

Today, you will have opportunities to speak the truth or to lie. What will be in your nature to do? Will the thought of telling a lie make you squirm, or will the idea of telling the truth be too unnerving? Will your struggle be over how to tell the truth in love and in a way that glorifies God? Or will your struggle be over how to fudge the truth convincingly and get your way?

Seeking Wisdom

Proverbs 14:6

A scoffer seeks wisdom in vain,
  but knowledge is easy for a man of understanding.

The sad irony that Proverbs teaches is that the people who need wisdom the most – the fool, the scoffer, the wicked – are the ones least likely to attain it, while the wise are the ones who find it and profit from it.

The scoffer/fool just doesn't get it. Like Simon the Magician who tried to buy the power of the Holy Spirit, the fool doesn't understand what wisdom even is. He sees the wise make right decisions to solve problems, and he confuses their wisdom for cleverness; he sees them profit from wisdom, and thus regards wisdom as a mere tool to use for his advantage. He does not understand that wisdom has to do with character. Wisdom comes out of a right character, and it molds character. But the fool doesn't want his character changed. He wants to change others to get his desires.

And so the scoffer seeks wisdom in vain. How is your wisdom hunting going? Understand that the issue is not so much you finding wisdom but rather having a character in which you invite wisdom to find you and to mold you. Pray that the Holy Spirit – the true Giver of Wisdom – will keep you still and open your heart and mind to him.

Leave the Room

Proverbs 14:7

Leave the presence of a fool,
  for there you do not meet words of knowledge.

We can save ourselves much frustration if we would heed this proverb. There are times in which, literally, we need to walk out of a room in which foolishness is spoken. There are many times in which we ought not to answer foolish words, be they spoken or written. With the advent of email, and the ability to forward email to masses, and the proliferation of websites, blogsites, electronic bulletin boards, and chat-rooms, there are many more avenues for foolishness to take.

Taking time to answer foolish words creates frustration in you because you spend time, effort, and emotional energy all for no avail. A fool is not after knowledge; his goal is to make a sensation; it is to gain attention. To respond to him merely plays into his intention. Other fools are not so much after attention, as they are merely taking in what they want to hear and then passing it on. You may be able to bother them with your responses, but you cannot win them over. Again, you are the one feeling the frustration. Even Jesus said not to cast pearls before swine.

What then can you do in response to foolish words? One, do not respond; two, do not pass the words on; three, if in the presence of a fool, either ignore his words or leave; four, do not let his words get under your skin; at least, do not show that they do. The fool wants either to win your admiration or your ire. He wants to know that he has impacted you. Leave the room; delete the email; hang up the phone.

And turn to wisdom. Turn to the words of Scripture. Pray and think about whatever is good (Phil. 4:8).

Discerning Prudence

Proverbs 14:8

The wisdom of the prudent is to discern his way,
but the folly of fools is deceiving.

Here is the great prize of the prudent – he can see where he is going. If he has strayed from the path of righteousness, he will catch himself and turn back to the path. If he is heading into trouble, he can see the danger ahead and act accordingly. Thus, the prudent turns to Christ in faith and repentance. Where others cannot see the calamity awaiting them, he sees and turns to his Savior. Where others cannot see the glory of the righteous path, he sees and keeps his eyes upon the prize. Where others cannot see the freedom of bondage to Christ, he sees and rejoices in his freedom to live for the glory of God. Where others can only see with their physical eyes, he sees what is unseen and moves forward with anticipation towards the unseen, eternal glory.

Meanwhile, the folly of fools deceives them into believing that their slavery to sin is freedom; that becoming slaves to their passions is liberating. They do not merely miss the hidden traps of their chosen paths, but refuse to see the clear signs warning them of danger. For the folly of fools is that they cherish their foolishness. They are happy; they believe they are on the right path. They do not want to see dangers that would make them have to change.

Pray for those whom you know who are blinded by folly. Only the Holy Spirit can give the spiritual sight needed and the faith to turn to Christ. And pray for yourself, that you not be led astray by the folly of the world which is telling you that you are the fool. Always we must depend upon the Spirit working in us to keep our eyes open and our path leading to God.

Mocking God

Proverbs 14:9

Fools mock at the guilt offering,
  but the upright enjoy acceptance.

Fools never apologize for their foolishness. Even when they make an attempt (which they do only from pressure), they always add "but" – but I did not intend to harm anyone; but I am trying to do my best; but I am misunderstood. Fools see admission of sin and mistakes as a sign of weakness. They want to be strong, or at least perceived as strong and confident.

Again, fools just don't get it. The strong are strong, not because they will not admit their failures, but because they are willing to bear responsibility for their mistakes. The strong man will say, "I blew it," but then he moves on, having learned from his failings. This is the mark of the upright. They accept responsibility and so enjoy acceptance of other people who respect their forthrightness.

But the tragedy for the fool is not that he doesn't win acceptance of his fellow man, but that he places himself under the wrath of God. It is God who calls for the guilt offering; it is God who must be appeased; it is God the fool is mocking, and God will not be mocked.

Know that we do not have to bring guilt offerings for our sins; we do not have to do penance to win our way back to God's favor. But we must pay God honor by turning to the Guilt Offering he has provided for us, our Lord Jesus Christ.

Lonely Is the Heart

Proverbs 14:10

The heart knows its own bitterness,
  and no stranger shares its joy.

Ultimately we are alone with our hearts. Even now, as you read this, sadness or joy that only you know lies in your heart. The closer we are to others, the more open our hearts; but even in the most intimate relationship the other person cannot see, and, more to the point, cannot feel all our emotions. Nor can he/she know the motives and feelings of our hearts except what we reveal. We may laugh when we are distraught. We may feign sorrow when really we are happy. We may feign reverence and love for God when in truth we have no feeling for him at all.

But it is God from whom we cannot hide our hearts. We may even hide our hearts from ourselves, denying what truly lies within us. But God knows the heart and Christ reveals the heart, that is, by our response to him and to the gospel. And it is the Spirit who changes the heart through rebirth and sanctification.

Be uneasy if you are trying to hide sin in your heart. God knows the sin. But then, turn to Christ's mercy and grace. And take hope in the Holy Spirit who will turn your heart of stone into a heart of flesh, and who will continue the work of sanctification in you. How wonderful it is to know that the very one from whom you cannot hide your heart is the same one who can truly transform that heart. God knows what you are feeling now. If it is joy, then give thanks to him for your joy. If it is sadness or anxiety or bitterness, then pray to him for help now. He will not be shocked by what you reveal, though you may be when you realize what is in you. For God's desire is to bless, to transform you that your heart may know the peace and joy of Jesus Christ.

The Tent That Flourishes

Proverbs 14:11

The house of the wicked will be destroyed,
but the tent of the upright will flourish.

The end of the wicked is seen every day. They cheat their way to success and yet end in jail, are killed, or experience some other kind of calamity. Because they build with worthless materials and through unethical practices, their very works lead to their downfall. But the upright, though they may experience trials, flourish. Many flourish materially because their integrity and wisdom bring success. Many may be poor and yet flourish in happiness through loving relationships. For many, they leave a flourishing legacy – their children succeeding beyond them, or, again, leaving a legacy of love.

One of our failures is to confuse who is rich and who poor even about ourselves. We may grumble that our unethical colleagues are doing better than we, failing to see the riches we have and their poverty. For anyone who has Christ is rich beyond all measure, and he who does not have Christ is utterly impoverished. Know what you have. Each day you should give thanks to God for the eternal glory and riches that belong to you, if you are clothed in the righteousness of Jesus Christ. For truly, living in the tent of Jesus Christ which flourishes eternally is wealth indeed.

Seems Right

Proverbs 14:12

There is a way that seems right to a man,
but its end is the way to death.

This proverb makes two matter-of-fact statements that, depending on who we are, we tend to ignore. One is that the man of the world lives the way he does because it seems right to him. We Christians seem to forget this.

We get angry with nonChristians who live what we consider immoral and unethical lifestyles. How can they live that way? They live that way because it seems right to them. It makes sense to them. Even the criminal will justify his behavior as the right thing to do in his circumstance. And given their worldview, their behavior makes sense.

The other statement is that such a way is the way to death. Their worldview, however much sense it may seem to make, is wrong. What God sets forth is truth, despite whatever perspective any person may have. People may argue against truth; they may reason to the best of their ability; they may rail against truth; they may curse it; they may ignore it. Nevertheless, their way ends in death.

Do not be angry with the world. Do not be resentful of your neighbor. But do pray for your neighbor, that he or she may not follow what seems right, but be awakened to what is right. Pray that the Holy Spirit will awaken, convict, and grant faith to your neighbor to follow the path of faith in Christ that ends in life.

Endless Joy

Proverbs 14:13

Even in laughter the heart may ache,
and the end of joy may be grief.

Not all is what it seems. That neighbor who is laughing may be experiencing immense anguish. That couple who seem so happy may be filled with sadness. The news of joy may be setting in motion great grief. This is the character of life in this world – that joy is either mixed with sorrow or is but an interlude between times of grief and anxiety. The story of the world is the story of Camelot. No matter how good a place and time may be, seeds of sorrow are always sown and bear fruit. Such is the story of every individual.

Nothing is certain. No joy is lasting. No sky is cloudless. Except...

Except the one thing that matters most – the guarantee of everlasting joy. It is the guarantee that there will come a time when the heart will never ache, that laughter will be of pure joy that will never end in grief. There will be a time when there shall be no "mourning nor crying nor pain anymore" (Rev. 21:4).

In your grief, Christian, remember your true hope which cannot be denied you. Your inheritance is everlasting joy in the presence of your Redeemer. Take joy in that hope now. Take joy in knowing that the laughter you experience here is but a preview of the laughter in eternal glory. Begin enjoying now the eternal life that is yours. There are trials in this life, to be sure. But you can withstand the trials if you but keep the hope that is before you, and you look for the signs of that "weight of glory" that is yours. You will find those signs in good joy, in the blessings of Christian fellowship, in worship, in meditating upon the sacred words of Scripture, in beholding the beauty of the world. The signs of eternal joy are all about you.

Bearing Fruit

Proverbs 14:14

The backslider in heart will be filled with the fruit of his ways,
and a good man will be filled with the fruit of his ways.

Once, I commented on the poor luck a certain fellow seemed to keep having. My companion replied that sometimes a person makes his own luck. He could have quoted this proverb. We often question why we are having so much trouble. It is true that trouble comes to the godly as well as the ungodly and that often there is no accounting for troubles. But much, if not most, of our troubles come as consequence to our behavior.

If we backslide in our faith, we can expect problems. God will discipline his children, but that discipline may be his allowing our conduct to receive its due consequences. This is a major theme of proverbs. If we start hanging out with ungodly friends, we will more likely experience more troubles. The wicked and the immoral draw trouble for themselves. But the backslider will experience more bitterness than the immoral who are living according to their character. The backslider will experience remorse; he will feel

173

uncomfortable in both worlds. He can neither find real happiness in the sin that the wicked enjoy nor in the pleasures of the righteous. Life is thrown off kilter. This is the fruit that he reaps.

The good man – the one who remains true to his faith – may experience troubles, but he reaps blessing. He reaps a good name; he experiences honest joy and peace. And he reaps the blessing of being productive in good things. He not only bears more fruit, but more pleasing fruit.

And Jesus tells us how to bear that fruit – abide in him. Abide in Christ and we will bear more fruit than we could expect. Abide in Christ and he will abide in us and keep us from backsliding. He will keep us from falling.

The Simple and the Prudent

Proverbs 14:15

The simple believes everything,
   but the prudent gives thought to his steps.

The simple believes the advertisements that happiness, sex appeal, and popularity are found in merchandise, especially expensive merchandise. The simple buys into the messages of pop music and media, because they are expressed with passion. The simple believes whatever appeals to his senses and promises him happiness without change or cost. He believes everything, not because he is intellectually incapable of sifting for the truth, but because he is most affected by flattery. As long as someone appeals to him in a flattering manner, he will believe the message, provided that the message also is flattering to him.

The prudent knows to hesitate over anything that appears too good to be true. But his real motivation is knowing and abiding by the truth. How real is that motivation? The simple test is his reaction to the Truth – Jesus Christ. Many profess a love for truth, but their response to Christ reveals how much love they truly have. Thus, there are many who seem prudent, who reject much of what popular culture teaches; nevertheless, they also are as the simple who yield to Satan's flattery that they are wise even while being blind.

Give thought to your steps today – all of your steps: your steps in your home, in your workplace, in your school; your steps that take you past a myriad of messages which purport to tell the truth. Give thought to your steps by directing your thoughts to God, filtering all messages through the Word and the gospel, keeping Christ as Lord, and seeking the leading of the Holy Spirit.

Reckless Living

Proverbs 14:16

One who is wise is cautious and turns away from evil,
  but a fool is reckless and careless.

Our culture today, at least our popular media culture, disdains such a proverb. It celebrates those daring to live on the edge because it considers that the one virtue that truly matters is passion. It makes no difference what one is passionate about. One person is passionate about serving the poor; another is passionate is about skateboarding. Each activity has the same value as long as the activity produces a rush.

The bride will dump her cautious fiancé and run off with the passionate lover. Obviously the latter must enjoy life more. It is the rule breaker who saves the day, while the rule keeper dies or at least is left without the girl. To be daring is what matters.

And yet, that is what the reckless are not. For if they were daring, they would risk giving up control of their life on their terms. They would engage in the most daring adventure of all – yielding completely to the control of Christ and living fully for the glory of their Maker. They may seem to be fearlessly reckless with their lives, but it is the control of their lives that they will not give up because of fear. They fear God's control; they fear what Christ would compel them to do.

And they have good cause. For God demands absolute control; Christ demands absolute obedience. All that is promised is eternal life; in this life there is no guarantee as to what a disciple will be called to do and to experience. Christ does not promise safety; indeed, he says to count the cost. For it is the life of the Christian who turns away from evil – that is, from the sin that is comfortable. It is such a life which is most "reckless" in this world as it gives in to the Lordship of Christ.

Temper, Temper

Proverbs 14:17

A man of quick temper acts foolishly,
  and a man of evil devices is hated.

This proverb points out the danger that comes with anger: we make fools of ourselves. More times than not, we regret our words spoken and actions committed in anger. We harm people we love; we lose or destroy possessions valuable to us. Anger makes us dumb. All the more trouble then for a quick tempered person.

Such a person may be zealous to serve; he may be compassionate; in other respects he may exhibit godly character. But his temper continually destroys what his good character produces. People are guarded around him, unable to receive his attempts to befriend them. He cannot be entrusted with responsibility despite his giftedness. He is regarded as a danger. If you have this problem, take steps to receive counsel and accountability. There is nothing more destructive in your life than a quick temper. Make it your daily prayer for healing.

A man may mean well but be distrusted for his quick temper. A man of evil devices is hated, for his very intent is to harm his neighbor. He devises ways to take advantage of others for his own gain. He may be able to master his temper, but he does so in order to get his way. The joke on him is that he thinks he is clever but is really a greater fool. Unlike the quick tempered man, he keeps his cool and plans ways to manipulate his neighbor. But though he is able to fool others for awhile, his evil heart becomes known through the hurt he causes, and so he wins hatred. The rest of his life he must keep devising schemes to offset the hatred he has earned and the attempts of others to harm him. He is a fool, thinking that losing the respect and love of his neighbors is worth winning the trinkets of money and power.

Inheritance

Proverbs 14:18

The simple inherit folly,
  but the prudent are crowned with knowledge.

The simple complains about his bad luck. He can't seem to the find the right job; he always gets the unfair teacher; he never gets a break. He can't see what everyone else sees – that his folly leads him into further folly. The prudent, on the other hand, because he is prudent, learns and benefits from his experiences so that he turns both bad and good experiences into opportunities for knowledge that benefits him.

This proverb indicates, however, that the simple and prudent do not merely produce their respective fruit. They are also rewarded accordingly. It teaches the lesson of Romans 1:18-28 that God gives up the foolish to their foolish ways. They inherit further folly. And the proverb teaches Jesus' lesson of "The Talents." To everyone who has, more will be given. The wise and the prudent will be given greater knowledge.

How does one move from being simple to becoming prudent and wise? The secret of the prudent is humility. The prudent know that in truth they are not wise before God. Because they are humble before him, and therefore become cautious about their own ability and wisdom, God grants to them knowledge and wisdom.

Bow Down

Proverbs 14:19

The evil bow down before the good,
   the wicked at the gates of the righteous.

How galling for the wicked! They are wicked precisely because they refuse to bow down before the good. We may be quick to point out that many do not bow down, that they get away with their wickedness. Perhaps. But many do have to bow down. Typically, the good do not end up in jail; quite often, the wicked are brought to justice. For every instance of injustice in the courts, they are many instances of justice carried out.

But for us Christians, the proverb should stir in us such a passage as Philippians 2:10: "at the name of Jesus every knee should bow, in heaven and on earth and under the earth." The day will come when all people, both the good and the wicked, will bow before the Good Judge as we all stand before the Gates of the Righteous One.

The Poor and the Rich

Proverbs 14:20

The poor is disliked even by his neighbor,
   but the rich has many friends.

This is an "observation" proverb, not one intended to instruct us on how we should be. It makes the unpleasant observation that a poor person must go through extra effort to prove himself to be a "good" person, while a rich person would have to make the effort to prove himself not a good friend.

We take quickly to the rich person for a couple of reasons. One, we more naturally take him to be a "quality" person. In our minds, he has proven himself to be a hard worker, smart, and so on. He must be a good person to be around. Two, it is advantageous to have him as a friend because he is in position to hand out favors, be it money, good references, etc.

The poor man – well, we want to know why he is poor – drugs?

laziness? There must be something about his character that keeps him in his position. If he is friendly, we must be suspicious that he wants something from us.

This is reality. The sober truth is that we reveal more about ourselves than the rich or the poor. We naturally gravitate to the rich and naturally shy away from the poor. We naturally will trust the rich and distrust the poor. It is true that we are to be discerning of both rich and poor; we are to be cautious in making ourselves indebted to others, as well as making others indebted to us. But because the deck is stacked against the poor, all the more we are to make the effort to know the poor neighbor so that we are in a position to be discerning. All the more we should take time to talk with our poor neighbor to know him as a person. We certainly will not be competing with many others for his attention.

Neighborly Sin

Proverbs 14:21

Whoever despises his neighbor is a sinner,
  but blessed is he who is generous to the poor.

This proverb is likely intended to complement the previous proverb:

> The poor is disliked even by his neighbor,
> but the rich has many friends.

The poor may be disliked by his neighbor, but that neighbor then is sinning. Here's the point. Our attitude towards our neighbor is not to be controlled by the condition of our neighbor. Remember Jesus' teaching through his parable of the "Good Samaritan." The question is not to be "Who is my neighbor?" but "To whom will I be a neighbor?" And the answer is that we are to treat everyone as our neighbors whom we are to love.

Again, the focus here is on the status of our neighbor. We don't choose to love or withhold love according to his income, social status, or other classification. Our neighbor's attitude toward us will influence our behavior towards him. If he is friendly, we will be friendly; if he is hostile, we will be guarded. Even so, we are still called by Christ to love him. If he is hostile, we are still to pray for him and look for opportunity to do him good. If he is reserved towards us, we are still to look for ways to befriend him. Let us be generous to our neighbors who are poor in social graces and poor in loving. For our Lord was generous to us while we were poor in righteousness and love toward him.

And let us love our neighbor especially if he is poor. We are to love poor and rich alike, but Scripture tends to speak up for the poor and to urge us to give special regard to the economically poor. We are quick to blame them for their poverty. Scripture is not blind to laziness and sin that leads to poverty; even so, again and again God's Word instructs us to be generous and compassionate.

What We May Meet

Proverbs 14:22

Do they not go astray who devise evil?
  Those who devise good meet steadfast love and faithfulness.

Those who devise evil certainly go astray from the path of righteousness; they also go astray and miss what they desire (unless they believe such things do not exist) – steadfast love and faithfulness. Who does not desire to have friends and family who love them and will remain faithful to them? The most wicked man wants someone to count on. If he claims that he doesn't, it is only because he is disillusioned, believing that love and faithfulness are empty dreams. He does not connect his behavior with his failure to find such things.

There are some who have been hurt after attempts of showing love and kindness; some who have been faithful to another, only to be turned on by that person. And so they become bitter. But the proverb is not teaching that those who devise good will always meet steadfast love and faithfulness in everyone. This will not happen in a world of sin, but the experience is more likely to happen and will

180

happen more frequently for the one who consciously seeks the good of others. It is worthwhile to devise good deeds, to plan ways to bless others.

And always remember that you will meet the steadfast love and faithfulness of the Lord. Indeed, let him be your model, he who remains faithful to his people, though we continually break his commandments; he who shows us steadfast love, though we often show petty resentment in the ways we respond to daily experiences. Let the Lord Jesus Christ be your model for devising good today. Who knows what you will then meet?

Profitable Labor

Proverbs 14:23

In all toil there is profit,
  but mere talk tends only to poverty.

Or to put it in modern terms – just do it! Be reluctant to make promises; be resolved to carry out commitments. And definitely let the making of excuses be rare. If you demonstrate through your actions that you keep commitments, that you labor conscientiously, taking pride in your work, then you do not need excuses for the few times you might fail. Your work reputation is developed by the actual work you do, not by your ability to talk about your ability and especially not by your ability to make excuses for yourself.

Learn to take pride in all toil (that is legitimate and moral). There is profit from all toil. It will usually be literal profits earned through labor; it may be the product produced which provides satisfaction. It may be the satisfaction of accomplishing difficult work; it may be pleasure in the very act of labor itself. It may be learning that a particular labor is not for you or is the wrong way of doing something.

And if done well, and if done for the glory of God; if done understanding that Christ is your Master whom you are pleasing, then surely all labor is profitable, not to earn merit with God, but to enrich your life as you take pleasure in serving and glorifying your God.

The Wealth of Wisdom

Proverbs 14:24

The crown of the wise is their wealth,
 but the folly of fools brings folly.

Wisdom often leads to literal financial wealth, for though the wise do not prize wealth, they nevertheless prize the behavior that is conducive to building wealth. They are not spendthrifts, wasting money on what is trivial, vain, and of low quality.

They set money aside, saving it for lean days, which rarely come, or at least to their standards rarely exist. Thus the money accumulates, and because of wise prudence is placed where it can accumulate with interest. The wise do not enter into foolish ventures. Though they may be generous, they do not co-sign notes or loan money easily, knowing the risk for them and the borrowers. They only spend what they have and avoid debt.

Because the wise are discerning of the character of other people, they know whom to trust and whom not. They cannot be scammed. Because the wise treat others with dignity and with wisdom, they earn the trust and respect of their neighbors, and so themselves are often given "breaks," receiving discounts, favors, and better quality service and products. Because the wise value wisdom above all else, they often receive wealth and other rewards through their wisdom.

Finally, as God rewarded Solomon with great wealth because he desired wisdom, so God will often bless his people who desire him above all else. The wise believer who desires to glorify God will often find many rewards not sought or expected. It is true that the faithful follower of Christ should expect persecution and sacrifice; but it is all the more true of the faithful follower that he will have the eyes to see the great riches of his inheritance.

Saving Truth

Proverbs 14:25

A truthful witness saves lives,
but one who breathes out lies is deceitful.

The witness who truthfully testifies to the innocence or guilt of a suspect...the witness who brings to light criminal conduct...the witness to truth who is willing to expose false teaching and refute false reasoning or accusations...the witness who speaks the whole truth, not merely what is critical or congratulatory...the witness who led by the Witness bears testimony to the truth of the gospel and to Jesus Christ – such a witness saves lives, be they physical, intellectual, or spiritual.

But the one willing to bend the truth cannot be trusted. If he is willing to bend the truth for one reason, however good it may seem, he may just as easily bend it for harm. That's what the movies and TV shows miss. The loveable characters lie to protect themselves or to win their lovers, but because they have good hearts and the lies are always uncovered, things turn out alright in the end. But in real life the lies build distrust and become ingrained in the liar so that he turns into a deceitful character, deceiving himself the most.

The truth shall set you free. Of course, it is the Truth, Jesus Christ, who sets us free. But understand as well, that living a life of truth-telling, however difficult it may seem, is the life of freedom.

Confident Fear

Proverbs 14:26

In the fear of the Lord one has strong confidence,
and his children will have a refuge.

The fear of the Lord produces confidence, for to properly fear the Lord is to recognize him as the Sovereign God who rules over his creation for his glory. It is to recognize that nothing takes place outside his control and that he always carries out his will, a will that is higher than our understanding as the heavens are higher than the earth.

To love the Lord without fearing him produces a mixed attitude of enjoying God in good times and feeling the same anxiety that unbelievers feel in hard times. Such an attitude is inevitable with a philosophy that God means well but can't guarantee our welfare. To fear God is to know his power to do as he pleases; and because we also know that God is love – because we know him as our Father – we can trust that whatever he pleases is for our good. All the more reason then to fear him. For unlike us who will defer doing what we know to be best for others because we don't have the heart to bear their suffering, God will do what is best regardless of how we may feel about it.

And so, as a good Father who chastises his children for their good, so our heavenly Father will put us through trials and suffering for our good. And so we fear God, but we fear him with confidence that in his hands only our good will be accomplished and that no one, especially the evil one, will ever snatch us out. That is the refuge that we may pass on to our children – to fear (and so to trust) the Lord.

Life Filling Fear

Proverbs 14:27

The fear of the Lord is a fountain of life,
that one may turn away from the snares of death.

Far from this fear being paralyzing and suffocating, it is life renewing; for the fear of the Lord is what overcomes the other fears that keep us enslaved and timid. The fear of the Lord gives us confidence in God's might and wisdom to provide and protect. It turns us to Christ for our confidence in finding mercy and away from ourselves. Thus we do not have to worry daily about whether we are doing a good enough job to be accepted.

And thus we turn away from the snares of death. By not trusting in ourselves and by not fearing what the world fears, we do not take matters into our own hands, which always leads us into snares. We can do what is right, not be worried about consequences, trusting our God to handle those things. We can do what is good and what is of real joy, not calculating what wins us favors or wards off penalties.

Fear the Lord and enjoy the fountain of life.

A King's Glory

Proverbs 14:28

In a multitude of people is the glory of a king,
but without people a prince is ruined.

A king cannot reign without a people. Indeed, without a people to rule over he is not a king. By its very definition, kingship is about relationship. A person may have great qualities, but if there is no one over whom and for whom to exercise those qualities, then he has no status. If a king is only great as a king in relation to the people he governs, then, however great he may like to regard himself, he is dependent upon those who are beneath him for his status. Thus the greatest of leaders is dependent upon the humblest of followers.

And thus a leader must lead well and govern well. If his glory is people and not wealth, then all the more he must give attention to the welfare of his people. This is a good principle for all leaders. The true glory of any leader is found in the commitment of those who follow him or her. Leaders do not merely get things done; they get things done is such a way that those under them gladly follow and carry out their responsibilities. They aspire to please their leaders.

Gladly do we follow our King who won our allegiance by being our Servant. Gladly do we offer up our service to the one who battled for us and who suffered on our behalf. And so this King has won multitudes of people for his glory.

Slow to Anger

Proverbs 14:29

Whoever is slow to anger has great understanding,
  but he who has a hasty temper exalts folly.

It requires wisdom to control anger. One must be wise enough, first of all, to know what circumstance calls for anger. Jesus knew when to act in anger and when not. Thus, he spoke in anger at the proper times against hypocrisy and injustice; and yet, when the greatest injustice was committed against him, he exercised control.

One must be wise enough to know how to control anger. Again, Jesus knew what words to speak to those who tried to ruffle him; he knew how to keep his emotions in check. And in his wisdom, he trusted in his Father. This alone is the greatest help to check one's temper. When you can trust God to vindicate, you don't have to get caught up in anger. When you can trust God to bring about good, you don't have to get angry over what you think you've lost. When you can trust God to protect you and provide for you, you don't have to get angry with your circumstances. And when in wisdom you humbly accept your own frailties and sinful state, you become more tolerant and patient of others.

A Tranquil Heart

Proverbs 14:30

A tranquil heart gives life to the flesh,
  but envy makes the bones rot.

This is a good proverb to post on your mirror or refrigerator, wherever you are going to see it daily. The Apostle Paul who faced more troubles and deprivations than most people found the blessing of a tranquil heart. Read what he says in Philippians 4:11-13:

> Not that I am speaking of being in need, for I have learned in whatever situation I am to be content. I know how to be brought low, and I know how to abound. In any and every circumstance, I have

learned the secret of facing plenty and hunger, abundance and need. I can do all things though him who strengthens me.

Let's be honest. What bothers us more than being in need is being in need when others have plenty. What makes us most discontent about our paychecks is not that it is hard to pay bills, but that others can buy more and be more financially secure with their larger paychecks. What bothers us more about not being "successful" is comparing ourselves with others who have done better than we.

But envy makes the bones, our bones, rot. It robs us of peace; it robs us of peaceful relations. It makes us less productive, less useful for the kingdom of God, and that is precisely what Satan wants. Recognize your enemy. It is not the other person who has climbed higher in success than you. It is not God who seemingly withholds blessings from you. It is not yourself with your limitations. It is Satan who hates you and wants to embitter you, making you unfruitful for the work God has given you.

Because Paul knew how to be content, he could not only endure his troubles, but through those same troubles be all the more fruitful in his labors. Pray for a tranquil heart; pray for contentment. The Lord is happy to fulfill such a request, and you will be surprised at the blessings that seem to fall your way.

Loving God and Neighbor

Proverbs 14:31

Whoever oppresses a poor man insults his Maker,
but he who is generous to the needy honors him.

God takes personally how we treat our poor neighbor. We cannot honor God if we do not care for the poor. We reason that we do not oppress anyone who is poor. This is where we need to critically examine ourselves. Perhaps we do not personally oppress anyone, but are the policies we support helpful or oppressive? We who are conservative must take this matter seriously. We rightly desire that policies of assistance be those that truly help the poor rise out of their circumstances and do not enable them to remain impoverished. But is that a pure desire? Or is it mixed with skepticism and indifference of the poor?

How much attention to give to the poor? How are you involved in activities that help the poor climb out of their poverty? Do you know anyone personally who is poor? Can you say that you have been generous in helping the poor, in helping anyone personally who is poor? It matters to your Maker.

Good and Bad Death

Proverbs 14:32

The wicked is overthrown through his evildoing,
but the righteous finds refuge in his death.

This is a recurring theme in proverbs. The wicked, who is seeking his advantage through evildoing, is actually causing his undoing. He is working against himself. Most of the wicked experience downfall in this life. They create enemies and make themselves enemies of the state, so that often they get caught and brought to justice, or are overthrown by other wicked competitors. Regardless of what happens in this life, all the wicked are overthrown in the next life. All receive their just reward which is everlasting. God will not be mocked.

The righteous, however, find eternal refuge in their death, for they enter into the eternal rest won for them by Jesus Christ. This is what marks the real difference between a good death and a bad death. It is not the circumstance of what caused death, but the state of the person when death comes. A person who dies in a horrifying manner dies a good death if he is immediately ushered into glory; a person who dies peacefully in old age dies a bad death if he is ushered into damnation.

Whatever we may think that we see in this life regarding the wicked and the righteous, what we are to live by is what God's Word teaches is the truth – the wicked are overthrown; the righteous do have a true and lasting refuge who is Jesus Christ.

Public Wisdom

Proverbs 14:33

Wisdom rests in the heart of a man of understanding,
  but it makes itself known even in the midst of fools.

The person of understanding possesses wisdom in his heart. He is wise because he is understanding of truth, of the ways of others, and most of all of God. To understand – to have the ability to listen and observe well so as to discern truth – that is the way and the source of wisdom. A person of understanding does not have to take courses to learn wisdom; he does not have to search for it; rather, wisdom already abides in him.

But wisdom is of such magnitude and possesses such fortitude that it makes itself recognized even in the midst of fools. It rises above foolishness, so that even the fools see the wisdom of others even though they may reject it for themselves. Wisdom may rest in the heart of the person of understanding, but it is not hidden. It cannot but be manifested in the possessor's conduct.

And so the Word of God shines in its wisdom and is acknowledged even by those who reject its author. So Christ is honored by those who do not recognize who he is. And even we may be respected if we walk by wisdom.

Righteousness That Exalts

Proverbs 14:34

Righteousness exalts a nation,
  but sin is a reproach to any people.

Righteousness exalts a nation. It is good for a nation to excel in liberty; it is good for a nation to become prosperous and to enable its people to prosper. It is good for a nation to protect its people from threats. But, as ultimately an individual is judged by his righteousness, so a nation. Thus, above all, we are to hold our leaders and ourselves accountable for ethical behavior, to act righteously within our country and in our dealings outside the nation. It matters what kind of neighbor we are and what kind of community we are.

Having said this, let us remember as Christians our citizenship in the kingdom of our Lord. God will judge the nations, including America, and we do well to call our nation to righteousness. But it is his own nation, the Church, that he will hold most accountable, for we represent the rule of God. Are we distinctive in our churches in the way that we treat our neighbors. Do we amaze our enemies by our love for them? Do we put to shame slander against us by our righteousness which is displayed by holy, moral living and by compassion, mercy, and pursuit of justice even for those who hate us? Do we demonstrate worship that is defined by God's standards and not the world's? Do we do business according to God's righteous law rather than the world's?

Righteousness exalts the Church, the world-wide nation of God. And always remember, that it is only the righteousness that is Christ's which exalts a nation, a church, and an individual.

Winning the King's Favor

Proverbs 14:35

A servant who deals wisely has the king's favor,
   but his wrath falls on one who acts shamefully.

The servant who has the king's favor deals wisely in two ways. The work that he carries out on behalf of the king is wisely done. He is efficient and fruitful in his labor; he makes wise decisions that benefit the king's welfare. Secondly, he is wise in his dealings with the king. He pays deference to him; he takes time to understand the king's personality and adapt to it. Thus, the servant is conscientious in his labor for the king and in his relations with the king.

The shameful servant fails in one or (most likely) both. He may be honest but thoughtless in his behavior. He may be extremely efficient and productive, but also arrogant and belittling of others. He may make wise decisions for the king, but then speak ill of him, even to him.

The point is that wisdom encompasses both the work accomplished and the manner in which the work is carried out. It is not only in your accomplishing the goal, but the way in which the goal is achieved that impacts how you will be regarded. If you want "the king's" favor – be he a boss, a teacher, even a spouse – act wisely in both work and relationships.

Now, let us give thanks for our King who, because already his favor was upon us, carried out his work of redemption, fulfilling both the labor necessary and in the spirit of absolute obedience for his Father, so that the Father could say, "This is my Son with whom I am well pleased."

Soft Answer

Proverbs 15:1

A soft answer turns away wrath,
but a harsh word stirs up anger.

Force and harsh speech only breed resentment and stir up anger. Indeed, the harsh word will stir up anger where there is peace. Many Christians are guilty of stirring up anger both within the Christian community and outside it because of the harsh manner in which they speak. It is not enough to value truth; one must value speaking the truth in love. It is not enough to have wisdom to know the answer; one must have the wisdom to know how to communicate the answer.

One can stir up anger by speaking the truth, as did Jesus. But most of us are guilty not of speaking the truth as needed, but of merely getting things off our chest or of wanting to put others down. Our zeal for striking a blow for truth is more motivated by a desire to

191

strike a blow for our egos. We desire not so much to win someone over to our side as to shame that person.

If our goal is the welfare of our neighbor; if our motivation is love for our neighbor, we will speak wisely. Begin today, praying for the welfare of your neighbor; pray that your speech will be controlled by your love for God and your neighbor. The best word you speak today may be your prayer to God to control your speech for his honor and your neighbor's good.

Commending Knowledge

Proverbs 15:2

The tongue of the wise commends knowledge,
  but the mouths of fools pour out folly.

The thought here is that the wise make good use of knowledge in their communication. Unwise use of knowledge is devastating and has a long history. From the childhood "friend" who shares that the other girls don't like you to the misuse of statistics and research, abuse of knowledge can wreak havoc. The wise, however, know what conclusions to draw from knowledge; they know how to communicate knowledge in such a way that it is received appropriately; they know when to keep silent, when they are casting pearls before swine, and when they are providing a cold cup of water.

Fools, on the other hand, pour out folly that is all the more dangerous when the folly contains truth. Gossip that is true is more harmful than if it is false as is the inappropriate leaking of secrets. This is why there are several proverbs that speak of the wise man keeping silent. He is not withholding information that needs to be heard, but he is being careful to speak only when doing so promotes good.

How will you use your knowledge today? In a world in which knowledge (and communicating that knowledge) is at the touch of a keyboard, it is all the more important to "commend" knowledge rather than abuse it.

Being Watched

Proverbs 15:3

The eyes of the Lord are in every place,
keeping watch on the evil and the good.

This is either bad news or good news depending on who you are and what you are doing. For the wicked, this is bad news. They can get away with nothing. God sees all; he cannot be deceived, cannot be mocked. For the righteous, this is good news. God sees all their good deeds; he sees their suffering. They are never alone.

For us Christians, this proverb serves to keep us both accountable and assured. Understand that there is no such thing as a private sin, not even a private thought. God sees all. Understand also that we are never in peril due to God not paying attention. He holds us in his hands all the time.

A couple of lessons we can gain from this. One, there is "no temptation that has overtaken you that is not common to man. God is faithful, and he will not let you be tempted beyond your ability, but with the temptation he will also provide the way of escape, that you may be able to endure it" (1 Cor. 10:13). God keeps his eyes on you, both to observe your faithfulness to him and to provide your way of escape. Two, God's grace is always with you as one who is righteous in Christ. He sees your righteous clothing. He sees your soul washed by the blood of his Son. And he watches you with love. Thus, even your sin results in grace abounding all the more. For the wicked, even their "good" deeds condemn them, for they do not profess Jesus Christ as Lord.

As you go through the day, be aware and give thanks that God's eyes are upon you.

Gentle Tongue

Proverbs 15:4

A gentle tongue is a tree of life,
  but perverseness in it breaks the spirit.

Seek a gentle tongue, which is another way of saying a gentle spirit. Seek a tongue/spirit that is a tree of life to the broken, the downtrodden, the person weighed down in suffering and/or in guilt. And this is the case of more people than you realize. It is often the case of the person who is acting arrogant, who may be on your case. People act out their tensions, often shifting those tensions on to others. A "soft answer turns away wrath" because its gentleness unarms the attacker. He wants a fight; instead he gets love; he gets a caring voice, and that alone can breathe life back into him. The heavy heart may express itself in poor work. More effective than the demanding tongue is the gentle tongue whose show of concern re-energizes the downcast worker.

The truth is that the gentle tongue is often more powerful than the harsh tongue in motivating better work. That, again, is due to wisdom. For the gentle tongue is not to be equated with merely being mild-mannered. It is the tongue that is under control of a wise mind and heart, which discerns what is needed by the other person. The gentle tongue is possessed by one of sound mind and heart.

The perverse tongue breaks the spirit of others because it is out of control and is coming out of a person whose mind and spirit are not sound. Such a tongue wreaks havoc on both the recipient and the speaker, for it stirs up anger, pain, defensiveness, and other unsound effects in the recipient, and it hardens the anger, pain, and other unsound elements in the speaker.

Pray for the Lord to guide your tongue today, that you may speak with a gentle tongue and promote healing and life. Don't miss the opportunities to speak words that express the gospel or flow out of the gospel, so that others may be drawn to it.

Prudent Listening

Proverbs 15:5

A fool despises his father's instruction,
  but whoever heeds reproof is prudent.

The fool despises his father's instruction, thinking that he is smarter than his father. In some ways he may be. He may know more than his father about technological gadgets. He knows more than his father about what is fashionable. He may have more street smarts. But what the son (or daughter) doesn't know as well are the experiences of a longer life. What he lacks is maturity that comes with experience, especially the experience of making mistakes. He lacks the experience of playing the fool and then becoming wiser. Such wisdom a father (and mother) has to give.

This proverb is probably thinking not only of wisdom from experience, but the father who follows the law of God and thus imparts that law to his son through instruction and reproof. The fool rejects such instruction, not so much because he thinks he is wiser but because he wants to sin. He wants to do what he wants to do and not be restrained by law. Is this not ultimately why people reject the instruction of God the Father? They want to do what they want to do.

But like the fool who walks into his own downfall, so will all who reject God's instruction and reproof in his Word. They are merely pronouncing their own sentence and shackling themselves to the bondage of sin. Heed instruction from the Word of God; bear willingly reproof based on God's Word. Examine your heart today by the scripture you read that you may heed reproof and be prudent.

Much Treasure

Proverbs 15:6

In the house of the righteous there is much treasure,
  but trouble befalls the income of the wicked.

There may very well be financial wealth in the righteous because he will be prudent with his money, will not spend it foolishly, and will put savings aside. He will also use his money righteously, tithing ten percent or more, being generous to the poor, not defrauding others, and so receiving blessing from God and from his neighbor.

The wicked, on the other hand, will spend foolishly, make reckless investments, and think only of today. He will try to take advantage of others, thus incurring the anger of God and neighbors, many of whom will try to achieve retribution.

The true treasure of the righteous in Christ is the inheritance of Christ – the riches of his glory, the "inheritance that is imperishable, undefiled, and unfading, kept in heaven for [them]" (1 Pet. 1:4). This is wealth beyond all earthly wealth, for it is eternal and to be eternally enjoyed without fear, without the presence of sin, and in the presence of God. Trouble befalls the wicked who at best can only enjoy earthly wealth. Then it vanishes when their bodies return to the dust, and it only increases their torment when they rise to the final judgment.

As Paul prayed for the Ephesians, so I pray for you this day:
> "that the God of our Lord Jesus Christ, the Father of glory, may give you a spirit of wisdom and of revelation in the knowledge of him, having the eyes of your hearts enlightened, that you may know what is the hope to which he has called you, what are the riches of his glorious inheritance in the saints, and what is the immeasurable greatness of his power toward us who believe..." (Eph. 1:17-19).

Spreading Knowledge

Proverbs 15:7

The lips of the wise spread knowledge;
not so the hearts of fools.

The wise spread knowledge that is useful, that makes one wiser, that is good. Fools spread information that is false or perverted or that harms. Fools often think they are spreading knowledge, not realizing that they are revealing their foolishness. They like to hear themselves talk, and they think others like listening to them. The wise speak only as necessary, weighing their words so as to speak appropriately and to meet their proper intention.

What knowledge will you spread today? Will you be quick to gossip, to pass on hearsay or hurtful words? Or will you weigh your words, being sure that what you speak is the truth and that it is good to say? Christians make mistakes often, thinking that we are being good witnesses for the gospel – the supreme knowledge to pass on. We spread tracts that are poorly written and stereotype unbelievers, causing unnecessary offense. We speak judgmentally or arrogantly, quick to engage in debate so as to score points. We are zealous with the gospel, unaware of how our presentation actually affects others.

The Apostle Paul – the great evangelist – had this instruction to give in spreading the gospel: "Conduct yourselves wisely toward outsiders, making the best use of the time. Let your speech always be gracious, seasoned with salt, so that you may know how you ought to answer each person" (Col. 4:5-6).

Abomination

Proverbs 15:8

The sacrifice of the wicked is an abomination to the Lord,
 but the prayer of the upright is acceptable to him.

It is bad enough to act wickedly and ungodly and to think you can get away with bad behavior. But to feign reverence for God, to pretend to love God or pretend to repent? God will not be mocked. And if it is possible for him to be angrier over one sin than another, be sure that his greatest anger is against those who try to drag him over to be identified with their wickedness. And there are many who profess believing the gospel, yet are filled with hate, vindictiveness, who cheat in business and school, and yet somehow justify their behavior as squaring with their faith. Their worship is received by God as an abomination.

There are others who regard themselves as upright, yet under the

197

name of Christian undermine the gospel faith. There are many who use the Christian pulpit to destroy confidence in God's Word. Their worship is an abomination.

God will not be mocked. He does not look with favor upon those who not only insist on going their own way, but either try to drag him along or make him conform to them. The reason the prayer of the upright is acceptable to him is that the upright conform to him. Their standard for what is righteous is what is established in God's Word. They call upon Christ not only as Savior but as Lord.

Righteousness

Proverbs 15:9

The way of the wicked is an abomination to the Lord,
  but he loves him who pursues righteousness.

God is not lukewarm, neither about sin nor righteousness. He does not look upon us with indifference; he does not find sin humorous, nor does he regard righteousness mildly. He hates sin and will judge in his wrath the sinner; he loves the righteous, preparing for them a place of glory. Therefore pursue righteousness!

But this can be a message of despair unless understood in the light of Christ's work of righteousness. Consider what we are taught about this in Romans:

> I find it to be a law that when I want to do right, evil lies close at hand. For I delight in the law of God, in my inner being, but I see in my members another law waging war against the law of my mind and making me captive to the law of sin that dwells in my members. Wretched man that I am! Who will deliver me from this body of death? Thanks be to God through Jesus Christ our Lord! (Rom. 7:21-25).

Thanks be that:

now the righteousness of God has been manifested apart from the law...the righteousness of God through faith in Jesus Christ for all who believe...[For we] are justified by his grace as a gift, through the redemption that is in Christ Jesus, whom God put forward as a propitiation by his blood, to be received by faith (Rom. 3:21-25).

Give thanks to God this day and every day for this gospel truth.

The Warning

Proverbs 15:10

There is severe discipline for him who forsakes the way;
whoever hates reproof will die.

Understand clearly that there may be two options to choose for how you want to live, but there is only one option if you want eternal salvation. Forsake the righteous way of the Lord and you will suffer punishment. Reject the reproof intended to put you on the right path and you will die. As the previous proverbs noted, the way of wickedness is regarded as an abomination to the Lord who is your Judge. And as the next proverb will make clear, this Judge sees all!

You can talk all you want about how you feel about this. You can shake your fist at God. You can turn your back on him... for now. But one day you will stand before him and give an account for your life. He will not give an account to you. He will not justify his ways to you. He will render judgment.

You can tell yourself there is nothing after death. You can assert that "my God" is not like that. But you have before you the warning of Scripture, and if you are wrong, you will have no excuse before God that you did not know.

Follow the Way. Follow Christ. Receive reproof for your sin, turn to the Redeemer, and live.

The Open Heart

Proverbs 15:11

Sheol and Abaddon lie open before the Lord;
  how much more the hearts of the children of man!

For the writer, Sheol and Abaddon represent the places of the dead, that which is beyond human sight and knowledge. They are the uttermost places far from human existence. If Sheol and Abaddon, then, are open before the Lord as though meadows under broad daylight, how much more then are our hearts open before the Lord.

God is not watching us from a distance. He sees our actions; he hears our words; he knows our very thoughts, even the motives from which all these things spring. Such knowledge should sober us and encourage us. We "get away" with nothing; we may fool even ourselves at times, but never God. Therefore it is useless to wear masks before him, useless to pretend what we do not feel. Our hearts lie open before him. All the more reason, then, to confess our sins and to express to him what we feel. Confession is good for the soul because God already knows our guilt; what he waits for is our coming to him honestly.

But be also encouraged. God knows every burden we bear; he knows whatever we suffer; and he knows whatever good we have done, even when we do not know. And he commends us for every time we honor him, however quietly and secretly. He knows and he blesses.

And because we are in Christ, know that God watches our hearts with love and compassion. He is not angry with you today. He is not looking for that sin in you for which to punish you. He looks upon you with love, knowing you fully as you are, fully as you are clothed in the righteousness of Jesus Christ and adopted as his child.

Receiving Reproof

Proverbs 15:12

A scoffer does not like to be reproved;
  he will not go to the wise.

The cynic, or scoffer, thinks he is wise because he is able to find fault in others, especially those in authority. And the greatest scoffers are those who have never held position of authority or responsibility. They despise reproof, they think because of the faults they find in authority figures such as parents and teachers. The reality is that they hate reproof because of their unwillingness to face their own faults.

Everyone has faults. Even the wise are not wise about some things, including their own behavior. Such is the doctrine of sin. But wisdom lies in recognizing one's own shortcomings and in recognizing the insight of others, whoever they may be. Even a fool can be right sometimes, and the wise person will recognize the rare time he is.

The wise also have the humility necessary to be discerning. Because they are not caught up in their egos, because they are not focused on looking wise, they can spend the effort on gaining further wisdom. All this the scoffer dismisses to his own loss.

And thus the reason so many never come to Christ. For such requires humility to be discerning, to hear and understand the gospel, to be cut to the quick, and to turn to the Wise Son of God.

Cheerful Heart

Proverbs 15:13

A glad heart makes a cheerful face,
  but by sorrow of heart the spirit is crushed.

This proverb can be taken as both descriptive and prescriptive. It describes the effect of the heart on the outer being and welfare of its owner. A glad heart cheers up the face and the spirit. It promotes well being. Sorrow, on the other hand, crushes the spirit, makes the face downcast, and adversely affects a person's health. We can read the same information in scientific studies.

The proverb is also, then, prescribing what is good for us. It is good for us to be cheerful. We cannot manufacture cheer, but we can choose to focus on what is encouraging rather than what weighs us down. We can be guilty of dwelling on our failures and losses, refusing to acknowledge the blessings that God has given. We can be guilty of focusing on the negative – what is wrong with others and bothersome in our lives – rather than looking for the good. We can choose cynicism over observing what is good. We can even choose feeling bad about ourselves because we are not cheerful!

There is a time and place for both gladness and sorrow. We should certainly grieve over our sin, and we are to grieve over loss, but godly sorrow over sin should lead to repentance and thankfulness for the forgiveness we have in Christ. And grief over loss or misfortune should drive us to the comfort provided by Christ and the Holy Spirit. Dwelling in continuous sorrow and indulging in depression is but to stiff-arm your Savior and Comforter. It keeps you from having a glad heart that gladdens the sorrowful heart of a friend in need.

Seeking Knowledge

Proverbs 15:14

The heart of him who has understanding seeks knowledge,
  but the mouths of fools feed on folly.

The point here is that the wise earnestly desire knowledge. Reading is not something they do when there is nothing good on TV. They do not catch up on the latest news in order to be conversational. They do not learn trivia to be competitive in games or make themselves sound interesting. They love knowledge because it gives them further understanding about things that matter.

Fools feed on folly because their heart is not into knowledge for wisdom's sake but for their own ego. They then reveal their foolishness by the way they spout off information that either is inaccurate or irrelevant.

What is your heart into? What do you seek: knowledge that is of value or information that you think will make you appear knowledgeable? What are you seeking when you read Scripture? A verse here and there that you can quote or do you seek truth that will lead you to a deeper relationship with God and a fruitful life in service to him? What are you seeking?

Dealing with Affliction

Proverbs 15:15

All the days of the afflicted are evil,
  but the cheerful of heart has a continual feast.

It seems here that the proverb is not contrasting those who are afflicted and those who have good things happening to them; rather, it is between those who live feeling afflicted and those who live counting their blessings. Sometimes the deeper philosophy lies in what seems fanciful.

Every life has its share of affliction and blessings. The decision for us is which of the two we will focus on. Though some people do live under worse afflictions than others, I've never been able to detect a pattern among people in general that connects the amount of suffering with a person's outlook on life. I've seen people mortally ill in great pain who are cheerful and thankful to God; and I've seen people in good health with much going for them and yet are continually downcast.

For most of these people, their unhappiness and happiness are choices they have made. For some, depression has become an affliction itself, unexplainable even to them. Even so, the decision to deal with depression becomes a choice to make. One must choose to get the help needed. You may not be able to choose what feelings you have, but you can choose what feelings you should have and take steps toward achieving them.

Scripture teaches, "in everything by prayer and supplication with thanksgiving let your requests be made known to God" (Phil. 4:6). Whatever our prayer, start with thanksgiving. That alone will help orient our thoughts and feelings as we recall before God his goodness to us. If we are in Christ, we should daily give thanks for our salvation, remembering this gift that is above all afflictions we might endure in this life. Thus Paul, who could claim the prize of most afflicted, could write, "this slight momentary affliction is preparing for us an eternal weight of glory beyond all comparison" (2 Cor. 4:17).

True Wealth

Proverbs 15:16

Better is a little with the fear of the Lord
  than great treasure and trouble with it.

In truth, the one who fears the Lord is the one who is wealthy, and the one without such fear is impoverished. To truly fear the Lord is to believe in Christ; to believe in Christ is to be born of God, adopted as his child, and made an heir of the glories of God's kingdom. It is to possess an inheritance that "is imperishable, undefiled, and unfading, kept in heaven" (1 Pet. 1:4) for the possessor. It is to be reconciled with your Maker; it is to be relieved of the burden of guilt; it is to be set free from the bondage of sin; it is to experience the full love of God. Will I trade having a nice car and a large bank deposit for such riches? Does not the very question sound absurd?

And yet we Christians often act as though these riches are not enough. Our attitude is "That's nice, God, but what would really make me happy is _____." The treasure of material prosperity is never secure. The wealthiest persons have lost their riches. Material prosperity brings with it the ever constant need to guard that prosperity, to protect from thieves, to withstand competitors. But more to the point is that it cannot bring peace, happiness, or true fulfillment. The wealthy have all the emotional troubles of the poor; indeed, their wealth can produce troubles in their families and other relationships. Their wealth can create stress.

But worse, wealth can create blindness and a false sense of security. It can dull the soul, making it seem that peace exists through material security and luxury. It can make the possessor addicted to it, so that he will trade his soul for physical pleasure and security. He is impoverished indeed who holds on to what he cannot keep and gives up what would have given eternal joy and peace.

A Good Meal

Proverbs 15:17

Better is a dinner of herbs where love is
than a fattened ox and hatred with it.

The message of the proverb is that love is supreme over wealth. Better to only afford a skimpy diet than to dine luxuriously if love comes with the former and hatred with the latter.

This proverb can also teach us an important lesson about hospitality. True hospitality is not the ability to prepare sumptuous meals for guests; it is the ability to provide an environment in which the guests feel that warmth and peace are present. It is not uncommon for parties and celebrations to be tense because of the anxiety of the hosts, an anxiety brought on by the preparation and worries about everything "going right." It is better to have a host who enjoys his guests than one who worries over them.

How wonderful it is for us to have a Host who enjoys us and provides a banquet overflowing with delicious food. Our Lord makes our cups overflow. But just as a feast can be spoiled by an anxious host, so it can be dampened by overanxious guests who refuse to be at ease. Our Lord invites us to his table every day to enjoy the blessings of his grace, and yet we so often bring to the table the worries and strife that beset us, either because we refuse to let them go or we can't believe that we are allowed to let them go.

Today, your Lord has prepared a feast of his grace, mercy, and love. He knows that you are not dressed as well as you should be; he knows the baggage you bring with you. All the more, he wants you to take his robe of righteousness and even of blessing; he wants to take away the load of your baggage. Don't go through this day missing his feast, but enjoy the fattened ox that is served with love.

Hot-Tempered

Proverbs 15:18

A hot-tempered man stirs up strife,
but he who is slow to anger quiets contention.

Note the opposite effects each man has. The hot-tempered man stirs up strife. Have you ever been in a Bible study where the discussion has been interesting and then, by the way one person interjects his opinions, an argument ensues? A hot-tempered man stirs up strife when there has been no tension present. On the other hand, the one slow to anger is able to quiet contention. Not only does he not promote strife; he is able to quell it.

Which are you? Do you have a history of losing your cool? Do you "set people off" by the way you speak? Do people have to be careful what they say around you because they don't know how strongly you are going to react? Most hot-tempered people know that they are that way, but instead of dealing with it, they seem resigned to it and accept that they are going to cause casualties. That is sin. We do not have the right before God to accept our anger.

If this is your case, please do something about it. Get help. Anger is not something that a person handles on his own. Explore why you have trouble with anger. Learn techniques to control your anger. The trouble of hot-tempered people is not that they have no sense of self-control but that they don't exercise control over that one area.

Finally, quit acting as though you must prove yourself. So much anger is the result of thinking that someone is against us and we must exert ourselves in defense. If you are in Christ, understand that God is not against you. Christ has reconciled you to God. And if you are reconciled to him, and if you believe that he is sovereign over your life, there is no reason for remaining hot-tempered. The peace of Christ is with you and in you. If you are born of God in Christ, it is peace, not anger that should be manifested in you.

Sluggards

Proverbs 15:19

The way of a sluggard is like a hedge of thorns,
but the path of the upright is a level highway.

For a lazy person there always seems some kind of obstacle to prevent him from making progress. He is an "unlucky"" person. For some reason he can't get ahead. With each job he takes, for some reason he gets an unreasonable boss or works with people hard to get along with. If he is a student, his teachers are too demanding and unfair. He would exercise but his schedule keeps him from it. Someday he is going to consider religion but there is too much going on right now to give it proper time.

For the upright, however, progress seems smoother. To the sluggard, the upright gets the lucky breaks or plays up to their bosses or teachers. It does not occur to him that they conscientiously commit to abiding by the rules, making no excuses, taking pride in doing good work. Nor does it occur to the sluggard that for the upright such behavior is a matter of ethics. That is why the proverb contrasts the sluggard not with the energetic but the upright.

The upright will seem more energetic because they do more work. But they are motivated, not so much by the need to get ahead, but by the desire to do what is right before the Lord. They want to please him as their Master. That is why they can work under unfair teachers and overly-demanding bosses. It is why they can work along disgruntled workers. Unlike the sluggard who looks for circumstances to excuse him from progressing, the upright does not let circumstances be the deciding factor for doing quality work. Because his or her relationship with God remains the same in Christ, it is that relationship, not changing circumstances, that moves him/her along.

Wise Children

Proverbs 15:20

A wise son makes a glad father,
   but a foolish man despises his mother.

This proverb presents a contrast between the wise and the foolish. The wise are the pride and joy of their parents; the foolish are their shame. But fathers need to consider what they should be looking for in their children.

Look, of course, for wisdom. More than athletic achievement and even more than good grades, look for wisdom. Cultivate in them early the way to make wise discernments – how to control their tongues, how to be conscientious in their work, the value of knowledge and understanding, all the things that the proverbs have been extolling. You may want to present a "proverb a day" to them. Surely a biblical proverb is as good as giving a daily vitamin.

But also note a sign of foolishness that ought to disturb the father – despising one's mother. Most likely what is meant is disregarding her instruction and discipline. The father, above all, is to protect the honor of his wife especially before his children. They should know that to speak back to their mother will result in dire consequences administered by their father. Never allow your children to show disrespect to your wife. There are no winners. Your wife is disheartened and hurt, and your children grow up foolish.

Applying this metaphorically, we should be reminded that not only are we to show respect to our Lord Jesus Christ, but to his Bride, the Church. To honor him is to honor his Bride.

Motivated by Joy

Proverbs 15:21

Folly is a joy to him who lacks sense,
   but a man of understanding walks straight ahead.

208

We may wonder how a person can play the fool, acting and speaking in embarrassing ways. The answer: he enjoys it. Most often he thinks he is demonstrating his sophistication or coolness or daring spirit. He enjoys the attention he gains, even if it is notoriety. What matters is being in the spotlight. He may get his kicks out of shocking others, thinking that he is making fools out of them. Whatever the reason, motivation is the pleasure, even the "high" that he gets from folly.

The person of understanding walks straight ahead, not distracted nor tempted by the follies of others. And what is he walking toward? The heavenly city; the glorious prize; eternal joy. He is keeping his eyes on his Savior. He walks, not rejecting joy, but finding his joy in his Lord and Savior. He rejects the joy of the fool because it is vaporous and sin-filled. It is a joy that harms and blinds. It is a joy that would shame his Lord. The wise person's joy is honoring his Lord.

And so the fool and the person of understanding move along motivated by joy. Who gets the better deal?

Counsel

Proverbs 15:22

Without counsel plans fail,
  but with many advisers they succeed.

Many of our plans seem right – the house to buy, the job to take, the strategy for carrying out a project, the method of settling a dispute, etc. But we show a plan to a friend or someone with more expertise and surprisingly see glaring mistakes in our thinking. Indeed, what were we thinking, we wonder. Or maybe we are near target, but with the review of others it is sharpened and made better.

This is the strength of counsel. By submitting our ideas, thoughts, and plans to others for review, our thinking becomes sharper. Counsel may reveal blind spots, or further refine good plans, or even reinforce our decisions as the questioning of others forces us to think through the defense of our plans.

The point of the matter is that seeking counsel is a sign of wisdom, not of weakness. People who fail at leadership often fail because they don't understand this principle. They think that seeking counsel signifies weakness, especially if counsel leads to exposing errors in their thinking or admitting that they need help. But good leaders get to their positions by listening well to others. They demonstrate their wisdom by how well they respond to counsel, be it discerning between good counsel and bad counsel. By accepting good counsel, they build loyalty among their counselors. They rise to the top because they have proven to others that they listen well and work well with others.

Don't be afraid to seek counsel, be it for work, or life decisions, or marriage/family matters, or spiritual.

Apt Answers

Proverbs 15:23

To make an apt answer is a joy to a man,
and a word in season, how good it is!

It is a blessing to give an apt word and to receive it. The blessing of possessing wisdom is giving an apt word that encourages a neighbor; or that saves the neighbor from disaster; or gives guidance that leads a neighbor along the right path. That is the blessing of possessing knowledge – to help others when they are in need. And wisdom is needed for giving such answers. Often an apt answer is a surprise even to the one giving it. But, in truth, the answer is not surprising because it comes from an inner source of wisdom and discernment. The surprise homerun at the bottom of the ninth happens because of years of conditioning and practice, so that even if it is the only homerun of the hitter, it is still the result of one he has developed physically and inwardly. Do you want to give "apt" answers? Then seek wisdom; store up wisdom through study of the Scriptures; through listening to and reading the works of wise people; through prayer.

And give thanks to God for the "word in season" that has come to you. Thank him for the word from a friend, a relative, a minister, and even a stranger that came at just the right time – the note, the email, the phone call, the sentence in a book, a song overheard. In so many ways God has sent to us a word in season.

And thank God for the "Word for all seasons," our Lord Jesus Christ.

The Prudent Life

Proverbs 15:24

The path of life leads upward for the prudent,
  that he may turn away from Sheol beneath.

The prudent is defined as a person who thinks through what he does. He considers his ways, where the path that any decision he makes leads him. He is careful with his remarks that they do not come back to haunt him. He is discerning in regard to the friends he makes, the places he frequents, knowing that there is always what is below the surface to consider.

This does not mean that he is indecisive, always taking a long time to know what to say or do. Rather, he knows what not to waste time on in making decisions. He immediately goes below the surface; he is quick to discern after-effects of his actions. And if he has trained himself for years in acting with prudence, then he becomes a very decisive person knowing by instinct what is right or wrong. And so his path takes an upward direction away from the Sheol of folly and disaster towards glory above.

This, of course, is because of his most prudent action – recognizing his inadequacy without Christ to save himself or to live a life of prudence. In Christ, he takes the attitude of the Apostle Paul who wrote:

> Not that I have already obtained this or am already
> perfect, but I press on to make it my own, because

211

Christ Jesus has made me his own. Brothers, I do not consider that I have made it my own. But one thing I do: forgetting what lies behind and straining forward to what lies ahead, I press on toward the goal for the prize of the upward call of God in Christ Jesus (Phil. 3:12-14).

The Widow and the Proud

Proverbs 15:25

The Lord tears down the house of the proud
  but maintains the widow's boundaries.

The contrast of what the Lord does in each situation helps explain who the proud is. He is not merely someone with an ego problem who looks down on others such as the widow; rather, he seeks to take advantage of the needy such as the widow. He is after her property; he enlarges his own possessions through taking away from those who are poor and do not have a protector.

The proverb warns the oppressor that the Lord himself protects the interests of the poor; whoever will go after the needy must answer to God. We may think to point out that oppressors often do go without punishment. But the truth of the matter is that they are likely to fall. Other proud enemies may undo them; the government may bring them to justice; ruin may occur within their own house. Even if they outwardly seem to be secure, their security comes with a price. They do not have freedom to live without worries about enemies.

But let this proverb also be a word of instruction to us in caring for the widow. James 1:27 says, "Religion that is pure and undefiled before God, the Father, is this: to visit orphans and widows in their affliction." From the earliest days of the church the care of widows was assumed as a responsibility of the Christian community. What widows do you know? A neighbor? A colleague? A church member? Perhaps God has placed you in her life so that through you he "maintains her boundaries."

Gracious Words

Proverbs 15:26

The thoughts of the wicked are an abomination to the Lord,
  but gracious words are pure.

The thoughts, the words, and the deeds of the wicked are detestable to God. However witty they may consider themselves, however clever and fashionable they may seem to themselves, even how right they believe they may be, their behavior is odorous to God who will not be mocked. The great illusion of the wicked is that they believe they are getting away with their schemes. "There is no god," they say to themselves as fools. Pray now that they will learn the reality and power of God while there is time to be saved. Pray for your neighbors, family, and colleagues who reject Christ.

And pray for your own words to be gracious to them and to your spiritual family. Colossians 4:5-6 says, "Conduct yourselves wisely toward outsiders, making the best use of the time. Let your speech always be gracious, seasoned with salt, so that you may know how you ought to answer each person." For your words to be gracious, you must be a person who lives under the grace of God, whose heart is transformed by grace. Your words and thoughts only reveal your heart. That is why the wicked, no matter what they think or say, cannot please God. Study God's grace; study what it is to live under grace and to be a person of grace; pray for God's grace to be manifested in your life.

Of Greed

Proverbs 15:27

Whoever is greedy for unjust gain troubles his own household,
  but he who hates bribes will live.

It is bad enough to be greedy. Such a person cannot be satisfied with having his needs met, and he is always discontent, wanting to have more. But to be greedy for unjust gain magnifies his own troubles and the troubles he creates for his household.

Now his discontent is mixed with fear, a fear of getting caught for his crimes. Like the addicted gambler he needs to experience risk, but that same risk creates stress. That stress leads to inner turmoil and to outer turmoil in the home. His family distrusts him; he loses their respect. His bad reputation is imposed upon them. They suffer the consequences of his actions.

But the person of integrity who hates bribes lives in peace. What he may lack in money, he is enriched by a good reputation and by respect in the home. His children look up to him; his spouse respects and trusts him. He is a model for others.

Greed leads to unjust behavior to satisfy that greed which can never be satisfied. Integrity springs from a love for righteousness and hatred for injustice. It leads to contentment in doing what is right. It leads to a fulfilling life.

Thinking before Speaking

Proverbs 15:28

The heart of the righteous ponders how to answer,
but the mouth of the wicked pours out evil things.

The heart of the righteous ponders when and how to give a soft answer that turns away wrath and avoids stirring up anger (15:1). It ponders how it will enhance the reception of knowledge (v. 2). It ponders how to speak in gentleness and so be life-giving (v. 4). It ponders how to spread knowledge (v. 7). The heart of the righteous is slow to anger and so avoids answering impulsively (v. 18). Such a heart ponders how to give an answer that is apt and timely to the occasion. Such a heart ponders how to speak gracious words that honor the Lord.

Such a heart has much to ponder, but then the heart of the righteous is practiced in giving right and good answers so that it becomes natural to know what to say. And such a heart does not find it a burden to take the time for weighing its words. It knows how important the right answer is. It knows how important words are to God. It knows how powerful words are for both good and evil. And it knows that the person receiving the answer is another person made in the image of God who matters to his or her Creator. Such a heart has already pondered such thoughts. Will you consider such thoughts today?

A Distant God?

Proverbs 15:29

The Lord is far from the wicked,
  but he hears the prayer of the righteous.

"Why won't God answer my prayer?"
"Why won't God listen to me?"
"Why is God so distant?"

Such questions are usually spoken as accusations against God for being indifferent. God is on trial. They would be wonderful questions if asked as a matter of personal examination. "If God is good and powerful, should I be examining myself for the reason he seems distant?" God will not bless the wicked, but he does desire for the wicked to repent and be blessed. "Have I any pleasure in the death of the wicked, declares the Lord God, and not rather that he should turn from his way and live?" (Ezek. 18:23)

It is not that the wicked must make himself righteous in order to be heard. He does not have to merit God's hearing; he needs, rather, to turn to God in submission. Yes, it is the righteous whom God hears, but then no one is righteous. Our blessing is to receive the righteousness of God the Son freely given to any who call on his name.

This is the gospel message for the lost but also for the saved. For so many times it seems to us that God is distant; he seems distant, not because he is, but because we keep placing between us and him idols

215

and works. We either do not want to be near because of wanting to hold on to sins and idols, or we put in the way obstacles that we somehow believe will aid us in getting God's attention. Like the believers at Colossae, we make up rules and restrictions that seem to have value, but in truth merely make us trust in man-made rules rather than resting fully in the work of our Lord. Righteousness is not about what rules we make up to appear reverent; it is about resting – resting on and in the Lord of Righteousness.

Healthy Practices

Proverbs 15:30

The light of the eyes rejoices the heart,
    and good news refreshes the bones.

This proverb gives two practices that make for good health. The first is a cheerful look. We speak of the "gleam in the eyes." It is the look that expresses happiness, approval, love, fun. It is the look of approval that the young student hopes for in the teacher as she looks over his essay, or that the child hopes for in her parents' eyes as they read the card she made. It is the loving look a couple gives to one another that assures each other of secure love. It is that brightening of the eyes of your friend or loved one because you came into sight. Or perhaps it is the look of forgiveness and reconciliation after a period of tension. Cheerful looks – bright eyes – have good effects on the heart.

For the bones, good news is very helpful. What is the "good news"? Like the look, it can be many things. Perhaps it is the long-awaited letter from a loved one; perhaps the good news of being accepted to college, or getting the job offer, or having one's proposal for an idea accepted. It may be the good news that the cancer is gone or that one's team won the championship. Whatever it is, good news has a powerful way of removing stress and making us feel better.

The simple, yet profound principle is that joy is a powerful, if not the most powerful, ingredient to a healthful life. Joyful people tend to live longer and healthier lives while being productive than gloomy

216

people do. The "cheerful look" and the "good news" are not trivial forms of entertainment; they are not devices to blind us and deafen us from sad and bad realities. They are, rather, the nurturing elements that sustain us through the sufferings of this world. The best of men and women who have devoted themselves to working for justice and ministering to the suffering need the cheerful looks and good news from others to keep them going. The child, in order to become an adult who can persevere through trials, must along the way be nurtured with bright eyes and encouraging words. Just as a healthy plant must have a measure of light and water to be durable and fruitful, so a person needs a measure of cheerful expressions and good news.

Perhaps you will be the nourishing "vitamin" today in someone's life with the light of your eyes and the good news of your tongue.

Listening Ear

Proverbs 15:31

The ear that listens to life-giving reproof
will dwell among the wise.

Here is the key to wisdom – simple as most deep truths are. One grows in wisdom as one is able to listen well and heed correction. All scientists know that the road to knowledge is paved with mistakes and then learning from those mistakes. So it is with wisdom. We are all born sinful; all born ignorant; what distinguishes the person who grows in wisdom from the one who grows in folly is this disposition to hearing and valuing reproof.

Most people would agree with the assessment, but, nevertheless, still fail to listen. Here are some reasons why we will not listen.

1. We choose what we will hear. Sin and pride keep us from hearing. We will listen to reproof about some sin but refuse to consider what are our deepest sins and blind spots because of pride and desire to cling to particular sins.

217

2. We choose whom we will accept reproof from. Some of the best reproof comes from our enemies who are not reluctant to point out our faults, but we will not listen knowing they do not seek our good. Some good reproof comes from fools who occasionally may be on the mark. A wise person knows how to sift the wheat from the chaff and thus benefit from the fool. But our real sin comes in refusing to listen to certain people out of pride – the husband who will not listen to his wife because he is supposed to be the head; the teacher who will not listen to her students because she should know best; the "expert" who will not listen to his critics because "what do they know?"

Of course, the greatest life-giving reproof is the giving of the gospel to those who are perishing. Ironically, God has chosen the weak and the foolish to be his messengers of the most profound truth. He has chosen us. We who are so poor at times at hearing good reproof are called upon to deliver life-giving reproof to our neighbors. Let us be mindful as we deliver what is reproof to the world – calling them to confess their sin – that we are no different from they. We also would reject what we hear except for the grace of God to open our ears and hearts to the truth. Pray that God would open the ears of our neighbors and continue to open our ears to receive the ongoing, life-giving reproof for ourselves.

Despising Oneself

Proverbs 15:32

Whoever ignores instruction despises himself,
   but he who listens to reproof gains intelligence.

This proverb states what every teacher has said sometime to his students, "If you don't study/if you cheat, you are only hurting yourself." The fool thinks he is cleverly getting away with something by "outfoxing" the teacher or the system, not realizing that he is only keeping himself ignorant, and indeed is falling behind others who are gaining knowledge. He also is losing out on sharpening his ability to

218

listen well and to think clearly. In short, he is acting like a person who despises himself, who is keeping himself from advancing.

The second part of the proverb indicates that the instruction includes the concept of addressing error. This is why the fool so despises instruction: he cannot bear the idea of being in the wrong, or really, of being wrong in the eyes of others. And so again, he loses out to the one who willingly listens to reproof and gains further intelligence.

How well will you listen today? If a student, will you pay attention in class and not begrudge having a "hard" teacher who won't go easy on you and who demands high standards? If a worker, will you pay attention to the instruction, even the reproof, given by a supervisor and not be defensive? As a Christian, will you listen to your minister preaching the Word, to your teachers teaching the Bible? Will you listen to your sister or brother admonishing you with Scripture? Will you listen to the Holy Spirit teaching you through the special revelation of Scripture and through the general revelation of creation and life's experiences? No lesson and no experience is wasted if you will head the instruction and reproof of the Holy Spirit.

Fear and Humility

Proverbs 15:33

The fear of the Lord is instruction in wisdom,
and humility comes before honor.

"The fear of the Lord is the beginning of knowledge" (Prov. 1:7). Listening to and reading the words of wise men and women will make you wiser. The keener you observe and learn from the experts in their fields, the more you will grow in knowledge and the more skillful you will become. But until you understand what it is to fear the Lord, you will never achieve true wisdom. Without fear of the Lord, you will never know true humility; and without fear and humility you will never know what it is to be honored by the Lord.

How you react to the above statement indicates whether you are on the road to wisdom or not. If you are troubled by the concept of fearing the Lord, then you either are young spiritually, not yet able to grasp the concept, or you are off the road of wisdom altogether, equating fear with being afraid of a mean entity. The truth is that the fear of the Lord has close semblances to being afraid of one who is terrifying because God is holy, all-powerful, a judge who will bring judgment against the unrighteous. And yet, the fear of the Lord is a delight to those who have grasped it, and they have grasped it because they have come into a true understanding of the God who is holy/terrifying and merciful/loving beyond degree.

Before such a God one joyfully is humble. And we humbly receive instruction from his Word through his Holy Spirit, rejoicing in the holiness and mercy revealed in his Son. If you react negatively to what was said above, pray for the Spirit to open your eyes and your heart to know true wisdom that brings with it true joy.

Best Laid Plans

Proverbs 16:1

The plans of the heart belong to man,
but the answer of the tongue is from the Lord.

The mystery of how this truth takes place is deep, beyond our understanding. Our question should be not how this can be, but why we are being told such a mystery. What message is God conveying to us?

If you are rebelling against God, if you are plotting against him, then know that your best laid plans are but serving his will. Joseph's brother's evil intentions were used to bring deliverance unknowingly for their families years later. Pharaoh's hardened heart against the Israelites only served to magnify the saving power of their God. Rehoboam's rejection of wise counsel led to the split of Israel, yet it happened in fulfillment of God's own words. Shake your hand as you will against the God in heaven; you cannot defy his ultimate, mysterious counsels.

If you are the victim of unjust actions, know that, if you are in Christ,

220

God uses all things for your good and for his glory. You do not need to understand the "why"; and, indeed, you will get caught in a never-ending tangle of trying to interpret every episode of your life if you make the attempt. We do not have the capability within ourselves to understand the deepest counsels of God. But we do have the capability to trust our heavenly Father who knows the number of hairs on our head. And we have all reason to trust him, seeing how he planned and carried forth the most mysterious, most wondrous plan of all – our redemption through Jesus Christ.

Let the rulers of this earth make all their plans; let the enemies of God shake their fists all they want. What will take place is what God will use for his glory and for the good of his people ultimately. Don't worry about the plans laid against you in court or at the office or among your neighbors. Whatever anyone intends for evil, God intends (and will see that it happens) for good.

The Spirit Weighed

Proverbs 16:2

All the ways of a man are pure in his own eyes,
but the Lord weighs the spirit.

All our ways, even our sinful ways, seem right at the time. Our anger seems justifiable; our fudging of the truth seems reasonable; our pride feels more like concern for God's honor; our idolatry seems harmless.

But we are to remember, it is the Lord who weighs the spirit. And the Lord weighs with accurate scales. Such a reality should be sobering and a relief. It should be sobering that nothing, not even the sin that we don't see in ourselves, is missed by God. If we examine ourselves in light of that knowledge, we will see what we have unconsciously covered over. If we shed the defensiveness that makes us hypocrites even to ourselves and ask with sincerity "search me, o God," then the clearer we will see ourselves and honestly weigh our motives.

This truth is also a relief in that it removes the burden of having to cover up our sinful motives. The Lord weighs the spirit with perfect equity. We gain nothing but grief and burden trying to justify ourselves; we gain nothing trying to make our ignoble ways seem pure. The Lord knows all. But if we strive for honesty with ourselves and the Lord; if we yield willingly to him our spirits to be examined, knowing that he will find much sin; then all the more we can revel in his grace and mercy. For our hope lies not in what the scales reveal about our sinfulness, but what they reveal about the weightiness of God's grace and mercy, and about the justice rendered on the cross of Christ.

Commit-Commend

Proverbs 16:3

Commit your work to the Lord,
  and your plans will be established.

Literally, the term for "commit" is "roll." We are to roll to the Lord what we do. The idea is similar to the expression "put in the hands of the Lord." We are to commit to the Lord what we do, placing in his hands the outcome of our actions, trusting him to preserve us, to cause good to come forth, and to glorify himself. It is to leave to God the results, trusting in his sovereign will.

To commit our ways requires that we have already committed ourselves to God. It may be helpful here to make a distinction. We tend to mean by commit that we act out of our own power to do something for God. To commit ourselves to God in the biblical sense is to give up trying to do for God and to turn to him to act for us. Think of it in terms of commending. To commend ourselves to God is to recognize that even when we make commitments, we are doing so under the power of God to make and keep us committed.

This trust in God to act for us is not a blind trust. The Jews founded their trust on God's deliverance from Egypt, preserving them in the wilderness, and leading them into the Promised Land. We establish our trust on Christ's deliverance wrought on the cross. He has delivered us, has preserved our souls, and has led us into his kingdom. Therefore, we trust him to continue to deliver, preserve, and ultimately glorify us.

If we commend/commit to the Lord whatever we do, if we show peaceful trust, then plans have a way of falling into place. Doors have a way of opening up and the wrong doors closing. If our motivations are right, the plans take the right form and achieve the right results. I think that is the primary point of the proverb. One who has commended himself and his ways to the Lord generally finds that his plans succeed, because those plans themselves are in line with God's will.

But understand that the very act of commending one's ways to the Lord implies that we accept the times when our plans do not succeed. Indeed, it means that we are trusting God to alter our plans as necessary and even to bring needed chastisement. Commending our ways to the Lord means that we are trusting God rather than ourselves to know our hearts fully, to know our motivations and for him to act accordingly. To commit our ways to the Lord is to keep in mind that we and our ways belong to him and are to serve for his purposes and glory.

A Purpose

Proverbs 16:4

The Lord has made everything for its purpose,
even the wicked for the day of trouble.

This proverb is for us to turn to when the wicked commit violence. Such events cause us to ask, "Where was God?" "Why did this happen?" "Is God in control?" "Will the wicked get away with this?" This proverb says that the wicked get away with nothing. It says that even their actions are under the control of God and serve the purpose or purposes he, not the wicked, intends.

Such a teaching might seem discomforting. How could God be involved in violence against the innocent? Consider the terrorist attack of 9/11 or the Boston marathon bombing. Religious leaders are quick to disavow God's involvement and cast him as a sympathetic onlooker. It is true that God is not the author of evil as James 1:13 teaches. But if God is merely a compassionate God who wishes bad things didn't happen, if God was watching the airplanes heading into the buildings simply wishing they would miss or that the bombs might malfunction, consider then the greater discomforting thought that we are on our own.

It is grievous to have loved ones die "before their time." But more grievous would be to think they died beyond God's timing. The one comforting thought in the midst of such tragedies is that their deaths fit into God's plans, that he is working all things out, including, especially including, all the bad, rotten stuff that goes on. He is working all things out for the purpose which he intended. The wicked are getting away with nothing. Whether they are acting in conscious defiance of God; whether they foolishly think they are pleasing God; whatever the case, they can do nothing but what he permits and what will serve his purpose.

That should give us comfort, because the most despairing thought of all is not that good people suffer and die, but that they suffer and die for no reason; that ultimately there is no reason for why anything happens, good or bad; that in time no one is remembered; nothing serves any purpose. Keep in mind, that whatever happens – and we have no guarantee what may happen – that the Lord has made everything for its purpose, even the wicked for the day of trouble.

Be Assured

Proverbs 16:5

Everyone who is arrogant in heart is an abomination to the Lord;
  be assured, he will not go unpunished.

Who is arrogant in heart? He is the one who is assured of himself. He is assured that his success is the result of his cleverness, his natural ability, his taking charge of his own life. He may even be assured that he has outwitted God and is able to act with impunity.

224

This proverb tells us that there is one thing of which we can be assured – and that is God's justice. God, the Judge, will carry out justice. He does not look on the wicked with indifference; be assured, all who are unjust will not go unpunished. And Proverbs does equate "arrogant in heart" with wickedness and injustice. Arrogance by definition is a crime against others and certainly against God. It causes one to despise others without cause and to promote oneself over others without just cause. It robs a neighbor of the love that is demanded by God. It distorts truth and creates an idol out of oneself. It mocks God and robs him of his glory.

Or more truthfully, it tries to rob God. Be assured, God will not be mocked, and no one can rob him of what belongs to him. Thus, God turns man's arrogance into opportunity for further glory. That glory is shown through God vindicating himself in justice and through the marvelous act of redeeming. Be assured, the arrogant in heart will not go unpunished if they do not repent. Whether in this life or the next, full justice will be rendered. Pray for justice to come in this life and that they be led to repentance and know God's glory through his redeeming power.

Sin Atoned

Proverbs 16:6

By steadfast love and faithfulness iniquity is atoned for,
and by the fear of the Lord one turns away from evil.

Yes, you can have a second chance. You can put the past behind you. You can turn from being identified with sin to being a child of God. You can have the ending of Scrooge. All it takes is a change of the heart. And God joyfully provides such a change: his Son makes atonement for all your sins; his Spirit gives you a new heart.

So you may now live a life of steadfast love and faithfulness. You may now turn away from evil by the fear of the Lord. Have you sinned today? Of course you have. But do not despair. It is your love that you possess in Christ that God keeps record of; it is your turning to him in faithfulness – turning to him for refuge, for forgiveness – that he holds dear. It is the fear of the Lord that causes you to grieve over your sin and turn to God. Grieve over your sin, but rejoice in the steadfast love and faithfulness of God to forgive and to hold on to you.

And in your rejoicing, continue to show such love and faithfulness to God (we love because he first loved us) and to your brother and sister in the Lord (by this we are known as Christ's disciples) and to everyone (love your neighbor as yourself). By such a heart and by such action, your sins are more than atoned for – that is, the good you do will overshadow the wrong, and you will be known not for hurts you have caused but for blessing you have given.

Peace with Enemies

Proverbs 16:7

When a man's ways please the Lord,
  he makes even his enemies to be at peace with him.

We are quick to assert that being obedient to the Lord will bring persecution by the world. Certainly there is much truth to that. But it is also true that pleasing the Lord leads to peace. Christ commands us to love our neighbor, even to love our enemy. He commands us to turn the other cheek, to give freely to those who would take. He commands us to bless our enemies and not to respond to evil with evil. Such pleasing ways would bring much peace.

We would win peace if we reacted to hostility from our own status of having peace with God; we would win peace if we spoke and acted out of the grace that God has shown us. We would win peace if we shared the heart of God for the souls of others. Consider the peace with our neighbors if we made their welfare our concern, if we strove to be good neighbors to everyone.

If we are honest with ourselves, much of our so-called persecution is the result of our own self-righteousness. Much of our so-called righteous anger has more to do with feeling personally offended. If we acted with patience and wisdom, and not out of stress or defensiveness, consider the peace to which we could win many of God's enemies to the gospel.

Wealth of Righteousness

Proverbs 16:8

Better is a little with righteousness
*   than great revenues with injustice.*

Consider the "little" wealth of righteousness.

There is the wealth of a good conscience before the Lord, which brings great peace.

There is the wealth of a good name and peaceful relations with one's neighbors.

There is the wealth of truly enjoying what one possesses.

There is the wealth of knowing and valuing what is of true value.

There is the wealth of time well spent.

There is the wealth of no regret.

There is the wealth of receiving the inheritance of everlasting life with the Lord.

Not a bad deal!

Established Steps

Proverbs 16:9

The heart of man plans his way,
*   but the Lord establishes his steps.*

Such words should be of great comfort to believers. It is comforting to know that however foolish my plans may be, ultimately the Lord will establish my steps to lead me to him. My heart always seems right to me and yet will always lead me astray if not for the Holy Spirit. Many of my "wise" plans have met brick walls because God has graciously placed those walls in the way; many of my steps have led through unplanned paths bringing me to places I never could have reached left to my own devices. And many steps led me from the dangers of my plans.

What peace it is to know as I wrestle over my plans that God will be faithful in carrying out his plans for me despite the choices I make. The result is that there is no wasted past; indeed there is no wasted time at all; for God has established my steps to take me through trials (even those caused by my sinful plans) and lead me to his glory.

Sinless Judgment

Proverbs 16:10

An oracle is on the lips of a king;
his mouth does not sin in judgment.

Such it should be for those in authority: the higher in authority, the greater the responsibility to conduct oneself in integrity, speaking with wisdom. He should speak as one representing the great King.

Do you pray for those over you that they will exercise wisdom in integrity? It is easy to "sin in judgment" even by those desirous to do what is right, even by those who follow Christ the King. There are many temptations luring them to make the easy decision. They receive threats. They receive enticing offers. Aside from temptations, it is often difficult to discern what is right and best. Who knows the full implications that piece of legislation will have? One may know the right moral principle but not know the best practical means of keeping that principle. Many times good intentions have brought about unwanted results.

And consider the individual who is a king in his own domain: the business owner, the supervisor, the school headmaster, the classroom teacher, the football coach, the dance instructor. He may not have power over many, but his words and actions have influence over individual lives. His sin in judgment can leave a scar that lasts a lifetime in its effects.

Pray for those you know who are kings in their domains, however small the domain may be. And pray for yourself. You likely are in position over someone. Pray for integrity; pray for wisdom in all judgments seemingly great or small you are to render. And pray with thanksgiving for your King, who truly did speak oracles when on earth, who because he did not sin will sit in judgment when he returns and deliver his people.

Of Balance and Scales

Proverbs 16:11

A just balance and scales are the LORD's;
all the weights in the bag are his work.

All ways in which justice is carried out come from the Lord. Anywhere and anytime there is fair play, its source is the Lord. The very idea of justice and fairness comes from him, and, indeed, serves as evidence for his existence and reign. Every time a charge is made that something is wrong is a testimony that there is such a thing as moral order in the universe, and such a reality cannot exist unless there is a Judge who sets that order. Justice is a phenomenon that belongs to the Creator.

With that in mind, understand that the Lord is working all things out to meet justice. Does injustice seem to be the order of the day? The day is not over. God is causing all things, even evil and sin, to work towards his just ends. Do you seem to be the victim of injustice? Be assured that God is working things out for your good. Your perspective is limited to your small world. You do not see the whole order. But when the Day of Judgment comes, all will be put right.

But then, this proverb may serve as a warning to you. If you are not practicing justice and fair play, know that you will be weighed on God's just balance and scales. However much you may rationalize your actions and try to hide your motives, all of your actions, speech, thoughts, and inner motives will be weighed.

Are you ready to be weighed on such scales? Don't fool yourself. Your only hope is the righteousness of the Lord provided for you through Jesus Christ. Now, while there is time, turn to him. Now, while you can, call upon the name of the Lord to be saved.

The Purpose of Thrones

Proverbs 16:12

It is an abomination to kings to do evil,
  for the throne is established by righteousness.

It is terrible enough to do evil. Man was made in the image of God, and every wicked act is a reminder of the great Fall. But to do evil from a position of authority magnifies evil's perversion. Whether one be a king or a low-level manager, such positions are created to accomplish good and to restrain wrong-doing. To use these positions to accomplish evil and to punish good is truly an abomination.

It is said that power corrupts. Closer to the truth is that power releases the corruption that is in us all. Be wary of yourself, whether you have authority over millions or one.

And all the more give praise and thanksgiving for our Righteous King who sits on the eternal throne. Give praise to the Sovereign God who is seeing that all things, even evil, work for his goals, which are good. Give thanks for our King who rescued us from our evil state. For we were an abomination, but we have been delivered from sin and are now justified. Give thanks for our King who will return in glory, who will raise us from the dead, who will give us glory, who will turn us and all things over to his Father. Give thanks for this great throne that is established by righteousness

Speaking What Is Right

Proverbs 16:13

Righteous lips are the delight of a king,
and he loves him who speaks what is right.

Do you wish to give delight to your King? Then let your speech be that which promotes justice and good. Speak the truth in love, as you are taught in Ephesians 4:15. How can you know what to speak?

Speak what is of Scripture. Read it and study it so that you will be able to share it when people turn to you for counsel, or when you need to know how to respond in a situation.

Speak what will build up others. If your concern is for what will build up your neighbor, you will more likely discern what you ought to say.

Speak prayerfully and thoughtfully. If you measure your words before the Lord, you are more likely to speak what is right.

Speak the gospel. Apply the gospel message – we are sinners, Christ saved us, God sent him in mercy and by grace; take such truths and principles and apply them in your speech.

Desire to please the King. The very desire to please your King will guide your speech. But it must be a desire based on gratitude and joy, not on trying to win favor. You will give him delight only as you take delight in him. From such a relationship, you will speak what is right.

The Kings Wrath

Proverbs 16:14

A king's wrath is a messenger of death,
and a wise man will appease it.

It is wisdom to recognize danger and to take measures for safety. We recognize the signs of a thunderstorm and take appropriate cover. So we should do the same when we observe the wrath of one who has power over us. Take measures to appease one with authority, especially when his wrath is a just wrath, that is, when we are guilty of wrongdoing.

This is the principle behind the sacrificial system. A person sins. He breaks the law of God the King and incurs God's wrath. He appeases the King's wrath with a sacrifice that receives his punishment. Sin must be punished. God's wrath is stirred up by injustice, and it is appeased not by bribe but by due punishment. Earthly kings might be appeased by bribes and favors; the divine King is only appeased by justice being carried out.

And so our wise Savior on our behalf has appeased the just wrath of God the King. We in our folly either took inappropriate and ineffective measures to appease God's wrath, or we even tried to defy it. But he who is supremely wise carried out the one effective means of appeasing just wrath by his own sacrifice. And his wisdom carried him back up to the King his Father who received him in love and with honor. This is the wise man who appeased the King's wrath.

A wise man now will recognize that he cannot appease the King's wrath. His salvation comes through the appeasing work of Christ the Savior. Turn now to that Savior. Recognize that the King's wrath is a messenger of eternal death. Recognize that your sinfulness draws that wrath to you. Seek cover now in the Savior.

The King's Favor

Proverbs 16:15

In the light of a king's face there is life,
and his favor is like the clouds that bring the spring rain.

If the previous proverb impresses upon us the danger of being under the thunderstorm of our King's wrath, this one stirs us with the refreshment of being under his favor. To know God's favor is to know life. And that is what Christ came to bring – life to the fullest

232

(John 10:10). He has removed our guilt so that our King looks upon us with divine favor.

We need not hide from God. We know that when we come before the throne we come before the mercy seat where we find mercy. We are not weighted down with the impossible task of making enough amends to make ourselves acceptable. Christ has done the work of reconciliation and of cleansing us. That work is done! And what we receive now, not some day if we work hard enough, is the favor of the great King!

Whatever this day may bring, know that God's favor is upon you. He is not angry with you. He is not punishing you. He is working all things even those which are hard to bear for your good (Rom. 8:28) because the light of his face shines upon you.

Better Than Gold

Proverbs 16:16

How much better to get wisdom than gold!
  To get understanding is to be chosen rather than silver.

Gold and silver are good for providing financial security. As long as one possesses these metals, he can feel confident that he has something of value if:
- he is willing to part with them when he is hungry or needs shelter or medical care
- they are not stolen
- they retain their value when economic conditions plummet
- they do not make him greedy for more
- they do not take the place of what should have been spent on taking care of others
- they do not prevent spending money on what would have blessed others
- he is not possessed with fear of losing them

Gold and silver are nothing but objects granted value by man. Wisdom and understanding are traits of man used to give or reduce that value. Objects are only as valuable as the wisdom of man knows how to use them. Gold does not add to wisdom and is likely to have a corrupting effect. Wisdom adds value to gold and to everything else. There is no greater security than wisdom. There is no likelier path to contentment than through wisdom. Certainly there is no other asset more valuable to make a difference in the life of others than that of wisdom.

And it is the wisdom that comes from God that will lead one to eternal life. How much better to get the wisdom of the gospel than to fall into eternal judgment while possessing all the gold of the world. How much better to gain understanding of the riches of Christ than to be deceived by the riches of the world.

Highway Driving

Proverbs 16:17

The highway of the upright turns aside from evil;
  whoever guards his way preserves his life.

The upright, when it comes to temptation, heeds the warning of his conscience: "don't go there." He does not listen to the various rationalizations that would take him into temptation and danger: curiosity, to become stronger, to protect others, to see what others struggle with, and so on. "Just don't go there," he says to himself.

In our modern day, the image lends itself to someone driving a car. Billboards are along the highway for adult entertainment, casinos, alcohol. Add others: signs for gluttony, for pride, for greed, for gossip, etc. All you need to do is pull over at the next exit. So easy to do; you are away from home; you've got some extra time...

The upright turns aside from the exits and travels on. Why is he able to do so? Because he has greater self-control, a greater capacity for self-denial? Perhaps it is because he has a greater destination to reach and can't be distracted by shallow, empty substitutions for true joy and fulfillment. Perhaps he has tasted that the Lord truly is good. He has drunk from the water of life given by Jesus Christ, and his thirst is for righteousness; it is for God himself.

If you are to turn aside from evil and guard your way, if you are to do this successfully, it will not be because you have developed enough willpower to resist temptation. It will be because you have tasted the Lord and found him good indeed; it will be because you love him and you are driven by the desire to know him more. Desire is not bad; what matters is the object of your desire. Seek after God; learn the joy of righteousness. Christ said he came to give abundant life (John 10:10). Take time, make the effort, to enjoy that life now.

Insidious Pride

Proverbs 16:18

Pride goes before destruction
and a haughty spirit before a fall.

This is a proverb that has proven itself time and time again yet seems to be the hardest to learn. Its principle is behind most of the upsets in sports events in which the clearly better team loses. One reason attributed to the "miracle" win of the 1980 US Olympic hockey team is that it was soundly trounced by the Russian team in a pre-Olympic game. The Russian coach said that he could not get his team afterwards to take the Americans seriously.

Pride affects more than sports. Its special strength is its subtle influence, for it infiltrates our lives at the holiest of times. It seeps into our worship as we are caught up in the feelings that our music and architecture inspire in us, which subtly shifts our feelings to pride in what we have. It seeps into the sermon time as we listen intently and then with pride of how we have the best preaching.

And that is the curse of pride. We do not merely enjoy what we have, but we enjoy that we have it better than others. We do not merely enjoy what we do but that we do it better than others. This insidious sin affects everything: our jobs, our education, our relationships in the home and in the community. We cannot simply enjoy, but we must do it in comparison with others. We then fall because we have taken our eyes off of what should have our attention and devotion, and shifted those eyes to others and ourselves. Pride thus robs us of pure joy which delights in something outside of us and further leads us to fall in our joyful pursuit.

All the more then we must keep our eyes focused on the One who is exalted far above us and who modeled true humility so that he could save us who were poor and even rebellious. It is then we gain right perspective and the burden of pride is lifted.

Spoiled Spoils

Proverbs 16:19

It is better to be of a lowly spirit with the poor
than to divide the spoil with the proud.

The second line gives the context for this subject of pride and humility – dividing the spoil with the proud. It is better to be oppressed than to be an oppressor; it is better to be without than to take away from others. The proud or arrogant in Proverbs is equated with the wicked, who in their arrogance oppress others and commit crimes. This proverb says that such gain is not worth the price. For the price is not a mere matter of being hindered in getting along in life; it is receiving the judgment of God.

We are given the image of a gang of men dividing the spoils they took after defrauding or beating up some victim. The victim is bemoaning his loss or even lying on the road while the proud thieves rejoice over their treasure. The Teacher, though, shakes his head, trembling not over the fate of the victim but of the perpetrators, for he knows the judgment coming for them. It may be soon through the hands of human justice; it may be in death or after death. But it is coming, and better to be of a lowly spirit with the poor than to be found with the spoil in your hands before God.

The fool says in his heart that there is no God, David wrote in Psalm 53. "They are corrupt, doing abominable iniquity; there is none who does good" (v. 1). He then asks this question in verse 4: "Have those who work evil no knowledge, who eat up my people as they eat bread, and do not call upon God?"

What are the wicked thinking? Evidently they either think there is no God who exists, or more likely the case in the ancient world and Israel, they think God doesn't see what they are doing. They think they are getting away with their crime. Many think that way today. They cheat and lie and do not get caught. They profit from taking advantage of others, and their road is as smooth riding as ever. Traveling through life is a pleasant drive.

But what are they thinking? Don't they realize that the odds are against them of the road remaining smooth? That more than likely they will become victims themselves of the same crimes they have committed? They should realize that, whatever happens, the road will end, and they will have to give an account to God who will judge with justice, not mercy.

Discovering Good

Proverbs 16:20

Whoever gives thought to the word will discover good,
and blessed is he who trusts in the Lord.

This proverb presents a recurring theme in Proverbs – that the mark of a wise and godly person is being a good learner. Just in the last chapter and a half, there are six proverbs that refer to this theme:

> A fool despises his father's instruction,
>   but whoever heeds reproof is prudent (15:5).

> A scoffer does not like to be reproved;
>   he will not go to the wise (15:12).

> The heart of him who has understanding seeks knowledge,
>   but the mouths of fools feed on folly (15:14).

The ear that listens to life-giving reproof
　　will dwell among the wise (15:31).

Whoever ignores instruction despises himself,
　　but he who listens to reproof gains intelligence
　　(15:32).

How much better to get wisdom than gold!
　　To get understanding is to be chosen rather than
　　silver (16:16).

The proverb that most closely parallels this proverb is 13:13:
　　Whoever despises the word brings destruction on
　　himself,
　　　　but he who reveres the commandment will be
　　　　rewarded.

The principle is simple: the way to succeed in life is to be a good learner. The second half of the proverb clues us into what type of word is meant: blessed is he who trusts in the Lord. The wisdom-word of Proverbs is the fear-of-the-Lord wisdom, that which comes from knowing God and how God would have us live. The one who gives attention to this kind of word and who trusts this wisdom will know the good life. The problem with the fool is that he doesn't want to learn, nor does he want to trust the Lord.

Why? It may be that he fears what he will have to give up or take up. He is comfortable being lazy; he likes the sins that he indulges in. The wisdom of Proverbs and Scripture does not encourage such behavior. It may be that he fears he will fail or will be let down. Maybe he doesn't have the ability to stay on the straight path and trying to do so would expose his weakness.

Maybe it will turn out that God (whom he cannot see) doesn't come through in the way he thinks God should. He leaves his old life only to find the new has more troubles. That does happen. There is a lot of risk to walking along the path that the wisdom of God would have one go. By definition, walking by faith is walking without clear sight. But this proverb teaches that the one who will walk by faith in the

238

Lord will find what is truly good, for what he finds is the eternal, joyful life given by Christ.

Sweet Talker

Proverbs 16:21

The wise of heart is called discerning,
  and sweetness of speech increases persuasiveness.

Here is our sweet talker. A wise person will be recognized for his wisdom, and because he is wise he will know how to speak in a persuasive manner. Our sweet talker is a wise guy! Do you want to be the person who, when you speak, people listen? There are two routes you can go.

The first route to take is to seek wisdom. Seek to understand right from wrong. Seek to understand God and his ways. Seek to understand the human heart. The more you understand, the wiser you will be, and the wiser you are the more respect you will gain. You will become one who is trusted, whose opinion is respected. This will happen because of what you know but also because your wisdom guides how you speak.

The wise person knows what to say and how to say it because he understands the human heart and how different persons respond to instruction. The wise person understands how God would have him speak, that it is important to God to build up others with the truth not blow them away with it. The wise person gives attention to his tongue, knowing when to speak and when to keep silent.

The easier route in which to gain influence is to take courses on speaking and salesmanship. There are excellent books and seminars that teach how to sell yourself. Public TV has built its success on featuring financial, health, and even spiritual gurus who are excellent communicators and have built successful careers of influence. As the best salespersons know, cultivating the ability to speak in a winsome manner paves the way for success.

One can counterfeit wisdom. This is not a secret, and, indeed, has become a science in the marketing and political world. Knowing how to use words and catch phrases, knowing how to use the inflexion of one's voice, how to use dramatic pause, body language, and so on – such knowledge can turn someone into a sweet talker without the wisdom. All of us at some time have fallen prey to such sweet talkers.

It is not wrong to learn techniques of speaking. A wise person may take advantage of such things to improve himself. But nothing replaces wisdom itself, and nothing stands the test of time like wisdom. Remember this. We can be anxious to have people acknowledge us for our wisdom, and, indeed, make fools of ourselves trying to impress others. But real wisdom has a way of coming to the surface to be seen. The counterfeit wisdom of others might take the spotlight for awhile, but real wisdom will be seen eventually, if not by the majority, at least by others who have wisdom as well. You will be able to persuade those who have the ears to hear and win the respect of those whose opinions are themselves respectable.

Good Sense

Proverbs 16:22

Good sense is a fountain of life to him who has it,
  but the instruction of fools is folly.

The good sense spoken of is good common sense, and certainly it is a fountain of life to the one who possesses it. Good sense is what makes one take heed to instruction and able to detect the wise from the foolish. It puts knowledge to practical use and makes sense out of information.

The opposite is true for the fool. This second line about the fool can be taken in one of two ways. One, as represented by the ESV, KJV, and NKJ Bible versions, is that instructing or punishing fools is fruitless. Unlike people with good sense who profit from instruction, fools will not learn no matter how they are taught. The other sense, as indicated by the NIV Bible, is that the folly of fools brings them their own punishment. Whereas the good sense of the wise is a fountain of life to them, the folly of fools is their punishment. The word for instruction could be translated as correction or punishment.

Whatever the case, the point is this: it is what a person has within him that determines what he gains from life's lessons. Two individuals can attend the same classes, have the same parents, and be given the same opportunities. The one with good sense will learn and benefit from what he is taught and experiences; the foolish one will not benefit and even pervert the lessons so that they are harmful to him. The one with good sense credits others for what he has learned and accepts responsibility for his mistakes. The foolish one congratulates himself for his cleverness and blames others for his errors.

In the western novel *Shane*, a farmer and his wife discuss hiring Shane as a farm hand. By his dress and manner they know that farming is not his line of work, and the wife comments that Shane probably doesn't know a lot about farming. Her husband, who has sized up Shane as a man of integrity, replies, "What a man knows isn't important. It's what he is that counts." Knowledge is important, of course, but the farmer understood that knowledge can be learned; what matters is the person having the spirit to learn.

The Wise Heart

Proverbs 16:23

The heart of the wise makes his speech judicious
and adds persuasiveness to his lips.

After the wise person speaks, his hearers believe they have heard someone who is fair and insightful. They benefit from his words; they admit where they have been wrong. Perhaps they were upset, and they walk away at peace.

What happened? The wise person spoke from a heart that was right. The heart of the wise does not react; it responds. What I mean is that the wise does not give a knee-jerk reaction; he does not speak out of feelings of stress or feeling offended; rather he thinks through a matter, determining two things: what truly is at issue and how to communicate in a way that wins a hearing. He is both just and persuasive.

Mishaps happen. How we respond to them determines whether these mishaps become opportunities for strengthening bonds or straining them. If we speak from an anxious or angry heart, we will strain relationships even as we think we are resolving matters. But if we speak judiciously (with careful thought) and speak persuasively (with the intent to win over our hearer), then the mishap turns into an occasion to build bridges and strengthen relationships.

What is your intent? To get people off your back? To get frustration off your chest? Then your words will be neither judicious nor persuasive. Your heart must be right. Its desire must be to glorify God, to build up the body of Christ, and to love one's neighbor, especially one's Christian brother or sister.

Gracious Words

Proverbs 16:24

Gracious words are like a honeycomb,
  sweetness to the soul and health to the body.

Consider the sweet effect of gracious words.

Compliment: This is a word we often deny we want, but we certainly do enjoy when we receive it. Isn't it nice to receive an honest compliment, especially to get one totally unlooked for? "You really look nice today." "You made a great contribution." "That is a great job you did."

Encouragement: "You can do it; I believe in you." "You're going to be okay." "That's the way to try." Such words give us the strength to go on.

Comfort: How good it feels to hear a sympathetic voice when we are hurting. "I'm here for you." "I'm so sorry." "I'm praying for you."

Helpful: "Can you use a hand with that?" "Let's think through this together." We don't feel alone. Someone is there with us and for us.

Good humored: Sometimes the best thing we can hear when we are down or worried or angry is a good humored remark. There is nothing like a little laugh to perk us up again and help us to see that the end of the world has not come.

Positive: In most bad events and discouraging news there is something positive. How heartening when someone helps us to see it.

Attentive: "How are you doing?" Spoken honestly, is a meaningful question. "You look like you could use a friend"... "could use some cheering up"... "are new here." "You seem to have reservations about what's going on." It's nice to have someone take notice when we are feeling too reserved to speak up.

Listening:" Tell me what you want to say; I'm listening." "Help me understand what you are going through." "Do you mean...?" It is satisfying to talk with someone who is foremost trying to hear what we are saying.

Thanking: "Thank you." "Thanks for helping me." "Thanks for your hard work." "Thanks for listening." How many times has our temper or depression been wiped away by the simple remark of thanks? I've been resentful, angry with persons who then come up to me and give a heartfelt thanks; all of a sudden, I switch to thinking how nice they are!

Gracious words are like honeycomb – sweet and healthful to the soul and body. They have tremendous power to change the course of a person's life for the good, to rescue people from despair, and to bring great blessing. You don't have to be rich or powerful; you don't have to have degrees or be eloquent. Just be gracious and you will significantly touch the lives of all kinds of people. What gracious word will you speak today?

My Way

Proverbs 16:25

There is a way that seems right to a man,
but its end is the way to death.

This proverb addresses the idea of this famous song:

> And now, the end is near;
> And so I face the final curtain.
> My friend, I'll say it clear,
> I'll state my case, of which I'm certain.
>
> I've lived a life that's full.
> I've traveled each and ev'ry highway;
> But more, much more than this,
> I did it my way.
>
> Regrets, I've had a few;
> But then again, too few to mention.
> I did what I had to do
> And saw it through without exemption.
>
> I planned each charted course;
> Each careful step along the byway,
> But more, much more than this,
> I did it my way.
>
> Yes, there were times, I'm sure you knew
> When I bit off more than I could chew.
> But through it all, when there was doubt,
> I ate it up and spit it out.
> I faced it all and I stood tall;
> And did it my way.
>
> I've loved, I've laughed and cried.
> I've had my fill; my share of losing.

And now, as tears subside,
I find it all so amusing.
To think I did all that;
And may I say – not in a shy way,
"No, oh no not me, I did it my way."

For what is a man, what has he got?
If not himself, then he has naught.
To say the things he truly feels;
And not the words of one who kneels.
The record shows I took the blows –
And did it my way! (lyrics by Paul Anka)

When the singer of the song faces the final curtain and states his case, of which he is certain, do you think he really will be certain as he stands before God the Judge? Often there is a way that seems right but ends in trouble and even death. All the more reason we need to go beyond what seems right to us and look for better guidance. For the Scripture writers that means going to God's Law or Word. Psalm 119:105 sums it up well: "Your word is a lamp to my feet and a light to my path." Sometimes God's Word may not be specific enough for a decision we must make. In such a case, Proverbs would have us seek counsel: "Without counsel plans fail, but with many advisers they succeed" (15:22).

The point is this. We have got to take into account that we are creatures of the Fall. We live in a fallen world and are ourselves bent, as we would be described in C. S. Lewis' world of Malacandra (*Out of the Silent Planet*). What seems right may very well be the course that leads to death, because the world itself is out of kilter and sets up illusions for us as to what is important, as our song demonstrates. Furthermore, our hearts are tainted with corruption. And so, though our culture teaches us that the one thing we can trust is the heart, in reality we must be most careful to examine to see if the heart is trustworthy. Finally, Satan and his forces are clever and seek through subtle means to lead us astray.

Christians, as we face the final curtain, may it be said of us that we turned from our own way to follow the one who is the Way. May our

245

song be, "I have fought the good fight, I have finished the race, I have kept the faith" (2 Tim. 4:7).

Good Appetite

Proverbs 16:26

A worker's appetite works for him;
  his mouth urges him on.

Our appetite motivates us to produce. Hunger will drive even the laziest of persons to work to satisfy his hunger pain. How can you get a stubborn mule to walk? Hold an apple in front of him. It is a basic principle that success is predicated on hunger. It has become a sports cliché. Who will be the winner depends on who wants to win the most, on who is the hungriest.

If appetite is a powerful motivator to work, then the control of one's appetite is important. The degree of the appetite and the direction of the appetite must be considered. An appetite for food is essential for getting the proper nutrients for our bodies. A person with a poor appetite is likely to be malnourished. However, too strong of an appetite can lead to overeating with the health problems it brings. Likewise, a poor appetite for what makes a comfortable and secure life can lead to poor work habits, leaving individuals and their families in poor conditions, whereas too great an appetite for wealth and luxury can lead to out-of-whack work practices and the breakup of relationships. Too little an appetite and too much of one each brings its share of troubles, whatever the appetite is for. We should desire the appetite expressed in Proverbs 30:7-9:

> Two things I ask of you;
>   deny them not to me before I die:
> Remove far from me falsehood and lying;
>   give me neither poverty nor riches;
>   feed me with the food that is needful for me,
> lest I be full and deny you
>   and say, Who is the Lord?
> or lest I be poor and steal
>   and profane the name of my God.

In the same manner, the direction of the appetite is significant. An appetite for financial wealth produces one pattern of behavior; an appetite for a happy family produces another. An appetite for a comfortable life produces certain behavior, while an appetite for serving God's kingdom yet another. For which are you hungrier – a pleasant, comfortable life or a productive, meaningful life? These things are not necessarily opposed to each other, but the appetite for one over the other will determine how you live.

Likewise, your appetite for God will affect how well you know and serve him. "Oh, taste and see that the Lord is good" (Ps. 34:8). If you find the taste of the Lord good, then your appetite will spur you on to know him better. "How sweet are your words to my taste, sweeter than honey to my mouth!" (Ps. 119:103). If that is your experience with God's Word, then your appetite for his Word will lead you to read and study it.

THE Bad Character

Proverbs 16:27

A worthless man plots evil,
and his speech is like a scorching fire.

Literally, the worthless man digs up evil. Like an archeologist diligently digging for precious artifacts, he labors to come up with something evil to do. Talk about bad breath; his is like scorching fire. He uses speech for wicked ends, to do harm. This is the first of three proverbs that speak of the "bad character" – the worthless man, the dishonest man, and the man of violence.

There are some people who stumble into sin through errors in judgment and yielding to temptations. But there are others who have bad characters and who delight in doing mischief. (Oddly enough, these are the characters who are glamorized in TV and the movies. We know they are bad, but we are fascinated by them and admire their boldness.) More can be said later, but today think about THE bad character – Satan.

Satan plots evil, and he plots against you. If you are in Christ, he cannot touch your soul but he will still work to render you ineffective for Christ's service. He will use whatever means he can to turn you away from the path of righteousness – temptation, sclf-righteousness, false humility, pride – whatever works to distance you from Christ.

Know your enemy. He is like a roaring lion prowling about trying to devour you (1 Pet. 5:8). Be on guard against him today. There are bad characters out there, and perhaps you will encounter someone today. But you will encounter THE bad character everyday. Don't be like Peter who trusted in himself. Pray even now for the Lord's protection and be alert.

Dishonesty

Proverbs 16:28

A dishonest man spreads strife,
and a whisperer separates close friends.

"Did you hear about Joe?"
"I probably shouldn't be saying this, but I thought you had a right to know."
"What's going on between that couple? I bet it has to do with..."

And so the poison works in creating doubt, suspicion, resentment. All it takes is a remark supposedly in innocence, even under the guise of concern. We need to examine ourselves about this. The truth is that I can be the dishonest man spreading strife because it is easy to be dishonest with myself. I can convince myself that I am speaking what is needed (and not because I am angry or jealous or hurt). It is easy for me to think that others are being oversensitive or spiteful or hypocritical in their response to my words. They are the real problem.

We must be careful of dishonest people and gossips. They can cause real harm. But today, I want you to be more alert to how dishonesty and hurtful words can come out of your mouth. It can happen. Remember, the heart is "deceitful above all things" (Jer. 17:9). Even our redeemed hearts have vestiges of the old nature remaining, and we can be blind to our sinful motive and behavior.

Pray that the Lord will prevent dishonesty and "whispering" from flowing out of your heart today. Be alert to the opportunities that will come your way to speak out of hurt and jealousy. Pray that you may have the discernment to look even into your own heart.

Enticement

Proverbs 16:29

A man of violence entices his neighbor
and leads him in a way that is not good.

First, the violent man must entice his neighbor. Somehow he must win his neighbor over, pretending to offer something pleasurable. How does he do that? The neighbor must either be completely deceived into thinking that he is being offered something honorably good or his own sinful desires must be stirred. Thus, we must be doubly guarded. There is the enticement of the magazine covers as we walk by the stands appealing to our lust. We must be on our guard not to yield to such temptation. There is also the enticement to help someone who seems to be in need yet really is taking advantage of our kindness to take from us or to assist him in doing wrong.

Once the enticement works, the second part of leading in the wrong way becomes relatively easy. If our sinful desires are being fulfilled, we will follow with no resistance and even keep following when we come under conviction. Shame or desperation may keep us following the violent man who has taken advantage of us. What then may we do? Throw ourselves at the feet of Jesus Christ. Call out for mercy. Turn to his people, especially his shepherds, for help. Do what you must. For the way of the violent man leads to destruction. It is not good for the soul, nor is it good for happiness and a meaningful life. It wrecks homes and relationships. It can lead to public shame as well as private shame and despair.

Turn to your Savior and confess to others who will come alongside you in the name of Christ to help come back to the path of the Way.

Be Aware

Proverbs 16:30

Whoever winks his eyes plans dishonest things;
  he who purses his lips brings evil to pass.

Be aware of the subtlety by which the wicked deceive – the unscrupulous salesman and the stranger who seem overly familiar with you; the caller who has a "great deal" for you; the "friend" who wants to show you something new. There are many people who wickedly want to harm you or take advantage of you. There are many more who just want to make an extra dollar or close a deal that is not necessarily bad but may not be best for you.

In this sinful world you must be on your guard, knowing that danger often comes from seemingly innocent and even good sources – the person who seems so nice, so sincere. Pay attention to signs that indicate questionable intentions. Do not be put into a position where you feel like you owe someone your business or a favor. The wicked take advantage of good people by making them feel like they owe them the favor of buying into a special deal or for being so attentive to them.

Be alert. If you have gotten caught in such an arrangement, go now to a trusted friend for help in getting out of trouble. If you are considering such involvement, do not act without turning to a trusted friend. Do not yield to pressure tactics.

And remember that dishonesty is rampant in the religious world and among so-called Christian evangelist stars who are happy to take your donations in the name of Jesus. If you are not connected to a church, you need to do so if only for protection against religious stars who are not accountable to anyone. I would say put your trust in God; but put your trust in God by putting trust in a sound church with faithful leaders who shepherd their people.

Glorious Gray

Proverbs 16:31

Gray hair is a crown of glory;
 it is gained in a righteous life.

Gray hair is a crown of glory. We think it is gained in a trying life. "You kids are enough to give me gray hair!" "I didn't have gray hair until I took this job." We envy the man or woman able to enter middle age with no gray hairs. If Solomon is trying to lure us into living a righteous life with the promise of gray hair as our crown, he needs to hire a marketing firm. This will not fly: "Would you like to turn your hair gray? Try living a righteous life!"

This proverb comes out of a culture that honors old age. The law, in Leviticus 19:32, commanded respect: "You shall stand up before the gray head and honor the face of an old man, and you shall fear your God: I am the Lord." In general, the older the person the more respect he or she was given for possessing wisdom. The elders of Jewish society were the authorities and judges. Thus the term, which originally refers to age, took on the added meaning of leader. Proverb 20:29, which says, "The glory of young men is their strength, but the splendor of old men is their gray hair," is not exalting a hair color but wisdom. Young men have strength; old men (and women) have wisdom.

Even so, the real focus is not wisdom but righteous living. It is about being a righteous person – that is, a person who is morally good, treats others justly, and is devoted to God. Long, productive life is often the reward for such persons, whose gray hair serves as evidence.

God rewards a good life with length of life. But also to the point is that living a righteous life avoids the pitfalls of the wicked and foolish life so that one is able to live out one's days. How many men and women have died young because of their foolish ways? Poor decisions about lifestyles and ways to pursue pleasure seemed right at the time, but in truth were ways to death (Prov. 16:25).

Do you want to live to the age of gray hairs? Then focus not on how to live longer, but how to walk along the path of righteousness. God already has your days numbered. What matters is how you live those days to his glory.

Slow to Anger

Proverbs 16:32

Whoever is slow to anger is better than the mighty,
and he who rules his spirit than he who takes a city.

This is an important principle to learn, and the ones who have learned it (both the righteous and the wicked) have achieved great success in life.

Even the wicked know the truth of this proverb. Anger is a powerful passion. Anger can increase strength due to the rush of adrenaline, giving an individual the power to accomplish more than expected. But it is the adrenaline, not the anger, that produces energy, and the key to success is harnessing the adrenaline so that you control it rather than be controlled.

I remember a basketball team of talented players that nevertheless struggled because of the inability of most of the players to handle anger. The most talented member often had to sit on the bench because of losing her anger during the game. She would get fouled, then get mad, and then get reckless. Another player would sulk if the ball was stolen from her. But there was another player who would get knocked down, perhaps have the ball stolen, but would immediately bounce back up and keep playing aggressively. Indeed, she would take advantage of the opposing players by getting them angry with her aggressive play. She did not need anger to motivate her. She simply kept focused on her goal.

It is the one who keeps focused, who remains patient and perseveres that wins and keeps the victory. That is the point of the second half of the proverb: "he who rules his spirit than he who takes a city." Many persons have won victories in sports or business or the military, only to lose what they gained. Their anger got them the burst of energy to win the battle, but they had not the wisdom to know what to do when they won. Essential to military success is knowing one's limits and not overstretching. An army can win too much territory too quickly, exposing itself to counterattack.

Anger can be helpful and even the right emotion to have depending on the circumstance. But the key is that we must control our anger to make it useful rather than let anger control us, which is what happens most of the time. We should be angry at injustice; sometimes it takes anger to get us doing something that normally we would be afraid to do or indifferent about. Even then, the anger needs to be harnessed, controlled by our wisdom. It is difficult to do; thus, we need to be those who are slow to anger.

The Cast Lot

Proverbs 16:33

The lot is cast into the lap,
  but its every decision is from the Lord.

And so we can have peace. We can drive ourselves crazy trying to sort out providence, but Scripture teaches providence and God's sovereignty so that we might give due honor to God and that we might learn to trust (and rest) in him.

Yes, your decisions today matter. They have real consequences for good and bad, and you will be held accountable for what you choose and do. But take heart in knowing that ultimately all that happens – all that you do – will ultimately work for God's glory and purposes, even for your good. This is not an excuse for you to cavalierly do whatever; rather it is your hope that your Lord controls your destination. He redeems and restores; he builds even from our destructive behavior. All our bad decisions are turned into purpose-full experience.

Whatever big decisions are before you, know that God is in control and that his purposes will be carried out. Step forward with the confidence that however the lot may fall, he controls the outcome; he will be glorified, and (amazingly) he will do what is good for you who love him through Jesus Christ.

The Quiet Spirit

Proverbs 17:1

Better is a dry morsel with quiet
than a house full of feasting with strife.

This is not a contrast between homes of quiet, mild-mannered families and those of boisterous families, but rather between homes of peaceful relations and of conflict. Quiet homes can have their share of conflict. But this kind of quiet is the quiet of peace. It is the home of families who are at peace with one another. Such a family is better, even if they may be poor, than a wealthy family with plenty on the table and yet filled with strife.

Peace is better than wealth; it is a greater security than financial possession. For with strife wealth can be lost; but with peace a family stays together and holds each family member up. With peace comes contentment; wealth without peace brings only anxiety, jealousy, and greed.

It is not better to be poor than wealthy, unless we place wealth on a pedestal. If wealth becomes the aim in life, then strife will naturally accompany it, for we will hurt our loved ones as our ambition and greed take over our lives.

The quiet spirit of peace is what we should desire, for by its very nature it means peace with others, especially our loved ones. That peace begins with the peace of the soul with God, the peace that only Christ can give. Meditate upon the peace that has already been granted you by Christ's work on the cross. You are reconciled with God now; how then will such peace be lived out in you today?

The Inheritance

Proverbs 17:2

A servant who deals wisely will rule over a son who acts shamefully and will share the inheritance as one of the brothers.

This is another way of teaching the primacy of wisdom. Other resources can put us in position to succeed, but it is wisdom that takes us to the top and keeps us there. As talented as pro athletes may be, there are others as athletic or even more talented who did not make it to the highest level because of foolish choices. And many a lesser talented team has won over its opponents by outwitting them. So it is in battle and in business and in any area of life. Wisdom can compensate for lacking innate talent or wealth or, as this proverb notes, station in life.

Consider this servant. He is under the command of the son whose shameful acts no doubt include mistreating the servant. But instead of dwelling in self-pity or resentment, he "deals wisely." He acts for the good of his master and offsets the foolishness of the son. It is necessary to note that the wisdom of the proverbs is never reduced to scheming. The servant does not scheme against the son. Rather, the wisdom of the proverbs is always the wisdom characterized by righteousness and the fear of the Lord. It is the wisdom of integrity. The servant is like Joseph, who regardless of his circumstance served his masters well so that he could be entrusted for his wisdom and his integrity.

Finally, note the application to the gospel. There are many who have grown up in the church as covenant sons and daughters, and yet have lost their birthright through their shameful choices and behavior. And there are many who grew up outside the church, yet when they heard the gospel, dealt wisely by repenting of their sins and embracing the Master. They moved from the status of servants of sin to sharing in the inheritance as one of the brothers or sisters of Christ. Such is true wisdom.

Tests

Proverbs 17:3

The crucible is for silver, and the furnace is for gold,
and the Lord tests hearts.

If the Lord knows our hearts, why does he need to test them? Consider Peter's teaching:

> In this (our inheritance) you rejoice, though now for a little while, if necessary, you have been grieved by various trials, so that the tested genuineness of your faith – more precious than gold that perishes though it is tested by fire – may be found to result in praise and glory and honor at the revelation of Jesus Christ (1 Pet. 1:6-7).

The simple lesson is this – our tests in life are not given as profile tests used by God to figure us out. Rather they are given to us to prove and to purify our faith. Just as the crucible and the furnace remove impurities, so tests remove our idolatries, our self-deception, and other sins that cling to us. But they also reveal in us and for us the faith and spiritual strength we did not know we possessed. And they serve as testimony before the world to the glory of God.

As Christians we are not exempt from trials. But we can know that our trials are meaningful tests that ultimately will result in praise and glory and honor for Christ, and even for ourselves as we reflect his image on that final day.

Bad Hearing

Proverbs 17:4

An evildoer listens to wicked lips,
and a liar gives ear to a mischievous tongue.

Have you ever been frustrated trying to convince others that a rumor is false? You encourage them to think positively about others, but they assume the worse. Maybe you are trying to clear up your own name. You think that if you can only explain clearly the facts, they will listen. If you can only reason with troublemakers, they will see the error of their ways. They must be acting out of misinformation.

The truth is that they are acting out of the information they want to believe. Romans 1:18 says, "For the wrath of God is revealed from heaven against all ungodliness and unrighteousness of men, who by their unrighteousness suppress the truth." The problem of the wicked is not that they did not hear the truth, but that they wanted to hear the lies and mischief.

Jesus bluntly said, "Why do you not understand what I say? It is because you cannot bear to hear my word. You are of your father the devil, and your will is to do your father's desires" (John 8:43-44).

What is the application for us? Understand what really is at issue for the wicked. Those who delight in falsehood and mischief are not misinformed people who need education. They are deluded by Satan and need the Holy Spirit to bring them into the light of truth. Pray for the wicked and liars. Pray against Satan who holds them in his grasp. Do not exasperate yourself with trying to reason with them. Concentrate more on giving the gospel and making it plain. Without the Spirit they will still reject you and your message; but do not then yield to frustration. Pray and trust God to do his work.

Furthermore, when your own reputation is under attack, trust God for vindication. You are called to act with a clear conscience before God. It is not on your shoulders to convince those who want to hear lies and mischief. When you are slandered and others believe the slander, what matters most is that you live honorably before the Lord. "Humble yourselves, therefore, under the mighty hand of God so that at the proper time he may exalt you, casting all your anxieties on him, because he cares for you" (1 Pet.5:6-7).

Mocking the Poor

Proverbs 17:5

Whoever mocks the poor insults his Maker;
he who is glad at calamity will not go unpunished.

This is a sober warning for us all. First, we should not be quick to mock anyone. Mocking may have its place, but such times are far fewer than we tend to think. We are quick to mock those whom we do not know and those with whom we differ. As Christians we should be distinguished by the respect we accord even to our opponents. And yet in matters such as politics or social issues, we mock, exaggerate, and misrepresent them. We rejoice over their calamities and are quick to believe the worst in them. This should not be. Our opponents should be surprised by the love and respect we show them.

This proverb specifically speaks of mocking the poor. Such sin is made worse when directed towards those in worse circumstances. "Ah," you might say, "but so many are in dire straits because of their own sinful behavior." Do you think we are any different? What do you have that you have not received from your gracious Maker? Would you dare pray to God, "Thank you that I am not like my poor neighbor; I make better decisions"?

How can we mock the poor, we who have nothing to bring to our Maker to pay for our sins? The poor represent outwardly our condition inwardly. Far from mocking the poor, they should serve as reminders to us how merciful is our Maker who did not mock us, but grieved for us and won us to him. How can we mock the poor when our Lord became poor for our sakes, who, indeed, endured mocking by his enemies that we might receive crowns of glory. Let mocking cease.

Of Grandchildren and Fathers

Proverbs 17:6

Grandchildren are the crown of the aged,

and the glory of children is their fathers.

This is a good reminder of what family relations should be. It is not merely a matter of having children who then have children. It is about investing in family relationships so that there is a strong, loving bond, and that your children live lives that are deemed honorable.

Fathers can forget this as they neglect their children. The result is the lesson learned by the father in Harry Chapin's song "The Cat's in the Cradle." The father is too busy to spend time with his son. When the son grows up and gets married, he then becomes too busy to spend time with his father. The father ruefully reflects, "He'd grown up just like me."

Do you need to do some investing? Perhaps there are some relationships that need recultivating. Grandparents, do not neglect investing in your grandchildren. It is fine to give them presents, but even more they need your wisdom. They may not listen to you now, but they will remember your words. Tell them your stories; tell them about your faith. In coming years that might be what brings them through tough times.

And thank God for the bond between the Father and the Son. Such a bond enabled the Son to go through the greatest trial of all. He could do so because he loved the Father who is his glory.

Fine False Speech

Proverbs 17:7

Fine speech is not becoming to a fool;
still less is false speech to a prince.

Fine speech from the mouth of a fool comes out as mockery and sarcasm. That which should be deemed honorable is made to seem silly. The speaker is embarrassing. Having said all that, even worse is for a person of high and noble position to lie. Thus, as bad as it is for a president to be lampooned, it is worse for a president to lie through his noble words. As bad as it may be for those under authority to mock their superiors, the greater sin is committed by those superiors if they abuse their positions through lying. The fools demonstrate their own foolishness; the "princes" betray the character that should be inherent in them. The fools withhold honor they ought to give; the princes betray the honor given to them.

Follow the teaching of 1 Peter 2:16-17:
> Live as people who are free, not using your freedom
> as a cover-up for evil, but living as servants of God.
> Honor everyone. Love the brotherhood. Fear God.
> Honor the emperor.

The Good Bribe

Proverbs 17:8

A bribe is like a magic stone in the eyes of the one who gives it;
wherever he turns he prospers.

This proverb is translated in different ways, and this particular translation can be given two different interpretations: it is observing the way and perspective of the wicked briber but does not agree with him, or it is commenting on the effective use of gifts, another translation of the word.

Other proverbs will comment on the evil use of bribes, but consider for now the appropriate use of gifts that in a sense are bribes. A husband who has offended his wife comes home with flowers to smooth the way for his apology. A new boss – wanting to break the ice his first day – comes in with coffee and doughnuts for his staff. A mother helps her child break into the neighborhood circle by inviting the children over for ice cream. There is a difference between paying off someone with a bribe or manipulating him for favors, and using gifts to smooth transitions and win goodwill.

Someone may reply, "I shouldn't have to give gifts to butter up anybody." Such an attitude fails to recognize the need that we all have to be encouraged. And we will respond positively to those who encourage us, and we will be turned off by those who show no interest in how we feel. The person who appropriately gives gifts is giving attention to others. It is true that wicked people do this to manipulate, but wise and good people do this because they truly regard their neighbor and are desiring good results.

Who can you "bribe" today with cheer?

Covering an Offense

Proverbs 17:9

Whoever covers an offense seeks love,
  but he who repeats a matter separates close friends.

"I probably shouldn't tell you this, but..."
"He didn't want me to tell anyone, but..."
"Did you know..."
"We should be praying for..."

And so begins many a repeating of a matter that creates anger and suspicion that never should have occurred. Every day we say and do things that we should not or did not mean to do. Someone gets frustrated and says something without thinking. Another gets nervous and acts in a way in which he knows better. But the sinful word or deed is now "out there." Will it be repeated? Will we pass it on, letting it be relived in our mouths and the ears of others?

It depends on how we respond to offense. Jesus said that when we are offended we should go privately to the offender. If that does not resolve the matter, then bring in a witness, then elders. In other words, seek to handle an offense privately with the intent for a peaceful resolution. But this proverb notes that there are times when it is best to overlook an offense. Indeed, if we were to bring up every offense we think we receive, our days would be marked by confrontation. Ephesians 4:2 tells us to bear with one another in love. This assumes that we will be offended, and we are called upon to take much of it in stride. After all, we (more often than we know) offend others. If we were confronted every time we erred in our speech and acts, we would be weighed down in discouragement.

And if our mishaps were repeated – if the unthinking remark was reported or foolish act passed on – then we would be devastated as hurt and anger were compounded. Stop and pray before you confront someone about their offense. And do not repeat a matter unless you are compelled after much prayer. Whenever you share an offensive remark or deed, you place a burden upon the hearer. This is not a matter of minding your own business. It is a matter of acting in love, thinking what is best for everyone. If need be, seek godly counsel what to do. But always keep before you what demonstrates love for neighbor – both the neighbor who offends and the neighbor you are about to tell. Seek love.

Of Rebuke and Blows

Proverbs 17:10

A rebuke goes deeper into a man of understanding
than a hundred blows into a fool.

The ultimate distinction between a man of understanding and a fool is not how well they do on an aptitude test but in how well they receive correction. Everyone will make mistakes; everyone sins. What then do they do when their mistake or sin is pointed out?

The fool insists he did not make a mistake or sin. Or he may acknowledge he is in the wrong but then continue in the same behavior. Even though he is reasoned with, even though he is disciplined, he only hardens his attitude. He has his own view of reality, and he will not change. In his folly he is filled with pride which only stiffens when rebuked and disciplined.

The man of understanding needs only a rebuke, and even then only a mild one, because knowing and doing what is right is of ultimate importance to him. He is grateful for correction even if the correction is harsh. It is better to him to be righted than to persist in error or sin. Because he possesses understanding, he is able to listen well and discern the truth of the correction. Because he is not full of foolish pride, he is able to give ear to what is said.

It is foolish, stubborn pride that makes fools out of us. "I don't need this." "I don't care what you say." "Punish me all you want; I'll do what I want." "Religion is for weaklings." "I'll live the way I want." Such pride keeps a man from the rebuke that would lead to repentance and everlasting life. Such pride leads a man into an eternity of blows.

Rebellion

Proverbs 17:11

An evil man seeks only rebellion,
and a cruel messenger will be sent against him.

Such a person looks at life from the perspective of me versus everyone else. He is in rebellion against everyone because he sees everyone as competitor. The competitor may be someone over him; thus he looks at the competitor as an oppressor, someone whose chains must be thrown off. The competitor may be an equal, whom he sees as a combatant fighting to get ahead of him. The competitor may be under him, whom he regards as someone trying to undermine him. That is the way life is to him - each person seeking power for himself. Rules are created by those in power to restrain those below them from rebelling. And so he rebels. He does not merely question authority; he seeks to undermine it.

Such a person must understand that his rebellious spirit and behavior bring the restraint he abhors. The more he rebels, the more competition will rise up. He is now seen as a threat to peace; certainly he is a threat to those over him. Whether those in power are good or evil, they cannot abide rebellion. The cruel messenger is the representative of the authority who comes to restrain the evil man. Whatever oppression he may have felt before, he certainly feels the weight of bondage now.

There is such a thing as righteous rebellion. There are righteous causes that call for rebellion against wicked rule. But be clear about that cause and especially your motive. Rebellion can seem glamorous.

It stokes the ego. It allows you to gloss over your own sin as you focus on redressing the perceived wrongs committed against you. It can embitter your soul so that you see life as you versus everyone else, including your Maker.

Rebellion is the mark of the unsaved soul. If that soul is not willing to bend the knee to the righteous Authority who paid the greatest price to win the rebellious and to deliver them from bondage, then know that someday it will be not the messenger of peace who comes to him, but the cruel messenger of wrath.

> *"Come now, let us reason together, says the LORD:*
> *though your sins are like scarlet,*
> * they shall be as white as snow;*
> *though they are red like crimson,*
> * they shall become like wool.*
> *If you are willing and obedient,*
> * you shall eat the good of the land;*
> *but if you refuse and rebel,*
> * you shall be eaten by the sword;*
> * for the mouth of the LORD has spoken"* (Isa. 1:18-20).

Dangerous Fool

Proverbs 17:12

Let a man meet a she-bear robbed of her cubs
* rather than a fool in his folly.*

We laugh at the fool and dismiss him for his nonsensical behavior. But just as we would run for cover when a gun is placed in the hands of a child who thinks he has a toy, so we need all the more to be careful around the fool.

An evil man is dangerous, but if he has his wits about him, he limits his wicked acts to attain his goals. The fool knows no such limits. The fool delights in the attention he receives and the chaos he causes. It is the fool who pulls the fire alarm for fun and pushes someone near the edge of a precipice. It is the fool who yells when silence is needed, who plays with danger. And when he is caught up in the midst of his folly, where others would pull back he all the more plunges ahead. He does not heed words of caution or rebuke. Reasoning with him only provokes him to more irrational behavior. He knows no boundaries.

And so be careful with him. Do not feed him opportunity to display his folly. Avoid him as much as possible and keep on your guard. Stay alert lest you are taken down or shamed by his foolish outbursts.

Evil for Good

Proverbs 17:13

If anyone returns evil for good,
evil will not depart from his house.

Wickedness is troubling in any form. Even so, there are degrees even for evil to climb. It is condemning to do mischief. It is wrong to take advantage of the innocent. But to return evil for good; to harm someone who has done you good – is it possible to sink lower?

The scam artist who takes money by posing to represent a charity or to be a person in need – that is wicked. He takes advantage, not merely of someone innocent, but of someone doing good. But to go a step further, to take advantage of a person who knows you, who has only been kind to you, and then to use that very kindness to take advantage of him surely that is to sink to the lowest depths.

It certainly is an affront to God who will see that evil will not depart from his house. This is a statement of how greatly offended God is by such behavior.

And what is man's position before God? He created man and blessed him; man in return turned against him. Even so, he continued to provide for man and by his grace give him many daily blessings. But man rebelled against him all the more, setting up false gods and giving to them the worship due God. Even so, God was patient. He sent prophets to reveal God and to teach what God wanted. But those prophets were themselves abused and murdered.

However much good God did, man returned it with evil. We are man. We are the guilty. But what have we received? Grace, mercy, the priceless gift of God's Son, his very blood shed for us to pay for our guilt. Instead of evil never departing from our house, we have been given peace. And so, we who have moved from returning evil for good, let us move from returning evil for evil. Let us return good for evil that those who are wicked might be awakened to their sin and turn to God. It is no less than what God has done for us.

Strife Like Water

Proverbs 17:14

The beginning of strife is like letting out water,
  so quit before the quarrel breaks out.

When a container of water cracks, when it is opened only by a hair, water seeps out and cannot be retrieved. Cover it with your hands, put a cloth tightly around it, the water continues to seep. It cannot be contained. And even if you do seal the crack, you cannot reclaim the water. It flows into every crevice nearby. Such is the problem when a pipe leaks. You may find water damage in one place – a wall, a ceiling, the floor – only to discover that the leak is elsewhere because the water flows to wherever there is least resistance.

So it is with strife. Once it is let out, it travels wherever it can in different directions, wherever there is least resistance. It stains the clean surfaces of the room. It cannot be put back in its container as though it had not spilled out. Wipe the surface dry, patch and paint the stains and cracks; nevertheless, the damage was made and memories keep the strife in storage. There is less trust now, less fellowship. Like undersurface damage that is never restored, so damage in the minds and souls of fellow believers and of neighbors and of family members remains through the years.

And that is assuming effort is made to deal with the strife. More likely the crack widens into an opening and as water pours forth, so strife pours forth. "Now I know where you really stand!" "I've never

266

trusted you and you have proven why!" Then the charges multiply and opportunity for recrimination is looked for.

And where all this is likely to happen is in the church amongst the fellowship of the followers of Christ. *So quit before the quarrel breaks out!* Whatever damage you think will occur because you hold your tongue, consider the damage that will occur when you speak in strife. And if you must speak up, consider what you will say and how you will say it before you speak. Consider how you will help your fellow believer with your words. Consider if that really is your motive. For once the crack is made, the water of strife will come forth.

Abominable Sin

Proverbs 17:15

He who justifies the wicked and he who condemns the righteous
  are both alike an abomination to the LORD.

God is not a moral relativist. There are the wicked who do bad, who break his moral law; and there are the righteous who do good, who follow his moral law. To flip them around to justify the wicked and condemn the righteous is an abomination to him.

We see that in our society. Abortionists are good; to oppose abortion is wicked. Sex of any variety is good; to proscribe that sex is reserved for a married couple of man and woman is wicked. To ignore or reject outright the God of the Bible is good; to take his Word seriously is wicked. It is one thing to wink and commit sin; it is another to uphold the sin as good and condemn righteous behavior.

But that is the way that a society that rejects God will go. There is no divine law to inform and restrain. All that is left is to do what seems right in one's own eyes, and the only measure is inner feeling. This will always lead off the righteous path laid forth by Scripture. For as Scripture explains, the heart itself is sick with sin. What can it do but lead us into sin? And how can we live in sin and remain happy? By calling what is sin good, and what is good sin. Now we are able to live in peace.

However much peace we may feel, God is not at peace with us. Rest assure that the righteous whom he regards as righteous will be justified, and the wicked whom he regards as wicked will be condemned. He will not tolerate abomination.

But how do we get out of our mess? For if we are honest, we still give in to what is wicked. Turn to the Judge and find that he is also the Merciful Redeemer. He does not desire the condemnation of the wicked, but rather that the wicked will turn from their evil ways. Don't justify your wickedness. Turn to God to save you, to change you.

Buying Wisdom

Proverbs 17:16

Why should a fool have money in his hand to buy wisdom
  when he has no sense?

Even if wisdom could be bought, it still would do the fool no good. But isn't wisdom exactly what a fool needs? True, but the fool's problem is that he does not know what to do with wisdom even when given to him.

He may obtain wisdom now. He may turn to a wise counselor now and receive the fruit of wisdom. He may open the Word of God now, the greatest source of wisdom. But his foolish mind will reject the wisdom or else twist it into foolishness.

The fool does not need to buy wisdom. He needs to be transformed by wisdom. How then can he be transformed? That is the work of the Holy Spirit. The wisest of counselors cannot change the foolish mind. At best the wise person can manage the fool. He can perhaps keep the fool from causing harm. But he cannot make the fool become wise. Only the Holy Spirit can do that kind of work.

Be wary of the fool, yet treat him with the love of Christ. Do what you can to alleviate the effects of his folly on others and himself. But do not reason with him as you would another rational mind. And do not give to him responsibility, such as the possession of money that he will only use for harm.

The best you can do (which is truly the *best* we should do) is to pray for him. Pray for the work of the Spirit in him. And love him with the love of Christ, a love that seeks his good. We were all fools when it came to knowledge of God and redemption. Only the Spirit working in us turned us away from folly to the wisdom of the gospel. Only the love of God pierced through our darkness.

Friend and Brother

Proverbs 17:17

A friend loves at all times,
    and a brother is born for adversity

How good it is to be a friend and to have a friend, a true friend. A friend always loves; that is, he always desires the good of his friend. To love at all times is to seek the best for one's friend at all times. That means sticking by him when others desert him. It means being there for him. And it means being truthful with him, telling him at times what he does not want to hear. Sometimes it even means not sticking by him when he chooses evil, that is, not entering into the evil with him or enabling him to do what is wrong; but then, always, being there for him when he suffers the consequences.

And then a brother (or a sister) has even a closer connection. Even though he (or she) may not seem as close as a friend, he literally was born for adversity. For he is a kinsman. Brothers and sisters are bonded by blood. They are not connected by their common tastes. And it is in the troubles of life that their bond most clearly is shown to protect, to deliver, to avenge. If a brother is disappointed in another brother, the very disappointment rises from the blood-bond. And should brothers be against one another, it is a greater tragedy than any other feud because of that bond.

Let us be thankful for the One who calls us his friends (John 15:15).

269

Let us be humbled by the One who is not ashamed to be called our brother (Heb. 2:11), who became our kinsman-redeemer:

> Since therefore the children share in flesh and blood, he himself likewise partook of the same things, that through death he might destroy the one who has the power of death, that is, the devil, and deliver all those who through fear of death were subject to lifelong slavery. For surely it is not angels that he helps, but he helps the offspring of Abraham. Therefore he had to be made like his brothers in every respect, so that he might become a merciful and faithful high priest in the service of God, to make propitiation for the sins of the people. For because he himself has suffered when tempted, he is able to help those who are being tempted (Heb. 2:14-18).

Risky Security

Proverbs 17:18

One who lacks sense gives a pledge
  and puts up security in the presence of his neighbor.

This is one of several proverbs warning against putting up security for another person (6:1; 11:15; 22:26). The concern is putting one's self at risk. Putting up security for another person is saying that I will make good what that person cannot, *even though I will reap no benefit from what I give.*

Are you able to say that with contentment? Are you able to part without harm and with contentment from whatever will be required of you? During the time that your neighbor, for whom you have put up security, is still under his obligation, will you be able to keep the relationship that you now have with him? Will you be able to do so if he is unable to meet his obligation? If so, then feel free to sign.

But if you will be harmed; if you will fret over your loss or possible loss; if your relationship will be tested by his ability to come through, then know that you are putting that relationship under strain, as well as your own peace. And if you have a family, then you are risking their welfare.

The pressure to put up security comes about because of the relationship, likely a family member or a friend. You do want to see him succeed. You don't want to let him down. Perhaps not signing will itself strain the relationship. And what if it does work out, and he does repay and is grateful because you helped him when he was in need? You showed faith when others would not!

Again, you must weigh the risk. Failing to pay his due, or paying only under the weight of a burden now owed to you – is that a risk worth taking? Again, if you are married or have a family, if others are dependent on you, can you put them at risk? For risk is the definition of a security put up for another person.

But what about Jesus? Did he not risk much for our sakes? He did, but as a gift not as a loan. And he definitely did not put up his life as our security in hopes that we might be able to pay back the debt. If you wish to be generous, then be generous with gifts, not with loans, not with anything that you must have back.

Bad Love

Proverbs 17:19

Whoever loves transgression loves strife;
he who makes his door high seeks destruction.

Consider the transgression of the Ten Commandments in reverse order. One who covets will experience strife with his neighbor through competition and resentment. One who lies presents opportunity for strife by deceit and breaking trust.

One who steals causes strife with the victim. One who commits adultery stirs up strife with the fellow adulterer, the spouse, the family, and others. One who murders is enacting the ultimate strife with one's neighbor. One who dishonors his parents brings strife into the family. One who takes the Lord's name in vain, brings strife for public religion. One who worships created images, creates strife directly with the Creator. One who puts other gods, including himself, before the Lord God is filled with strife within himself and with God. Transgression and strife go hand in hand. How different from the love of friendship and kinship (17:17).

The lover of transgression is essentially arrogant, believing he is above the law and setting himself above his neighbors. This is what "makes his door high" means. He exalts himself. He believes he is invincible, secure. But his very insolence will lead to his destruction. His transgressions will catch up with him, usually in his own lifetime; always in his death. Destruction is his destiny.

Crooked Heart

Proverbs 17:20

A man of crooked heart does not discover good,
and one with a dishonest tongue falls into calamity.

The problem for such a man above is not bad luck, as he would think is the cause. Nor is the problem one of circumstances – if only he had money, a good job, a job without a boss, neighbors who appreciated him, etc. Jesus stated clearly his problem: it is his heart. "For from within, out of the heart of man, come evil thoughts..." (Mark 7:21).

If only we "good" people could understand this principle; then we would not be perplexed about the sins of others, nor the bad things that happen to us. We wonder how "bad" people can keep behaving badly. Bad behavior is the mark of a crooked heart. It neither seeks good, nor (should it be under the illusion that it is seeking good) can it find it. And the dishonest tongue is dishonest because of the heart that is crooked. Thus, if you link up with an ungodly neighbor, understand that your neighbor will expose you to, and try to lead you into, sin.

Understand more that many of our own calamities are the result of our own sin. Christians will often ask if their suffering is the result of sin. Even then they are following the wrong trail, for they try to connect their suffering with sin that is not a direct cause. "I am having a hard time at work because I must learn to trust God more...I need more faith...I need to be more disciplined..." Often our hard times are the result of direct sin – speaking rudely to our neighbor, showing dishonor to our supervisor, complaining, doing poor work. Indeed, where many times we credit suffering to being "bold witnesses for Christ," the real truth is that we have been arrogant and obnoxious.

Check the heart. It is the hardest work to do, but the most necessary.

A Fool's Father

Proverbs 17:21

He who sires a fool gets himself sorrow,
  and the father of a fool has no joy.

Too many parents can nod their heads to this proverb. Others may laugh at a fool, shake their heads in disdain or pity. The parent (father or mother) weeps. The father hangs his head in shame and the mother in sorrow. They had hopes for their child; their delight was in the pleasure he would bring. And especially in ancient times, they looked to him to provide for them in their old age. But the fool becomes their thorn in the side. When they see children devoted to their parents, they ache. When they see children grow up to be mature men and women, they cannot help but contrast their foolish child. The fool robs his parents of joy.

The fool does not think about this. He thinks only of himself, and if he thinks of his parents, he blames them for all his calamities which are many. If they had given him what he wanted...

How can we meditate on this proverb without thinking of our heavenly Father who must put up with our foolish ways? For though he has saved us and adopted us, though his Spirit dwells within us, we continue to act foolishly. Do we not cause him shame? Does he not grieve over us for whom he paid such a great price?

273

No? What is this? "God shows his love for us in that while we were still sinners, Christ died for us. Since, therefore, we have now been justified by his blood, much more shall we be saved by him from the wrath of God" (Rom. 5:8-9). Is this our Father running to meet us from a distance? Is this the Father seeking after us after wandering away from his flock? Is this our Father loving us with a steadfast love that cannot be deterred, not even by our foolishness, because it is in Christ Jesus our Lord?

Perhaps our greatest folly is to doubt what he has done for us in adopting us as his children. The more our confidence is founded in the work of God for us, and not our work for him, then the less folly we will fall into. God has sired no fools.

Good Medicine

Proverbs 17:22

A joyful heart is good medicine,
but a crushed spirit dries up the bones.

Centuries before the advent of scientific medicine, this proverb recognized a key element of good health and even for curing illness – a joyful heart. Being happy is not a cure-all, of course, but it does play a significant role in reducing the ill effects caused by stress, depression, anger, self-pity, and resentment.

Perhaps this was how the Apostle Paul was able to deal with all his sufferings, including some kind of chronic physical ailment. He said, "Rejoice in the Lord always: again I will say, Rejoice....do not be anxious about anything, but in everything by prayer and supplication with thanksgiving let your requests be made known to God" (Phil. 4:4, 6). You may not be able to rejoice in being ill or going through a trial, but you can always rejoice in your salvation, in the grace and mercy of God, in his steadfast love, in his promise of eternal glory, and on and on.

Paul goes on to say, "whatever is true, whatever is honorable, whatever is just, whatever is pure, whatever is lovely, whatever is commendable, if there is any excellence, if there is anything worthy of praise, think about these things" (4:8). You cannot keep bad things from happening, but you do have a choice on whether or not to let such things dominate your mind and spirit. What are you thinking about today – your trials or your blessings? Are you counting what you wish you had or what all God has blessed you with?

And by the way, are you being medicine for someone today? Are you passing on a good word, a kind act that will refresh someone's spirit? Let the blessings which God has poured out on you in Christ Jesus be passed on to others.

Bribes

Proverbs 17:23

The wicked accepts a bribe in secret
  to pervert the ways of justice.

Truly there is nothing new under the sun. The giving of bribes has a long history. Bribes are given to sway judges' rulings; to fix betting events; to obtain advantage over business competitors; to gain money and power. It is wicked to give such bribes, but as this proverb points out, it is also wicked to accept bribes. For the one giving bribes in one sense is not the one perverting justice; rather, he is giving a bribe to one who has the power to pervert justice. The very reason he must give a bribe is that he lacks such power.

Thus, we see the danger of power. Many "good" persons have taken positions of power in the courts and in government with the desire to enforce justice, only to be corrupted by the lure of money or another form of bribery. And we are all susceptible to bribery in our own small spheres of influence. The teacher is tempted to reward "pets" in the class; the parent to favor the "nice" child of the family; the boss to favor the employee who brings snacks to work. We don't need to receive thousands of dollars to misuse our authority. Small favors that make us feel special will do.

We are all susceptible to bribery, however great or small the bribe or our power. Thanks be to God that he, the Great Judge, is swayed by nothing other than his own just character; and all praise to God that he is moved by his own mercy. Our God will always do what is right; he will always do what is for our good. We may consider that there is one "bribe" that he always accepts – the intercession of his Son who is our High Priest. He will never turn down his Son who ever pleas for us.

Setting One's Face

Proverbs 17:24

The discerning sets his face toward wisdom,
  but the eyes of a fool are on the ends of the earth.

The contrast here is between the discerning who keeps focused on wisdom and the fool who chases after each fad that pops up from everywhere. Today he would be the one fascinated with the "new discoveries" of the *Da Vinci Code*. His home library is an archive of each year's most popular self-help and new-thinking books. He's taken all the newly discovered ancient Asian exercises and meditation practices. He's dabbled in Indian Hinduism and Tibetan Buddhism. He's got the latest book by the Dalai Lama. And there is his collection of crystals and other New Age paraphernalia.

But the discerning "sets his face toward wisdom." He does not lose focus; he does not waver from the one true source of wisdom – Scripture. He does not lose sight of his one true hope – the redemption of Jesus Christ. He does not waver in his faith in the one true God. Like Christ when tempted by Satan, he does not waste time with fruitless debate about what is right or wrong for him but merely cites the teaching of Scripture. And like Christ, his trials do not discourage him, for he keeps his eyes on the joy set before him.

For Christ is his wisdom. In Christ wisdom becomes simple and profound. To abide in Christ is all that he needs.

Grief of a Fool

Proverbs 17:25

A foolish son is a grief to his father
and bitterness to her who bore him.

Fools annoy others; they make others angry. Others enjoy fools, finding them to be entertainment. But fools grieve their parents who are filled with shame by the public disgrace and filled with sorrow for the path their children are following. They may also be angry, but their anger is stirred by disappointment and the loss of hope for their children.

It is a wondrous feeling to hold one's own newborn, to know that this is not just a baby but one's own child. There is no question for a parent at that moment that he or she will do anything to protect him and to do what is best for him. And no parent cannot but help to invest their own happiness and hopes in the child. This is the reason why parents can seem to be more reasonable with other children than their own. Just as we do not lose sleep over the investments of others but are anxious about our own, so parents are anxious for their own children.

Your hope for your children and for yourselves is to entrust them to God. You have responsibility to raise your children in the path of righteousness, but you cannot control their hearts nor be with them everywhere. And you must remember that they ultimately belong to God. You can do nothing better than to hold them up before your Lord in prayer. Certainly there is much you can do to learn how to raise your children and relate to them, but always be faithful in prayer. God grieves also for his wayward children. You do not love your children more than he. And so you can share your grief in prayer with one who understands. For after all, you are his child and he has had plenty experience dealing with your foolish ways.

Not Good

Proverbs 17:26

To impose a fine on a righteous man is not good,
   nor to strike the noble for their uprightness.

Injustice occurs in two ways: not punishing the guilty and punishing the law abiding. It is one thing to be lax about prosecuting the guilty, but it is more grievous to take action against the person who is upright. Indeed, this proverb presents not merely a person who is innocent of a crime, but who consciously lives an upright life and promotes justice.

Understand that the writer is not merely shaking his head at injustice. His moral stance is based on God's law, and God will enforce his law. In essence, he is pronouncing doom on the judge who imposes injustice. To do what "is not good" is to incur the wrath of God, and God will not be mocked. All the more, he will mete out his justice against those in authority abusing their offices. The ruler who is a tyrant; the judge who is unjust; the boss who takes advantage of his power over others – such persons should take warning that what they do "is not good," and God will avenge his law, especially when injustice is carried against the upright.

Pray that the unjust will receive their due punishment in this life, not simply so that you can see it happen, but that in this life they still have time to repent. Final judgment will take place when there will be no chance of repentance. For God is just and he will see that final justice is delivered.

Of Few Words

Proverbs 17:27

Whoever restrains his words has knowledge,
   and he who has a cool spirit is a man of understanding.

How is being few with words connected with being knowledgeable? First of all, the person of knowledge and understanding knows that his value is not found in making others see how knowledgeable he is. He is not compelled to speak louder, quicker, and more often than others. His self-esteem is not wrapped up in being thought smart by others.

His understanding is seen in his cool spirit that keeps him from aggravating problems and allows him to calm others. By his cool spirit he can act with wisdom and apply his knowledge productively. He controls his anger because it is the wise thing to do.

He restrains his words, knowing when and to whom to speak, and thus not wasting words or having his words used against him or being misunderstood. This restraint actually raises him in the estimation of others. He may not be recognized for his wisdom early on, but time will provide the occasion and prove his understanding, whereas, the quick talker will eventually prove how little he really knows.

But note: the man of knowledge and understanding is not praised for keeping his knowledge and wisdom to himself, but rather knowing how to impart them effectively by restraining his impulses. A quiet person does not necessarily know more than the talker. The key is having control over one's impulses and especially one's tongue.

Silent Value

Proverbs 17:28

Even a fool who keeps silent is considered wise;
when he closes his lips, he is deemed intelligent.

The point of this proverb and the previous one is that the best use of words comes from a measured restraint, or to use a common phrase – think before you speak. The problem with the fool is that he speaks quickly without considering his words. He speaks on impulse. He does not consider how others perceive him as he is speaking.

Think through what to say and how to say it. And if you can't think of what to say, then be silent. You will be considered wise until you prove otherwise. Indeed, your silence can be a very tool for communicating that you have something to say. It is better to have others cajole you into sharing your thoughts, than for you to impose them on reluctant hearers. Words that are not readily given become more sought after than the words spilled out quickly.

Isolation

Proverbs 18:1

Whoever isolates himself seeks his own desire;
  he breaks out against all sound judgment.

The thought here is not that it is wrong to seek solitude or even to work alone. Rather, it speaks to the person who has fortressed himself against companionship. He may be like the hurt lover of Paul Simon's song "I Am a Rock," who isolates himself from relationships so that he might not be hurt again. He may be the disenchanted idealist who gives up his dreams and loses respect for his neighbors. Or he may be the epitome of the American hero – the person who "goes it alone," who lives for himself.

Whatever may be the motivation, to isolate oneself either physically or emotionally goes against the way God made us, which is to be communal creatures. We are made to desire companionship. Our dreams are meant to be shared with others. This is especially true for us as Christians, who when we come to faith in Christ are made members of his one body. To isolate ourselves from one another is like the eye wanting to isolate itself from the head or the hand from the arm.

Whatever experiences you may have had that would lead you to isolate yourself from the body of Christ, know that the true help for you is not isolation, but connection. The hope for us all in living productive lives for the Lord is to be attached to him through his people.

The Opinionated Fool

Proverbs 18:2

A fool takes no pleasure in understanding,
  but only in expressing his opinion.

It is hard to get in a word in a conversation with a fool. Even when he asks you a question, he interrupts before you can say much. He must give his opinion, tell his story, listen to his own voice. And all the while he thinks that he is earning your good opinion of him. Surely he must be wise to be able to have an opinion about everything; certainly he must be intelligent to know so much. Of course the truth is that he has revealed his foolishness and ignorance. If only he would heed the counsel of Proverb 17:28 and keep silent; at least then some may mistake him for being intelligent.

It is difficult to help such a fool, due to his being wrapped up in himself. He finds himself entertaining. He likes listening to his voice; his pleasure is in expressing his opinion. If you contradict him, he only talks more in self-defense. If you stay quiet, he interprets your silence as being enrapt with his speech.

Again, the problem of the fool, regardless of his type of folly, is that he loves his folly. Education will not help him. Whatever information and skill he gains he only turns into means to further his folly. He simply does not like what is wise, what is sensible. Wisdom does not appeal to him. He cannot be reformed. You cannot change him by reasoning with him or scolding him. The only hope is that, like the prodigal son, he will come to his senses on his own; or rather, that the Holy Spirit will do what is necessary to convict him. Pray for the fools you know. Have pity on them and lift them before the Lord.

What Wickedness Brings

Proverbs 18:3

When wickedness comes, contempt comes also,
  and with dishonor comes disgrace.

One would think that a truth so obvious would have a sobering effect on the wicked. And yet, far from avoiding behavior that leads

281

to disgrace, they all the more pursue their immoral and wicked ways, even basking in the notoriety that results. For the wicked are also fools who mistake shame for honor and contempt for respect. They value the praise and respect of other fools and disdain the opinion of the wise and honorable. They also value being in the spotlight for whatever reason. If it must take wicked behavior to stand out, then so be it. Indeed, that is the behavior they enjoy most.

But we should desire an honorable reputation earned by exhibiting integrity, love for our neighbor, and devotion to our Lord. As Christians, we can expect to be slandered, but it should be just that – slander, and not a true report. Our neighbors ought to be perplexed by us, finding our beliefs odd and yet acknowledging that we are trustworthy, caring neighbors.

But the reputation most important is our reputation before God. He alone knows fully our hearts; he alone judges rightly; before him alone we will stand to give an account for our lives. Desire now to live in such a way that honors our Lord; for truly no better reward can we gain than to hear him say, "Well done, good and faithful servant."

A Bubbling Brook

Proverbs 18:4

The words of a man's mouth are deep waters;
    the fountain of wisdom is a bubbling brook.

This proverb is presenting a contrast between the words of sinful man that hide motive, like the deep waters which hide what is underneath, and the words of the wise which are refreshing and clear like a bubbling brook. We are as likely to use words to miscommunicate than to communicate. We use words to hide our true feelings, to camouflage our real intentions. We sometimes use words to disguise our ignorance. So-called intellectuals and scholars will at times rely on esoteric (hard to understand) words merely to seem deep.

How refreshing to hear clear wisdom spoken. We've been in "discussions" that only grow more confusing, and then, some word of reason is spoken, and the answer so difficult to discover becomes so simple that we marvel we did not know it all along. A question is raised that brings light to what seemed a complex dilemma.

And so Jesus' words must have been like a bubbling brook to so many ears as he cut through the verbal entrapments of the religious leaders; as he spoke "with authority"; as he taught truth. The paradox of Jesus' teaching is that many turned away from him, claiming, "This is a hard saying; who can listen to it?" And yet others attested, "Lord, to whom shall we go? You have the words of eternal life." And so wise words reveal the wisdom of the speaker and the wisdom of the hearer; for only those so tuned to truth can recognize it, so that even if they do not understand all they hear, they nevertheless recognize when it is spoken and desire to hear more. They find its cool stream delightful and refreshing.

Delight in the bubbling brook of God's Word today, especially in the words of Christ which are words of eternal life.

Guilty?

Proverbs 18:5

It is not good to be partial to the wicked
or to deprive the righteous of justice.

Surely we all agree with this proverb, but then, how might we be guilty of such injustice? By placing ourselves before God and others. We will ignore political policies that hurt others but either help us or at least do not harm us. We will avert our eyes when confronted by injustice if what is required of us is sacrifice or inconvenience. When our world is just that – "our" world – then right and wrong get redefined to what makes us feel comfortable or uncomfortable. We are partial to the wicked when we ignore their wickedness. We deprive the righteous of justice when we fail to strive for justice.

And then there are our actions. We are partial to the wicked when we speak like them and hurt others. We deprive the righteous of justice when we fail to speak well of them and encourage them. We must remember that the Judge of all the earth sees our every action (and inaction) and that his standards are far beyond human laws. What we consider trivial, he regards as great offenses or great deeds of kindness; and so much of what we think to be of great magnitude, he finds to be small.

All the more then, let us do the daily difficult work of examining our hearts before the Lord; and let us daily fall on the grace of God in Christ for forgiveness and for the power to live righteously to his glory.

Fighting Words

Proverbs 18:6

A fool's lips walk into a fight,
  and his mouth invites a beating.

What a funny proverb and so true! The fool will even be warned: "You're asking for it. You'd better stop talking." But he won't stop. He must rant and rave; he keeps provoking, keeps sounding off until the listener either literally or figuratively gives him his beating.

Why does the fool invite punishment? Because he is caught up in himself. He has worked himself into a fit, and it feels good to vent. He loves the sound of his voice and cannot see the real effect his words are having. He likes hearing himself talk more than being heard. He does not consider how to communicate; he simply wants to make sound.

The exasperating part of it all is that he does not understand why he receives a violent reaction. He blames the listener for being impatient or mean or unjust or a fool. "All I did was ask a question." "I was only trying to reason with him." "I don't know why he should get so upset." He does not learn from the reactions of others, even when he

284

develops a history of angering others. He blames bad luck with getting jobs that have difficult co-workers and bosses. His church is filled with problem people and leaders who don't care. His wife thinks only of herself and his children are moody. He does not make the connection between their behavior and his foolish speech.

We will all at times speak foolishly. Let us at least learn from our mistakes and develop the ability to listen to others.

Snare to One's Soul

Proverbs 18:7

A fool's mouth is his ruin,
  and his lips are a snare to his soul.

By his mouth the fool shows lack of wisdom and thus loses the respect of others. He irritates others with his thoughtless remarks; he offends; he makes himself a bore; he betrays confidences; twists the words of others; shows arrogance; stirs up trouble. And all the while is troubled that he does not get a fair hearing!

Sometimes a fool can tell the truth, but because he has developed a reputation of a fool he will not be believed. His mouth has become his ruin. He grows in resentment; he turns to other fools who will hear him. And thus his lips become a snare to his soul as he leaves the path of life and wanders into the way of the wicked.

If you have a history of getting into trouble because of your mouth, do whatever you must do now to control your tongue. Seek accountability with respected brothers and sisters; read books on the subject; seek counsel from those known for their good speech. Do it now; do not put off getting help, for your tongue is a snare for your soul; it will bring you to ruin. James 3:9 warns of those who with the same tongue bless God and curse those made in the image of God. This is not to be taken lightly.

Whispering Morsels

Proverbs 18:8

The words of a whisperer are like delicious morsels;
  they go down into the inner parts of the body.

Such is the danger of the whispering tongue. We are enticed by it. We like hearing secrets "confided" in us. We like being in the know, being brought into the inner circle. But those words go into our "inner parts." We mull over them, and they begin to seep into our unconscious and eventually conscious thoughts. We become distrustful of the people we have heard about; we worry over the inside information we've been given. Others' reputations are tarnished in our minds. Complainers whisper their complaints, and before we know what is happening, we become complainers.

We need to learn how to say no when the whisperer comes around. We need to walk out of the room. We need to understand that the persons hurt the most by whispering are us, the listeners. The whispers go down with a delicious taste, but they poison the soul.

The Slacker

Proverbs 18:9

Whoever is slack in his work
  is a brother to him who destroys.

The slacker destroys productivity. Products, service, goals are sacrificed. He destroys morale, as others are influenced to have the same attitude or frustrated so that they become less productive. He destroys teamwork, as others become not only angry with him but with supervisors for not managing him well. He destroys his own future, his laziness becoming the obstacle that he cannot get around.

But the problem of the slacker is that he does not recognize that he is one. He attributes his lack of productivity to others – to the bureaucracy he works under; to the supervisor who doesn't manage well; to his colleagues who don't understand how he works; to his parents for not raising him well; to his spouse who doesn't appreciate him; to whomever he can remotely place blame.

He may even think that he is productive. He is pleased with his output, especially if he works with others who also have low productivity. That is why he and others are resentful of the worker who comes in and immediately out-performs them. His laziness is played out in different ways: he simply moves slowly; he is easily distracted; he is unmotivated and shows his disinterest; he enjoys talking; he may work busily but disorganized (too lazy to organize himself).

You are likely to be thinking of some lazy workers now. But be sure to examine yourself. Remember, the slacker's problem is not recognizing his own laziness. Also examine how you are influenced by the slacker. Is he affecting the way you do your job. Are you blaming him for your poor attitude? Remember, the slacker is quick to blame others for his failings. Your Master for whom you work is Jesus Christ: "Whatever you do, work heartily, as for the Lord and not for men, knowing that from the Lord you will receive the inheritance as your reward. You are serving the Lord Christ" (Col. 3:23-24).

The Name

Proverbs 18:10

The name of the LORD is a strong tower;
the righteous man runs into it and is safe.

What's in a name? How can a name be a strong tower? What's in a name is what is in a person. According to that person's character and relationship to us, the name may evoke joy or sadness, peace or fear. And so it is with the LORD – Yahweh, I AM WHO I AM. Those who are without Christ may despise and fear the Name. To those made righteous in Christ, his name is a strong tower. The mere mention of the name evokes joy and peace and confidence, as expressed in this hymn by John Newton:

How sweet the Name of Jesus sounds
In a believer's ear!
It soothes his sorrows, heals his wounds,
And drives away his fear.

It makes the wounded spirit whole,
And calms the troubled breast;
'Tis manna to the hungry soul,
And to the weary rest.

Dear Name! the Rock on which I build,
My Shield and hiding place,
My never-failing Treasury filled
With boundless stores of grace;

Jesus, my Shepherd, Brother, Friend,
My Prophet, Priest, and King,
My Lord, my Life, my Way, my End,
Accept the praise I bring.

Weak is the effort of my heart,
And cold my warmest thought;
But when I see thee as thou art,
I'll praise thee as I ought.

Till then I would thy love proclaim
With ev'ry fleeting breath;
And may the music of thy Name
Refresh my soul in death.

The Imagined Wall

Proverbs 18:11

A rich man's wealth is his strong city,
*   and like a high wall in his imagination.*

Note the contrast with the previous proverb. The righteous man
looks to the LORD to be his strength; the rich man looks to his

wealth. The righteous man turns to the LORD and finds safety; the rich man turns to his wealth and finds an illusion. For wealth can save no one. It can create an illusion of safety, but it not only fails to protect; it creates its own dangers.

A wealthy man must take measures to protect his wealth. He must protect himself from others who seek his harm because he is wealthy. He cannot distinguish for sure those who are his friends and those attracted to his wealth. His wealth cannot protect him from slander nor from jealousy. He can fall in disgrace and lose his family.

Or even more dangerous, his wealth can make him happy all his days. It can protect him from constructive criticism and keep him entertained enough so that he does not consider his heart. It can deceive him into thinking he really is powerful. And thus he learns only at his death that his "high wall" was an imagination all along.

The Haughty Fool

Proverbs 18:12

Before destruction a man's heart is haughty,
  but humility comes before honor.

There are several reasons why this proverb bears out, but consider one reason today. Haughtiness is foolishness; humility is wisdom. To be haughty is to be "scornfully and condescendingly proud." It is not merely to recognize your own skill to be better than others, but to actually consider others as lesser beings. You despise them merely because they are not as adept in some particular skill as you are or because they have backgrounds that seem beneath you.

This is a poor attitude for a number of reasons, but again, it actually makes you foolish and thus more likely to take a spill. You will overestimate your ability and take foolish risks. You will deny yourself the benefit of other persons' skills. You will cut yourself off from good relationships and partnerships. You will not prepare for the future, failing to see that you are likely to lose whatever great gift it is that you possess. Thus, you are setting up your own destruction.

Humility is wisdom because it frees you up to see clearly what are and what are not your strengths. It allows you to seek the help of others. You forge strong relationships and partnerships; you think now how to prepare for the future. You win the respect of others, and, thus, you are likely to receive honor.

But where foolishness and wisdom are most realized is in one's standing before God. Scripture makes plain that he will destroy the proud and raise up the humble. This may play out in one's earthly life (which it often does); it certainly will occur in the Day of Judgment, at which time there will be no opportunity for repentance. Thus we see the greatest folly of the haughty person who thinks that he can actually outwit God.

The Foolish Answer

Proverbs 18:13

If one gives an answer before he hears,
it is his folly and shame.

Strong but true words. We do this on different levels. There is the surface level in which we actually begin answering before the person has completed the question, only to find that we wrongly anticipated what the question would be. "No, that is not what I was trying to ask."

We give unasked for answers, such as when a person is sharing a concern, and we take it upon ourselves to give solutions when all the person wanted was a listening ear. "Thank you, but I already know what to do."

And there is the level in which a question has been asked, and we miss the target in our response. "No, you don't understand." And the reason we don't understand is that we did not hear well. This might be for a number of reasons. The person did not articulate himself well, thus misleading us. But we could have dealt with that by asking good questions first that helped the person communicate better.

Quite often the reason we do not hear well is that we are formulating an answer while the person is still communicating. We don't want to be caught without a wise answer, so we begin thinking through a reply while he is still speaking.

Don't worry about having answers. It is better not to have an answer than to have a wrong one. If you must disappoint your inquirer, it is better to disappoint by confessing that you do not know the answer, rather than to disappoint by leading the person astray and making the matter more befuddling and leading to greater shame.

But you are more likely to have a wise answer if your primary concern is to listen well. Take the time to listen. Ask good questions. Do not be in a hurry to reply. And most importantly, pray for wisdom. You will be surprised by the answers that you did not have the wisdom for but were given at the right time by the Holy Spirit.

The Crushed Spirit

Proverbs 18:14

A man's spirit will endure sickness,
but a crushed spirit who can bear?

Undoubtedly many of you reading this proverb will sadly nod in agreement because of your own crushed spirit. The weight of depression, of anxiety, of feeling unloved feels unbearable and you focus on merely surviving each day. This proverb lets you know that God understands. It is placed in Scripture for you to know that you do not suffer alone. God is with you and even now is bearing your great weight. You are not alone as a sufferer. Many others throughout the ages and in the present have known the "crushed spirit." Stop at this very moment and offer a prayer for those whose spirits are crushed.

All the more reason it is so important to be about the business of encouraging others. Husbands are told not to be harsh with their wives and do not discourage their children (Col. 3:19, 21). Why? Because such behavior crushes their spirits. So it is in all relationships. Venting anger and criticizing freely crushes. And we willingly crush the spirits of our brothers and sisters all the while claiming to do so for their good because telling the truth is what matters most. We are to speak the truth, but we are to speak the truth in love with the intent to build up one another in Christ (Eph. 4:15-16). And if we must correct a brother or sister of sin then we are to do so in a spirit of gentleness (Gal. 6:1).

Examine your heart today especially in your relationship with those closest to you. Are you building up those closest to you or crushing their spirit? Remember your Lord of whom it was said "a bruised reed he will not break, and a faintly burning wick he will not quench" (Isa. 42:3). Surely he had cause to crush you for your sin and yet chose to become crushed himself (Isa. 53:5) that your spirit might live.

Seek Knowledge

Proverbs 18:15

An intelligent heart acquires knowledge,
  and the ear of the wise seeks knowledge.

Note the precondition of the person who gains knowledge. He is already intelligent, already wise. It is his intelligence and wisdom that spurs him on to attain knowledge. He becomes knowledgeable because he values knowledge. Unlike the student who raises his hand in class and asks the teacher, "Is this going to be on the test," the intelligent person inquires deeper into the subject. He is interested in what he is learning; he wants to learn.

It is this attitude towards knowledge that separates the students who perform well from those who do not. The difference has little to do with ability; it has everything to do with desire.

But even then there is a distinction between the wise and the mere hard worker. The latter will gain knowledge merely as a means to gain a goal such as good grades or a promotion. The wise person seeks knowledge because of true love for knowledge. The result is that the "hard worker" only obtains his particular goal; the wise person becomes wiser; his intelligence is enhanced. Thus his very quality of life and usefulness are magnified.

Seek knowledge. Do not be content with learning as little as needed. Strive to know as much as you can. Strive to know God as deeply as you can. Desire to know the knowledge of his Word. Seek the knowledge of the gospel and of the grace found in Christ. For there is true wisdom and intelligence.

The Giving of Gifts

Proverbs 18:16

A man's gift makes room for him
   and brings him before the great.

What is the difference between a gift and a bribe? Is this proverb permitting the offering of bribes to get one's way? The proverb may not be giving permission for anything. Many proverbs are mere observations about life, adding no comment about the moral value. That is true of this one.

And yet, there are many situations in which a gift may be used wisely. In this proverb the gift is used to win an audience with someone in a greater position. It is mere bribery – that is, a payoff – to pay a sort of fee and obtain unfair advantage over others, especially in the matter of justice. And yet a wise person will take the time to give a pleasing gift that softens an otherwise stony composure and thus win a fair hearing. It is also appropriate to give gifts that express true sentiment of appreciation, such as giving a gift to someone whom you admire.

Again, this is not the case of a rich man able to give a higher cost bribe than his poorer opponent, or deliver secret bribes. Rather, it is the wise paving of the way that allows him to receive his hearing and to enhance good relations. Thus, Jesse sends David to his brothers not only with food for them, but for their commander; Jacob sends gifts to Esau and the brothers bring gifts to Joseph on behalf of their father. The givers are expressing to the recipients that they acknowledge their position of being under the recipients' authority or power. They are not demanding rights but appealing to generosity.

It is in such spirit that we come before our Lord in worship, offering gifts of worship, perhaps our tithes, and certainly offering ourselves in service. Such gifts, the Lord is pleased with, and in his generosity continues to overflow our cup with blessings.

Examination

Proverbs 18:17

The one who states his case first seems right,
*   until the other comes and examines him.*

What a true observation! How many times have we heard one speaker lay forth an argument that seems the epitome of commonsense, only to hear someone else give a different opinion or examine the first speaker, and we then completely change our opinion? Perhaps the first speaker omitted pertinent information; perhaps he operated from presuppositions that needed questioning. Whatever the case, it took another examiner – either one impartial or with a differing opinion – to present a fuller picture.

Thus, we need ourselves not to be quick to form opinions nor to assume that the speaker on our side is always right. This happens in politics and theology where we presume that our guy is the one with the right facts and opinion. Take time to listen to the examiner, regardless of his position. The truth can reside even in the one with the wrong motivation or perspective. We are not to judge by what "seems" right but by the evidence itself. Oftentimes we need someone with another perspective to help us consider what the evidence may be.

A common scenario is our taking sides in a dispute before listening to each party. Take, for example, a marital conflict. One spouse shares with you how he or she has been wronged. You are sympathetic and now become angry with the other spouse. You either hold a grudge or even confront the other spouse with his or her wrongdoing. What then happens? The conflict escalates. Before you bothered to hear the other side, you made accusations which only increased the trouble between the couple. Do not be quick to judge. The proverb is right: The one who states his case first seems right. But seeming right and being right are not the same thing. It is fine to be sympathetic but not to rush to conclusions.

Finally, give thanks that we have a Lord who judges not by what his eyes see or ears hear, but only with righteousness and equity (Isa. 11:4). And give thanks that we have God's Word that gives, not an opinion, but truth by which we may judge the opinions of others, including ourselves.

Casting the Lot

Proverbs 18:18

*The lot puts an end to quarrels
   and decides between powerful contenders.*

It is interesting how the casting of lots or drawing straws or flipping coins settles matters that could produce controversy or are already controversial. Rival teams let a coin flip decide who gets the ball first; kids arguing over who has to take the worse job will meekly accept the result of drawing the shortest straw. There is an odd sense of fairness to committing a decision to chance. That is when there is no clear reason for choosing one side or person over the other, or sometimes simply to avoid the ill will that choosing will cause.

There is some kind of resignation to a "higher" decision through committing decisions to "chance." All the more then, Christians ought to accept the seemingly random events that result in pleasant and unpleasant consequences. We are to accept our lots as coming from the Lord to be used for his purposes for his glory and our good. Scripture is not teaching us to cast lots to make our decisions, but it is teaching us to accept the consequences of all decisions, however random they may seem, as God working out his purposes.

Instead of wallowing in self-pity or anger over "bad luck," we should be exploring how God wants us to live for his glory. Instead of swelling with pride over our "good luck," we should be moved to humility and exploring how God wants us to live for his glory. What matters in life is not so much what lot we get, but what we do with whatever lot is ours. Whether we get heads or tails, the short straw or the long straw, what matters is what we do in the circumstance. And what we do will ultimately lie in our confidence in God's sovereignty and goodness. And our confidence will ultimately lie in how much we treasure Jesus Christ and the grace shown to us through him.

Breaking Through Bars

Proverbs 18:19

A brother offended is more unyielding than a strong city,
  and quarreling is like the bars of a castle.

The closer a relationship the deeper an offense is felt. It may or may not be easier to offend a brother, but when he is offended the wound goes deep, as is the witness of many, many family divisions. The offense only goes deeper and the brother more unyielding when the offender tries to argue his case which ends up in quarreling.

How to break through the city wall and the castle bars? Here are practical steps to take: Listen. Take the time to hear out the offended brother. Ask good questions that help you understand what he is saying and how and why he feels the way he does. Don't be satisfied until you are able to articulate to his satisfaction his side and feelings.

That's about it. You will be amazed at how easily your brother's defense system comes down when he believes you really understand him. Because he is your brother (or sister), he wants resolution and reconciliation. But he cannot bring down his defenses until he knows you understand him and that you will not attack once he brings them down.

It sounds too simple, but you will be surprised at how effective it is.

The reason? You are having to put down your attack weapons and your own defenses in order to listen well. You are having to make changes in yourself. And the best chance of our brother making the changes we think he needs to make is when he sees us making our own for his sake.

Fruit of the Mouth

Proverbs 18:20

From the fruit of a man's mouth his stomach is satisfied;
  he is satisfied by the yield of his lips.

This proverb is based on the assumption that the fruit is good. When our speech produces good fruit by blessing others and conveying wisdom and knowledge, then we receive blessing, as when satisfied by a good, healthy meal. Conversely, when our speech stirs up trouble and offense, we will experience our own stomach aches.

To delve deeper, Jesus pointed out that it is what comes out of a man that defiles him. Thus, the fruit of a man's mouth does not spring from the mouth but from the heart. Most of what we say, we say without conscious thought. We merely react with our mouths to what we see or hear. Those reactions will reflect the condition of our hearts. Do we speak carelessly often causing offense? Do we speak foolishly? Do we find ourselves having to apologize regularly for offending others, even though we really don't understand what all the fuss is about?

Good fruit ultimately reflects good soil. Give attention to the soil in your heart that you might bear good fruit in your mouth and be satisfied.

The Power of the Tongue

Proverbs 18:21

Death and life are in the power of the tongue,
  and those who love it will eat its fruits.

Bad and good result from the power of speech; those who love speech will reap the consequences of how they use it. This proverb carries the weight of a warning to those who love to talk and those who skillfully use speech for bad ends. Sooner (usually) or later (for those who are skilled), one will eat the fruit of one's wicked ends.

Over and again the proverbs teach the power of the tongue for good and ill, and thus the necessity to exercise godly wisdom. Do not be quick to speak. Think before you do speak. Seek such a heart that the words which pour out of it will be good and true. Death and life are in the power of the tongue both for those who hear your words and you yourself.

Those of you who are given the gift of speech, such as teachers, trainers, preachers, and counselors, all the more you must use your gift wisely. For as you use your gift of speech, so your reward will be measured out to you, good or ill. The same holds true for anyone in a position of authority over others – parent over child, teacher over student, supervisor over employee, elder over church member. Your speech carries power for death or life. A momentary comment can lift up the spirits of a person that he will never forget; it can also tear him down and be a bitter memory.

Such power should humble us and lead us each day to pray for wisdom to use our tongues wisely and for good, and for mercy for the times we misuse them. Such power should lead us to the wise words of truth found in Scripture. For it is there that all words spring from and lead us to the life that is in Christ.

A Good Thing

Proverbs 18:22

He who finds a wife finds a good thing
and obtains favor from the LORD.

God instituted marriage as a blessing to man. It was "not good" for man to be alone, and so God created and brought the woman to the man. And he realized it was good, for "she is flesh of my flesh and bone of my bone." Marriage is not a trap; it is not a mere social convention to procreate and keep order. Marriage is good. Blessed is the man who finds a good wife, and the woman who finds a good husband.

The husband, who may be wishing for freedom, should especially take note. Your wife is a blessing from the Lord. It does not seem so? Instead of focusing on what you consider her shortcomings, perhaps you need to examine yourself. As head of the marriage, you have the greater control and responsibility for the health of your relationship. Are you taking charge by making the sacrifices of a Christian leader for the person under your care? Are you aware that God is using your wife for your own sanctification? Are you letting your wife know that she is a good gift from the Lord? Understand an important principle in leadership – those for whom you are responsible are likely to live up to or live down to what you communicate about them.

Husbands and wives, give thanks today for your spouses. See the good that the Lord has given you, and communicate to your spouse how good you have it because of them.

Entreaties

Proverbs 18:23

The poor use entreaties,
but the rich answer roughly.

Our status often determines our behavior. If we are poor, we will rely on entreaties to coax help from others. If we are in a position of power or wealthy enough to procure the help we need from many, we are likely to speak roughly or be more demanding.

Think about this in our relationship with the Lord. It is those who recognize their poverty who will humble themselves before him; those who think they are rich in life see no need for him and are offended to be told otherwise. They patronize and ridicule those who are spiritually humble. Their riches – be it of money or talent or pleasures – blind them to their true position. They are impoverished, believing they are rich.

Are you rough sometimes in your speech or thoughts towards the Lord? Do you find yourself at times demanding the help you want? Are you ever resentful, thinking that your good behavior merits better response from God? What do you have that you have not received, even the ability to behave well?

Blessed are the poor in spirit, for theirs is the kingdom of heaven. They turn to their Savior and Lord humbly for all things. They are not blind to their poverty, nor are they blind to the blessings that are theirs in Christ. They make entreaties like the poor, but they receive the blessings of heirs. Entreat the Lord today for his favor and know this – that to all who entreat humbly he answers tenderly and generously.

Closer Than a Brother

Proverbs 18:24

A man of many companions may come to ruin,
but there is a friend who sticks closer than a brother.

It is not the number but the depth of relationships that matter. It is good to have many companions. We are meant to be social creatures, and we should seek and enjoy the acquaintance of many people. And yet, what will sustain us through the trials of life and enrich our happiness is deep, meaningful friendship.

Such friendship arises both out of active and passive experience. You ought to desire and seek close friends. Many of us are reluctant to do so for various reasons, mostly out of timidity and fear of becoming vulnerable. But once a close friendship is formed, then it is a great blessing. For it is good to have a friend who sticks closer than a brother, who can understand and tolerate your moods and failings, who will encourage you when you are down and reprimand you when you are at fault.

But always remember the One who calls you his friend and is not ashamed to be known as your brother. No human friendship is guaranteed to last. We can offend both brother (and sister) and friend, and they can offend us. There is the one friend, Jesus Christ, who has already demonstrated a steadfast love that will never die. Keep up your relationship with him today; he is already sticking closer than a brother.

Better to Be Poor

Proverbs 19:1

Better is a poor person who walks in his integrity
than one who is crooked in speech and is a fool.

There is too high a price to pay for crookedness. The loss of integrity is worse than the loss of money and position. The world considers a person not willing to compromise the truth to achieve a goal to be a fool. So be it. God, through his Word, declares a person who compromises integrity to be a fool. Whose judgment is more likely to be correct? In the end, who more likely will see that his judgment is vindicated?

This applies to politicians who are crooked in speech and promises. It applies to preachers who are crooked with Scripture. It applies to business people crooked about their services and products. It applies to teachers crooked with their responsibilities to their students. The list goes on. Where is the person willing to sacrifice election, promotion, fame, money, or job for the sake of integrity? Where is the "fool" who counts favor with God as greater value than achieving worldly success?

There is only one – Jesus Christ, who walked in integrity even unto his death. Let us walk behind him, leaning on him, until we reach the destination he has prepared for us in our heavenly city.

Desire Without Knowledge

Proverbs 19:2

Desire without knowledge is not good,
  and whoever makes haste with his feet misses his way.

Is this not the cause of our troubles? We desire without knowledge. The young man desires the Forbidden Woman, not knowing that she leads to death. The fool desires fortune and fame, not knowing that he chooses ignominy and destruction. The wicked desire to take advantage of others, not knowing that they are entrapping themselves. Man desires to exalt himself, not knowing that he is debasing himself. Pride, greed, ambition all serve to make us ignorant.

Then we haste to fulfill our desires and thus miss the signs that would lead us aright. Our desires not only blind us but compel us not to look, not to use discernment. The result of all this is that we miss The Desire instilled in us – the desire for God. We substitute it with the trivial and the profane; we substitute it with desires which, if they did spring from desire for God, would be good; but now that we have made idols of them in place of God they become soiled and lead us astray.

Desire is good – desire that is with the knowledge of the fear of the Lord. Such desire leads to what is truly fulfilling, what is lasting, what raises one up to glory. Desire that springs from the love of God found in Jesus Christ – such is abundant joy.

Why, God?

Proverbs 19:3

When a man's folly brings his way to ruin,
  his heart rages against the Lord.

This is so true of Christians. "Why can't I get a job?" "Why are my workplaces always so difficult?" "Why is this ministry by which I serve God filled with so much trouble?" "Why, when I am devoted to God, am I having so much trouble in my marriage, in my family, with my health, in my church?"

Doesn't God keep his promises to bless his children? Doesn't he reward those who serve him and make sacrifices for him? Why won't he/can't he control the behavior of others (especially other believers) who are making our life so difficult? Doesn't God care? Doesn't he see what our troubles are? Can't he be merciful to us? What have we done so wrong?

What we will not do is examine our folly. Sometimes the folly is direct and obvious. I am in trouble at work because I lied about my performance. My marriage is in trouble because of my unfaithfulness. Oftentimes the folly is subtle or the consequences follow folly committed long before. My marriage is in trouble because of my sins committed long before leaving me with disease or in debt. It could be the folly of unwise decisions. I can't get good work because I decided not to get the education needed when I was able to get it.

The point is that we are always more quick to put blame on someone else, including God, than to own up to our folly. "Bad" things do happen to good people and even because we are doing what is right. Suffering will happen to those who follow God. But suffering is as likely to happen because of our folly. We made foolish decisions; we gave way to foolish behavior, spoke foolishly, panicked foolishly, acted with pride foolishly, doubted God foolishly.

And then we questioned God about his goodness, his faithfulness, his mercy. Folly leads to folly.

True Friendship

Proverbs 19:4

Wealth brings many new friends,
but a poor man is deserted by his friend.

If the writer of this proverb had access to quotation marks in his day, he would have added them around "friends" and "friend." In each instance the friends are nothing of the sort. The friends of the wealthy person hang about to get what they can. The poor person has but one other person willing to "be a friend." Such a friend is obviously not hanging about to share in the wealth, but he is a "fair-weather" friend, the kind of person who will not be dependable. Indeed, he will desert his poor friend as soon as he thinks the poor man wants something from him.

Are there true friends? Yes, but such friends are cultivated. The bonds of friendship are forged through sharing experiences and through learning to give-and-take with each other. And one more ingredient is necessary – the friend himself must have integrity, at least regarding the friendship. A trusted friend must be trustworthy. And, again, that trustworthiness can only be tested through experience.

How do you find such a friend? The most sure way is to cultivate trustworthiness in your own heart. It is more difficult than it may seem, for your own trustworthiness is purified through the fires of trials.

Give thanks for our Friend, Jesus Christ, who walked into the fire of trial to demonstrate his trustworthiness and to make us trustworthy.

No Escape

Proverbs 19:5

A false witness will not go unpunished,
    and he who breathes out lies will not escape.

The irony in this proverb is that people lie for the express purpose of escaping punishment. We lie to cover up other sins. We fudge the truth so that our spouses will not get upset; so that our bosses will not blow up at us, etc. We will lie so that suspicion is passed on to others. Our lying so that we can get ahead is a form of escape. We think that our present status, our present financial state, our present job and position in life is not as good as it should be. We want to escape it and climb higher. We lie on our tax forms to escape more taxes   to   pay.

But such lies, though they may seem to provide escape, are merely leading us into entrapment. As often as not, our sins are found out and our lies prove only to magnify their gravity. But more to the point, we cannot lie before or to our Maker, who sees all things even into our hearts. Furthermore, we cannot lie about our faith. We can fool others about our faith, but we cannot fool God.

Before you can exercise faith, you must exercise honesty. You cannot be inwardly convicted about what you will not own up to. You cannot repent what you will not admit. You cannot turn in faith to your Redeemer if you will not confess your true need. And you cannot grow close to your Lord if you try to deceive him. Remember then that your goal is not to escape, except to escape from the clutches of sin and lying. You want to be caught by your Lord who is your Redeemer. You want to be forced to confess your sin and your need for your Savior. Like the father caught in his own lie – "I believe" – you want to be caught in mid-sentence and cry out – "Help me in my unbelief!" (cf. Mark 9:22ff)

Seeking Favor

Proverbs 19:6

Many seek the favor of a generous man,
and everyone is a friend to a man who gives gifts.

"Generous man" could be translated "nobleman" or "prince." Whatever the case, the point is that the person in a position to bestow gifts – be it of money, of position, of power – will have many "friends" who in truth are lovers of what he can give. The person may understand this and so all the more love his position because he can get "friends" to show him attention. The end result, however, is his own downfall from the ego that swells up in him, and the desertion of such friends when the downfall comes.

The irony of such behavior is that the One who rules over all and is more than generous is the one such "friends" are least likely to turn

305

to. What does God offer? All the riches in Christ Jesus. He offers not only escape from damnation, but eternal bliss. He offers food and drink without cost. He paid the greatest cost in order to offer these marvelous gifts. Furthermore, he guarantees what he gives. Think about this. The one thing that is the most important – eternal joy – is the one thing that he gives away and guarantees that we cannot lose.

And how do most people respond? "No thanks." C. S. Lewis was right. Our problem is not that we desire too much, but that we are satisfied with so little. Seek the favor of this generous King who gives costly gifts beyond measure. You who have turned to Christ: why do you act as though you do not have his favor? Why do you act as though you are poor, that your King does not give you gifts? It is such an attitude that keeps the lost from turning to our King, because they look at you and conclude that he is a poor giver. Make them envious of the gifts of peace, of love, of so many other gifts that you have in Christ.

The "Poor" Man

Proverbs 19:7

All a poor man's brothers hate him;
  how much more do his friends go far from him!
He pursues them with words, but does not have them.

If a wealthy, generous man has many friends, a poor man with nothing to give has none. They not only do not hang around him; they stay far from him. Of course, such "friends" are neither true friends of the generous man nor the poor man.

These "friends" are the true losers. At best they may gain some material favor. But what they gain with it is a bad reputation for lacking integrity, for not being trustworthy, for selfishness, and other shameful traits. They also miss out on what is of greater value than material prosperity – true friendship. They have no one they can count on, no one for comradeship, no one who will be for them in time of need. They will ever experience loneliness, ever live in suspicion of others who share their same worthless values.

And they are made blind to who truly is wealthy and rich. The reason many turned away from Jesus is that he was perceived to be poor. The reason many keep away from him now is that his Body is perceived to be poor. All his Church has to offer is the gospel, which seems a poor substitute to the "wealth" that Satan and the world have to offer. Such "friends" miss out on the riches that are in Christ Jesus as they move forward to their destruction.

Got Sense?

Proverbs 19:8

Whoever gets sense loves his own soul;
  he who keeps understanding will discover good.

Do you love yourself? Do you want what is good for you? Then pursue wisdom! Seek commonsense. Value understanding and discernment. Get knowledge. For it is through attaining good sense – the skill to discern what is right and true and good – that you will discover and enjoy the good in life.

How do you get sense? You pray for it; you study God's Word; and you observe. You observe what God reveals through natural revelation. You study the knowledge he gives to anyone through his common grace. You learn from the experiences – all the experiences – he takes you through.

More importantly, you study the knowledge God's Spirit gives through his special grace of revealing the gospel. It is through the gospel that you may now look at everything else. Explore redemption; explore what salvation entails; explore what it means to be adopted in Christ, to be sealed by the Holy Spirit; explore justification and sanctification. As you dig deeper into gospel truth; as you delve into the holy attributes of the God who made you and saved you; as you seek such wondrous knowledge, so you will grow in good sense and understanding.

And then keep understanding as you would keep any treasure you may possess. You hold on to it, take pleasure in it, work to protect it and add to it. For the more understanding you have and the greater care you take to keep it, the more useful it becomes in leading you to discover good. Indeed, the more useful it becomes in leading you to the One alone who is Good.

The Liar's Destiny

Proverbs 19:9

A false witness will not go unpunished,
  and he who breathes out lies will perish.

This is the same proverb as 19:5, except that it spells out what is alluded to in the previous one which states that the liar will "not escape." He will perish. However much he may try to lie his way out of such a destiny, his lies only serve to secure that destiny. Punishment will come, judgment will take place, and the verdict will be death.

The biggest lie of the liar is the one he makes to himself – that he will escape such an end. He is the fool who has bought into the lie of the first liar Satan – "You will not die." If only he would listen to the words of the one who is Truth – "You shall know the truth and the truth shall make you free" (John 8:32).

What is Fitting

Proverbs 19:10

It is not fitting for a fool to live in luxury,
  much less for a slave to rule over princes.

It is not fitting for a fool who has done nothing to earn or deserve wealth to live in wealth. Like a pig with pearls, he will treat his wealth with disdain, not merely indulging in worthless pursuits but turning what is beautiful and noble into base objects. There is something to appreciating what is of value and beauty. Unlike the tragic figure who appreciates such things, but cannot restrain his vices, the fool neither appreciates what is good nor recognizes his vices.

It is not fitting for a slave to rule over princes, for princes ought to fit their position by truly being noble, wise, and just. They ought not to be subject to manipulation by those under them. This is not a comment on slaves being kept in their places but, rather, on those given positions of power to use their positions wisely and ably.

Indeed, the rise of the fool and the slave is more a comment about the failure of those entrusted with power and influence to use that power for the good, assuring that those who rise to wealth and power are those who earn such reward, and not merely obtain them by luck or deceit.

What is fitting? For us who are princes and princesses by virtue of belonging to Christ, it is to use our position for good. If we have wealth, then use it responsibly both in terms of helping others and in valuing what is truly admirable and beautiful. If we have power and influence, then use such possessions for the common good, dispensing justice. We are to display the justice and the nobility of our Prince Jesus Christ.

Good Sense and Anger

Proverbs 19:11

Good sense makes one slow to anger,
and it is his glory to overlook an offense.

Here is a good measure for how much good sense you have: How do you respond to offenses? Are you quick to retaliate? Do you quickly throw back a verbal jab? Do you get easily flustered? Do you dash off curt emails or text messages? Then good sense is lacking.

What is the connection between good sense and controlling one's temper? For one thing, the person with good sense understands that angry responses are more likely to worsen a given situation rather than resolve it. Because he knows his goal is to bring resolution and understanding to the matter at hand, he controls his temper.

Also, the person with good sense understands what should and should not bother him. Injustice committed against those who cannot defend themselves will make him quick to be angry. Personal offenses thrown at him by those who are foolish or by those caught in a foolish moment will have little effect on him. Such offenses have no weight and thus will not harm a person with good sense.

So today, when a car pulls in front of you; when the co-worker at the office makes a curt remark; when you get a silly email, show good sense. Show that what really matters to you is the regard of Christ for you, who is your model for one who knew his goal and loved his Father and thus could endure the foolish offenses of many.

Like Dew

Proverbs 19:12

A king's wrath is like the growling of a lion,
but his favor is like dew on the grass.

Consider the wrath of our King. When he acts in wrath against the wicked, no one can withstand his ire. For it is not that he acts with an uncontrollable rage, but precisely because his anger matches justice. God is to be feared because he is just, and as Supreme King he is able to carry to the fullest the just wrath that the wicked deserve.

But his divine favor is all the more blessed to receive for it comes freely and generously. His favor is not distributed arbitrarily nor is it earned by ingenuity or hard labor. His favor is mercy; his favor is grace. By his grace he extends his mercy to those whom he has called to be not merely his subjects, but his very children.

And so today, give thanks for his favor, which like dew on the grass, refreshes you each day, not merely to get through the day but to take delight in your King. Your trials are not the result of his wrath bringing forth punishment; but as a father disciplines his beloved son for his good, so your King brings trials your way to purify your faith, to all the more increase your yearning for the day of glory to come, to let you share in the sufferings of your Lord, to make you compassionate toward others, to protect you from sin. Your King, if he is your Father, turns toward you the face of his favor. Give thanks.

Bringing Ruin

Proverbs 19:13

A foolish son is ruin to his father,
and a wife's quarreling is a continual dripping of rain.

The way to break the spirit of a man is through his family. It may be through the folly of a child or through the grumbling of a wife. There is much to be said in Proverbs and Scripture to admonish the husband and father, but this proverb is directed to the impact of poor behavior on the man.

The foolish son is ruin to his father in two ways. One, his folly often leads to financial repercussions, as well as impacting the father's reputation in the community. Thus a son can literally bring his father to ruin. But then there is the inner ruin of spirit. The son's folly drives grief into the father's spirit. Whatever else may be fulfilling in the father's life, the grief over his son stays with him.

Regarding the wife, however much she may have cause to quarrel about her husband's behavior and attitude, the effect of the quarrel is to drain him of desire to change. Like the incessant dripping of rain, the quarrels steadily wear him down.

We all have more power than we realize. Though the father and husband supposedly have the power to exercise authority, nevertheless, they can be brought down through those who are closest to them. So we may impact anyone through our folly and grumbling. We can bring down the best of leaders and destroy the morale of the best teachers. We can ruin those who love us, who in some way care for us. We can ruin them by breaking their spirits.

311

Today, will you lift up the spirits of those you love and those around you, or will you pull them down?

The Blessing of Prudence

Proverbs 19:14

House and wealth are inherited from fathers,
  but a prudent wife is from the Lord.

If a foolish son and a quarreling wife are ruin to a man, all the more blessed it is to have a prudent wife. Why prudent? Why not loving? A prudent wife is a loving wife, for she takes care of her husband and home. The epitome of such prudence is found in Proverbs 31:10-31. A prudent wife is one who exercises wisdom and discretion in practical matters. Her home is kept in order. She takes care of the children. She strives to be a helpmeet to her husband. Truly a man with such a wife is blessed by the Lord.

Likewise, men are to be prudent, as the first part of the proverb demonstrates. The man receives a house and wealth as an inheritance from his father who exercised prudence in providing for his family. The father heeded the proverbs which taught to be industrious, to use discretion with money, to slowly build up wealth and not to spend it foolishly. Truly a wife and children with such a husband and father are blessed by the Lord.

Slothfulness

Proverbs 19:15

Slothfulness casts into a deep sleep,
  and an idle person will suffer hunger.

Laziness makes a person weary. Inactivity slows down the body's metabolism. Taking it easy causes even the easy to become laborious. And as activity grows more wearisome, so then one is unable to produce a living.

312

We see this in the workplace. There is the employee who drags into work. He then takes a long time to "settle in." He needs his coffee; he needs to chat a bit. He needs to ease into his work. He then needs to take breaks, check his email, check the news, see how others are doing. He always "has a lot to do"; if only the company would hire more people. In essence he is in a deep sleep even during his waking hours.

Then he wonders why others get promoted over him. He thinks his supervisor doesn't understand his situation. Nor, now that he thinks about it, did the supervisor in his other job, nor any of the supervisors in the jobs he bounces around in. He suffers hunger in that he cannot afford the things he wants or advance as he thinks he should. But even his hunger cannot move him to do what is necessary because it is more comfortable to rest, to sleep than to be productively active.

So it is with many spiritually. There are many who are quite active in attaining worldly success, but are in a deep sleep spiritually because, well...they just aren't "religious." They move about in their dream world unwilling to wake up from their comfortable beds. They too suffer hunger, but their idleness keeps them from seeking God. They also easily come up with excuses: Who can know the truth? Too many religions. A God of love will not condemn. I have a good heart. Religion is just too much work.

What will mark you day today? Slothfulness or productive activity?

Despising Life

Proverbs 19:16

Whoever keeps the commandment keeps his life;
  he who despises his ways will die.

Most likely the sense of despising one's ways is that of being careless about how one lives. Such a person is not so much defiant against

God's commands as he is uninterested in the subject. His motto is "go with the flow."

Such a person ultimately is defiant, and he would be surprised to learn to whom it is he shows disdain. It is himself. He is willing to forfeit eternal happiness to go with the flow. Many persons would be surprised to find that they fit the category of such a lackadaisical person. There is the 92 year-old man renown for physical fitness. He exudes vitality. There is the young entrepreneur who in his thirties has achieved wealth through hard work and tenacity. But both will die, and they do not seem to be interested about keeping the commandment that will give eternal life. They are careless about their ways.

What kind of witness are you to such persons? They would have to see in you someone as committed to the gospel as they are to health and wealth. They would have to see in you someone who is as exuberant about the gospel as they about their passions. Would they see in you something to envy?

God and the Poor

Proverbs 19:17

Whoever is generous to the poor lends to the Lord,
  and he will repay him for his deed.

The lesson of this proverb is not about how to place God in our debt and make him give us what we want. It is about caring for the poor. It shows the compassionate heart of God for the poor, what we often lack.

We want to see a return for our money. We want to be assured that the poor will spend the money wisely. We would prefer a background check. Did this person become poor out of circumstances beyond his control or did he contribute to it by his behavior? If so, what is he doing productively to get out of his situation? Will he be asking for more money?

Generosity to the poor is more than giving money. It is taking time to treat them as people precious in God's sight. It includes treating them with dignity. To be generous means to go beyond what is convenient and to give of ourselves as we would to those close to us.

Remember, the poor represent outwardly our inward condition before God who was and is generous to us. He already pours out his riches in Christ, not because he has ascertained we are a worthwhile investment, but because he is generous to the poor.

It is true that we should give wisely and give in a way that helps. But don't let that become an excuse to be cold-hearted and to resent the poor. Be generous in deed and in spirit.

Right Discipline

Proverbs 19:18

Discipline your son, for there is hope;
 do not set your heart on putting him to death.

As a high school principal I learned how to discern which poorly performing students had potential of turning things around and which were likely to remain mired in their self-defeating behavior. It was the response of their parents to discipline. If their parents were quick to defend their children when disciplined, it was a sign of doom for the students. If their parents supported discipline and added their own, then there was hope that at some point the students would catch on to where their behavior was leading them and begin to apply themselves.

Right discipline is what parents do because they love their children and have hopes for their success. The absence of discipline is a sign that parents have given up hope or have never had special hopes to begin with. In essence their unacknowledged intent is their children's deaths – figuratively and even literally. Their hope is not to be bothered by their children.

Give thanks that we have a Father who loves us enough to discipline us, who allows for our bad behavior to bring upon us difficult consequences. Give thanks for a Father who leads us through trials that our faith may be purified. Give thanks for a Father whose sure hope is our eternal life, and thus will do whatever is necessary to lead us to our destination, causing all things to work for our good.

Give thanks that we have a Brother who received the discipline of death that we might live; whose sufferings led to our blessings and turned our sufferings into loving discipline of a kind Father.

Of Wrath and Consequences

Proverbs 19:19

A man of great wrath will pay the penalty,
for if you deliver him, you will only have to do it again.

You will have to bail the angry man out of jail again, or defend him in the principal's office again, or speak up for him at work again, or whatever the circumstance may be. A person whose temper explodes gets himself into trouble time and again.

He may be a well-intentioned person; he may even be kind. But if he cannot control his temper, all of his good intentions and kindnesses are lost in the wave of his temper tantrums. It is the wrath that is remembered. It is the wrath that lingers about him. And sooner or later, he must pay the penalty. He lands in jail and does not get out. He is expelled from school. He is fired from his job. And it is his reputation as a "man of wrath" that stays pinned on him. He is disqualified for leadership; he cannot serve as an elder (1 Tim. 3:3).

At best he is tolerated. "You know _____. That's just the way he is." The best hope for him is to receive the consequences of his wrath, and thus be stirred enough to get the help he needs. Only humility is powerful enough to control anger, and humility comes through bearing the consequences of one's behavior.

316

Do you have a problem with wrath? You will not make headway until you own up to your sin and do not excuse it nor try to minimize its severity. Do not underestimate its power to ruin your reputation and destroy your successes. Humility is your only hope.

Listen and Accept

Proverbs 19:20

Listen to advice and accept instruction,
*   that you may gain wisdom in the future.*

The wise understand this principle, for it is what led them to a higher plane of wisdom. Their desire to learn allowed them to seek instruction in the first place. Their interest is not in being perceived as knowledgeable, but rather they value knowledge itself. Furthermore, they understand that what may seem to be useless knowledge when they first learn it, becomes valuable in the future. The advice of the father to his son that seemed pointless in younger years is what came to their rescue in later years. The seemingly useless facts learned in school became applicable years later.

But it is not only the information itself that enhances wisdom in the future. The more the skill of listening to advice and accepting instruction is honed, the greater will be one's advance in wisdom. Listening is a skill, and the earlier one develops and practices it, the better equipped he will be in the future to gain the knowledge and wisdom needed.

Learning information is important. You build each year upon the knowledge of earlier years. But knowing how to listen to advice and having the temperament to accept instruction are invaluable for equipping you throughout your life to handle the challenges you will face. The best insurance for the future is wisdom, and the route to wisdom is listening well and accepting instruction.

How well will you listen today? Will you listen to some advice and automatically tune out the advice that is good because it doesn't come from the source you expect? Will hurt feelings keep you from receiving instruction that will help you and increase your wisdom? Listen and accept.

The Purpose of the Lord

Proverbs 19:21

Many are the plans in the mind of a man,
but it is the purpose of the Lord that will stand.

What a humbling and comforting statement. It is humbling to remember that, however clever and powerful we may think we are, our plans only serve *the* plan of the Lord. The rebellion of the wicked serves God's purposes. The service of the righteous is carried out by his sovereign will. How he carries out his will is mystery. What his plans are remain hidden to us except the purpose of his glory through our redemption. Let us remember this as we plan and try to maneuver outcomes to fit what we think should be. It is the purpose of the Lord that will stand.

This is a comforting statement to the redeemed. We are comforted to know that, however it may seem that Satan's purpose is being carried out, all is working to fulfill the Lord's purpose. Our redemption is secure, for the purpose of the Lord will stand. And it is comforting to know that all that is required of us is to do what is right and not to resort to what we think will be effective. We do not need to lie to protect ourselves; we do not need to manipulate others to get them to make a confession; we do not need to use the means of the world to get the world on our side and defeat our enemies. We simply need to be obedient to our Lord. It is he who will see that his purpose will stand.

Steadfast Love

Proverbs 19:22

What is desired in a man is steadfast love,
and a poor man is better than a liar.

It is better to have a poor friend who shows steadfast love through all circumstances than to have wealthy friends who are false. It is better to be a person who shows such love than to attain wealth and friends through deception. Money cannot compare in value to friendship, and friendship is only as valuable as the steadfast love that bonds it.

But understand that what matters is what God desires to see in a person. It is God who desires to see steadfast love. He could care less for the wealth a person has; he values highly the love a person possesses. He detests a liar. Offer to God your wealth, but that wealth should spring out of your steadfast love.

And understand that God values what he possesses. He values steadfast love, for he supremely holds such a trait.

> The steadfast love of God endures all the day (Ps. 52:1)

> Answer me, O Lord, for your steadfast love is good (Ps. 69:16).

> It is good...to declare your steadfast love in the morning (Ps. 92:2).

> Oh give thanks to the Lord, for he is good, for his steadfast love endures forever! (Ps. 106:1).

> And how has he supremely demonstrated such love? "In this is love, not that we have loved God but that he loved us and sent his Son to be the propitiation for our sins" (1 John 4:10).

Fear of the Lord

Proverbs 19:23

The fear of the LORD leads to life,
  and whoever has it rests satisfied;

319

he will not be visited by harm.

The "fear of the Lord" is not a popular concept in modern Christianity. We associate such an idea with pagan religion in which worshippers cringe before an idol in terror or a slave trembling before a cruel master. And yet Scripture portrays the fear of the Lord as something to desire. As the proverb says, it "leads to life."

Some say "fear" should be understood as "respect." Fear does include respect, but there is more to it than that. When Isaiah "saw the Lord" (cf. Isa. 6:1ff), he did not pay his respect to God; he cried out, "Woe is me!" When John saw "one like a son of man" (cf. Rev. 1:12ff), he did not politely bow his head. And yet, neither man experienced the sense of terror one feels in the presence of mere power or of evil.

C. S. Lewis' depiction of a holy fear is helpful in understanding the fear of the Lord. In *Perelandra* he describes the feeling of coming in the presence of an "eldil," what we would know as an arch-angel.

> My fear was now of another kind. I felt sure that the creature was what we call 'good,' but I wasn't sure whether I liked 'goodness' so much as I had supposed… Here at last was a bit of that world from beyond the world, which I had always supposed that I loved and desired, breaking through and appearing to my senses: and I didn't like it, I wanted it to go away. I wanted every possible distance, gulf, curtain, blanket, and barrier to be placed between it and me. But I did not fall quite into the gulf. Oddly enough my very sense of helplessness saved me and steadied me. For now I was quite obviously 'drawn in.' The struggle was over. The next decision did not lie with me."

Lewis picks up on why the fear of the Lord allows one to rest satisfied. For what really happens is not that we break through to good, but that "Good" breaks through to us, forcing us to be helpless, forcing us to let the "next decision" lie with God. There is a sense that we cannot trust God until we fear him; we cannot really love God for who he is until we understand what it is to fear him. We cannot really know fear until we behold the "one like a son of man" dying on a cross for our sin.

320

The Impact of Laziness

Proverbs 19:24

The sluggard buries his hand in the dish
and will not even bring it back to his mouth.

The sluggard begins a task and does not complete it, even the simplest task. "I'm tired," he says. Everything is work; it takes too much effort.

But if the hand does not bring back the food to the mouth, then the sluggard will become only more tired and even malnourished. What is the prescription for feeling tired? Doctors say exercise. The very thing a tired person doesn't want to do is what will cure him of his tiredness.

Extend this to productive labor. If the sluggard will push himself to work, he will reap the benefit of affording food and even labor saving devices. He will earn the opportunity to rest if he works productively. His very laziness prevents him from doing what he desires most, which is to rest from strenuous activity.

Thus the sluggard creates worse conditions for himself, which makes the smallest activity strenuous. The energetic person can afford rest, but now that he is energized he enjoys activity. And that becomes the true payoff. The true difference between the sluggard and the active person is that the latter has the energy to enjoy life.

The Scoffer and the Simple

Proverbs 19:25

Strike a scoffer, and the simple will learn prudence;
reprove a man of understanding, and he will gain knowledge.

Strike the scoffer and at best he will curtail his behavior; yet he will not learn. As Proverbs 9:7- 8 notes: "Whoever corrects a scoffer gets himself abuse...Do not reprove a scoffer, or he will hate you." A scoffer is someone to be controlled. His attitude prevents him from actually changing. He only grows more hardened.

The simple, however, might change, whether he be the one receiving punishment or observes it in others. He is the foolish teenager who cleans up his act when a friend dies in a drunken car wreck; he is the person who hangs out with the wrong crowd but wises up when they get arrested. He has a chance to change for the good because he is marked more by folly than by a hardened heart.

The man of understanding welcomes and improves from being reproved. Because his desire is for knowledge rather than to be thought knowledgeable, he benefits from correction. Because he desires more to give than to receive, to be useful than to attain luxury, he benefits from lessons regardless how they are delivered to him.

This is a theme that runs through Proverbs. It is attitude that matters. To be wise one must desire wisdom, and as one grows in understanding then he will all the more grow in wisdom and knowledge. In the matter of wisdom and knowledge, it is true that he who has little will lose what he has, while he who has much will receive all the more.

Pray for the scoffer to be restrained; pray for the simple to learn prudence; pray for yourself that you may be a person of understanding who gains wise knowledge from each day's lessons, however those lessons come your way.

The Rebellious Child

Proverbs 19:26

He who does violence to his father and chases away his mother
  is a son who brings shame and reproach.

Rebellion against parents is an especially grievous offense in Scripture. Striking one's father or mother is punishable by death.

Rebellion against proper authority is wrong, but there is something more involved in the rebellion against parents. Proverbs speaks of the sorrow, bitterness, and shame that parents of a foolish son experience. There is something sacrilegious in committing actual violence against one's parents.

All the more then consider the offense against our heavenly Father. Earthly parents are themselves sinful and can exasperate their children so as to lead to violence. But our Father is righteous. Thus to rebel against him is to do violence against rightful and righteous authority. But more so it is to do violence against one with even closer connection than a parent – the one who created us and keeps watch over us. For we who belong to Christ, it is to rebel against the one who has redeemed us and loves us with a steadfast love.

How great indeed is this steadfast love of the Father. For it is while we were sinners that Christ died for us; it is while we were rebellious enemies that Christ reconciled us. How much more then, now that we are reconciled, shall we be saved by his life (cf. Rom. 5:6-11). How great is the patience of God who forgives all our sins, even the ones committed today! This is not an excuse to sin, but it is an excuse to daily be in awe of our Heavenly Father who loves us with a steadfast love!

Cease and Stray

Proverbs 19:27

Cease to hear instruction, my son,
and you will stray from the words of knowledge.

Stop hearing instruction and you will not only stop learning, but you will stray from the path of knowledge. Ceasing to learn more is not a matter of slowing down and letting others pass you by. Rather, it is straying off the path of knowledge altogether. A patient who stops receiving physical therapy too soon not only stops improving but regresses. So it is for anyone who thinks he no longer needs to hear instruction.

James says that if anyone is a hearer of the word and not a doer, he will forget what he learned (Jas. 1:22ff). Solomon is saying that if anyone thinks he no longer needs to hear, he will begin to do what is wrong. He will stray. He begins to interpret wrongly what he sees. He will make mistakes in judgment. And worse, he will lose his ability to discern when he makes mistakes. He no longer has the ability to hear.

The mark of wisdom is not reaching a plateau where you no longer need instruction. It is reaching the point where you delight in hearing instruction. Certainly for the believer, it is the delight in hearing instruction in the Word of God. The true person of knowledge cannot hear the gospel enough; he cannot receive enough instruction in the teachings of grace nor of the law which guides him in the way of righteousness; he cannot hear too many times about the greatness of his God and the wonders of his works; he cannot desire too much to live a life that glorifies his Lord.

Devouring Iniquity

Proverbs 19:28

A worthless witness mocks at justice,
  and the mouth of the wicked devours iniquity.

This is yet another proverb recognizing the inner nature of the wicked. They do not act wickedly out of ignorance. They do not have a misguided sense of justice. Showing them the error of their ways does not bring repentance. Rather, they are pleased that the error of their ways is receiving recognition.

They like wickedness. As the proverb points out, they eat it up. To get away with a lie makes their day. A lie is not merely a tool to get out of trouble or to gain something they value. As a craftsman delights in the work itself, so the liar delights in his art of lying. The wicked sleep well at night. Like the righteous who lie in bed satisfied with having done good, the wicked are satisfied by having done evil.

Therefore pray for the wicked who believe the one big lie – that they are getting away with their wickedness. For the day of retribution will come. Pray for the wicked, for their only hope is that the Holy Spirit will turn their hearts of stone into hearts of flesh. Pray for the wicked whose evil deeds illustrate what we still do in our thoughts and too often in our own deeds, however subtle they may be. We all sin because we want to sin. Pray for the wicked, for such were we without Christ. Our hearts too were hearts of stone, and we are counted righteous only by the work of Christ for us.

The Scoffer and the Fool

Proverbs 19:29

Condemnation is ready for scoffers,
and beating for the backs of fools.

Condemnation and beating is what scoffers and fools prepare for themselves. Scoffers will not win hearers (unless they are other scoffers and fools). For a brief time, some may try to listen to them, but they will quickly realize that the scoffers have nothing constructive to say. They will see that scoffers delight in mocking rather than building up. Similarly, some will try to reason with fools but will learn the very folly of such effort.

Thus, all that is left for scoffers is condemnation. They will not listen to reason and even chastisement has no effect. They cannot be re-educated or reformed. What remains is to ignore them, and, if they make themselves too much of a nuisance, then to punish them. The best that can be done is to restrain them until their time of condemnation.

With fools there is at least the possibility that a beating will sober them. They may possibly change some behavior to avoid punishment. Reason, however, is of little avail, as the earlier chapters about lady Wisdom calling out to the foolish and not being heard demonstrated.

All the more wondrous then is the work of God in us. For we scoffed at his commandments and foolishly thought ourselves wise

325

to ignore him. Yet, instead of condemnation, instead of beating, we received mercy. The Son of God was wounded for our transgressions; he was crushed for our iniquities; upon him was the chastisement that brought us peace, and with his stripes we are healed (Isa. 53:5).

The Mocker and the Brawler

Proverbs 20:1

Wine is a mocker, strong drink a brawler,
  and whoever is led astray by it is not wise.

The drinker takes on the personality of what he drinks. He becomes silly, turns foolish, and loses all sense of control so that he becomes a brawler. Many drink because alcohol releases natural inhibition. The shy person becomes extroverted, but he also loses control of his commonsense. He may feel uninhibited, but in truth the alcohol controls him. He cannot make his own decisions.

For many, alcohol gives them a mean personality. They easily take offense when others do not see how wonderful their lack of inhibition makes them. They are surprised to find others taking offense when they mock people. Can't everyone see how witty they are? Can't everyone take in the fun?

The drinker certainly is not wise while intoxicated, but his real lack of wisdom lies in not seeing that he cannot control his drinking. Scripture does not condemn the enjoyment of wine, but it does warn of the danger of intoxication. The immediate danger is turning over control of one's own personality. The long range danger is losing control when one is sober. The drinker cannot stop his drinking. He cannot handle reality while sober. He cannot even recognize that he is an alcoholic.

Wine is a mocker and strong drink a brawler, and their primary victim is the one who delights in them.

Provoking to Anger

Proverbs 20:2

The terror of a king is like the growling of a lion;
*   whoever provokes him to anger forfeits his life.*

This proverb is giving warning to those subject to another's power. Just as the person with power should take heed not to be provoked, so the person under another's power needs to exercise proper wisdom not to provoke. Many people have lost jobs, they claim because of principle, but in truth because their pride was hurt or they simply would not do their jobs. See how unreasonable their bosses are! Students may be given "one last" warning to come to class on time or turn in homework and they fail to do so. They are surprised by the anger of the teacher or principal. Even Christians are guilty of such behavior, excusing themselves by claiming religious persecution.

And so it is with many people in their attitude toward God. They hear warning after warning about provoking God's wrath, and they ignore or even mock the very warnings. Like the student who ignores the principal's warning and continues his ways, or the worker who keeps trying to get away without working, they believe they can continue to go their own ways.

But God will not be mocked. His judgment will come. Therefore, pray for such persons. Pray that they will receive such mercy so as to hear and heed the warnings of judgment. Pray that their eyes will be open to their sin that provokes. And pray that we will bear witness through our lives of the good fear of our God who shows a love that is wondrous precisely because of his powerful wrath. For what wondrous love is this that God the Son would forfeit his own life and receive such anger for us?

Of Quarreling and Strife

Proverbs 20:3

It is an honor for a man to keep aloof from strife,
*   but every fool will be quarreling.*

327

To a fool it is dishonor to walk away from a fight. It is shameful to "back down." The fool believes he is protecting his dignity to respond to every perceived slight. The fool believes that he must correct every perceived error, that he must argue every point. He is quick to debate in any setting and with anyone. He feels that if others are offended by his behavior, it is because they are hypocrites who don't want to hear truth; they are cowards who won't take a stand, who are too fearful to speak up or fight for their name.

And yet, what the fool is really demonstrating is his own folly and arrogance. Whether it is the street thug who is quick to pick a fist fight or the intellectual quick to pick a verbal debate, what each reveals is that he is a fool.

It is not only practical to keep from strife; it is not only counted as wise to avoid arguing and fighting when possible; it is honorable to do so. What is being brought out here is not the unwillingness to take a stand for what is right, but avoiding unnecessary strife. It is knowing when to speak and when not to. It is knowing what is and what is not appropriate to say. It is knowing when to walk away and when to remain.

In reality the fool will be quarreling because he likes strife; he likes to offend. The honorable person engages in a fight or a debate only for the purpose of winning over an opponent to his cause or for protecting others. He stands up for justice because he truly cares about justice, not because he likes to make an impression of being for justice.

It gets back to the difference between pride and humility. The goal of the proud fool is to fit an image that he thinks is noteworthy; the goal of the humble wise is to do what is right and honorable before the Lord. Thus the fool will be seen by God for what he is and the wise person will be held up in honor by the Lord.

Empty Harvest

Proverbs 20:4

The sluggard does not plow in the autumn;
  he will seek at harvest and have nothing.

The sluggard does not plow in the time when the cold begins merely because it feels cold. No season is a good time for him to plow. Either it is too cold or too hot, too dry or too wet. And if the weather is ever right, then it is too nice a day to work!

The odd thing about the sluggard is that he still expects to find a harvest. He is surprised to find no fruit from his non-labor. He was sure he had plowed or that someone else had done it for him. He certainly thought about plowing and intended to get around to it.

And yet all his intentions served no purpose. All his hoping that someone else would do the work has resulted in nothing. He may seek, but he will not find, for he sought the fruit of no work. And as sure as this sluggardly example is repeated over and again through the years, so it is repeated at the end of many lives when souls seek the heavenly reward that does not exist. All the reasons for not studying the Word of life; all the excuses for not laboring for heavenly fruit – they will do the seeker of a harvest no good.

In truth, God will brand all who did not have time for the gospel, who did not have time to find the truth, as sluggards. For it is not so-called intellectual honesty nor scientific inquiry that keeps a person from the truth. Rather it is the laziness of the soul that is content with the ease of not living for God that keeps the field unplowed and the harvest empty.

In Deep Water

Proverbs 20:5

The purpose in a man's heart is like deep water,
  but a man of understanding will draw it out.

Every counselor should know this verse by heart. But the skill is not reserved for professional counselors. It is for anyone with understanding – understanding of what?

It is understanding the biblical teaching about the human heart. That it is sinful and deceptive even to the owner of the heart. That even the redeemed heart will have vestiges of sin which will inflict the owner until he is received into glory. That, nevertheless, all individuals are created in the image of God and receive a measure of God's common grace, so that as wicked as they may be, they also possess great potential for creative, intelligent, even kind acts.

It is understanding biblical teaching about the struggle against the flesh, the world, and the devil – all three are at play tugging at an individual's heart. Every decision he makes is either a giving in or a standing against one or all of these three.

It is understanding the ways individuals have developed to protect their hearts from being examined by others and even themselves – the defenses they put up, the masks they wear, the rationalizing they do, and so on. It is understanding their fears, what motivates them, what arouses them and discourages them.

It is understanding one's own heart and what one needs to do to patiently listen, to love the other person, to let down one's own defenses and be attentive.

A person of understanding is like a good fisherman fishing in deep water. He quietly, patiently, and knowledgeably casts his line and waits.

Steadfast Love and Faithfulness

Proverbs 20:6

Many a man proclaims his own steadfast love,
but a faithful man who can find?

This is a proverb that would have been as an arrow into the heart of Peter, who after proclaiming his willingness to die for his Lord

330

denied him a few hours later. It is a proverb that haunts us all. Over and again we profess our steadfast love for God, and then each day betray ourselves consciously or unconsciously through our sins. We might remain faithful to our tasks of service but are unfaithful in our hearts as we sin in the midst of our service.

Who is faithful? Who has put his hand to the plow and not looked back? Who has stepped out upon the water and not looked at the waves about him? Who in honesty can say that his love has always been steadfast?

All the more then to look to the steadfast love of the Lord and his faithfulness.

> For your steadfast love is before my eyes, and I walk in your faithfulness (Ps. 26:3).

> Your steadfast love, O Lord, extends to the heavens, your faithfulness to the clouds (Ps. 36:5).

> As for you, O Lord, you will not restrain your mercy from me; your steadfast love and your faithfulness will ever preserve me! (Ps. 40:11).

> For your steadfast love is great to the heavens, your faithfulness to the clouds (Ps. 57:10).

> It is good to give thanks to the Lord, to sing praises to your name, O Most High; to declare your steadfast love in the morning, and your faithfulness by night (Ps. 92:1-2).

Blessed Children

Proverbs 20:7

The righteous who walks in his integrity –
blessed are his children after him!

331

Blessed are his children who grow up in a home under his influence. They have a father who models the righteous life before them. They have a father who instructs them in the way of righteousness. They have a father who shows them steadfast love and faithfulness, who loves his wife, and who fears the Lord. For all of this is to walk in integrity.

It is error to restrict integrity to being honest and even to following one's principles. Such "integrity" is defined as being true to oneself. What matters is to be true before the Lord. Honesty that shows no regard for love of one's neighbor is sin. It is a misuse of true honesty. And it is sinful to follow one's principles if they are not God's principles.

A man who will not cheat a client, but who also will not love his children, is not walking in integrity. A man who leaves a legacy of being ruthlessly honest and yet no concern for encouraging others is not walking in integrity. However much money he may leave his children due to his integrity in business, he has not shown integrity before his children and thus leaves them poor in spirit. And if he has left them a legacy of strict law abiding with no understanding of mercy and grace, he has failed to walk in integrity.

Bless your child by integrity that is marked by the fear of the Lord and the love of the Lord; by integrity that nurtures your children and bears the mark of Christ's love.

The Just King

Proverbs 20:8

A king who sits on the throne of judgment
  winnows all evil with his eyes.

So is the task of a just king or a just judge. He listens well and he is a keen observer. He notes the wink or eyes averting his gaze. He sees the smile of arrogance and the nervous twitching of the liar. He sees

332

through the exterior into the heart. Such is the task of the one who rules and judges justly.

If only we had many such judges. It is a skill few have, either out of ineptness or corruptness. How difficult it is to rule and judge well when one has his own guilt and sinfulness to deal with, as well as limitations.

All the more be thankful for the King and Judge who rules in perfect justice and righteousness. Such a thought should bring terror to our hearts, except that this same King and Judge is merciful and wise. In his mercy and by his wisdom he has provided the means by which we who are wicked may stand before him and be declared just. Those who do not understand this mercy will claim that it is a cheap grace that lets sinners off the hook. Those who do understand it are simply moved to bow before such incredulous mercy and wisdom, and all the more strive to live righteous and just lives. There are those who try to "work the system" and make his mercy work for them while they secretly hold on to their sin. But, the "King who sits on the throne of judgment winnows all evil with his eyes."

Who?

Proverbs 20:9

Who can say, "I have made my heart pure;
  I am clean from my sin"?

Let us give thanks now that there is one man who in his human nature was able to say this – Jesus Christ. And because he was able to do so, he qualified to be our sacrificial lamb who made atonement for our sins. Because his heart was pure, he was able to purify our hearts. Because he was always clean, he was able to cleanse us from sin. His sacrifice once and for all removed the guilt of our sins, so that though we cannot claim we have made our hearts pure and cleansed ourselves from sin, we can nevertheless come before our God with hearts that have been purified and cleansed by our Lord. He was not ashamed to call us his brothers and sisters; he is now our sympathetic High Priest who is heard by his Father as he intercedes for us.

All praise be to our Lord Jesus Christ who alone could answer this question with a resounding, "Here I am; I have come to do your will." Because he did, you may now "with confidence draw near to the throne of grace, that you may receive mercy and find grace to help in time of need" (Heb. 4:16).

Abominable Measures

Proverbs 20:10

Unequal weights and unequal measures
are both alike an abomination to the Lord.

Cheating customers is an abomination to the Lord; so is cheating clients and cheating anyone to gain an advantage. What is particularly offensive here is cheating through means that of themselves signify fair play. What can be trusted if we abuse the very seals and symbols that are meant to guarantee good faith?

All cheating is wrong, but its offense is heightened when scam artists take extra care to give a pretense of fairness – presenting false credentials, showing false information, etc. They prey on the poor and the elderly, anyone whom they can take advantage of through their deceit. They are the false advertisers who suffer no twinge of conscience for making fools of others.

They are just like us when we use unequal weights and unequal measures to justify ourselves before the Lord. For that is what we do when we measure ourselves against our neighbors in order to appear righteous before the Lord. The behavior of our neighbors is a false scale, but even then we will use false measures by which to judge them.

How fitting that this proverb follows the previous one: "Who can say, 'I have made my heart pure; I am clean from my sin'?" They are many who dare to make such a claim, but to do so requires using unequal weights and measures; so then, even while trying to prove one's purity of heart, the individual is sinning.

Whatever measuring tool we want to use, understand that the Lord measures with perfect accuracy. We will be weighed on true scales. We will be measured with a true measuring stick. How then will we compare? Here is one way to measure what is in your heart. When you hear such a question, do you begin to think of ways to improve your chances, or do you turn for mercy to the One who alone can justify?

Making Known

Proverbs 20:11

Even a child makes himself known by his acts,
  by whether his conduct is pure and upright.

How do we "make known" what is in our hearts? How do we reveal our faith? By our behavior.

But one can deceive through his actions. One can pretend to be pure and upright. Not a child. He invariably gives himself away even if he wants to deceive. And not even an adult, not if he is observed closely. He will give himself away as well, for he is unable to constantly keep up the pretense. Those whom he fools are those not paying attention.

The bottom line of this proverb, as with other scriptures on the same theme, is that the condition of the heart is revealed through how one lives. When we protest, "What you see is not really me," we are deceiving ourselves. The burst of anger is not produced by outside causes; it springs up from within. As Jesus said, "For from within, out of the heart of man, come evil thoughts" (cf Mark 7:14-23).

It is fine to work on conduct, but we will make the most progress by being keen observers of our conduct and then looking into our hearts. Behavior is my best diagnostic tool for knowing the heart. Don't go by feeling. Go by what is observable.

Eyes and Ears

Proverbs 20:12

The hearing ear and the seeing eye,
the Lord has made them both.

"Who has made man's mouth? Who makes him mute, or deaf, or seeing, or blind? Is it not I, the Lord?" So spoke the Lord to Moses (cf. Exod. 4:10-12). What do we have that is not from the Lord? And what has he given us that is not to be used for his glory?

God has given us ears by which we may hear the gospel and live. He has given us ears that we may hear instruction and obey him. He has given us eyes that we may see the path of righteousness and follow it; eyes to see the stumbling blocks and dangers to avoid.

He has given us the hearing ear and the seeing eye to hear and see that which is good. To use the ear and the eye for sin is to abuse his creative gifts. We are to use our faculties to receive that which is good and true; we are to use our faculties to follow along the paths of goodness and truth; and we are to use them to speak and to show to the ears and eyes of others the goodness and truth of the gospel.

What will you hear and see today?

Sleep Deprivation

Proverbs 20:13

Love not sleep, lest you come to poverty;
open your eyes, and you will have plenty of bread.

Don't suffer sleep deprivation, that is, the sleep that deprives you of being industrious. It is healthy to get a "good night's" sleep, but it is hurtful to linger in bed and block the sun out of your eyes. However comfortable you may feel for the moment, you are robbing yourself.

How so? For one thing, you are robbing yourself of hours of work – work that will produce food or money for food. You cannot earn your pay while sleeping in bed. Another thing is that you are robbing

336

yourself of energy to work. Sleep is necessary to restore a body's energy, but too much sleep tires the body; it tires the mind as well. Activity is necessary to generate energy for body and mind.

And then, too much sleep increases the likelihood that you will miss opportunities that come your way for success. As another proverb outside the Bible says, "The early bird catches the worm." How many opportunities have you missed because sleep kept your eyes closed?

Finally, understand that "sleep" represents more than closed eyes. It is closing the eyes of your mind and of your heart. You can walk around with your physical eyes wide open and still sleep through the opportunities God has provided for you to see him and to see his work. Indeed, your prayer in the morning should be "Lord, open my eyes to all the opportunities you will give me to glorify you this day." The Lord has much bread to give you today if you will but open your eyes and be active serving and enjoying him today.

The Greatest Bargain

Proverbs 20:14

"Bad, Bad," says the buyer,
  but when he goes away, then he boasts.

The savvy shopper does not reveal how much he truly values the object he wants. He is critical of the object. He points out its flaws. He doesn't need it and certainly can't afford what is being asked. All the while he inwardly prizes it. When he does acquire the object, he then may boast of its value. This is how we normally conduct business. We look for a "good deal." We try to get the best bargain we can.

But then there is that rare object whose value is so clear that one would be ashamed to bargain for it. Indeed, the buyer is only too ready to pay full cost. So it is with the gospel, the pearl for which the knowing buyer eagerly gives all that he possesses. Such a pearl the "savvy" buyer cannot buy. It is not available to bargain hunters, even though it is the greatest of all bargains. Even when we give away all

337

that we possess, its value is such that we grow only the richer for possessing it.

The gospel is not an object to haggle over. God cannot be bartered with and certainly not over the matter of the value of his Son's atoning death. He offers the gospel, but not for bartering. He offers it free, but will only give to those who recognize its costliness. And those who obtain it boast only in the Lord's great mercy to them who do not deserve such a gift.

The Precious Jewel

Proverbs 20:15

There is gold and abundance of costly stones,
but the lips of knowledge are a precious jewel.

Like the previous proverb, this one presents a scenario that goes against the common wisdom of the marketplace. There are those who train to become experts in identifying pure gold and costly jewels. Such items are valued for their beauty, but their market value is based on their rarity. However beautiful a jewel may be, if there are many comparable gems then its value diminishes.

The lips of knowledge are a precious jewel. In comparison to the amount of gold and costly stones, they are more rare and all the more to be valued. There are many persons who know lots of information; many who are clever. But the lips of knowledge that Scripture has in mind are rare and valuable beyond these others. For this knowledge is that which teaches the fear of the Lord and leads those who listen and obey along the path of eternal life. This knowledge imparts wisdom that is able to discern what is of true value and what is mere imitation. This knowledge blesses and reaps blessing. It cannot be stolen, and the more it is given, the purer and more abundant it becomes in the giver.

But again, it is also rare. For even those who have found the truth of the gospel still mix in false teaching. Even those who think they are imparting the true Word are often imparting worldly wisdom. The

338

lips of knowledge – of gospel wisdom – are precious; and when you hear them, value them for what they are, and adorn yourself with them through obedience. Those are the costly stones most beautiful to adorn.

Risky Investment

Proverbs 20:16

Take a man's garment when he has put up security for a stranger,
  and hold it in pledge when he puts up security for foreigners.

Protect your risk. When even someone you know vouches for a stranger, it is appropriate to ask for some token of assurance that your loan will be protected. This protects not only you, but impresses upon the securer the seriousness of what he is doing. Perhaps he is being too quick or feeling pressured to co-sign for the stranger. Perhaps he needs to back out of the transaction and your requirement allows for him to do so. The point is that we are not to be hasty in putting ourselves or our friends in situations that incur such a risk that leads to heartache and conflict if the third party does not come through.

Always count the cost whenever you take a risk. If you are willing to loan money, count the cost of not getting it back. If you cannot handle the loss, then don't take the risk. Don't make any loan that you are not willing to lose; especially do not involve a friend in such a risk.

Now consider the investment that God the Father has made in us. He invested in our salvation with the intention that we would be made holy. Does it not seem to be a bad risk? It would have been had it not been for the one who gave up his garment of righteousness as a surety for us. For now we are counted as righteous with his garment. And more, Christ has given us the Holy Spirit as a seal for our salvation until that day we are fully sanctified and God's investment is realized.

The Father and the Son could take that risk not because they trusted in us, but in each other. They knew fully the cost and paid the full price before the risk of loss.

A Mouthful of Gravel

Proverbs 20:17

Bread gained by deceit is sweet to a man,
  but afterward his mouth will be full of gravel.

Consider the gravel. There is the gravel of a painful conscience. What at the moment seemed to be exciting comes back to haunt the heart that is not given fully to wickedness. The transgressor worries about breaking God's law and its consequences. If he is not too far gone, he is troubled by the wrong done against his neighbor.

There is the gravel of consequences. Even if his conscience does not bother him, he now must deal with the trouble of keeping up his deception. If he is found out, he must take the trouble of avoiding capture or avoiding conviction. He must take caution to protect himself from retribution. He may avoid legal prosecution but then must suffer the loss of his reputation. His neighbors do not trust him nor respect him. He himself is now avoided.

And then he may well find that the bread he stole is not what he thought it would be. It actually is not satisfying; it does not accomplish for him what he thought it would. He finds that his eyes and reasoning had deceived him.

What is the bread you desire? A good career? Wealth? Good looks? Break the law of God in obtaining them and you will find their sweet taste turn to gravel in your mouth.

Of Counsel and Guidance

Proverbs 20:18

Plans are established by counsel;
  by wise guidance wage war.

What are the benefits of counsel? One, the mere act of pausing to seek counsel reduces impulsive behavior. You are likely to give the matter more serious attention and to think more deliberately. Two, consulting with others sharpens your thinking as you explain your thoughts and as you listen to the thinking of others.

But this proverb also presents the benefit of wise guidance. It advocates seeking the counsel of persons who are wise and who possess the expertise needed for the matter at hand. Therefore, as you seek counsel, seek it from those who have demonstrated wisdom and knowledge. Also seek it from those who will be forthright with you. There is nothing to gain from seeking the counsel of those who only affirm your ideas. The counselors should be wise enough to speak in such a way that does not tear you down, but in such a way that also communicates the truth.

This proverb also presents the benefit of wise listening. You may gather about you wise counselors, but if you do not listen well then it is a waste of time, and you only make yourself out to be a fool. If they consistently give you counsel that contradicts your thinking, are you willing to examine carefully your heart? Are they seeing what you refuse to see? Many unnecessary wars have been started precisely because of matters of the heart rather than of strategic thinking.

Of Slander and Babblers

Proverbs 20:19

Whoever goes about slandering reveals secrets;
  therefore do not associate with a simple babbler.

Be a realist when it comes to confiding in certain people. The proverb does not advise that we be careful how we tell something confidential to a babbler. We are not given tips on how to assure that the babbler will not reveal our secrets. We are simply to stay away from him. We are to keep our secrets to ourselves when in his presence.

341

The motive of the babbler is irrelevant. He may want to hurt you or even think he is helping you. The result is the same. Information that should not have been passed on was and will cause hurt. Do not try to reform the babbler by entrusting him with private information; don't try to come up with ways to make him keep your confidence. Keep silent.

You will find this simple counsel very helpful in the workplace, home, church, and other areas where there is a web of relationships. You cannot control what others say, but you can control what you say. You can also control avoiding situations that lead to compromise. If you are in a room where gossip is being spoken, excuse yourself and leave the room. Again, focus on what you can control and avoid what you cannot.

Of Parents and Children

Proverbs 20:20

If one curses his father or his mother,
his lamp will be put out in utter darkness.

It is wrong to curse anyone, but to send curses in the way of one's parents is especially appalling. Indeed, it is regarded here as sacrilege. The special nature of bond between parent and child is recognized by everyone. The reason there is much dysfunction in families is because offense between parent and child (particularly parent against child) carries more significant impact. Scripture understands this; Scripture teaches that it should be so. A parent is not a mere provider for the child until he reaches adulthood. "Father," "Mother," carries with that name a profound bond.

So what is your regard for your father and mother, be they living or dead? Whoever you are reading this, you have your own context in thinking about this. You may have had a wonderful relationship with your parents or a terrible one. Even so, it is vital that you recognize the peculiar relationship of a parent to a child. You may know others who are like a father or mother to you, others who may legally have taken that role. You should of course show them due deference. But if you struggle about your feelings towards your biological parents, even so, do not fall into the sin of cursing them. You do not have to excuse their sin or deny their offense. You do not have to conjure up loving feelings. But still, for your own sake, do not fall into the pit of bitterness that leaves you desiring judgment to fall upon your parents. They must answer to their own sins before God. Your curses are not needed for them to get their due. But your prayers are needed for the hope of the Spirit's work in their hearts.

Is this not what the gospel is about – bringing hope to those who do not deserve it? It was for his crucifiers that Jesus asked his Father for forgiveness. It was for his enemies that God sent his Son to die. If the gospel has penetrated your heart, then forgiveness (not curses) is what will come forth. You cannot change your parents; you cannot create new feelings; but you can offer the blessing and forgiveness in Christ to your parents that have been given to you.

An Inheritance

Proverbs 20:21

An inheritance gained hastily in the beginning
   will not be blessed in the end.

Sudden wealth – whether it be through inheritance or winning the lottery or through some scheme – as often as not creates trouble. Wealth, as with power and fame, carries its own dangers of corrupting the owner and creating anxiety over its protection. Jesus noted how difficult it was for a rich man to enter the kingdom of heaven.

Sudden wealth brings with it further troubles. Because it does not come from the fruit of his labor, the recipient does not measure its true cost. Not knowing what it takes to earn the wealth, he also does not know how to maintain it. He either becomes overly protective of it or too loose with it. It is difficult to be wise with something gained without wisdom.

343

But wisdom is needed for the effect one's wealth has on others. The suddenly wealthy person discovers friends and relatives he did not know he had; he also finds that the ones he has known change in the way they treat him. He is regarded more highly. He is praised and befriended by many. Pride rushes into his head which inevitably leads to his downfall. But these friends and relatives are not merely infatuated with him; they want a share in his wealth and do their own scheming to get it. There are others who now resent him for his luck. Why should he get the inheritance? What did he do to earn it? And so troubles come from them.

We all dream of what it would be like to come into sudden wealth, to be surprised by the uncle we did not know existed but who left his money to us. Let us dream, rather, of what it would be like to see the fruit of our labors. Let us be spurred on not by winning the lottery, but by the steady progress and fruit that comes from wise planning and diligent labor.

But then do dream and do give thanks for the one inheritance that has come without labor and quite surprisingly. Dream of that inheritance that awaits us in heaven, given to us by our Lord Jesus Christ, protected by God the Father, and for which even we are protected by the Holy Spirit. Is it not wondrous that the greatest inheritance is the one most secure and the only one in which the more we dream of it and value it, the more blessed and productive we become (cf. 1 Pet. 1:3-9)?

Wait for the Lord

Proverbs 20:22

Do not say, "I will repay evil";
wait for the Lord, and he will deliver you.

The sense here is not about bringing the wicked to justice. It is about exacting our personal revenge. This is a proverb for the worker outmaneuvered unjustly for a job promotion. It is for the student who is beat out for an award because of another student cheating. It

344

is for all of us in our daily experiences of being slighted and taken advantage of.

Wait for the Lord. Wait for the Lord because vengeance belongs to him. And it belongs to him because any offense is an offense against him. He alone is Judge, and offense against him is infinitely more serious than offense against us.

Wait for the Lord because he will exact the proper measure at the proper time. We will not. We inevitably sin in our attempt at retribution, and thus end up in the same position as our offenders.

Wait for the Lord for your own peace of mind. Your offender gains even more advantage by your fretting and scheming. You have lost not only the goal the offender won but your contentment as well.

Waiting for the Lord means putting the matter, including the results, in his hands and not worrying about the outcome. That is not only victory but the best kind of payback – not letting your offender take away your peace and joy.

Wait for the Lord for the sake of your relationship with the Lord. How can you learn to trust him if you will not wait on him? How can you learn contentment without waiting on him in all circumstances? How can you experience his working in you and around you if you do not wait for him? Wait for the Lord.

An Abomination

Proverbs 20:23

*Unequal weights are an abomination to the Lord,
    and false scales are not good.*

Just thirteen verses before there is an almost identical proverb: "Unequal weights and unequal measures are both alike an abomination to the Lord." Perhaps the repetition is to reinforce the seriousness which God attaches to cheating.

Consider this proverb with the one preceding it: "Do not say, 'I will repay evil'; wait for the Lord, and he will deliver you." Have you been cheated by unequal weights and false scales? Wait on the Lord. You see how he regards such offenses. He will deliver you. Justice will be carried out in exact measure to the offense of the crime.

Do not take matters into your own hands by trying to out-cheat the one who has done you wrong. Do not try to even the playing field. The cheater will eventually be exposed. Even if he is not exposed as timely as you desire, know that God sees all and works all for your good. The cheater will receive his due reward.

Your focus needs only to be on doing what is right and honest. Do not act in reaction to evil doers; act in response to your righteous Judge and Lord who desires to see righteousness displayed in your life.

How Can Man Understand?

Proverbs 20:24

A man's steps are from the Lord;
  how then can man understand his way?

How can a man understand his way apart from the Lord who works all things for his glory and purposes? The secular philosopher, despite his intellectual prowess, takes the wrong first "step" in his contemplation as he tries to understand his way. One may build insight upon insight, but if the foundation is not the Word of God, it is but a make-believe building.

Our own lesson as Christians is to accept that the mystery of God's secret counsels and his way of ordering man's steps is beyond our ability to understand. How is it that we will make our decisions today about the steps we take only to find that every step will serve God's purpose? How is it that today we will ponder how to answer someone, what weighty decision to make, and then later look back and see God's purpose in what took place?

346

Even then we will not have full insight. It is good to explore the ways of God and of man. But it is critical to do so in humility, even more so to do it in trust – trust that God is good and in control. If you are tempted to doubt, then look to the Cross. For there is the mystery of election and freedom, of wrath and mercy, of violence and justice, of sin and love; there is the mystery of God's way that is higher than ours as the heavens are higher than the earth.

Rash Vows

Proverbs 20:25

It is a snare to say rashly, "it is holy,"
and to reflect only after making vows.

Be cautious in making vows. Be cautious saying that you will set something apart for God. Be cautious because God takes seriously your word. He will hold you accountable for what you say.

Because we are only as good as our word, our words should be carefully chosen and few in number. Making a vow requires the following:

It requires humility. We too often make vows out of pride. We overestimate our ability and determination. Like Peter, we are quick to vow allegiance when we really need to be pleading for mercy.

It requires discernment. We should be able to count the cost accurately and our assets accurately before committing.

It requires a calm spirit. Again, vows are often made in the heat of the moment, in being caught up in emotion. We are more likely to carry through what we decide to do while calm.

It requires leaning upon God's Spirit. We can only fulfill what the Spirit gives us the wisdom and strength to do. We should only carry out what we know the Spirit is leading us to do. We can do nothing of ourselves; we can do all things through the Spirit of Christ.

Finally, we are to rest and find our hope in the vow our Lord made for us – to be our sacrifice, to assure for us the salvation to which we were elected. Our hope rests not in the seriousness by which we have made our vow to God to surrender everything to him, but in Christ's vow to surrender everything. He carried out his vow and will continue to carry out his promise to safeguard us until the day of his coming.

The Wise King

Proverbs 20:26

A wise king winnows the wicked
and drives the wheel over them.

The wise king is able, first, to discern between the wicked and the righteous (or innocent). Secondly, he is able then to act against the wicked in judgment. Many rulers exercise power but do so indiscriminately, harming both wicked and righteous; indeed, many rulers are especially brutal against the righteous. And there are rulers who know who ought be punished, but they lack the power or willingness to act. A wise king is able to do both – discern and act; for it takes wisdom to know how to act in such a way as to carry out due punishment and not be overthrown.

How wise are you in whatever capacity you might have – a job supervisor, teacher, parent, or other such position? Do you discern wisely? Do you discern how to act? A wise king does not bemoan how difficult his responsibility is. He uses his energy to consider how to act in wisdom. He studies wisdom. He gathers around him wise counsel. He turns to God and prays for wisdom. He studies the Scriptures for wisdom.

And he puts his own life under the Lordship of his wise King – Jesus Christ. He lays his heart before this wise king, willing to be chastened, zealous to please, and fully trusting for saving mercy. May the Lord grant you such wisdom today.

The Lord's Lamp

Proverbs 20:27

The spirit of man is the lamp of the Lord,
*   searching all his innermost parts.*

This is our conscience which bears witness that the law of God is written on our hearts (Rom. 2:15). God has placed within all of us – those inhabited by God's Spirit and those who are not – his inner moral compass, or, as this proverb notes, his inner moral lamp that searches our thoughts and actions. This is why everyone is without excuse in their rejection of God's law. We all know better, however much we may protest to the contrary.

Such a truth puts into perspective those who are most "moral." Their very interest in doing what is right betrays the fact that they know there is a God who requires righteousness, and yet they cannot bring themselves to acknowledge his existence; or if they believe he exists, then to acknowledge his rights over them; or if they believe he has such rights, then to believe in him as he demands – through Jesus Christ; or if they profess to believe in Christ, they nevertheless do not acknowledge his true work on the cross – to save sinners like them who cannot save themselves.

And then there are those of us who profess all these things about God and about Christ; who acknowledge our dependence upon our Lord and love for him; who profess obedience to him, but will not expose our darkest corners to God's lamp. We fear too much what we will see. And so we will look at the sin we can "handle" and congratulate ourselves for being severe with our sin.

Use the lamp for its purpose – to fully examine yourself. And use your inner lamp with that greater lamp – the Word of God – so that you might examine all your innermost parts with the clearest light. Are you afraid of what you will see? You will see nothing that God does not know already exists. He sees you completely and loves you completely. Your spirit will find nothing that his Spirit has not already exposed. And that same Spirit is already at work within you to bring cleansing and light and hope.

Good Protection

Proverbs 20:28

Steadfast love and faithfulness preserve the king,
    and by steadfast love his throne is upheld.

This is certainly a different perspective from the world's understanding. What preserves a king or anyone else in a position of power is power. Also needed are shrewdness, the willingness to eliminate the competition, a large ego to fuel the drive for fame and power. Even if a kinder view is taken, it would be expected that wisdom and knowledge would be the protecting forces. Love and faithfulness are good but can be so easily taken advantage of.

Consider what this proverb presents. However powerful the wicked king may be, what must he always be concerned with? Protecting himself. But then so do good kings, King David being a case in point. Most of his psalms include some reference to his enemies who were out to get him. On the other hand, it was his steadfast love and faithfulness to his people that helped provide his protection. Even when his own son turned against him, many remained on his side and provided the help needed to win his battle.

Furthermore, he did not unnecessarily create enemies. The wicked king's greatest enemies are those he betrayed. It is broken love, broken trust that stirs up wrath. It is love that remains true and faithfulness that is steady through all circumstances that stirs up devotion. When it comes to battle, better to have soldiers fighting out of devotion to their ruler than those disillusioned by their ruler.

It is steadfast love and faithfulness by which our Lord rules and thus has won our devotion. Though we have stumbled and failed, he remains true to his word. All the more then we desire to please him.

Start today knowing that whatever befalls, your King will love you with a steadfast love; he will remain faithful to his promises. Does not such knowledge stir in you zeal to stand by him?

Glory and Splendor

Proverbs 20:29

The glory of young men is their strength,
  but the splendor of old men is their gray hair.

There is glory and joy in being young. It is good to be young and strong, and the young should delight in what their youthfulness gives them strength to do. They have vitality; they are idealistic. They act with passion. They are able to move mountains by their strength.

And there is glory and joy in old age. It is good to be older and wise through experience, and the "old" should delight in what their knowledge gives them wisdom to do. They have calmness; they are discerning. They act with patience. They are able to move mountains by their wisdom.

Whatever your age, delight in it. Neither be anxious to grow older nor wistful to be young again. Your days are laid out by your Lord, and now is the best time in which to live. Do not live waiting for tomorrow, nor live wishing for yesterday to return. Live today; use whatever gift your age has given you; and delight in the Lord for what he has given you now.

Blows That Cleanse

Proverbs 20:30

Blows that wound cleanse away evil;
  strokes make clean the innermost parts.

Blows that come from one who loves you and hates the sin that binds you are essential for your welfare. It is right to be concerned with abuse, but it is as deadly to be denied the chastisement that awakens you to your sin and spurs you to action. It is deadly to be denied love that will not tolerate your sinking into the pit. So the loving parent will inflict punishment on his child to train him in the way of righteousness, however much pain the parent endures to do so.

So it is with our heavenly Father who loves us perfectly. Because he is good and because he loves us thoroughly, he will send the blows that cleanse away evil and makes clean our innermost parts. He will not be satisfied with our half-hearted righteousness and our superficiality. He will not tolerate our disease, however contented we may be. He will carry to completion the good work he began in us, whether or not we want further progress.

If you should think that his blows are too hard, that it is bringing death instead of healing, remember the Cross where our Lord "was wounded for our transgressions; he was crushed for our iniquities; upon him was the chastisement that brought us peace, and with his stripes we are healed" (Isa. 53:5).

The Heart in the Hand

Proverbs 21:1

The king's heart is a stream of water in the hand of the Lord;
he turns it wherever he will.

As a farmer irrigates his fields by creating canals to control the direction of the water, so the Lord provides for the fields of the earth by directing the hearts of rulers. Whether these rulers may be righteous or wicked, devout or profane, they nevertheless serve the deeper purposes of God. So it was with Pharaoh, Cyrus, and Artaxerxes. This was the lesson that Nebuchadnezzar learned. However events may appear to be occurring, however mighty the wicked may appear to be and the righteous appear not to be, understand that the very heart of everyone is in the hand of the Lord.

Thus, when you must appear before a "ruler" in your life, pray for God to direct his heart. God is not like us who must hope that by

352

acting one way, he can get a ruler to act as he wants. God controls the very heart. He is not dependent on outside influence. It is amusing to hear a pray-er give God counsel about how to get someone to do his will. Instead of bidding God to do what he deems is necessary, we will advise God as to what events are necessary to take place. We let God know that "the only way to get Bob to change is to..." God merely needs to change the heart, impossible for us but simple for him.

Pray for God to do his will, without giving advice on how to accomplish it. And trust God to do his will. Just as we do not have the wisdom to give God counsel, neither have we the discernment to understand all the ways his will is being carried out. It is not necessary for us to understand all of God's ways. We need merely to be like the child who trusts his father to know what is best and do what is best. We need to know that not only the king's heart is in the hand of the Lord, but that we are held in the palm of his hand.

Hearts Weighed

Proverbs 21:2

Every way of a man is right in his own eyes,
 but the Lord weighs the heart.

Note two insights in this proverb in relation to a Christian. First, a Christian will defend his behavior either through using scripture texts for justification or by appealing to conscience. There is the husband who defended being critical of his wife by appealing to Ephesians 5:25-27, which refers to Christ sanctifying the church. Likewise, Christians have defended rude behavior as being bold for Christ and zealous for truth. In every case, the person believes he is doing what is right. In his own eyes, he is being faithful to God.

Second, the Lord weighs the heart. He weighs the heart not the action. He weighs the true motive of the Christian not what the Christian thinks is his motive. The mistake of the Christian is to believe that he looks within his own heart with clear sight. That is precisely what we are weakest at doing. We cannot weigh our own heart. Only God can do so.

What is the practical input of this reality that we see a favorably distorted view of ourselves and only the Lord weighs with accuracy the heart? It should make us humble. It should make us slow to make judgment of others, especially to make unfavorable judgments of others in relation to ourselves. We should be zealous to study God's Word so that it shines a light on our hearts. We should never be quick to defend our hearts, knowing that we may very well be wrong. Even when we may be accurate about what we do see in ourselves, we never do know the full picture. Again, only the Lord weighs truly the heart.

Finally, it should lead us to rely wholly on the mercy of God. If God were to measure out justice according to what he weighs in our hearts, we would all perish. God weighs and then he measures out to us according to his mercy. Have you thanked him today for such mercy?

Better Than Sacrifice

Proverbs 21:3

To do righteousness and justice
  is more acceptable to the Lord than sacrifice.

For commentary, read these other scriptures:

> When you come to appear before me,
>   who has required of you
>   this trampling of my courts?
> Bring no more vain offerings;
>   incense is an abomination to me.
> New moon and Sabbath and the calling of convocations—
>   I cannot endure iniquity and solemn assembly.
> Your new moons and your appointed feasts
>   my soul hates;

354

they have become a burden to me;
    I am weary of bearing them.
When you spread out your hands,
    I will hide my eyes from you;
even though you make many prayers,
    I will not listen;
    your hands are full of blood.
Wash yourselves; make yourselves clean;
    remove the evil of your deeds from before my eyes;
cease to do evil,
    learn to do good;

seek justice,
    correct oppression;
bring justice to the fatherless,
    plead the widow's cause. (Isa. 1:12-17).

"With what shall I come before the LORD,
    and bow myself before God on high?
Shall I come before him with burnt offerings,
    with calves a year old?
Will the LORD be pleased with thousands of rams,
    with ten thousands of rivers of oil?
Shall I give my firstborn for my transgression,
    the fruit of my body for the sin of my soul?"
He has told you, O man, what is good;
    and what does the LORD require of you
but to do justice, and to love kindness,
    and to walk humbly with your God? (Micah 6:6-8)

Lamp of the Wicked

Proverbs 21:4

Haughty eyes and a proud heart,
    the lamp of the wicked, are sin.

Scripture makes clear God's displeasure of pride which is the root sin of the wicked. They will not humble themselves before God. This is played out in various ways, most notably through the violence committed against others.

The proverb reveals how pride mars their perspective on reality. Pride is the lamp by which the wicked see what is outside themselves. What do they see? They see people to despise who don't measure up to their distorted standards. Conversely, they see others to admire who in reality model arrogance and wickedness. A notable author whose works are rife with licentious sex visited a city noted for its licentiousness. Whereas most people would see the obvious vulgarity, broken lives, and despicable behavior, he saw it as the ideal city. Compare this proverb to verse 2, three verses earlier: "Every way of a man is right in his own eyes..." The proud wicked believe they are acting in accord to what is right, but it is the right in their own eyes which see by the lamp of haughtiness and pride.

All the more then humble yourself before the Lord. The Christian, too, is guilty of pride when he views his neighbor with haughty eyes, like the Pharisee looked upon the publican. We are easily proud that we see what our unbelieving neighbors do not. We act with great surprise that they do not see what we do. Why can't they understand the gospel? Why can't they know what is right from wrong? The answer is that they are no different from us. Without the work of the Holy Spirit in our hearts providing the lamp of God's truth, we would not "get it" either. And even with the Spirit within us, we still see too much with distortion out of our own pride. Indeed, we have less excuse than our unbelieving neighbor for our pride.

Plans of the Diligent

Proverbs 21:5

The plans of the diligent lead surely to abundance,
  but everyone who is hasty comes only to poverty.

This is a practical proverb to guide you today. It could make the difference between an action that leads to long-term blessing or long-term regret. Like a beautiful house built on poor land, many options look appealing but hide disastrous consequences. Many ideas seemed

356

good "at the time," but proved to be foolish as time went on. Remember verse 2: "Every way of a man is right in his own eyes." All the more reason then to prayerfully study, seek counsel, and plan. Many couples who come to me with troubled marriages are those who hastily married. Their passion at the time made marriage seem right and easy. How many people have switched jobs on impulse or moved to another town because at the moment they felt restless, only to become even more miserable?

Impulse is not necessarily bad and can provide a healthy spice in our routine. There are times when "the Spirit moves" and we should act. But when acting on impulse becomes the routine way of making decisions, we are setting ourselves up for disaster. We will make bad decisions, and we will earn a reputation of not being trustworthy. There are persons who master diligent planning in the workplace, but let their emotions lead them in their personal lives. It is a mistake to treat family and friends as workplace projects for diligent planning; but it is a greater mistake to "wing it" in choosing a life-long mate, keeping a marriage vibrant, and raising a family.

When we think about it, we reveal how important anything is to us by the careful thought we give to it. Whatever grabs our interest is what we will plan to get, keep, and nurture. What has your interest now?

Fleeting Vapor

Proverbs 21:6

The getting of treasures by a lying tongue
is a fleeting vapor and a snare of death.

The liar thinks he is setting a snare or escaping it by lying. To gain treasure he thinks he escapes like a fleeting vapor. He tells his lies in order to snatch the treasure. But he is merely setting up his own snare and insuring that his treasure will escape. Ask the white-collar executives in jail now because of their deception how much good their lying did them. Ask those who are bankrupt how much good cheating did for them.

357

The shocking surprise is that most of them will rue that they did not do a good enough job lying. Even now while lying in their snares they are mulling over how they should have covered their tracks better. That is the way of the fool. He does not learn from his consequences – especially the liar. Is there a more difficult pattern of behavior to break than that of lying? It is easy to do, and when it becomes so engrained as to be instinct, it is difficult to break.

All the more reason then to confess this sin now if it has you in its grasp. Husbands lying to wives, employees lying to supervisors, students lying to teachers – and all to gain treasure: affection, promotion, good grades. Break the habit now, for it will only grow more difficult and the snares will multiply.

How do you break the habit? By desiring true treasure – the grace of God – and by trusting in the one whose promise is not fleeting – God. How do you get to God? Through the one who has never lied and is truth personified – Jesus Christ.

Without Excuse

Proverbs 21:7

The violence of the wicked will sweep them away,
because they refuse to do what is just.

As we have learned in other proverbs, the wicked bring on themselves their own destruction. They suffer the consequences of their own violence. It is easy enough to see how they create trouble for themselves, but *the* consequence is that they place themselves under the judgment of God who will not be mocked and will see that justice is carried out.

Note here the real problem of the wicked. It is not that they do not know what is just, but that they refuse to do what is just. Compare this proverb to Romans 1:18: "For the wrath of God is revealed from heaven against all ungodliness and unrighteousness of men, who by their unrighteousness suppress the truth."

Before we apply this proverb to our neighbor, let us look at ourselves. Romans goes on to say that such persons are without excuse because what can be known about God is made plain through natural revelation. But we have the special revelation of Scripture, and we have within us the Holy Spirit to open our minds to the truth. Will God excuse our sin because we did not know better? Will he accept that we ever act in ignorance?

Give praise to God that there is no condemnation for those who are in Christ Jesus, for our sin would not only be held against us, but our guilt would weigh upon us even more heavily because of our lack of excuse. Every day we are living testimonies of the unfathomable mercy of God and of the inestimable power of Christ's work on the cross.

Of the Guilty and the Pure

Proverbs 21:8

The way of the guilty is crooked,
but the conduct of the pure is upright.

What is within us will come out in our behavior. The guilty's way will be crooked; the conduct of the pure will show in their very demeanor – standing upright with a clear conscience. The guilty must lurk about, hiding in the shadows, checking their backs, slipping across from side to side of the road, never walking down the middle. The pure walk straight and tall. They have nothing to hide and are not planning wicked deeds.

What a difference there is for the two types. One sleeps peacefully at night; the other tosses and turns in worry. One looks his neighbor in the face; the other averts his eyes. One walks with a sense of purpose and confidence; the other slinks about wary of his enemies. One is moved by the mercy of God, desiring to please him; the other despises God, wanting to escape him.

Being pure in heart is understanding that it is Christ who makes us righteous before God; it is the Holy Spirit sanctifying us; it is the mercy of God that makes it all happen. With that kind of knowledge, we will find walking straight and standing upright more natural to do.

A Quarrelsome Wife

Proverbs 21:9

It is better to live in a corner of the housetop
  than in a house shared with a quarrelsome wife.

Husbands, of course, can also be quarrelsome, but since this proverb speaks specifically of the wife, let's consider her case. Someone has made the wry comment: "A man marries a woman and is surprised to find that she changes. A woman marries a man and is surprised that he doesn't change." She is surprised that he still puts off the work he needs to do – whether it be house chores, or paying bills, or even for his job. After months and years, he still is clueless about his lack of affection, how he takes her for granted, and how he hurts her feelings.

She is especially frustrated because she has corrected him and reminded him time and again. She has even scolded him, even tried to shame him into action. Indeed, she becomes upset with herself. She doesn't like quarreling; she doesn't like hearing herself fuss. Why can't her husband understand this and just change a little?

The husband does need to change and will be held accountable before God for his sin. Meanwhile, the wife needs to exercise wisdom. If quarreling does not achieve results, stop quarreling. It only increases frustration for both wife and husband. Take time to understand what really motivates your husband. Study him. It is better for the wife's welfare for her to act wisely through understanding than to stew over his laziness.

More importantly, she should take time to focus on the Bridegroom who is preparing her as a bride to be spotless and in splendor. She will only be able to love her husband well as she loves her Bridegroom. She can only love her husband according to how well she knows the love of her Bridegroom. She can only be as wise as she understands her Bridegroom's wisdom by which he is working in her life.

No Mercy

Proverbs 21:10

The soul of the wicked desires evil;
his neighbor finds no mercy in his eyes.

Some people are simply mean-spirited. They laugh at the misery of others. They derive pleasure at insulting anyone. They revel in being bullies, connivers, and cheaters. To see a neighbor in need arouses spite rather than sympathy.

It is our responsibility to protect others from them and to seek justice against them. And it is our responsibility to love them and to seek their salvation. Seek God's mercy for the merciless wicked, as mercy was shown to your wicked soul.

Three Persons

Proverbs 21:11

When a scoffer is punished, the simple becomes wise;
when a wise man is instructed, he gains knowledge.

This proverb parallels 19:25: "Strike a scoffer, and the simple will learn prudence; reprove a man of understanding, and he will gain knowledge."

Punishment has its place, though its effect will differ according to the individual. The scoffer is punished and at best is restricted from further wicked behavior. His heart will not change; he does not grow wiser from the correction. The simple, whether he is the one punished or observes the punishment of the scoffer, may be sobered into seeing what the consequences of his sin are. The premise is that he really does lack education and needs to be shown the right ways.

The wise man does not need to be punished to learn. Education is all he needs. He wants to do what is right; he desires more knowledge. He welcomes instruction, even correction.

Which of the three describes you?

The Wicked Observed

Proverbs 21:12

The Righteous One observes the house of the wicked;
he throws the wicked down to ruin.

The critical mistake of the wicked is to believe that he is keeping unobserved. Think of the image of law officials staking out a house hoping to see or hear something that might give evidence of the wicked's guilt. The great challenge of the law is to come up with clear evidence and in a way that will be accepted in court. The wicked knows how to cover his tracks and use the legal system to suppress evidence.

But what he does not take into account is the Righteous One who observes his house even into its secret places, even into his own heart. His outwitting human justice only serves to blind him all the more to *the* justice that awaits him, whether it be in this life or after death. Ruin is his certain end precisely because all that he does, says, and thinks is observed by the Righteous One who is his Judge.

The tragedy is that his Judge could be his Savior and Advocate if he would but repent. His freedom is free for the receiving, but his pride over outwitting the "system" keeps him from seeing what even the simplest can see.

Silent Response

Proverbs 21:13

Whoever closes his ear to the cry of the poor
will himself call out and not be answered.

In a way, this proverb is more sobering than the previous one that warns of being ruined. There is a unique fear of being alone, of calling out for help and receiving only silence. The wicked may scoff at such a thought but that is only because they have yet to be desperate. The time will come when their strength and wit cannot save them. The time will come when they know they need help. And help will not come. No one will answer. The time will come when they stand before the Judge at Judgment Day and no one will be their advocate. As they responded to others, so they will receive the same response.

Note who the others are – the poor. We should not walk easily by the poor. We should not easily ignore their plight and blame their troubles on themselves. Whatever our political or social convictions may be on how to address poverty, we must personally care about our poor neighbor and be generous, whether it is a handout or, if that seems wrong, then giving generously to a ministry that helps the poor.

Scripture is consistent in portraying God as sympathetic towards the poor. We then must follow his example and his commandments. After all, the time may come when we need to cry out for help, and the time will come when we stand before the Judge and will be in need of our Advocate.

Secret Bribes

Proverbs 21:14

A gift in secret averts anger,
  and a concealed bribe, strong wrath.

This proverb speaks of a specific purpose in the use of bribes – averting anger. Most likely the situation is that of averting unjust anger. The king or some other authority has become overly angry and is about to harm someone. The offender, or a friend who steps in, gives the gift that appeases that anger.

The bribe is not a means of cheating others in competition; here, it is a means of protecting the innocent or of preventing an injustice taking place. Bribes are not to be used indiscriminately and never for the purpose of advancing one's own selfish cause. They are not to be used in place of trusting in God for one's circumstances. But again, they may be needed to avert violence.

Consider Abigail. Her foolish husband Nabal stirs up the fury of David, so much so that David gathers his men to attack Nabal's servants. When Abigail hears of the matter, she goes behind her husband's back and takes gifts to David, by which she is then able to reason with him. David responds,

> "Blessed be the LORD, the God of Israel, who sent you this day to meet me! Blessed be your discretion, and blessed be you, who have kept me this day from bloodguilt and from working salvation with my own hand! For as surely as the LORD, the God of Israel, lives, who has restrained me from hurting you, unless you had hurried and come to meet me, truly by morning there had not been left to Nabal so much as one male." Then David received from her hand what she had brought him. And he said to her, "Go up in peace to your house. See, I have obeyed your voice, and I have granted your petition" (1 Sam. 25:32-35).

Abigail saved the lives of innocent men through her "bribe." She kept David from great sin. She did not lack trust in God; rather, she used the discretion God had given her to see that mercy and justice won the day.

When Justice Is Done

Proverbs 21:15

When justice is done, it is a joy to the righteous
  but terror to evildoers.

When justice is done, the righteous are vindicated and the wicked are punished. But the righteous also rejoice in justice for its own sake.

They do not obey God's laws to keep from being punished, but because they actually delight in God's law. The wicked fear punishment, but they also are disheartened to see justice winning over evil which they delight in. A world in which justice prevails is not a desirable place in which to live. They must live in fear in such a world.

And that world will someday come when our Lord returns to establish full justice, and a new heaven and a new earth are established. In such a world, God "will wipe away every tear from [the eyes of the righteous], and death shall be no more, neither shall there be mourning nor crying nor pain anymore, for the former things have passed away" (Rev. 21:4).

"But as for the cowardly, the faithless, the detestable, as for murderers, the sexually immoral, sorcerers, idolaters, and all liars, their portion will be in the lake that burns with fire and sulfur, which is the second death" (21:8).

Thus, joy for the righteous and terror for evildoers.

Good Sense

Proverbs 21:16

One who wanders from the way of good sense
will rest in the assembly of the dead.

Do you want rest? Do you want to escape the hassles of life? Then wander away from good sense. Throw off your responsibilities and act according to instinct, and you can live a contented life. It is fairly easy to be contented when you have no responsibility for anyone and do only what you feel like doing at the moment. You will find rest.

Your contented rest, however, comes at the cost of a living death. You are dead spiritually, dead to what is of eternal value and joy. And it is likely you will find an early rest in death literally. Living for the moment usually leads to a shortened life. The catch there is that death does not provide rest. However peaceful a cemetery may seem, the souls of the dead find anything but rest.

The way of sense requires taking on responsibility for how you live and for loving your neighbor. We will practice good sense in some parts of our lives, but it is difficult to exercise good sense in every area. This is not because it is difficult to know what to do, but that we have limits to how much thinking we want to do all the time. Thus, we may practice good sense at our job and wander from good sense at home, or vice versa.

Will you practice good sense today in the home and work or school and everywhere else you may be? Or will you take a stroll away from good sense when it seems inconvenient or too tiring?

The Lover of Pleasure

Proverbs 21:17

Whoever loves pleasure will be a poor man;
  he who loves wine and oil will not be rich.

This would seem to be a proverb supporting the ascetic, stoic life. Its emphasis, however, is not contrasting pleasure with stoicism, but warning about a life devoted to physical pleasure. In such a pursuit the individual loses common sense. He thinks only of today and does not prepare for tomorrow, thus ending up in poverty. He slacks off from work and stops working altogether. The person who lives for the weekend or the happy hour is not giving due attention to his labors which he devalues.

Indeed, the irony of the lover of pleasure is that he misses out on what is truly pleasurable. True pleasure is found in doing what is meaningful and in taking delight in what is of greater value. And the real poverty that awaits the lover of physical pleasure is that he becomes impoverished spiritually. Nothing is more tragic than to look back over one's life and realize it was a wasted life.

Love pleasure, but love the pleasure of pleasing your Lord by doing his will. Love the pleasure that comes from knowing the love of the Lord, from knowing his majesty, from exploring his character and his work. Such a pursuit only enriches you whatever may happen physically. Better yet, such a pursuit leads you into eternal pleasure.

A Ransom

Proverbs 21:18

The wicked is a ransom for the righteous,
  and the traitor for the upright.

There is a sense in which the wicked receive the punishment that was to have been visited on others, including the righteous. Thus, Judah was spared when Sennacherib was moved by God to attack the Egyptians rather than his covenant people. And God could say,
          For I am the LORD your God
               the Holy One of Israel, your Savior.
          I give Egypt as your ransom,
               Cush and Seba in exchange for you.
          Because you are precious in my eyes,
               and honored, and I love you,
          I give men in return for you,
               peoples in exchange for your life (Isa. 43:3, 4).

This type of language expresses the justice of God in which we often see the wicked meeting destruction of some sort and the righteous being spared. Thus comes the expression, "There but by the grace of God go I." And so will we say when the Day of Judgment comes and we are spared the judgment of God.

All the more then, ought we to tremble as we contemplate the real ransom made for us. For it was not by the substitute of the wicked that the righteous were ransomed; rather, it was by the substitute of the Righteous One that we the wicked were ransomed. Christ ought to have been spared the cross and we serve as his ransom. That would have been just.

367

What mysterious mercy is this that brought forth a profound justice in order to ransom wicked people?

A Fretful Woman

Proverbs 21:19

It is better to live in a desert land
than with a quarrelsome and fretful woman.

Consider Peter's counsel to wives in light of this proverb:

> Likewise, wives, be subject to your own husbands, so that even if some do not obey the word, they may be won without a word by the conduct of their wives-- when they see your respectful and pure conduct. Do not let your adorning be external--the braiding of hair, the wearing of gold, or the putting on of clothing-- but let your adorning be the hidden person of the heart with the imperishable beauty of a gentle and quiet spirit, which in God's sight is very precious. For this is how the holy women who hoped in God used to adorn themselves, by submitting to their husbands, as Sarah obeyed Abraham, calling him lord. And you are her children, if you do good and do not fear anything that is frightening (1 Pet. 3:1-6).

Wives, consider what fretfulness ultimately conveys. You may think it conveys that your husbands are not acting wisely or loving. But it further conveys that you cannot trust God. Scripture teaches us to be content in all circumstances. That includes marriage. That is a difficult command to observe, but nevertheless it is the call for wives and for husbands.

Husbands, consider seriously how you contribute to your wives' quarrelsomeness and fretfulness. You may wish you were in a desert, but you are not. You as head of your marriage have the obligation to help calm your wives' fears. Just as her resorting to quarreling and expressing her anxieties do not help you to achieve more and be more responsible, neither do your reprimands help to quiet her fears.

Women should not nag and men should not escape. And neither of them should blame the other for their behavior. Follow the command given in Ephesians 5:33: "However, let each one of you love his wife as himself (regardless of her behavior), and let the wife see that she respects her husband (regardless of his behavior)." You will be surprised how much respect and love positively affects behavior when they are given irrespective of behavior.

To Devour or to Nurture

Proverbs 21:20

Precious treasure and oil are in a wise man's dwelling,
  but a foolish man devours it.

The wise person saves and exercises restraint. For that reason he accumulates an abundance. The fool consumes whatever he gets.

Compare this proverb with verse 17: "Whoever loves pleasure will be a poor man; he who loves wine and oil will not be rich." The seeming paradox is that the lover of riches and pleasure will be poor, while the wise person who understands restraint and proper value of fleeting pleasure will have more than he needs.

The consumer devours what he obtains. His motto is to enjoy the day at hand, to take now whatever is given. But he does not understand that he is not obtaining the full pleasure he desires. Restraint is not putting off pleasure to protect against an unknown future. Restraint is training the body and the mind to enjoy more fully an experience or object. Which wine lover truly enjoys the pleasure of wine – the drunkard or the one who lingers over one glass? Who really knows the pleasure of sexual intimacy – the person who goes from partner to partner seeking only a sensation or the person who enjoys sex in a loving, lasting relationship with a spouse?

Wisdom is not about putting off pleasure. It is about nurturing

369

pleasure, building it up to be a lasting experience. What is of real value is worth nurturing.

Will Find

Proverbs 21:21

Whoever pursues righteousness and kindness
* will find life, righteousness, and honor.*

This is the promise of the gospel – our pursuit of righteousness and kindness will not be in vain. However you may feel at the moment: if you despair of good winning out; if you see about you only death, wickedness, and shame; know that life, righteousness, and honor is what you will ultimately find. You will find more than you expect here in this world in your earthly lifetime, and you will find these things in their full glory in the presence of your Lord.

Do not despair as those who are without hope, who believe that there is nothing beyond this world and this life. Do not grow cynical; do not give way to bitterness. Rather open your eyes to the good that is around you. Take joy in the life you now have in Christ; delight in the righteousness that has been given to you in Christ; be humbled by the honor accorded to you in Christ.

For remember, it was not because you pursued righteousness and kindness that God sent his Son to die for you. You despised righteousness; you were not kind. But God showed his love for you in that while you were still a sinner, even an enemy of God, he sent his Son who brought to you abundant life, who clothed you in his righteousness, and bestowed the honor of being called a child of God. How much more now that you are pursuing righteousness and kindness, will he see that your faith "may be found to result in praise and glory and honor at the revelation of Jesus Christ" (1 Pet. 1:7).

Fighting Strongholds

Proverbs 21:22

A wise man scales the city of the mighty
   and brings down the stronghold in which they trust.

Wisdom is stronger than physical strength. In sports, the smarter team is more likely to defeat the better athletic team. So it is in the military. In business, it is the company that is cleverer that wins over the company with more money and resources.

And so it is in the spiritual life. It is not the amount of Bible knowledge that causes growth in sanctification, but the ability to discern biblical truth. One can memorize these proverbs and learn little from them or even misapply them. The wise are discerning about what these proverbs mean and how they apply.

How is it that Christians can know the gospel and know much Scripture and theology, yet have troubles in their relationships with others? Because they do not exercise wisdom. They try to bring down the stronghold of others by yelling at the wall or beating it with their fists. And they wonder why they cannot succeed. Jesus said, "The sons of this world are more shrewd in dealing with their own generation than the sons of light" (Luke 16:8).

Be wise; be discerning; think through your goal and how to achieve your goal. Strongholds can be scaled and even brought down. All that is needed is wisdom.

Keeping Out of Trouble

Proverbs 21:23

Whoever keeps his mouth and his tongue
   keeps himself out of trouble.

Do you seem to get enmeshed in trouble a lot? The problem may be your tongue. Don't be quick to deny it. The denier claims that the real problem is that he is misunderstood. Other people are too sensitive. They misread his intentions and need to examine themselves. He is sure that other people are spreading rumors about him so that others also misunderstand what he is saying. He sees a pattern in everyone else. For whatever reason, he cannot pick up on himself being the common element of the pattern!

One reason may be that he doesn't view his tongue as the problem is that he does not raise his voice. Indeed, in his mind he is quite courteous. He does not pick up on the tone of his voice. He is not sensitive to how insensitive his remarks are. He makes the fatal flaw of not being able to read (or choosing not to read) the emotions of others or the particular circumstances. What can be said in one place at one time cannot be said in another. What can be said to one person cannot be said to another. What can be said to a person feeling a particular emotion cannot be said when he feels another emotion.

To properly control the tongue requires being attentive to others and one's circumstances. It requires thinking and taking into consideration how what one says will be received. Sounds like a lot of work, but the real work that must be done is the examination of the heart. Controlling the tongue requires examination of one's love for God and for neighbor. It is a lot of work. But controlling the tongue so that blessing rather than trouble comes out produces great blessing to one's neighbor and for oneself.

What will your tongue bring forth today – trouble or blessing?

The Scoffer

Proverbs 21:24

"Scoffer" is the name of the arrogant, haughty man
who acts with arrogant pride.

The arrogance of the scoffer goes beyond believing that he is better than others. Even the prideful man can respect the accomplishments and ability of others. Indeed, his pride grows greater with the more credit he gives to those who come in second to him. The scoffer disdains others. He is not merely better than his neighbors; he is above them. He sees what they cannot see. He regards his neighbors as fools. He mocks them.

Christians fall easily into scoffing. We are incredulous that our neighbors cannot see what we see, somehow crediting ourselves for seeing what in truth we would be blind to without the Spirit. The Christians at Corinth fell into this sin. Paul had to write:

> I have applied all these things to myself and Apollos for your benefit, brothers, that you may learn by us not to go beyond what is written, that none of you may be puffed up in favor of one against another. For who sees anything different in you? What do you have that you did not receive? If then you received it, why do you boast as if you did not receive it? (1 Cor. 4:6-7).

Scoffing is sinful. Its ugliness is magnified in the Christian faith. Examine yourself today regarding this insidious sin. Are there Christian brothers and sisters you scoff at because they just can't "get it"? Do you believe you have insight because you are smarter or more spiritually advanced? Are you unable to see yourself in them?

It is actually good to be discerning spiritually and see into the folly of others. But grief rather than scoffing should be our response. We should grieve over the folly of our brothers and sisters. We should all the more examine our hearts for our own guilt. Folly is not unique to a certain group of people; it afflicts us all and we are most blind to what lies within us.

Killing Desire

Proverbs 21:25-26

The desire of the sluggard kills him,
for his hands refuse to labor.
All day long he craves and craves,
but the righteous gives and does not hold back.

How is it that desire kills the sluggard? Being lazy is the obvious cause. Being a slacker is a serious flaw, to be sure, but combining that flaw with ungodly desire is deadly. Think of the addicted who crave and crave for a fix. Their very addiction makes them sluggards, while all the more it is critical for them to earn money to satisfy their cravings which can never be satisfied. Unless their addiction is broken, they will inevitably die. Think of the person craving for wealth, but lacks discipline. He tries foolish scheme after another, trying to find the route to quick, easy wealth. Each scheme leads him further into debt until the day of reckoning comes. Think of the individual lost in his daydreams which prevent him from applying himself to his work. His very desire keeps him from achieving his goal.

That is why the sluggard is contrasted with the righteous rather than merely the industrious. The righteous desires the right things. He desires to please his Lord. He wants to be like Jesus. He does not curb his cravings so much as he craves good things such as doing good and expressing the love of his Savior. Thus he gives and does not hold back; and thus he receives all the more from his Lord. The desire of the righteous strengthens him rather than weakens. As he blesses, he is blessed.

Intent

Proverbs 21:27

The sacrifice of the wicked is an abomination;
how much more when he brings it with evil intent.

The sacrifice of the wicked is an abomination even when he does so with (in his mind) good intent. The wicked will contribute to charity. They will attend church and contribute to its causes. They will offer up prayers and even volunteer to help others. But because they do not repent of their sins, because they do not submit to the law of God, their sacrifices and "good" deeds are regarded as an abomination.

How much more then when the wicked bring their sacrifices with evil intent. They may give to a church in order to have control or to cover up their wickedness or to win the adulation of others. Attending church may be a means to win political favor or to gain new clients or even to prey upon the unsuspecting. They may pretend to worship while inwardly mocking those who are worshipping.

God will not be mocked. It is better for the wicked to offer no sacrifice. Consider then the false ministers who turn their office of Minister of the Gospel into Salesmen of Prosperity or even Deniers of the Gospel. Tremble for such persons who must give an account before the Almighty Judge. Take not lightly what God calls an abomination.

And take not lightly what our Lord has done for us. For without his sacrifice, our "sacrifices" would be an abomination to God no matter what our intent. His sacrifice was his own precious blood that he presented with the only pure intent ever shown by any man. Let us humbly give him thanks even now.

The Word of the Listener

Proverbs 21:28

A false witness will perish,
  but the word of a man who hears will endure.

Yet another unexpected contrast. We would think the second clause to say something like, "but the word of a man who tells the truth will endure." This contrast draws out the heart condition of the false witness. Such a person lies because he is not interested in a fair hearing of a case but in getting his own way. Some lie to take advantage of another; some lie to avoid being taken advantage of. In either case, the false witness is more concerned in getting the outcome he desires than for the truth to be known.

This proverb also notes what is in the heart of the truth teller. He is interested in the truth. That is why he first takes the time to listen well before speaking. To speak before one has listened is to betray that one's real motive is merely to draw attention to oneself. Will you speak the truth today? The better question is, "Will you listen carefully for the truth?"

A Bold Face

Proverbs 21:29

A wicked man puts on a bold face,
  but the upright gives thought to his ways.

Wickedness does take a certain courage. After all, the wicked man risks getting caught and punished. He is willing to incur the wrath of others. He takes these things upon himself all for greed and spite. And so he puts on his bold face to deceive and to mock, and to show his bravado. But a bold face can do little more than buy some time. Justice will come, either through the law or vengeance of his enemies, and ultimately when he stands before God. At that time there will be no bold face.

A bold face is no replacement for wisdom and righteousness which win favor with God and man, and which provide true security. It is not the bold face, but the upright heart that wins the day. Better to be strong than to feign strength; better to be wise than to pretend cleverness; better to give thought to what pleases God than to act with bravado.

Of No Avail

Proverbs 21:30

No wisdom, no understanding, no counsel
  can avail against the Lord.

Let Psalm 2 provide the commentary for this proverb:
      Why do the nations rage
          and the peoples plot in vain?
      The kings of the earth set themselves,

and the rulers take counsel together,
  against the LORD and against his Anointed, saying,
"Let us burst their bonds apart
  and cast away their cords from us."

He who sits in the heavens laughs;
  the Lord holds them in derision.
Then he will speak to them in his wrath,
  and terrify them in his fury, saying,
"As for me, I have set my King
  on Zion, my holy hill."

I will tell of the decree:
The LORD said to me, "You are my Son;
  today I have begotten you.
Ask of me, and I will make the nations your heritage,
  and the ends of the earth your possession.
You shall break them with a rod of iron
  and dash them in pieces like a potter's vessel."

Now therefore, O kings, be wise;
  be warned, O rulers of the earth.
Serve the LORD with fear,
  and rejoice with trembling.
Kiss the Son,
  lest he be angry, and you perish in the way,
  for his wrath is quickly kindled.
Blessed are all who take refuge in him.

God's kingdom will prevail.

The Victory

Proverbs 21:31

The horse is made ready for the day of battle,
  but the victory belongs to the Lord.

It is good to make plans. It is good to prepare well for whatever battle one faces. But always remember that the victory belongs to the Lord. His will *will* be done. With such knowledge you should:

1. Maintain an attitude of prayer throughout your preparations and battle. You may pray for victory, but more importantly that you will honor Christ in the battle.

2. Neither bemoan your weakness nor be puffed up in your strength. It is by your weakness that God's strength is made known. Whatever strength you may have is what God has given to you.

3. God has his own purposes beyond your battle. You do not know what those purposes are. But you do know that all things are to work toward his glory, and you know that as his child those purposes include your good. God is not distant, indifferent to your battles. But God is also not contained in your small world.

4. Whatever success you may experience, the victory belongs to the Lord and he is to receive all credit and glory.

Now go forth to your battles today.

A Good Name

Proverbs 22:1

A good name is to be chosen rather than great riches,
and favor is better than silver or gold.

This is the lesson George Bailey learned in the movie "It's a Wonderful Life." One earns a good name by living a good life, and that name becomes a sound investment. The person with a good name is more likely to receive help when the time comes. He is more likely to receive the benefit of the doubt should he be slandered. He is more likely to be defended by his neighbors when attacked. Others will speak up for him; people are pleased to do favors for him. Even his opponents will give him respect.

A good name does not guarantee security, and sometimes the good life actually leads to a poor reputation, as even Christ experienced. All the more then the importance of having a good name before God who is our true judge. And all the more important to find one's identity in Christ. It is his name that gives us a good name before God.

And let us exalt now the name of Jesus before whom every knee shall bow, in heaven and on earth and under the earth, and every tongue will confess that Jesus Christ is Lord, to the glory of God the Father (Phil. 2:10).

The Rich and the Poor

Proverbs 22:2

The rich and the poor meet together;
the Lord is the maker of them all.

Whether rich or poor, we are all creatures made by God to glorify God. There is nothing we possess that we were not given – neither money nor the ability to make money, neither favorable circumstances of birth nor the wit to climb out of unfavorable circumstances. There is no such thing as a self-made man nor an unlucky man.

The Lord is the maker of us all. That means we share the same value before him and the same status of sinners. We may look at one another and say, "There go I," for we both bear the image of God. It is for mankind, which includes us all, that Christ became man and died. It is to man in every circumstance – rich or poor, slave or free, male or female – that the gospel is freely given.

Therefore, no one can boast of what he possesses or has attained. He would have nothing unless granted by his Maker. Nor can man boast of how he deserves favor. Nor can anyone complain about his circumstance, as though he deserved better. For our Maker does not reveal his secret counsels and makes clear that what anyone receives is out of grace and mercy.

It is said that contentment lies not in what we possess but in accepting our circumstances. That is not quite true. Real contentment does lie in what we possess. The trouble of the rich is that they think of the wrong possessions; the trouble of the poor is that they fail to understand what they have. Whether rich or poor, they are "rich in faith and heirs of the kingdom, which God has promised to those who love him" (Jas. 2:5).

Seeing Danger

Proverbs 22:3

The prudent sees danger and hides himself,
  but the simple go on and suffer for it.

This is the same message as the proverb: Fools rush in where angels fear to dread. The simple "go on" either because they do not see the danger or because they estimate themselves too highly, thinking they can withstand harm.

The prudent does not hide himself out of cowardliness. Rather, he is able to discern the danger *and* discern the appropriate action to take, which will at times be to hide or walk away. As an old Kenny Rogers song says, "You've got to know when to hold them (cards) and know when to fold them." There are times to speak up and times to remain quiet; times to stand one's ground and times to give in. There are times to fight and times to make peace. The prudent understands the times; the simple does not.

And thus the simple person oftentimes suffers for his actions. He is admonished for his speech and punished for his behavior, and he actually does not seem to know why. He cannot look about him and see how his action is inappropriate.

Certainly the lesson is for us to develop our ability to discern. We are to be prudent. But all the more let us thank our God who watches over us. For the most prudent person is still unaware of most dangers. We do not see the future; we do not see the unseen spiritual

380

world. We do not grasp fully our depravity and frailty nor the power of the evil one. How many times have we been oblivious to the dangers about us and God has protected us from suffering? Let us thank God for the prudent One who saw our danger and put himself forward to suffer on our behalf.

Riches, Honor, Life

Proverbs 22:4

The reward for humility and fear of the Lord
  is riches and honor and life.

What riches? Every spiritual blessing in the heavenly places in Christ, the riches of God's grace, forgiveness of sin, redemption, the indwelling of the Holy Spirit, the riches of his glorious inheritance in the saints, adoption by God as his child, God's steadfast, unmerited love.

What honor? To be called a child of God, to hear "well done, good and faithful servant," to be called brother or sister by Jesus Christ, to actually receive "praise and honor and glory at the revelation of Jesus Christ," to someday receive an "eternal weight of glory beyond all comparison," to wear the crown of life.

What life? Abundant life in Christ, a forgiven life, a redeemed life, an eternal life of joy, a meaningful life, a transformed life, a life to come in which we will not sin nor be sinned against nor feel any effect of sin, a life spend in the presence of God and of the Lamb.

Not a bad deal.

Thorns and Snares

Proverbs 22:5

Thorns and snares are in the way of the crooked;
  whoever guards his soul will keep far from them.

This proverb has the similar message of 22:3: "The prudent sees danger and hides himself, but the simple go on and suffer for it." The new contrast is between the crooked (the wicked) and the righteous who take care to guard their souls. But the results are the same. Like the simple, the crooked find trouble in the path they have chosen to take. Like the prudent, the righteous is alert to where danger lurks and stays away from it.

One might say that the crooked and simple are the more daring, while the prudent and righteous are afraid to be risk-takers. Yet at the heart of both proverbs is not about being daring but being foolish. The simple is foolish in his estimate of the danger; the crooked is foolish in choosing a path that is wicked. The prudent and the righteous are both wise in sizing up danger and honorable in choosing what risk to take.

One man walks into a seedy neighborhood thinking that he can flirt with danger and temptation. Another walks into the same neighborhood to befriend someone, well aware of the danger but more intent to do what is right. Both take risks. Both put themselves in situations where trouble could come. But who is more likely to get into further trouble?

The simple and the crooked are lured by the excitement of temptation. That is why they fail to see their danger. That is why obstacles keep popping up. Their eyes are fixed on sin. The eyes of the prudent and the righteous are fixed on Christ, which makes them all the more alert to the greatest danger – the attacks against their souls.

Remember the greatest danger before you today. It is not that you might get hit by a car or robbed. It is that situations will catch you off guard and lead you to sin. Satan is not so interested in making you physically suffer; as revealed with Job, what he wants is to lead you astray. Be alert to the real enemy and the real danger.

Train Up a Child

Proverbs 22:6

Train up a child in the way he should go;
  even when he is old he will not depart from it.

Literally, the first line reads "according to the way he *will* go." Some then have interpreted the meaning to be that if you raise a child according to his inclination, he will set on a crooked path that he will not depart. Certainly that is true, and many parents bemoan that their children did actually depart from the way they should go.

Nevertheless, there is much truth to our traditional understanding of the proverb. Covenant children are likely to grow up in Christian faith and keep it. Even if their faith remains a second-hand faith inherited from their upbringing, they nevertheless keep along the law-keeping path. And even if they consciously reject their parents' faith, they still have ingrained in them Christian instincts hard to shake off.

Indeed, the testimony of many covenant children is that of wandering from the faith and returning to it precisely because of what they learned as children. They remember the Bible stories and verses. They remember the hymns. One covenant child turned to God in the midst of overdosing on drugs because hymns popped into his mind at the time and kept him sane.

Raise up your children in the way they should go. Remember that the way to go is to Jesus for grace and mercy. They should see that that is where you go. They should see that as law-abiding as you might try to be, what really motivates you is the mercy found in Christ, that it is Christ's strength that makes you strong, that it is the forgiveness found in him that gives you hope. It is such hope and love for our Savior that will keep many a child on the right path and not depart from it.

Slavery

Proverbs 22:7

The rich rules over the poor,

and the borrower is the slave of the lender.

The rich man rules over the poor man who is dependent upon him. The lender has control over the man who borrows from him. This is the disadvantage we should strive to avoid. What difference does it make that I owe money to someone else? That someone else has a claim on me. In a sense I work for him, for I am earning money to turn over to him.

Desire for comforts and pleasures leads us into indebtedness and keeps us from financial independence. But that very desire then is frustrated because we must work all the harder to satisfy the debt it has created. The rich man and the lender are the ones who get their desire through our labor.

What then do we do? For one, we should follow the teachings of the proverbs to be industrious, to build wealth slowly, and to walk along the righteous path. And then we would do well to follow James' admonition: "Let the lowly brother boast in his exaltation," that is, in his standing in Christ (Jas. 1:9). In Christ we are free; in Christ we are rich. If we would see who we are and what we have in him, then our desire for worldly gain and pleasure would diminish; then, oddly enough, we would do the things that actually lead to greater security and freedom.

For in truth, it is what gives us most pleasure that we become slaves to. If it is of the world, then we become slaves of the world and its lenders; if our pleasure is in Christ, then we become his slaves where we find ultimate freedom.

Reaping What We Sow

Proverbs 22:8

Whoever sows injustice will reap calamity,
  and the rod of his fury will fail.

We reap what we sow. The employer who sows injustice among his employees will reap poor performance. The seller who sows injustice

384

among his customers will reap business failure. The parent who sows injustice within the family will see his children turn rebellious. The employer may threaten to fire, the seller may act offended, and the parent may yell but their rod of fury will lose its force. A person will endure injustice only so long. Either he will retaliate or he will leave.

Are you sowing injustice? As a Christian you may actually have more difficulty seeing what you are doing. We are quick to admit when we lose our temper or overreact or some other sin that we explain as a momentary relapse. What is more difficult to see (and to admit) is a pattern of sowing injustice in our relationships. We then are surprised to learn that a spouse or a child or a friend or a colleague has harbored resentment against us.

Perhaps it is time to do a reality check. Pay attention to others and how they respond to you. Ask if there is something you need to examine and do not get defensive if they do have something to say. You don't want to find out years later what you are reaping.

A Bountiful Eye

Proverbs 22:9

Whoever has a bountiful eye will be blessed,
  for he shares his bread with the poor.

What is a "bountiful" eye? It can be translated good or generous. It is evidently an eye that looks about and sees ways to bless others. The man with the bountiful eye bestows bounty to others, but also included is the thought that he reaps bounty.

Compare this proverb with 11:24: "One gives freely, yet grows all the richer; another withholds what he should give, and only suffers want." Generosity is a virtue; furthermore, it is a virtue that reaps its own reward.

But generosity means taking delight in giving. One may give a generous amount, but do so begrudgingly or with the intent to earn reward or assuage guilt. This proverb is upholding the person who

385

looks for opportunity to give because he delights in giving. He shares his bread with the poor because he delights in heartening others, and because he delights in pleasing his Lord, who delights in our giving to the poor.

So in the same manner our Lord Jesus Christ has a bountiful eye. He delighted in doing God's will; he delighted in giving himself for us who were poor; he delights even now in sharing his riches with his people who believe in him.

Of Scoffer and Strife

Proverbs 22:10

Drive out a scoffer, and strife will go out,
   and quarreling and abuse will cease.

This is a proverb that has been proven many times in all kinds of settings. One person can sow discord throughout a team, a staff, a class, any group. He does not have to be openly rebellious. All he needs to do is consistently say a few words of discontent and disrespect, a few sarcastic remarks. At first others may shake off his words; they may quickly mark him as being a problem. But after a while the words begin to have their effect.

For there are always some things that are not right, that could be better. But whereas, before, the others may have overlooked such problems, they begin to get bothered. "John may be a complainer, but he is right about Tom being too harsh sometimes." "I hadn't thought about it before, but John does have a point." "Maybe John is right; maybe I should file a complaint." "John is being too sarcastic, but that was funny the way he made Tom sound."

And then John leaves. As if a fresh wind had blown through a room and driven away a foul odor, so the atmosphere changes.

Is there a scoffer on your team? Are you the scoffer? Christians can be just as guilty and actually worse because we cannot admit to ourselves that we are guilty. Do you have a complaining attitude?

386

Does everyone in your workplace or class know what disgruntles you? Are you a person that other complainers are attracted to? Better to change than to have to leave for peace to come.

Gracious Speech

Proverbs 22:11

He who loves purity of heart,
and whose speech is gracious, will have the king as his friend.

Note the addition of gracious speech. Shouldn't purity of heart be enough for friendship, even with a king? It is speech that conveys what is in the heart. Speech can be used to deceive, and other proverbs warn of flattery, but the point here is that one with a pure heart considers his words carefully.

Paul uses this same concept in regard to witnessing: "Conduct yourselves wisely toward outsiders, making the best use of the time. Let your speech always be gracious, seasoned with salt, so that you may know how you ought to answer each person" (Col. 4:5-6).

Does graciousness characterize your speech? Are people encouraged after speaking with you? Even in disagreements, do they acknowledge that you demonstrate due respect and fairness? Do they respect you?

What is gracious speech? It lacks grumbling and sarcasm. It certainly is void of profanity. It pays sincere compliments readily. It is encouraging. Its focus is on the welfare of others. It flows from a mind that is consciously thinking of the right and good thing to say. It flows from a heart that truly cares to honor God and respect one's neighbor.

Have such a heart; speak with gracious words – you must be a friend of the King.

Words Overthrown

Proverbs 22:12

The eyes of the Lord keep watch over knowledge,
  but he overthrows the words of the traitor.

God watches over knowledge as a shepherd watches over his flock. Far from fearing knowledge, Christians should above all nurture it and strive to grow in knowledge, for God is the God of truth. It is good to grow in all the fields of knowledge, except for learning the ways to sin. That is really the only knowledge that Adam and Eve gained. They learned to think like Satan.

Such knowledge God despises, and he will turn against the one who uses it. Let us remember this as we worry over evil men getting away with wickedness. God will overthrow them, most often in this lifetime but with ultimate finality after death. It is that second death that Christ tells us to fear which awaits the wicked.

The traitor thinks he is getting away with his treachery. All that he is doing is storing up God's wrath that will be carried out. God is not blind to our sin nor will he be mocked. Do not be jealous of the traitor or anyone who uses deceit. Rather, all the more determine to speak the truth and to uphold knowledge, especially the knowledge that is of Jesus Christ.

Lion in the Streets!

Proverbs 22:13

The sluggard says, "There is a lion outside!
  I shall be killed in the streets!"

He does have a point. We may not worry about lions, but there are cars and trucks that could hit us. It may be best not to go outside to work. And, for that matter, there are dangers in the home – tripping down the stairs, stumbling over shoes, or stepping on a ball. It may be best to remain in bed. Too bad the sluggard in Solomon's day did not have TV and a remote. Today's sluggard does not even have to come up with excuses for not doing work. The distraction of 24 hour television with literally hundreds of channels saves him from having

388

to think up rationalizations for lying in bed or the couch. He can get by with the dull thought of "I'll get up in just a minute."

Peter tells us that there is actually a lion out there ready to devour us (1 Pet. 5:8). The problem is that he is also within our home, even within our room, even under the bedcovers! Whatever imaginary lions the sluggard has to keep him from doing something with his life, he should be taking into account this very real lion – Satan – who is devouring his very soul. Inactivity is a killer of the soul; for we were made to act, to produce, to glorify our Maker through being makers in his image.

Whether healthy or ill; whether bold or timid, do whatever God has given you the ability to do that he might be glorified. Who knows, maybe today you will meet a lion in the streets and slay him!

The Deep Pit

Proverbs 22:14

The mouth of forbidden women is a deep pit;
he with whom the Lord is angry will fall into it.

A kiss is not just a kiss when the purpose is to lure into sin, a sin that leads into the pit of destruction. Words of invitation to pleasure are words of poison when that pleasure is forbidden passion. The folly of men is to believe that the sin is harmless and that they have the discernment and willpower to avoid the pit. But if money is the root of evil, then understand that sex is the root of folly. Sex makes a man foolish. An otherwise cool-thinking man becomes stupid when his sexual passion is aroused. He actually believes that illicit sex will give him satisfaction. He is actually willing to risk his reputation, his career, and his family for the sake of momentary pleasure that vanishes immediately and which leaves him craving for more, never fulfilled.

What then is the second line of the proverb saying? Is God angry with men who fall into such a pit, or does he allow men with whom he is angry to fall into it? Sometimes our punishment is to be allowed to go where our passions lead us.

Men, don't be stupid. Know your weakness when it comes to sexual temptation. Know that you cannot think straight and walk away. The best way to deal with such temptation is not to brace yourself against the temptation but to walk away from it. The best way to avoid falling into the pit is to get away from the edge of it.

A Child's Folly

Proverbs 22:15

Folly is bound up in the heart of a child,
  but the rod of discipline drives it far from him.

This proverb presents a premise that corrects the idea that a child merely needs to be educated as to what is right. Education is necessary, and much of the time children do merely need to be instructed as to what is right and they will then do it. But children are also like adults in that they are sinners. Much of their folly comes from their sinful desires. And so, oftentimes without any instruction that something is wrong to do, they will nevertheless act in secret. They have a conscience, just as adults, and like adults will violate it.

This is where discipline comes in, which is necessary for children and adults. The essential difference is that discipline has a greater chance of driving out the folly in the child than the adult. If discipline is exercised wisely and consistently, the child is likely to learn his lesson and become a wiser person.

Even so, however much good discipline can do regarding folly, it still cannot cleanse the heart. A child may grow into a mature adult with a good head on his shoulders through the help of proper discipline. But he cannot be disciplined to love the Lord; he cannot be disciplined to see his need for a Savior nor given the desire to follow his Lord. That is the work of the Spirit.

And so as parents, we need to exercise wise, consistent discipline to drive out the folly that is naturally inherent in our children. We are to instruct them in the Word of God and teach them the gospel. And we are to pray for the Holy Spirit to blow into them the breath of God that they may have life.

Real Poverty

Proverbs 22:16

Whoever oppresses the poor to increase his own wealth,
  or gives to the rich, will only come to poverty.

A lot of rich people will dispute this proverb. It is precisely by taking advantage of the poor (that is, those who do not how to or are incapable of making wealth) that wealth is achieved. Furthermore, a key to wealth-making is knowing to whom to give and so open doors for getting even more back.

But this proverb is not about how to get rich; it is about justice. As we have already seen, Proverbs does not despise wealth but how one obtains it. Steady accumulation over time is praised; get rich quick schemes are frowned upon, especially when such schemes (as most do) depend upon taking advantage of the poor and others who cannot fend for themselves. This proverb addresses that injustice, plus the added element that goes with it, which is forming a good old boy network of the haves against the have-nots.

The ugliness of the scenario presented is that of relationships formed – both adversarial and friendly – based purely upon what one's neighbor can and cannot do for one's own financial advancement. The one who has money is a friend; the one doesn't is a sucker. In both cases the neighbors are merely means to an end. They have no other significance.

Treating both the poor and the rich like this, you will certainly end up in poverty regarding relationships. You will be impoverished spiritually. You can only end up cynical, and you die with no satisfaction. And, for that matter, you stand a good chance of dying financially impoverished. For when difficult times come, your so-

391

called "friends" want to take advantage of you. Grow rich in relationships and you cannot really be poor.

Trust in the Lord

Proverbs 22:17-21

Incline your ear, and hear the words of the wise,
and apply your heart to my knowledge,
for it will be pleasant if you keep them within you,
if all of them are ready on your lips.
That your trust may be in the LORD,
I have made them known to you today, even to you.
Have I not written for you thirty sayings
of counsel and knowledge,
to make you know what is right and true,
that you may give a true answer to those who sent you?

Note the central motivation for learning the proverbs: that your trust may be in the Lord. Knowing what is right and true, gaining wisdom and knowledge – these things lead to trust, not skepticism. Faith in God is not based upon superstition, myth, and old wives' tales. It flows out of knowledge from the Scriptures which is then reinforced by knowledge from natural revelation and experience.

Why, then, do educated people not turn more naturally to faith? For the same reason uneducated people do not – sin. Man fails to trust God because he does not want to trust God. He wants to take pride in himself, to boast of his own wits. He therefore chooses his own path to knowledge, proving in his own mind that knowledge leads him from God.

But for you who believe, who want to grow closer to God, then seek knowledge; seek wisdom. Study the Scriptures; continue to study the Proverbs and meditate upon them so that your trust may be in the Lord alone.

Pleader for the Poor

Proverbs 22:22-23

Do not rob the poor, because he is poor,
or crush the afflicted at the gate,
for the Lord will plead their cause
and rob of life those who rob them.

How can one rob the poor? Why bother to crush the afflicted? Why bother, even if one is wicked, to do what brings no gain? Perhaps there is a robbery and an affliction that occurs by ignoring the plight of the poor and the afflicted. Concerning the commandment not to steal, the Larger Catechism contends that this means we are to "endeavor, by all just and lawful means, to procure, preserve, and further the wealth and outward estate of others, as well as our own" (A. 141). The poor and the afflicted are the class of people least likely to be given consideration. For we condemn them for the ills they have brought on themselves or else are embarrassed by them. As there may be no gain in robbing the poor or crushing the afflicted, so we do not see gain in helping those who "won't help themselves" or those who have given up in despair.

We need to take note of the class of people that Scripture time and again says God is on the side of. We need to do some soul-searching, because God evidently is quite willing to search our souls about this. He is taking sides. He becomes the pleader of their cause. He is not an indifferent judge on this matter. Indeed, he is ready to judge us according to our response to them. Whose side do you want to be found on?

Anger's Snare

Proverbs 22:24-25

Make no friendship with a man given to anger,
nor go with a wrathful man,
lest you learn his ways
and entangle yourself in a snare.

What might you learn from a man given to anger?

You might confuse a temper tantrum for forceful action. Men given to anger think that the expression of anger shows they mean business when it merely means they are immature. Those on the receiving end of the anger lose respect for such a man. If they seem to jump to orders at his rage, it is because of his position of power not because of the anger itself which they resent and behind his back will mock.

You might believe that anger is necessary to motivate yourself. This really is a danger, because such an idea has even become institutionalized. Athletes buy into it wholesale, as do many others in competitive situations. They believe that anger gives them the competitive edge. They don't understand that it is not anger that marks the champion, but the commitment to excellence. Anger may give spurts of energy, but more often than not it gives the competition the edge as the wise competitor knows how to use the other man's anger to his own advantage.

You might discover too late that you have unconsciously taken on the traits of the angry friend, just as children of angry parents take on their parents' anger. You don't notice how the tone in your voice has changed, how quick you are to take offense. What you begin to see is how sensitive your friends are becoming, how impatient they seem to be with you, how irritating small things become. And then you are caught in the snare of losing those closest to you and lacking the patience to win them back.

Insecure Security

Proverbs 22:26-27

Be not one of those who give pledges,
who put up security for debts.
If you have nothing with which to pay,
why should your bed be taken from under you?

The proverbs are quick to encourage generosity. They are also quick to discourage foolishness. It is generous to give and to give sacrificially. It is foolish to tie oneself to another man's questionable ability to handle his money properly.

The very fact that a person needs another signer means something about him carries risk. Perhaps he simply has yet to build a credit history. Perhaps his credit history is poor. Perhaps he does not have sufficient equity to cover a loss. Whatever the case, there is risk. You should decide beforehand whether or not you can sufficiently cover the risk. If you decide that you can, you should already in your mind treat the co-signing as a gift given. If the other person comes through and you lose no money, then that is an added bonus.

Lending name or property that you cannot afford to lose, but that you do out of loyalty or guilt, helps no one. You put yourself in a worrisome position. Even should the other person come through, you meanwhile are anxious. If he does not come through, if he is late in coming through, there will be inevitable tension in your relationship and likely a break in it. Then there is the very real financial loss. If you are married and if you have children, your loss becomes theirs.

Again, it is not giving generously that is the issue here. It is committing to something that you have no control over – the ability of your neighbor making good on what he has committed to – that is the issue. Do not make commitments that, should they cause financial loss, you are not willing to accept such loss gracefully.

Remember, the gospel is about giving treasure away. It is not about making loans that remain valuable to you and which will bring harm if not repaid.

Ancient Landmarks

Proverbs 22:28

*Do not move the ancient landmark
    that your fathers have set.*

This refers to the boundary lines marking the property belonging to a family. Its application is that we are to honor all contracts and agreements made before us. We do not move property lines; we do not revise contracts – that is, not without appropriate agreements. An appropriate agreement is not merely a legal one, but one in which we are assuring fairness for the other party.

It means that we take responsibility for the agreements that our fathers and grandfathers and great-grandfathers made. As citizens, we take responsibility for the agreements made by our government both past and present. So do we as members of a church. So do we as members of God's kingdom.

Consider some of the ancient landmarks set by Christ – turn the other cheek, do unto others what you would have them do unto you, go the extra mile. Such agreements we inherited when we took our inheritance. We may not revise the lines; we may not add conditional clauses. As our fathers accepted these lines, so must we, knowing as they did the property awaiting us in heaven.

Skill

Proverbs 22:29

Do you see a man skillful in his work?
  He will stand before kings;
  he will not stand before obscure men.

Skill is admired. Whether it be skill with one's hands and one's mind; whether it be artistic work or that of the laborer, a person of skill is admired especially by his peers. It is they who will bring him before "kings" for recognition.

The skillful person not only has the skill but delights in using it. That is what separates him from others. Such delight compels him to perfect his craft. He is dedicated to his work because the very work itself (perhaps even more than the finished product) gives him pleasure. The tragedy for many persons of skill is letting the recognition of "kings" divert their attention to fame and thus lose their focus and pleasure in their work. They become more interested in being known for their skill than in exercising their skill.

The proverb is not dismissing recognition. It is presenting recognition as a reward for skill. But remember – it is the skill, not promotion that leads him before the kings. Keep attentive to what you do well. For some day you will stand before the King to present your work. Take pleasure in that work now; take joy in the ability given you now to serve your King.

Table Manners

Proverbs 23:1-3

When you sit down to eat with a ruler,
  observe carefully what is before you,
and put a knife to your throat
  if you are given to appetite.
Do not desire his delicacies
  for they are deceptive food.

These verses open a section that goes through verse 8, presenting the scenario of a person being brought into the circle of the higher class. It seems the teacher disapproves of enjoying good fortune. What he is really addressing is how moving up to a "higher" class or entering into an "inner ring" can blind us to realities that accompany this seemingly better life.

Why be so careful at the dinner table of a person of higher rank? For one thing, you are being watched and judged. However friendly the "ruler" might seem, however much he may seem to want you to feel at home, he is watching and judging your behavior. You are not sitting among old friends who accept you as you are. You are sitting among persons who are still determining if you are worthy of being with them. You have to strike a careful balance – showing due appreciation without getting too excited, appreciating good food without over indulging.

Another thing to be careful of is what will be expected of you afterwards. Once you accept the hospitality of the "ruler," you are now in his debt. He may be expecting favors from you later. All the more, you need to watch that you do not over indulge in his generosity.

How good it is to sit at our Ruler's table of the most precious food – the bread and the wine that represent the body and the blood of Jesus Christ. How good it is to know that there are no strings attached. At this table is where our Ruler communicates that we are fully accepted.

Taking Flight

Proverbs 23:4-5

Do not toil to acquire wealth;
  be discerning enough to desist.
When your eyes light on it, it is gone,
  for suddenly it sprouts wings,
  flying like an eagle toward heaven.

Is it wrong to desire to be wealthy? It is wrong if wealth is the objective for working. Work is good. Managing your money well so that your assets grow is good. You ought to aim for financial security. You ought to think ahead so as to provide for your retirement and not be a burden to others if possible. You ought to provide for your family.

But wealth itself should not be your object. Why? The reason given here is its transitory nature. Wealth can be lost and, indeed, is likely to be lost if you have single-mindedly worked towards it. It is one thing to become wealthy out of wise, thrifty handling of your money; it is another because you have figured out some get-rich scheme. It is one thing to become wealthy because of a devotion to the product you are producing or the service you are providing; it is another because you are only devoted to stuffing your own pockets. It is one thing to become wealthy because you have treated others fairly; it is another because you used people as means to your advantage.

The lust for wealth skewers our values. And if we are on the outside of the wealthy circle trying to get in, our tendency will be to take unethical means to get inside. Keep in perspective what really matters for happiness. It is not wealth. It is not being with the "in" crowd. It is in doing work that itself is fulfilling. It is in providing properly for your family. It is in honoring the Lord. This is where true, lasting happiness comes that does not fly off.

After Dinner Effects

Proverbs 23:6-8

Do not eat the bread of a man who is stingy;
  do not desire his delicacies,
for he is like one who is inwardly calculating.
  "Eat and drink!" he says to you,
  but his heart is not with you.
You will vomit up the morsels that you have eaten,
  and waste your pleasant words.

We come back to the table of verses 1-3. The host, be he a ruler or not, is also observing you. He gives the impression of being generous but is not. He is calculating how much you are costing him. He says to eat and drink, but he is taking note of how much you actually are. He is seething that you are taking him at his word. He thinks you should know better, or else he is risking (in his mind) that you are worth the investment. For that is how he perceives you – a risk investment. He is hoping that his "generosity" will pay off and that he will get back from you more than he has had to put out.

Perhaps you will prove to be a good investment and end up doing favors that you find you cannot get out of. Perhaps you will be a poor investment, thinking that mere expressions of appreciation are enough, only to find you are no longer welcome in his house.

How do you know whether a man is truly generous or inwardly stingy and calculating? You have to do your own share of observation. You cannot let displays of wealth blind you. Observe the man. Observe the way he is with his servants, with his family. Are those who are constantly around him happy and at ease? Are they generous? A truly generous man will rub off on those around him, just as a truly stingy man will do so.

Be discerning. This is what all the proverbs are about. Look beyond yourself and pay attention to what is going on around you. Be a good listener and a good observer. Don't let delicacies cloud your seeing and impair your hearing. Don't let sensual pleasures befuddle your discernment. See through to the giver. Observe him. From him judge whether the delicacies are to be truly enjoyed or turned away. It is the giver, not the delicacies who makes the feast.

A Fool's Perspective

Proverbs 23:9

Do not speak in the hearing of a fool,
  for he will despise the good sense of your words.

This proverb repeats a recurring theme. A fool is a fool not because he has yet to be taught wisdom but because he despises wisdom. His problem is not that he lacks education. Indeed, there are many well-educated fools. Nor is his problem a mere lack of understanding to be solved by someone patiently reasoning with him. He despises wisdom. He is offended by it.

The love of wisdom requires a greater interest in truth than in self, which the fool cannot give up. The irony is that his interest in himself works against him as he regularly makes choices that make his condition worse. But he cannot see that. He cannot see what others see clearly because he cannot get outside himself to look. He certainly cannot put himself in the place of others and see from their perspective. He can only view others from his own self-interest perspective. Thus, what you might say to his benefit, he interprets as you acting from your self-interest.

How then will the fool ever learn? Experientially, he is more likely to learn through facing the consequences of his actions – receiving

400

punishment, experiencing poverty or physical pain through his own abuse, seeing the pain he has inflicted on others, etc. Where reason fails, painful consequences can sometimes succeed. If not, they can at least curb behavior and restrain the fool to a degree.

He may never learn. He will never learn unless the Holy Spirit works in him to effect a change. After all, that is the only reason we turned from our foolishness to receiving the gospel.

The Fatherless

Proverbs 23:10-11

Do not move an ancient landmark
or enter the fields of the fatherless,
for their Redeemer is strong;
he will plead their cause against you.

The wicked prey upon the weak and defenseless precisely because there seems to be little risk in doing so. They have little to no influence with the powers-to-be; they have no money to "buy" justice. They have no kin – at least kin who can do anything – to stand up for them.

But such persons do have an advocate to plead their cause, an advocate who never loses his case. Their advocate is their Redeemer who buys them, thus making their property his own. The crimes committed against them are crimes committed against him.

Judgment will be rendered against all perpetrators. Almost all will experience judgment in their earthly life; all will experience complete judgment after death. It is this second death that the Redeemer said to fear the most. However terrible the loss of physical life may be, it is the casting of a soul into hell that is the great horror, a judgment from which the wicked cannot escape.

The only hope of such escape is to recognize that one is poor and an orphan. It is to acknowledge that you are the neediest of all and the most wicked of all. For to make such confession now will result not

401

in judgment but in being bought by your Redeemer. Confess now. Repent now. By acknowledging that you are fatherless, you will find your Father and know your Redeemer.

Heart Instruction

Proverbs 23:12

Apply your heart to instruction
  and your ear to words of knowledge.

This is a good proverb to heed in a culture which teaches that the one thing we can trust is our heart.

"Go with your heart."
"What does your heart tell you?"
"Follow your heart."

Movies, TV, and the pop music industry (the real instruction institutions of our society) invariably teach that the heart is to be trusted over anyone and anything, especially in times of crisis. By listening to the heart, we will know when to go against conventional wisdom and when to defy the instructions even of the people we respect and love the most. The heart is supposedly the place of instinct, of innate knowledge.

For the Scriptures, the heart needs instruction just like the mind, indeed, more so. As Jesus said, "Out of the heart of man, come evil thoughts" (Matt. 15:19). Due to the fall, the heart loves sin. The heart "feels good" about the things God hates. Consider the bigoted mind that hates others of different races. Such a person acts on what his heart feels right. Even the wicked oppress the weak out of what feels right. They despise the weak and don't understand why others do not as well.

Thus the heart needs instruction as to what is right and wrong. And more. For instruction, as essential as it is, cannot change the heart. The proverb says to apply your heart to instruction. There's the rub. You must first desire instruction, and that takes a heart change.

Where then is your hope? It is in God's Spirit who can change your heart. Pray for such a work, and don't fool yourself into thinking that because you have been regenerated by the Spirit all the work needed has been done. The toughest case is the Christian who thinks by virtue of being Christian his heart is all right. Sanctification – the process of cleansing the heart from all sin – is a lifetime work. Start each morning praying for that work to continue in your heart, applying it to instruction.

Discipline

Proverbs 23:13-14

Do not withhold discipline from a child;
  if you strike him with a rod, he will not die.
If you strike him with the rod,
  you will save his soul from Sheol.

"Do not withhold discipline" implies that discipline is necessary for the health of the child. To withhold discipline is to withhold care; it is to shirk one's responsibility to provide for the welfare, in this case, of one's child. To withhold discipline signals that the parent either does not truly care for the wellbeing of his child or that he is too fearful to carry through on what is right.

It is heartless not to let one's child experience repercussion for his sin. It is cowardly to avoid setting and enforcing rules of behavior. No adult has ever thanked parents for failing to discipline or for not setting boundaries.

Parents can abuse and too often even good parents mishandle discipline. Thus, parents are to continually examine themselves. But they nevertheless cannot escape their responsibility before God. They must be the ones with an eye to the future, something their children cannot see.

And they must be willing to accept discipline themselves. Do they accept discipline from authorities – government, the workplace, the church? All who have some measure of authority have the same responsibility to exercise discipline. We are all willing, so we say, to accept the discipline of the Lord, but we rarely are willing to accept the Lord's discipline that is meted out through his human instruments. If you expect your children to accept your discipline, let them see you model how that is done.

Parent and Child

Proverbs 23:15-16

My son, if your heart is wise,
  my heart too will be glad.
My inmost being will exult
  when your lips speak what is right.

So speaks a father and so concurs a mother. Parents want what they perceive is good for their children. Most want their children not to suffer and to succeed in life in the various forms by which success is measured. Mostly, they want their children to be happy. They may differ with their children about what makes up happiness or how to attain it, but to see their children content and happy contributes to their own happiness.

This proverb gets under the surface of outward happiness to what really matters to most parents – to have a child who is wise. It is the goal of the parent to guide a child to maturity, to discern between right and wrong, to make wise choices regarding friends, to apply oneself in education, to be dependable, to take a career that is fulfilling and provides for one's needs, to choose a good spouse should one marry, and to wisely raise good children should children be granted.

The parent cannot disconnect his or her happiness from his child. He will grieve over a child's foolishness and rejoice over the child's wisdom. That is how it should be, for that is the natural relationship God has established between parent and child. We are connected to our children and to our parents. We cannot control others, but we can care about honoring our parents through our own pursuit of wisdom and care about blessing our children through teaching and modeling wisdom. And we can honor our Father through pursuing the wisdom he has revealed in his Word and living out the "foolishness" of the gospel.

Our Hope

Proverbs 23:17-18

Let not your heart envy sinners,
   but continue in the fear of the Lord all the day.
Surely there is a future,
   and your hope will not be cut off.

It is easy to envy sinners. Consider what they have. They may sin without guilt. They may even recast sin as good and natural. They have no commands to obey. They have no responsibility for their neighbor. The only responsibility they have is what they place upon themselves, which they may remove at any time. They may give thought to their pleasure without considering anyone else, including an omniscient God who watches them. They can make life to be the way they want it to be.

Believers, on the other hand, are saddled with the two great commands: to love God with all that one has and to love one's neighbor as oneself. We cannot do anything without taking these commands into account. We live in the world but are not allowed to be of the world, which greatly complicates our lives. Furthermore, we have an omniscient God whom we know will judge us.

What do we get in return? We are given a sure future; we have a secure hope of eternal joy and even glory, living in the presence of our God. But if we are perceptive enough, we will see that our hope lies not only in the promise of God about the future, but in the present blessings of today. Blessed is the man now who walks in the path of righteousness because his life now is filled with purpose. Now he is a blessing to others. Now he is rendering profitable service to his Lord. Now he is filled with the Holy Spirit, knows God as his Father, and experiences the blessings found in his Redeemer. It is because we glimpse present glory that we can feel in our hearts the future glory and know that our hope will not be cut off.

Be Wise

Proverbs 23:19-21

Hear, my son, and be wise,
and direct your heart in the way.
Be not among drunkards
or among gluttonous eaters of meat,
for the drunkard and the glutton will come to poverty,
and slumber will clothe them with rags.

"Be not among" – that is, do not be as one of them. Be wise and direct your heart; do not follow your heart. Do you want to be your own decision maker? Then be it now while you can. Choose to follow the way of righteousness now. For once you choose to be among the drunkards and gluttons, you will find your will to choose gone. Drunkards do not choose to remain drunkards. They do not choose to lose their willpower and destroy all their relationships. They do not choose to be fired and to end up sick on the street. The same holds true for gluttons. They do not choose to keep eating and destroy their health. They do not choose to be sated with food or other forms of pleasure. They cannot give up what they thought they would not want to give up. They find themselves slaves to what they thought was serving them.

Be wise now. Direct your heart now. Choose now while you still can.

The Parent Bond

Proverbs 23:22-25

Listen to your father who gave you life,
and do not despise your mother when she is old.
Buy truth, and do not sell it;
buy wisdom, instruction, and understanding.
The father of the righteous will greatly rejoice;

he who fathers a wise son will be glad in him.
Let your father and mother be glad;
  let her who bore you rejoice.

What is the special bond of parent to child? The bestowing of life. The proverb begins and ends with this observation. Is there any greater, more significant act than to bring another life into the world? Is there any other human bond that is more sacred than that of parent-child as a result?

What do parents want for their children? Certainly they desire success and happiness, but more so, they want their children to have noble traits, which begins with wisdom and the desire to be instructed. With such, he will acquire what he needs for life, but more to the point he will become a person of worthy character. For parents understand that they cannot control the future of their children. They cannot guarantee good things will happen. And so they hope to instill good values that will equip their children to handle the circumstances of life and to be worthy people.

Do you want to honor your parents? Then buy truth and do not sell it; buy wisdom, instruction, and understanding. But that is not what your parents want, you say? Then do not forget your heavenly Father. This is what he wants; for true wisdom and knowledge come from him and glorify him. And he, after all, is the true giver of life – physically and spiritually. May he rejoice in the wisdom you learn and impart today.

Entrapment

Proverbs 23:26-28

My son, give me your heart,
  and let your eyes observe my ways.
For a prostitute is a deep pit;
  an adulteress is a narrow well.
She lies in wait like a robber
  and increases the traitors among mankind.

Understand the motivation of the prostitute – it is to get your money. That is all she is about and nothing else. She wants your money and as much as she can get. The pleasures she gives, and makes believe that she receives, are merely a scheme to take money. And it works. You will come back. You will defy the principles you hold dear. You will risk the loss of your closest relationships and the respect of those you respect the most. You will risk disease. And all the while you will give your money, even going into debt. You will become a traitor to your faith, your spouse, your friends, even to yourself. And you will continue to give your money to the one who has ruined you.

So it is with other worldly pleasures. Beware of anything that leads you to live a double life while it takes your money. Understand that all these pleasures are given out for one purpose – to take your money. The prostitute does not enter her line of work out of the desire to give pleasure. She does so because it is good money. The casinos do not exist for people's pleasure. They exist to take money. Prostitutes and casino owners do not go to bed at night satisfied with how happy they have made others. If they go to bed happy, it is from counting their profits made off of you and which they have entrapped you to keep giving.

What a contrast to our God. People turn away from him because he is "demanding." And yet he is the only one who truly gives with our happiness in mind. He gave to us while we were his enemies, and he continues to give to us as his children. He will top it all off with eternal glory. He turns our very giving into receiving, for we find the very act of giving to be a blessing. He will give to you throughout today. He will only do what is for your good. He will turn suffering into wellbeing. You will always be in his thoughts; your good will always be his plan. Why become a traitor to such a God? It is wrong and it is also foolishness. Why get caught in a trap where you must always be spending more money to get your fleeting pleasures, when you can buy the everlasting pleasures of God without any cost?

Delusion

Proverbs 23:29-35

Who has woe? Who has sorrow?
  Who has strife? Who has complaining?
Who has wounds without cause?
  Who has redness of eyes?
Those who tarry long over wine;
  those who go to try mixed wine.
Do not look at wine when it is red,
  when it sparkles in the cup
  and goes down smoothly.
In the end it bites like a serpent
  and stings like an adder.
Your eyes will see strange things,
  and your heart utter perverse things.
You will be like one who lies down in the midst of the sea,
  like one who lies on the top of a mast.
"They struck me," you will say, "but I was not hurt;
  they beat me, but I did not feel it.
When shall I awake?
  I must have another drink."

The key in understanding this teaching lies in the phrases "Who has wounds without cause?" and "they struck me...but I was not hurt." Inebriation creates delusion. The deeper the inebriation the deeper the delusion and more frightening it turns. It exaggerates experience; it brings out one's fears. These verses describe a nightmare. Even then, one might think that the experience would waken a person to his senses. He will say to himself, "I'll never do that again." But instead, he wants another drink.

This is the way it is with worldly pleasures. They make their appeal to our senses, giving us the feeling of being in control. They then remove our self-control and take us over. So is the way of drinking, of drugs, of illicit sex, of gambling, and of anything that draws us from pleasure in our God.

"I must have..." Is there anything in your life for which you would say these words? Then beware. Already delusion is affecting you. Esau thought he must have a bowl of stew. Achan thought he must have silver. Amnon thought he must have his sister Tamar.

409

The Lord is the only one whom you must have. Without him, we have nothing; with him, we have all that we need. Without him, we live in a delusion; with him, we see clearly the way things are and what we truly have.

Of Evil Men

Proverbs 24:1-2

Be not envious of evil men,
  nor desire to be with them,
for their hearts devise violence,
  and their lips talk of trouble.

Sometimes we are envious of the wicked. They seem to prosper. They seem to be happy and contented. They have traits that seem admirable – daring, decisive, even generous at times. Some even rise to the status of heroes and legends.

But don't forget what they are about – trouble, violence. They are wrong-doers. It is easy to be daring and decisive without a conscience. It is easy to be generous as an oppressor and possessing riches that one can maintain through stealing from others. It is easy to be kind to some people while ruthless with others.

And remember what it is to become the friend of evil men. You move yourself into the position of owing the duties of friendship as they define it. You are expected to do them favors – from hiding them from the law or helping them to break the law. They scheme trouble – not trouble to get into, but trouble to cause for others, and they have no troubled conscience about you getting caught in those troubles.

Do not envy the wicked but rather delight in the path of righteousness and in the Righteous One who acts only for your good.

Building Wisely

Proverbs 24:3-4

By wisdom a house is built,
and by understanding it is established;
by knowledge the rooms are filled
with all precious and pleasant riches.

How is the house of your life being built? Does it have a sturdy foundation composed of the wisdom from God's Word, or does it wobble on the weak foundation of secular culture? Who has established your code of conduct, your foundational principles of the way things should be – God's Word or the secular media? And don't think that can be measured by how conservative or liberal your political views may be. The most conservative person politically can be the one most off the mark about the gospel.

How are you filling your rooms – with what is meaningful or what is superficially pleasing? With what has long-term value or what fits the momentary fad? Or are your rooms bare because you do not do anything to fill it with memories?

We are all called to do something with our lives. Some of us may be materially rich and some of us poor. Some of us may have many abilities, some of us few. But we are all called to build homes. And we need wisdom. If rich, we need wisdom on how not to be wasteful; if we are poor, we need wisdom on how to make the most of what we have. The rich fool thinks whatever is expensive must be good; the poor fool excuses himself from doing anything because of what he lacks.

Seek wisdom. Pray for it. Study it in God's Word. Learn from others who have it. For it is not as you grow in wealth that you will prosper nor even as you grow in information. It is how you grow in wisdom that you become a wise builder.

Wise Strength

Proverbs 24:5-6

A wise man is full of strength,
  and a man of knowledge enhances his might,
for by wise guidance you can wage your war,
  and in abundance of counselors there is victory.

The first half of the proverb seems to be extolling individual wisdom. The wise man alone is full of strength. But the latter half unveils more about wisdom. The true wise person seeks wise counsel. Wisdom leans on wisdom. A wise person knows that he alone does not have all wisdom. He knows his limits. He values others who see what he cannot see. He is not hampered by pride that refuses to acknowledge what others may possess and he lacks.

This is a primary reason that the wise achieve victory over those who are stronger. Unhampered by pride, they can think through carefully what is the best action to take. They are not weighed down by petty disputes and jealousies. Wise counselors think what is best for the one receiving their counsel. Wise rulers listen humbly to wise counsel and act accordingly.

How are you guided – by what appeals to your ego or by what presents clear, scriptural truth in light of the real circumstances? From whom do you seek counsel – from those known for wisdom or from those you can count on to take your side and flatter you? If you want to be strong, then humbly seek the wise counsel of those wiser than yourself. Out of such humility one finds wisdom and becomes strong.

Wisdom Too High

Proverbs 24:7

Wisdom is too high for a fool;
  in the gate he does not open his mouth.

The image here is that of men sitting at the gate of a city. This is where the elders of the town gather to discuss the Law and judge disputes. The fool does not join in because he cannot follow the discussion. He cannot comprehend their logic. It is not that they use esoteric words, but that he does not know how to reason and so cannot follow their reasoning. Though they are discussing practical application of the law, they may as well be speaking of deep mysteries, as far as he is concerned.

This is a growing problem today. Young people are growing up learning to read words without comprehending what is being said. They cannot follow a continual line of argument. The constant exposure and movement of images have added to the problem of deliberate reasoning. This can be seen in TV and movies in comparison to older shows. The camera angle and focus move much more often. We cannot tolerate a still camera. We lose our focus on what is being communicated.

This affects our whole society. As politicians already know, their task is not to use logic well but to evoke feelings that make the hearers think they are hearing good reasoning. Sermons are made shorter because hearers cannot listen to a sustained discourse for a long period unless the sermon is propped with changing visual images.

We have the capacity to reason well, but with media relying on emotional manipulation to communicate and the education system dumbing down what is being taught, we are becoming fools unable to comprehend wise discourse. If only we would then be silent at the gate. Instead, we are taught to open our mouths more loudly so that folly can be heard by all.

The Schemer's Plans

Proverbs 24:8-9

Whoever plans to do evil
will be called a schemer.
The devising of folly is sin,
and the scoffer is an abomination to mankind.

Wickedness is wickedness however it is carried out. But as the law affirms, it is especially repugnant to devise wickedness. Some people fall into sin, yielding against their better judgment. But the schemer plans his evil. He uses his ability to reason for the express purpose of causing mischief.

Consider the drug dealer who uses business acumen to run an elaborate, sophisticated business complex. Consider the thief who studies how to carry out a crime with the same meticulous attentiveness as any scholar. There is the businessman who out of greed and ambition uses his talent and expertise to manipulate the system and gain undue advantage over others.

There is a sadness about such persons, as one considers not only the crimes committed but the good that goes undone that these persons were capable of. What if such schemers used their abilities for good? What all could be done? How much good goes undone?

And then there is the scoffer who is an abomination. Again, the problem is not merely that he ridicules but that he uses his mental skills to mock rather than for productive good. Scoffing is the lazy man's use of mental wit. Unlike the schemer who turns to wickedness out of ambition, the scoffer turns to destructive ridicule out of lack of ambition. Both live wasted lives.

What are your plans today – to advance your own cause or the cause of Christ? To shoot down the efforts of others or to build others up? It is good to know that the plans of your Lord today for you, whatever exactly they may be, are for your good.

Strength to Rescue

Proverbs 24:10-12

If you faint in the day of adversity,
  your strength is small.
Rescue those who are being taken away to death;
  hold back those who are stumbling to the slaughter.
If you say, "Behold, we did not know this,"
  does not he who weighs the heart perceive it?
Does not he who keeps watch over your soul know it,

and will he not repay man according to his work?

What a sobering text! We are to be judged not only by the bad we do but by the good we fail to do. Even more sobering, we will be judged by the One who knows fully our hearts which we daily hide from ourselves. "I didn't know," we may say. But God sees that we did not want to know.

This teaching is invasive. It searches out every place of our hearts. What would happen if we honestly looked about us and saw those "who are being taken away to death"? Who would we see? What would we do about it? How would we "hold back those who are stumbling to the slaughter"? Who are stumbling to physical slaughter? Who are stumbling to spiritual slaughter? Who are physically beaten? Who are emotionally being broken? What would we see if we saw "slaughter" through the eyes of God? What would we see if we saw our own hearts as he does?

He saw sheep stumbling to slaughter and gave up his Son to hold them back. What do we give up?

The Honeycomb

Proverbs 24:13-14

My son, eat honey, for it is good,
*   and the drippings of the honeycomb are sweet to your taste.*
Know that wisdom is such to your soul;
*   if you find it, there will be a future,*
*   and your hope will not be cut off.*

We tend to contrast wisdom with pleasure. The wise man avoids pleasures so that he might pursue righteousness or keep his head to make good decisions. But wisdom lies really in choosing true pleasure. Wisdom itself is pleasure, and the wise man will not part from it, not so much out of self-discipline and denial but because he has tasted the honey and likes it.

He reads the "classics" and writings that typically take effort to comprehend fully, not so much to improve his mind but because they engage his mind. What we regard as an effort to be "above the rest" is simply his ability to delight in what we will not make the effort to understand. Our tendency is to go with whatever immediately catches our attention. That is why the mass media uses constantly changing images. It knows that we will press the remote quickly to another channel the moment we are bored. And we are bored when we have to use mental energy to grasp what we are seeing or hearing or reading.

Like the child who develops a fuller taste for foods as he grows up, so we could do the same if we would develop our minds. What may seem to be tedious at the beginning becomes a pleasure that tastes like honey.

The Righteous' Protection

Proverbs 24:15-16

Lie not in wait as a wicked man against the dwelling of the righteous;
* do no violence to his home;*
for the righteous falls seven times and rises again,
* but the wicked stumble in times of calamity.*

This proverb takes a twist. Instead of counseling against committing violence against the righteous as a moral issue, he addresses it from a standpoint of practicality. Conventional thought is that preying upon the righteous is easy work. The righteous are naive; they do not strike back; they tend to believe the best in people. Who better to take advantage of?

The righteous might seem easy prey, but they also prove themselves to be resilient. They may fall down, but they rise again. Why do they?

The proverbs equate righteousness with wisdom. Thus they have the wisdom necessary to carry on. And they are not as naive as they may seem. A common mistake of the wicked is to believe that courtesy and generosity are symptomatic of naiveté when instead they actually signify confidence. The righteous have not put their hope in

416

possessions. Thus to lose such things does not undo them. The wicked, on the other hand, do put their faith in material possession and earthly power; thus to lose such things completely undermines their confidence. They miscalculate what is of real value; they underestimate the strength of others who are unlike them.

But the underlying cause of the righteous' resilience, and the wicked's lack thereof, is God. The Lord protects and delivers the righteous. He attacks the wicked. Never take God out of the equation. With such a perspective, David won victory over Goliath:

> "Your servant has struck down both lions and bears, and this uncircumcised Philistine shall be like one of them, for he has defied the armies of the living God... The Lord who delivered me from the paw of the lion and from the paw of the bear will deliver me from the hand of this Philistine" (1 Sam. 17:36-37).

As with David, there is more than meets the eye with the righteous. Even more so, the Lord is their deliverer.

Attitude Check

Proverbs 24:17-18

Do not rejoice when your enemy falls,
*   and let not your heart be glad when he stumbles,*
lest the Lord see it and be displeased,
*   and turn away his anger from him.*

This proverb seems to contradict other Scripture that speaks of rejoicing in one's victory over enemies. Indeed, doesn't the very desire for justice require joy over the downfall of wicked enemies?

We recognize the attitude of God here, especially if we are parents of more than one child. We ourselves after punishing one child, will turn to the other and rebuke him for gloating over the offending sibling. And that is what this proverb is about – gloating over another's downfall. In movies, when the bad guy gets "what's coming to him," his devious plans are not merely foiled, but he suffers a humiliating or especially horrible death. The producers know that the audience is not contented with evil being checked or the innocent being vindicated. The wicked must suffer. That is what will fill the audience with satisfaction. The audience must be able to gloat.

And that is what we want in real life. We want the driver who swerved in front of us to be pulled over immediately so we can gloat over him. (We wouldn't even mind if he had a wreck.) We want whoever offends us to be humbled, not because we desire the welfare of their soul but because we want to gloat. It is right to desire justice; but we too often confuse such a desire with our sinful desire for personal vengeance. Our attitude for justice is found precisely in our attitude toward the wicked. Do we rejoice over their downfall or do we mourn that they would not repent? Justice must come, and we should rejoice over justice. But we should mourn the soul that is lost.

We forget that we too are sinners deserving God's wrath. God's displeasure could easily and rightly be turned against us if it were not for our Lord, who instead of gloating over his enemies (us) gave himself for us and made us God's children.

No Future

Proverbs 24:19-20

Fret not yourself because of evildoers,
and be not envious of the wicked,
for the evil man has no future;
the lamp of the wicked will be put out.

It is proper to concern ourselves with seeing that justice is carried out and that the oppressed are protected. In such a spirit we are to concern ourselves with thwarting the deeds of the wicked. However, we are not to live with jealousy of the wicked or with general anxiety about them. It is good to see a wicked person brought to justice, but understand that the real justice takes place before the throne of God who rules with perfect knowledge and power.

No one is getting away with anything. The wicked are digging their own graves and sealing their own doom. God sees all; more to the point, God is working out all things for his glory to be displayed in his justice and in his mercy. All persons will receive what he has ordained and in such a way that all mouths will be silenced at the time of their hearing before the Almighty Judge. All knees will bow before the King.

Nothing can stop that inevitable conclusion. Certainly no wicked creature can thwart God's purposes. They, who spent their lives mocking their Creator; they, who believed they were outwitting the law, will find their "lamps" put out. They have no future, that is, no future of blessing. They will wish they had no existence, that they had never been born. Keep this in mind the next time you fret over the way the wicked seem to be winning and prospering. And pray for their souls.

Who to Fear

Proverbs 24:21-22

My son, fear the Lord and the king,
  and do not join with those who do otherwise,
for disaster from them will rise suddenly,
  and who knows the ruin that will come from them both?

It is our tendency to separate the authority of the Lord from that of the king. The "king" could be our President or mayor or boss or teacher or parent – anyone who has responsibility for us. We are quick to point out the deficiencies of the "king," claiming that we follow only God. And so we neglect the tendency of Scripture to equate obedience to earthly authority with that of obedience to God. Read Romans 13 and 1 Peter 2. Consider the scriptural principal that we are to respect positions of authority in whatever circumstance that may be – parent to child, official to citizen, master to servant, husband to wife. Certainly there are many in authority who abuse their position, and they will be held accountable to God. But we are not to be quick to reject the authority of others who have been duly placed in their positions.

Apply this to church. Everyone who joins a church is happy to say that he will abide by the authority of the church leaders. But let the moment come when elders hold a person to account for his actions, and he will quickly reject their "presumption." He thinks he must be faithful to God and reject the counsel of the elders who are God's undershepherds responsible for the flock. The same pattern follows in the workplace and school and other areas. We know best. We know what God wants. It is up to us to stand against appointed leaders.

Take to heart the final warning: "Who knows the ruin that will come from them both?" People have gone from job to job, from church to church, even from marriage to marriage because everyone else is being unreasonable; no one else seems to understand what they alone can see. Fear the Lord and the king – the person placed in authority over you. If indeed that person is wrong, then all the more fear the Lord who is in control. Ultimately, the question is a matter of trust. Will we trust the Lord to have placed certain people over us for our ultimate good? Will we take the time to examine our hearts and discover what our Lord would have us learn about ourselves?

A Good Kiss

Proverbs 24:23-26

These also are sayings of the wise.

Partiality in judging is not good.
Whoever says to the wicked, "You are in the right,"
    will be cursed by peoples, abhorred by nations,
but those who rebuke the wicked will have delight,
    and a good blessing will come upon them.
Whoever gives an honest answer
    kisses the lips.

Partiality in judging happens because of fear or greed. There is fear of repercussions by the wicked. They are often powerful and usually ruthless. There is danger in opposing them. There is greed for the bribe offered by the wicked. Being a "friend" of the wicked can lead to wealth and high position.

But the proverb is right. If it is known that a judge rules in favor of the wicked, he is usually maligned by the public. He may get his money and secure his safety, but he loses the blessing of a good name. He may save his body but lose his soul – both figuratively and literally. He helps to spread cynicism and discouragement in the population. Others lose faith in the justice system and many give in to corruption. The wicked only sink further into their wickedness, since they go unchecked and their belief that there is no one good is reinforced.

It is in such a climate that an honest answer is like a kiss on the lips. Like the kiss that refreshes and delights, so an honest answer refreshes and delights the soul. "There is someone honest, someone who will speak the truth and face the cost. If so, there must be some good in this world. And if one person can speak honestly, then I can as well." And so, just as partiality poisons the environment, so honesty can restore it.

What will you do today – poison or refresh the people around you? Will your speech be as a dagger or a kiss?

Prepare

Proverbs 24:27

Prepare your work outside;
  get everything ready for yourself in the field,
  and after that build your house.

Before building your house, see to it that you are providing the income necessary to afford and maintain it. Before marrying and creating a household, get everything ready to support a family. Do not let your dreams and ambition carry your emotions and move you to setting up a home to support, when you have yet to make preparation for that support. Take the time to get the education needed, to develop the necessary skills, to put your finances in order, and to earn an income.

Are you eager to serve the Lord in his kingdom? Then take the necessary time to prepare yourself well. Eager to be serving, many of the Lord's servants fall by the wayside or never serve to their potential because they were quick to build the house before getting ready in the field. Marriages and families have suffered because the man and woman were too eager to get married before good preparation – be it education, finances, or preparing themselves to sustain an intimate, complex relationship. They quickly fall into debt; the husband is unable to get the job necessary to provide for the "house" they have built; both are unequipped to handle the pressures that come with marriage and raising a family.

Prepare. Prepare each morning the day before you. Prepare your heart before the Lord before you go out into the field or take care of your home. After that, begin building.

Pay Back

Proverbs 24:28-29

Be not a witness against your neighbor without cause,
  and do not deceive with your lips.
Do not say, "I will do to him as he has done to me;
  I will pay the man back for what he has done."

Here is where the Christian is to be distinguished. It is the natural reaction to get even with the person who has harmed us. We say to ourselves that we are only seeking what is fair. Our neighbor is only getting what is coming to him. This seems just.

We should seek justice... for others. For ourselves, we are to be concerned only with the welfare of our neighbor and return his wrong behavior with the kind that will bear witness to the gospel. For our hope is to be the salvation of our enemy. That is why Jesus taught the following:

You have heard that it was said, "An eye for an eye and a tooth for a tooth." But I say to you, Do not resist the one who is evil. But if anyone slaps you on the right cheek, turn to him the other also. And if anyone would sue you and take your tunic, let him have your cloak as well. And if anyone forces you to go one mile, go with him two miles. Give to the one who begs from you, and do not refuse the one who would borrow from you.

You have heard that it was said, "You shall love your neighbor and hate your enemy." But I say to you, Love your enemies and pray for those who persecute you, so that you may be sons of your Father who is in heaven. For he makes his sun rise on the evil and on the good, and sends rain on the just and on the unjust. For if you love those who love you, what reward do you have? Do not even the tax collectors do the same? And if you greet only your brothers, what more are you doing than others? Do not even the Gentiles do the same? You therefore must be perfect, as your heavenly Father is perfect" (Matt. 5:38-48).

This is hard teaching to live out. But nevertheless, it is what our Lord teaches. To live such a life today is what will honor him.

A Little Sleep

Proverbs 24:30-34

I passed by the field of a sluggard,
by the vineyard of a man lacking sense,
and behold, it was all overgrown with thorns;
the ground was covered with nettles,
and its stone wall was broken down.
Then I saw and considered it;
I looked and received instruction.
A little sleep, a little slumber,

a little folding of the hands to rest,
and poverty will come upon you like a robber,
and want like an armed man.

The "little sleep" and "little slumber" and "little folding of the hands to rest" end up being the primary activities of the sluggard. He does not tell himself that he will loaf and do no work. He thinks to himself that he will work, and very hard, but first just a little rest. Or better yet, "I think I will watch TV for just a few minutes, just to relax for a moment."

We see such workers in the workplace. He comes in late. When he does come in, he needs time to settle in. He likes to chat. He glances at his email before he gets started in his work. There's a funny article he's found. He looks at the day's work and comments on how much he has to do. They need to hire more workers. How can they expect one person to do all he has to do? The previous employers he worked for had the same unreasonable expectations as did the employers before. In fact, he has had the unfortunate luck of always working for unreasonable bosses.

What describes you? Are you known for the consistently good work you do, whether it be in the workplace or home or school? Or are you "plagued" with people having too many expectations? Circumstances do play in, to be sure. But more often than not, the work you produce or fail to produce has more to do with your attitude than anything else. The little breaks you take add up to more than you realize. And these breaks may be the real reason you fail to get the promotion or make the grade. Examine yourself before you blame your circumstances.

The Glory of Searching

Proverbs 25:1-2

These also are proverbs of Solomon which the men of Hezekiah king of Judah copied.

It is the glory of God to conceal things,

but the glory of kings is to search things out.

God in his glory transcends the ability of man to know all his ways. He must come down to man to reveal even a part of his nature and his will. His glory is impressed upon us because of his mystery. Even as we grow in knowledge of him, we are filled all the more with wonder as we realize how little we know. One great wonder is God's knowledge. He knows all things. He does not search out knowledge as we do. When Scripture applies such language to God, it is not meaning that he must learn what he does not know, but rather is impressing upon us that we and nothing can escape God. Such is his glory.

For the king, and anyone placed in a position of authority, his glory is displayed not in what he conceals but in his ability and zeal to know what is taking place under his rule. The wicked conceal their wicked behavior. It is the task of the righteous king to find them out. The oppressed suffer without help; it is the king's role to see them and come to their aid. It is the glory of the king to find good people and place them in responsible positions. It is the king's glory to search out what is good and bring it to light.

Before the king can act, he must know. And to know, he must search. Are you searching? Are you looking to know what is going on about you so that you can act responsibly? Are you searching for what is true, what is honorable? Are you searching for what is wicked so you can avoid it yourself and act to thwart it? It is the glory of everyone to be a searcher. What will you learn today?

The King's Heart

Proverbs 25:3

As the heavens for height, and the earth for depth,
  so the heart of kings is unsearchable.

Consider this proverb in light of 23:1-3:
    When you sit down to eat with a ruler,
        observe carefully what is before you,

and put a knife to your throat
    if you are given to appetite.
Do not desire his delicacies,
    for they are deceptive food.

The mistake of the diner who dives into his food is that he thinks he understands the ruler. He thinks the ruler offers the food merely out of friendship, not realizing that the ruler is using the meal as a test of the diner's character.

The point of our proverb is that kings do what they do out of calculation. They are not free with their hearts. That would be dangerous for them. They speak and act with design, as did Solomon when he pretended he would split a baby in two. And so it is with persons in position of responsibility. The greater the responsibility, the more careful they will be in speech and conduct. They are not being malicious; they are being cognizant that what they say and do have far-reaching implications.

This is a message to us, on the other hand, not to exert our energies in "out-calculating" the ruler. Act on what you know to be right, not on what you think will endear your "ruler" to you. If an employee, then do your work well as unto the Lord. If a student, act likewise. It is the Lord whom you are to be concerned with pleasing, and he has made clear what is appropriate speech and conduct.

Dross Removal

Proverbs 25:4-5

Take away the dross from the silver,
    and the smith has material for a vessel;
take away the wicked from the presence of the king,
    and his throne will be established in righteousness.

The metaphor is apt in two ways. First, the matter of the dross being gone. Without the dross, the smith has pure silver and with that material something beautiful can be crafted. So for the king. With the wicked away from him – that is, wicked counselors and others near

426

the throne trying to influence him – he is able to craft policies that produce something of value. Leaders have often found this the case. When advisors who are looking out for their own welfare are gone, wise decisions become easy to make. And when the employee or student who is poisoning the atmosphere leaves, then the workplace or class environment becomes productive and good-spirited.

But the metaphor leads us also to consider how the dross is removed. It is through a "fiery" process. The smith cannot take a cloth and rub the dross away. He has to expose the dross and the silver to the fire. So it is with the selfish advisor and the poor worker or student. The process of removing such a person requires wisdom and steadfastness to see the process of removal through, and usually it does not happen without pain. What keeps the leader steadfast is his eye on the goal, just as Jesus was able to endure his suffering because his eye on the "joy that was before him" (cf. Heb. 12:2).

But another understanding of this proverb comes from 1 Peter 1:6-7, which speaks of our faith being tested by fire. Sometimes the wicked dross that needs removal is the dross in our own hearts. We think work is such a terrible place or school an awful place. We complain about everyone else about us, not realizing that the real problem is within our own hearts. It is when that dross is removed that we will truly be established in righteousness.

Exalting Self

Proverbs 25:6-7a

Do not put yourself forward in the king's presence
  or stand in the place of the great,
for it is better to be told, "Come up here,"
  than to be put lower in the presence of a noble.

Let's turn to Jesus for application of this proverb:
    Now he told a parable to those who were invited, when he noticed how they chose the places of honor, saying to them, "When you are invited by someone to a wedding feast, do not sit down in a place of honor,

lest someone more distinguished than you be invited by him, and he who invited you both will come and say to you, 'Give your place to this person,' and then you will begin with shame to take the lowest place. But when you are invited, go and sit in the lowest place, so that when your host comes he may say to you, 'Friend, move up higher.' Then you will be honored in the presence of all who sit at table with you. For everyone who exalts himself will be humbled, and he who humbles himself will be exalted" (Luke 14:7-11).

Be Not Hasty

Proverbs 25:7b-10

What your eyes have seen
 do not hastily bring into court,
for what will you do in the end,
 when your neighbor puts you to shame?
Argue your case with your neighbor himself,
 and do not reveal another's secret,
lest he who hears you bring shame upon you,
 and your ill repute have no end.

This counsel is similar to that of Jesus' in Matthew 18:15: "If your brother sins against you, go and tell him his fault, between you and him alone. If he listens to you, you have gained your brother."

Being quick to bring a charge against your neighbor, whether in court or to anyone else, is foolish for several reasons. For one, you may be wrong in your charge. You did not see what you thought you saw. You did not know the extenuating circumstances. As a result, you are guilty of bringing false charges and losing the trust and goodwill of your neighbor and those whom you told. Another reason, and the one which Jesus points out, is that you should give your neighbor opportunity to repent. By going to him privately, you provide a way for him to confess his sin and deal with it appropriately, so that he becomes grateful to you. Not only do you help him to repent, but you win your neighbor over to be a brother or sister.

Being quick to bring charges demonstrates a spirit contrary to Galatians 6:1: "Brothers, if anyone is caught in any transgression, you who are spiritual should restore him *in a spirit of gentleness.*" There may be a time for charges to be presented, but we should not be hasty to get to them. And then, there are times in which we should overlook what we see. We should not overlook crime, but as weak sinners we would do well to show sympathy and commit our fellow sinners to prayer and to God's dealings. Galatians 6:7 says, "God is not mocked, for whatever one sows, that will he also reap." No one is getting away with anything.

Let us be thankful that Jesus, who easily could have brought charges against us, became instead our Redeemer and is now our Advocate against the evil one who does bring charges. Let us learn from him the spirit of mercy.

Fitly Spoken

Proverbs 25:11

A word fitly spoken
  is like apples of gold in a setting of silver.

The key term is "fitly." A word can be spoken with the intent to bless but ends up being like a curse. One can speak with the intent to heal but instead wounds. One can say a word for peace and produce turmoil.

The word must be "fitly" spoken. It matters what word is chosen. It also matters how the word is spoken – whether softly or harshly. It must be spoken at the right time – either immediately or delayed. How then does one know what or how or when? The way that anyone applies his craft – through observation. What does a medical doctor do when you come in with a complaint? He examines you. He listens to you explain your symptoms. Then he determines the treatment. The same is true of the car mechanic and the new coach of the football team and the salesperson. If they are good in what they do, they listen and observe well before they act.

So it is necessary for the person speaking a word fitly. He listens and observes the person and the circumstances surrounding the person, and then he speaks the word needed that becomes like apples of gold in a setting of silver. Its value and beauty are understood. How fitting will your words be today?

A Listening Ear

Proverbs 25:12

Like a gold ring or an ornament of gold
is a wise reprover to a listening ear.

The key term here is "listening." Let the reprover be wise, but if the listener is not listening then it will be to no avail except in the future to serve as a reproach for not heeding. Most of us, most of the time, do not listen well to reproof. We quickly judge the reprover to be mean or ignorant, certainly not sensitive to our feelings.

Response to reproof shows the condition of our heart. For if we desire above all else to be pleasing to God and to be following his will, then we will welcome any reproof that alerts us to our error and puts us back on the right track. If, as we traveled to our destination, someone yelled to us that we were going the wrong way, we would thank him for saving us from a great inconvenience. How then should we react when someone points out a moral or spiritual error?

But how stubborn we can be! We will reject the reproof of person after person, even elder after elder, claiming all the while we are right before God. We alone know what God is saying. Be aware. Some day we must appear before God, and he will ask where are the gold rings and ornaments he graciously sent to us through our brothers and sisters. Learn now to listen and to value wise reproof.

Faithful Messenger

Proverbs 25:13

Like the cold of snow in the time of harvest
is a faithful messenger to those who send him;
he refreshes the soul of his masters.

Here the key term is "faithful." The messenger is faithful by
delivering a true rendering of the message and by representing his
masters favorably. A poor messenger distorts the message either
through inaccuracy of what he conveys or by a presentation that
dishonors those he represents.

How good of a messenger are you for your Lord? Do you faithfully
impart his message? Do you use Scripture well in its context or do
you distort it by poor interpretation or application? To both believer
and unbeliever, are you conscientious in conveying what Scripture
says and only says?

How well do you represent your Lord? Do you convey Scripture
accurately, only to distort it by your careless behavior? When you
speak of the love of God, do you also convey that love by your life?
When you deliver the message that God is holy, do you demonstrate
your own concern to be holy?

You are a messenger. You cannot escape being such if you are a
disciple of Christ. Pray that you will be one who is faithful in word
and deed, one who blesses your Lord as the cold of snow refreshes
the soul.

Clouds Without Rain

Proverbs 25:14

Like clouds and wind without rain
is a man who boasts of a gift he does not give.

The day is hot, as it has been for weeks. There has been no rain. A
breeze picks up; you look into the sky and see clouds coming, dark
clouds. Finally, rain is on the way. The clouds are now overhead;

431

already it feels cooler and you can smell the moisture. But the clouds pass on, the sun returns, and your hopes are dashed. So is the feeling when someone makes a promise that he does not keep. It would be better to make no promises.

What kind of cloud are you? When you say that you will provide help to someone, do you follow through? When you promise to make an event, can you be depended upon to keep your word? When you boast of what you can give or do, are you boasting of what you really have or are capable of doing?

What will you be today? Will you bring rain to a thirsty soul? Will you say the kind word needed? Will you bring a gift that lifts a sad spirit? Will you be the rain cloud that the Lord sends which does bring the needed rain, or will you pass over leaving hopes unrealized?

We all have our different gifts. Some can give more than others. But if we promise only what we do have, and if we carry through on our promise, then we can all be the refreshing rain that our neighbors need.

Patient and Softly

Proverbs 25:15

With patience a ruler may be persuaded,
and a soft tongue will break a bone.

Water, with patience, will quietly break a rock. A wise person, with patience, speaking softly can win over the minds of others and thus accomplish his will. How does he accomplish this?

As a patient man, he takes the time to observe and to listen. He takes the time to understand the person he persuades. We may waste many words arguing our point, not having realized that the argument we are making has no relevance to the hearer. We also in our haste unknowingly work against ourselves, because we are actually offending our hearer.

The patient man also understands the power of the soft tongue. Words spoken softly may take longer to achieve their effect, but they have the advantage of softening the resolve of the hearer. If you speak to me loudly or harshly, you cause me to raise my defenses against you. Even if what you say is right, I want you to be wrong. But if you speak to me softly, I will give you a hearing, and though I reject your counsel then, I am inclined to mull over what you have said and to be open when you patiently choose the time to speak to me again.

Patience and a soft tongue make a powerful combination. Think about this the next time you want to "make your point" by fussing at whomever you are frustrated with. It is not the intensity of your emotion that will win someone over, but rather the patient, soft word spoken with wisdom and in love.

Enough

Proverbs 25:16

If you have found honey, eat only enough for you,
  lest you have your fill of it and vomit it.

The lesson is "moderation in all things." Apply this to food. What are you eating now, not because you need it but because you cannot restrain yourself? Honey is healthy food until you eat too much of it. And as with any food, eating too much of anything will cause your body to react. The result is that the very thing that was good and which gave pleasure turned into an enemy against your health and pleasure.

There is a purpose for exercising restraint, which is precisely to enhance pleasure not reduce it. The person who learns to savor food by not overeating enjoys much more the eating experience. To indulge in food is to deny ourselves the full enjoyment of food.

This lesson applies to every experience. The more we indulge, the less we savor. The more repetitive an experience, the less satisfying it

433

becomes. And worse, the experience takes control of us, forcing us to insist upon more while receiving less satisfaction.

If you have found "honey," take delight in it and restrain how much you eat. Enjoy it fully by not getting bloated by it. Then it will give you further delight in your memory and the next time you taste. Learn to savor your experiences by measuring your intake. It will heighten your senses and enrich your memories.

Respecting Boundaries

Proverbs 25:17

Let your foot be seldom in your neighbor's house,
  lest he have his fill of you and hate you.

A common mistake in social relations is to presume too much upon courtesy and neighborliness. A good neighbor will be courteous and friendly, but that does not mean he desires to have the kind of close friendship which allows us to step into his house at all occasions. A colleague may be friendly with us, but that does not mean that he welcomes us to stop into his office or at his desk frequently to chat.

There are relational boundaries which an observant person sees and respects. Even in close friendships there are still boundaries, and we are to respect them. That is how we build trust and develop closer friendships. If I know you will respect my boundaries, I am more likely to remove them for you. If I see you crossing over them, I will keep myself at more of a distance.

A friendship is not measured by how often one may "step into the house" of a neighbor. Rather, it is measured by the blessing of the time that friends are together. Like the person in the previous proverb who gets sick from too much honey, so a friendship may sicken from over exposure. A healthy friendship allows space between friends so that when they are together the time is savored.

False Witness

Proverbs 25:18

A man who bears false witness against his neighbor
    is like a war club, or a sword, or a sharp arrow.

Note God's standard of justice. To slander another person is equal to striking him with a weapon. To lie with the intent to damage a neighbor is an act of violence. Think about this the next time you are tempted to exaggerate the truth or fail to tell the whole truth.

Like the effect of a weapon, the damage lingers and may be permanent. The lie spreads and the neighbor's reputation cannot be reclaimed. Or if it is, the damage against his well-being has already been made.

Consider the term "false witness." It infers that you are a witness and as such to be trusted. This is not passing on gossip. It is making a claim that you witnessed the deed or the evidence. How much more then will you be held accountable before God when you become a false witness.

"But he lied about me!" All the more reason not to resort to the same tactic and thus lend credence to his slander. All the more reason to carefully speak the truth, even speak the truth in love to the honor of Christ whom you represent. Remember that God sees and knows perfectly all that takes place, even the motives of the heart. It is for him to justify. Our responsibility is to be a true witness for the cause of Christ.

Trusting

Proverbs 25:19

Trusting in a treacherous man in time of trouble
    is like a bad tooth or a foot that slips.

We must trust others. Walking down the street, we trust drivers not to swerve into us. Ordering our food, we trust the cook not to contaminate our dish. Unconscious trusting is necessary simply to go through an ordinary day. We raise the trust level as we consciously are aware of the role others play. Thus the laborer trusts his supervisor to give directives that will not lead to injury. The employee trusts his employer not to fire him without cause. Likewise, the employer and supervisor trust their workers to do their best and not undermine them.

But these common day experiences still require a measure of alertness. It is imprudent to walk down a street when you see cars swerving dangerously. You ought not to eat in a restaurant that has been cited for food poisoning. Employers and employees may take advantage of one another.

Where alertness is most needed is where the risks are greatest – putting your savings into the hands of an investor; following counsel about your future; giving your heart to another. Pay attention to the person you are trusting. Learn his reputation. It is the gift of treacherous persons to appear trustworthy. All the more reason then to learn his past.

The world is dangerous and we must be wary of whom we trust. But all the more reason to give thanks to God that the greatest risk of all – the welfare of our souls – is placed in the most trustworthy of hands – God the Father (John 10:29). He who controls our destiny is the one who will always do what is best and see that all things work out for our good (Rom. 8:28). The world is dangerous, but the Creator and Ruler of the world is good and sovereign. We may not be able to know who and when to trust, but we can always trust the one who holds us in his hands.

Feeling Sorrow

Proverbs 25:20

Whoever sings songs to a heavy heart
is like one who takes off a garment on a cold day,
and like vinegar on soda.

By the waters of Babylon,

> there we sat down and wept,
> when we remembered Zion (Ps. 137:1).

There is a time to mourn. There is a time when it is appropriate to grieve. The religion of Scripture is not one that condemns or even tries to escape sorrow. We live in a fallen world and grief is the natural and appropriate response to the trials it brings.

> On the willows there
> we hung up our lyres.
> For there our captors
> required of us songs,
> and our tormentors, mirth, saying,
> "sing us one of the songs of Zion!" (Ps. 137:2-3).

There is a time for grief, and when friends insist upon happy feelings they become our tormentors. They take off our coats, leaving us exposed to the raw cold. They hope to arouse us out of our pain, but only intensify the turmoil as vinegar on soda.

What are we to do when our neighbor mourns? Mourn with him. There is a time when mourning needs to end, but before we can insist upon that we must earn the right to lift someone out of his doldrums. We must mourn with him. And we cannot mourn until we ourselves have felt our own sorrow.

There are worse things than not being happy. It is worse not to feel sorrow when a love is lost; it is worse not to connect with another's pain. It is worse to expend energy trying to avoid every risk of pain. The reason that avoiding pain at all costs is worse is because it deadens the joy of the hope to come.

> When the Lord restored the fortunes of Zion,
> we were like those who dream.
> Then our mouth was filled with laughter,
> and our tongue with shouts of joy;
> then they said among the nations,
> "The Lord has done great things for them."
> The Lord has done great things for us;
> we are glad (Ps.126:1-3).

437

It is good to feel sorrow precisely because sorrow is not the final emotion. It is not sorrow, even when we feel it, that defines our life. It is joy, not the happy feeling of shutting out our sad thoughts, but the deep, real, everlasting joy of the hope that is in us, the hope secured upon a dreadful cross, that breaks through even now as the sun's rays through the clouds, that will come down out of heaven in full splendor and end all sorrow. Until that time, do not be afraid to grieve and to mourn with those who mourn.

Burning Coals

Proverbs 25:21-22

If your enemy is hungry, give him bread to eat,
and if he is thirsty, give him water to drink,
for you will heap burning coals on his head,
and the Lord will reward you.

Here is the Apostle Paul's application:
> Bless those who persecute you; bless and do not curse them... Repay no one evil for evil, but give thought to do what is honorable in the sight of all. If possible, so far as it depends on you, live peaceably with all. Beloved, never avenge yourselves, but leave it to the wrath of God, for it is written, "vengeance is mine, I will repay, says the Lord." To the contrary, "if your enemy is hungry, feed him; if he is thirsty, give him something to drink; for by so doing you will heap burning coals on his head." Do not be overcome by evil, but overcome evil with good" (Rom. 12:14-21).

Our goal in all circumstances is to glorify God. When we are ill-treated, our thought should be to glorify God. How do we do so? We bless those who treat us ill. We pray for them. We do good deeds for them.

Our good deeds are likely to have a positive impact, causing our "enemy" to repent of his bad behavior and change his ways toward us. He will feel our good deeds as burning coals of shame. "But what if he does not change?" That is the Lord's concern. He is the judge of hearts and the changer of hearts. He will see that justice is carried out, whether or not he allows us to see how that justice is played out.

We flock to Rambo style movies where the "good" hero gets vengeance through violence. Our model for vengeance is to overcome evil with good. As Jesus said, "You have heard that it was said, 'You shall love your neighbor and hate your enemy.' But I say to you, Love your enemies and pray for those who persecute you, so that you may be sons of your Father who is in heaven" (Matt. 5:43-45).

Jesus, not Rambo, is our model, thank goodness. He overcame our evil with his good. His "burning coals" on our head changed our hearts. And we who were his enemies became his brothers and sisters.

Backbiting Tongue

Proverbs 25:23

The north wind brings forth rain,
and a backbiting tongue, angry looks.

The backbiting tongue is the tongue that speaks behind another person's back. It is the negative remark, the insinuating comment that inevitably reaches the ears of the subject, striking him in the way that the north wind strikes with cold biting rain.

Such a tongue is easy to wield, so easy we are unaware that we are guilty of speaking in such a way. A quick comment to another person, maybe in terms of a joke – however it is done, the word gets back to the subject of the remark, who responds with "angry looks."

It is possible for someone to be over-easily offended, but you need to ask yourself if there is a pattern of people getting offended with you. If you periodically get angry looks or angry remarks, perhaps the problem is not that you are around overly sensitive people, but you are unnecessarily offending.

Again, the backbiting tongue is not so much a calculating tongue. The offender is not so much trying to be offensive, as he is letting his natural reactions be made known. The backbiter does not exercise control over his tongue. Well, actually he does exercise enough control to save his comment for a third party. But he feels he must tell someone, like a person having to hold his breath until he can get outside; he "has" to let it out.

If you must let it out, then let out your thoughts to God. Then be willing to listen to what God has to say. You might get angry looks back from him, but at least they will be for your chastisement.

A Quarrelsome Wife

Proverbs 25:24

It is better to live in a corner of the housetop
than in a house shared with a quarrelsome wife.

Some wives are quarrelsome by temperament. They are quick to find fault in anyone. Their husbands have the unfortunate position of being the closest target. Other wives grow quarrelsome out of unfulfilled expectations. The men they expected to be wise, loving, and godly husbands fail to meet those expectations. And so they begin to complain.

Whatever the situation, the reality is that complaining is not effective. A husband is not reinvigorated to repair the house or to lead family devotions because he has been berated. What then for the wife? First, the wife needs to examine herself. Is she doing her job of being a helpmeet who encourages and supports her husband? Secondly, she needs to examine what really bothers her. Is she primarily concerned for the welfare of her husband and his relationship with God, or is she primarily put out that he is not fulfilling her personal expectations? Thirdly, she needs to examine her own relationship with God. Like Martha who was impatient with Jesus for not making

440

Mary help her, so it is easy to become impatient with God for not making one's husband more responsive. Fourthly, she needs to exercise wisdom. Many proverbs, such as verses 11-15 in the same chapter, teach the necessity of speaking "fitly" so as to be effective. And the consistent theme is that it is the "soft" speech that is more likely to get the result intended.

The quarrelsome tongue drives away; the soft tongue draws near. The berating tongue steels the resolve of the other not to change; the soft tongue will break through that resolve. But the key is patience. Will you, can you patiently win over your husband?

Good News

Proverbs 25:25

Like cold water to a thirsty soul,
  so is good news from a far country.

The letter or email or the phone call from a loved one or about a loved one – that good news from a "far country" is indeed like cold water to a thirsty soul. Sometimes we don't realize how thirsty we were until we get the communication.

What news do you have and to whom? To whom can you give a cup of cold water? Is there someone you can take time today to write or email or phone and give the good news of your greeting? Pray now about this. Ask the Lord to place someone on your heart now and determine to send your good news.

Or maybe your recipient is your neighbor with whom you have communicated very little. You can live close to someone and yet be at a distance. Perhaps today is the day of sending good news of greeting.

Maybe the recipient needs to be a loved one in your own house who needs to hear the good news of your love, and you are unaware of how distant you have been.

Perhaps the good news you need to be sending is the good news of the gospel. Is there someone you have withheld it from? Is there someone who needs to hear your story? For we are the recipients of good news from a far country. Our Lord left heaven and traveled to us to deliver the good news of salvation. He has sent the Holy Spirit to us to carry this news into our hearts, and it indeed has refreshed us. Let us also determine to be messengers of such good news.

Muddy Water

Proverbs 25:26

*Like a muddied spring or a polluted fountain
  is a righteous man who gives way before the wicked.*

You are hot and thirsty. You hear the splashing of water; you look ahead and see the fountain. Eager to splash the water on your face and drink, you run up to it only to find it polluted. The disappointment is great. What held such promise has proven to be false. So it is with the righteous who give in to wickedness, who compromise with the wicked.

We know what to expect from a mud hole. It is the fountain, the spring that had held out hope to us and then dashed our expectations. All the more reason then for us who are righteous in Christ to be the spring of fresh water for our neighbors. They see in us the Spirit of Christ. They hear us speak of the Living Water of the gospel and testify that we drink of it and that it has made all the difference in us.

We may not use the excuse of our unbelieving neighbors. We cannot excuse bad behavior on being tired or having a bad day. We cannot "get even" when harmed. We cannot retaliate. We cannot appeal to what anyone or anything has done to us as an excuse for our muddy behavior. For we are to be springs of water to the thirsty and fountains for the weary. If they come to us and find us polluted in their time of need, then we muddy the very gospel we boast of.

442

Because you do not know what this day will hold and who will be watching and needing you to be fresh water, pray for the Spirit to keep you clean throughout this day. Many are weary and thirsty, and it may very well be you they look to for the Living Water.

Vain Glory

Proverbs 25:27

It is not good to eat much honey,
nor is it glorious to seek one's own glory.

Like Winnie the Pooh who ends up too fat and a sticky mess from eating much honey, so is the person who seeks his own glory – his ego becomes bloated and his life becomes a mess. Unlike Pooh who has friends to help him, the vain-glorious person loses his friends.

People obtain glory not because of seeking glory itself but out of striving for a noble cause or a far-reaching goal. Those who do strive for glory itself and have the misfortune of obtaining it will experience the devastation of finding such glory a small and bitter possession. It is the deed itself that is fulfilling; it is the competition itself that exhilarates. And should one obtain recognition for one's accomplishments, it will still be remembering the deed itself that will be the reward. The Super Bowl quarterback looks back not on the act of receiving the trophy but of throwing the touchdown pass.

Take delight in what you are doing, not in the recognition you hope to receive. By doing so, you will find pleasure each day, and you are likely to get the added benefit of being recognized. The glory is more likely to come to those whose attention is on the present – on what they are doing now. So it is for us in serving our Lord. Focus on the service you are given the privilege to do. Delight in what he permits you to do for his glory.

What will come, and often when you least expect it, is the glory of being recognized for your service. And ultimately you will receive the everlasting glory when your Lord returns. Let that knowledge take you through the times of feeling under appreciated. Your time will come when the Lord himself will acknowledge you. If you want the hours and days and weeks to pass more quickly until that time, then focus on the joy of serving now. Lose yourself in the present deed, and the time for glory will quickly and suddenly come.

Self-Control

Proverbs 25:28

A man without self-control
   is like a city broken into and left without walls.

Lack of self-control renders a person defenseless. It is self-control that allows him to keep his wits about him. Self-control gives him the discernment to know what to do and what to say. Lack of self-control gives him over to his emotions so that he acts blindly and exposes his vulnerable side. Lack of self-control leads him to actions that will result in retribution or injury.

We blame our lack of self-control on outside forces – on another person who enraged us or on circumstances that were impossible to deal with. But the very term "self-control" belies the cause being outside. Our problem is not with being unable to control outside forces but the inside force of our hearts.

The sad truth is that we cannot fully control our hearts. Some of us are more successful than others in controlling our expressions; some of us have learned patience. But the kind of self-control needed to guard our sinful passions is not ours to claim. We must look to the Holy Spirit to guard our hearts. We must pray daily to the Lord to keep us from straying. Good intentions will not give us the self-control needed. Only the transforming power of the Holy Spirit can do that kind of work.

Pray today for self-control. You don't know what will happen, and it is certain that your Adversary will try to bring out your sinful passions. Pray for protection by the Holy Spirit and that he will give to you the strength at the time needed to exercise control and to turn what could have been meant for evil into something that brought about good.

Unfitting Honor

Proverbs 26:1

Like snow in summer or rain in harvest,
  so honor is not fitting for a fool.

There is a season for everything but never honor for a fool. Perhaps a society can be best understood accordingly. Who receives adoration and for what purpose? Consider a society that rates individuality above all other traits. What is more likely to set apart a person's "individuality" than foolish behavior? In sports it is the "bad boy" who wins fame through his notoriety; likewise in entertainment. For that matter, so it happens in every strata of life. The fool gets his share of disapproval, but he gets with it an equal or greater share of praise from adoring fans who not merely excuse his behavior, but praise him precisely for it.

All the more reason then to praise the wise, to praise the good, to praise those persons least likely to garner attention. All the more reason to praise our Lord – the epitome of all that is good, wise, and holy. Especially praise him for the last quality, as well as any who bear such a mark. Holiness is distained by the world, unless the world first distorts the trait to its own liking. Praise those whom the world distains as prudish, as fanatical, as intolerant. Remember, we who follow the world will be counted as foolish. If our faith is counted as reasonable, even exemplary, to the world, then it is time to examine our hearts to see if we have not slipped into foolishness.

Of Curses

Proverbs 26:2

Like a sparrow in its flitting, like a swallow in its flying,
  a curse that is causeless does not alight.

445

Picture the small birds flitting about – up and down, back and forth, quickly darting from one direction to the next. So is the curse sent out without valid cause. It does not harm the intended victim. Thus, we should not superstitiously fear the curse sent our way. In particular we are not to fear the curse of Satan who certainly does desire our damnation. Remember who is your Advocate – Christ Jesus himself. Remember in whose hands you belong – God the Father. Remember who inhabits you – the Holy Spirit.

Nor then are we to blame our troubles on the curse of another. The troubles we face in life are mostly of our own making. We need to own up to that. Much of the troubles we face are those common to everyone else. We have not been singled out. The one curse that we can say with certainty has hit us directly is the curse of the Fall, making us sinners and the victims of sin. We don't need "special curses" to account for life's troubles. This one curse is enough to do the job.

Be thankful today and filled with awe, meditating upon our Lord who deserved no curse, yet took the Curse of the Fall upon himself, experiencing its full condemnation. Curses aimed at us may dart about missing us because he took the direct hit.

The Rod for Fools

Proverbs 26:3

A whip for the horse, a bridle for the donkey,
* and a rod for the back of fools.*

What do all three have in common? They need physical force to do what is needed. It is of no good to reason with a horse or a donkey about the direction it should take. Likewise, a fool does not listen to reason. He needs to be prodded. In particular, he needs to be disciplined in order to act the right way.

The fool is not necessarily wicked, nor even rebellious. He is, well, foolish. He does not recognize the signals that everyone else sees, and so he acts foolishly in front of others. He thinks he is being suave when he is really making a monkey of himself. He thinks he is especially discerning when he is most delusional. Subtle suggestions do not register with him. Even direct statements have little effect because he thinks you are the one who doesn't get it. Thus, discipline comes in. He is rewarded when he does right and punished when he does wrong. Hopefully in time he will, through enforcing right behavior, learn to do what is right.

And so God patiently disciplines us. Each day we act foolishly. Each day he disciplines. Each day we go our own way. Each day he pushes us in the right way or cuts off our stray paths to get us back on the right one. "Why, why?" we keep asking, like the fool who does not understand why he must be disciplined. "Can't God see?" we ask, like the fool who wonders why no one sees what he can so easily see.

Like a Fool

Proverbs 26:4-5

Answer not a fool according to his folly,
*   lest you be like him yourself.*
Answer a fool according to his folly,
*   lest he be wise in his own eyes.*

Here are two proverbs side by side contradicting each other. Which is correct? Both, depending upon the situation. When the proverb says, "Answer not a fool according to his folly, lest you be like him yourself," it means do not lose your own wit because a fool got under your skin and caused you to act irrationally. The second proverb is speaking of keeping your wit and thinking through how to answer the fool. Sometimes it may be to the advantage to use the terms and rationale of the fool (for in his mind he is being rational) to lead him to reason.

The Apostle Paul keeps his wit and uses two different tactics in speaking to the Corinthians. Here were Christians foolishly puffed up by their spiritual gifts. They thought the manifestation of gifts meant

447

they had arrived spiritually. They were wise above all others including Paul.

How does Paul address their delusion? He first denounces their folly by reminding them where they came from, declaring that the gospel of the cross is folly to the world and that such a folly of the cross is what he declares to be true wisdom (1 Cor. 1:17ff). In his second letter, in response to the Corinthians continuing to pit "super-apostles" against him, he compares himself favorably against them (2 Cor. 11:11ff). He is embarrassed even as he does so, but he believes it is necessary to use their terms to show their foolishness.

Paul uses discernment to advance his arguments, sometimes directly denouncing folly, sometimes even using folly to denounce folly! The mark of the real fool is that he has no discernment and thus blunders with his speech. The wise person turns even the speech of a fool into a tool for teaching.

The Foolish Messenger

Proverbs 26:6

Whoever sends a message by the hand of a fool
  cuts off his own feet and drinks violence.

This is graphic imagery, to say the least. It gives a clue about the message. This is not a message about remembering to take the shirts by the cleaners. It is of great import. Perhaps it is a message to an enemy about reconciliation. Perhaps two friends are at odds, and one friend is sending a message confessing his sin. Perhaps the message is from a military officer to another, giving vital news about the enemy's position, or of one general trying to set terms for surrender to another general.

The list, of course, can go on. The point is that the import of a message is not to be entrusted to someone known to be foolish. He may lose the message. He may distort the message. He may arrive too late. He has earned a reputation for not being trustworthy.

The fool never understands this. It does not occur to him that he has established such a pattern. He is eager to volunteer for the job without thinking of how to carry out the job or what the consequences may be. And as such, he is most dangerous.

It was through trustworthy men that God sent his own messages. It was through the most trustworthy of all that he sent his greatest message. Indeed, the Messenger was the Message. Ironically, he was regarded the fool. Just as ironically, this Messenger would send out his own messengers with the same valuable Message, and they also would be regarded as fools, even as we today are so regarded.

Of Proverbs and Fools

Proverbs 26:7

Like a lame man's legs, which hang useless,
  is a proverb in the mouth of fools.

Like a man given a tool for which he has neither knowledge nor skill to use, so is the rational proverb for a fool. He does not know what to do with the knowledge. Indeed, he is likely to twist the proverb to mean the opposite of what it teaches. The problem of the fool is not that he is rebellious and refuses to learn, but that he is delusional about truth. He cannot see what others so clearly see.

Why he is that way is another matter. Some are born with mental deficiencies and cannot process accurately the world around them. Others are made foolish. They are raised in ignorance and taught wrongly. Then others make themselves foolish by rejecting submission to God. As Romans 1:21 states, "For although they knew God, they did not honor him as God or give thanks to him, but they became futile in their thinking, and their foolish hearts were darkened."

What then can be done for such fools? Foremost is to pray for them. Ultimately, it is not their minds that need educating but their hearts that need transformation. That is the work of the Holy Spirit. But we are to use discernment in communicating with them. That includes

449

knowing when not to speak. It includes processing what the fool is able to handle and thinking through how to communicate. Simply speaking the truth may not be the answer. Sometimes you may have to speak "according to his folly"; at other times you may need to speak sternly against his folly.

The bottom line is to avoid the mistake of the fool which is to speak without thinking clearly. You need to be in control of your heart and mind; you need to be observant. You need to let the proverb you have learned to settle in your soul, so that you are not merely passing on a proverb but letting it pass through you.

Foolish Honor

Proverbs 26:8

Like one who binds the stone in the sling
  is one who gives honor to a fool.

It is of no purpose to bind a stone in a sling. The very purpose of a sling is to hurl a stone. It makes no sense. Nor does it make sense to honor a fool, at least not to honor him for his very foolishness.

We live in a society that seems to make a point of honoring fools. Making outrageous, offensive remarks or performing the same sort of stunts earns accolades. Our society confuses offensive and foolish behavior with freedom and creativity. The clown is upheld for making his mark.

Society plays the fool just as the person who binds the stone in the sling. Gaining attention is the honor a fool most craves. It makes little difference whether the givers sincerely honor him or think they are having the last laugh. They play into the fool's hands.

Understand this principle the next time you are tempted to respond to foolish behavior or speech. The media thrives on controversy. Of greater importance than being respected is to garner attention, and no threat is greater to its wellbeing than to be ignored. The same is true of all fools. You may honor or mock them; what they fear most of all is being ignored.

The Thorny Mouth

Proverbs 26:9

Like a thorn that goes up into the hand of a drunkard
  is a proverb in the mouth of fools.

Whether we visualize a thorn pressing into the hand of a drunkard or of a drunkard wielding a thorn branch, the reaction is "Ouch!" So is the reaction of hearing a fool speak a proverb. What comes out of a wise person's mouth sounding profound and noble comes out like the sound of fingernails on a chalkboard from a fool's mouth.

Why is this? For one, the fool obviously does not keep the proverb and so the irony is felt. The fool is not quite like the hypocrite who knows that he does not live what he preaches. The fool thinks he is wise. He thinks he truly models the proverb he speaks. He would agree with all the previous proverbs of this chapter, hoping that fools would heed them.

Another reason for the "pain" of hearing a fool speak a proverb is that he invariably misapplies it. He is like the sluggard who delights in quoting Jesus' remark not to worry about tomorrow, or like the greedy person quoting Jesus, "Ask, and it will be given to you." It is such abuse of wise teachings that is painful to hear.

Let us then be careful ourselves when we quote Scripture. It is better to have nothing to say than to take God's truth and turn it into a false teaching.

The Wounding Archer

Proverbs 26:10

Like an archer who wounds everyone
  is one who hires a passing fool or drunkard.

When we take risks we must first count the cost not only for ourselves but for others. It may seem humorous at the time to give a fool or drunkard a job to do; it may seem compassionate. But we must consider how others will be affected.

There are those better equipped for the work who lose jobs because of an impulse to hire a fool. There are the fellow workers whose work is now made more difficult because the fool not only cannot carry his load but interferes with them. There are the recipients of the fool's work – customers, passersby who are endangered, and others whose welfare is endangered.

The circumstances here are far different from those in Jesus' parable about the man who hires laborers at different times of the day and pays them all the same wage. Some might call that owner a fool to part with his money so easily, but he alone incurs a risk. It is his money to do with as he pleases. But one ought not to use his money to place risks in the lives of others.

The bottom line is that we are to carefully consider the consequences of our actions, especially those actions that seem like a compassionate thing to do. Misguided compassion produces the opposite of its intent. The fool is not made wiser, the drunkard is not reformed, and those who are innocent and well-deserving are harmed. Do good works, but count the cost for others and act with discernment.

Repeated Folly

Proverbs 26:11

Like a dog that returns to his vomit
  is a fool who repeats his folly.

There are some images we would prefer not to enter our minds! It is nauseating behavior. What possesses a dog to do such a thing? Whatever it is, it is common in dogs. So it is with the fool. Indeed, this is what marks a fool as being a fool. He repeats his foolish behavior as though it is instinct.

All of us commit foolish behavior. We say and do things that afterwards we rue: "What was I thinking?" The mark of a maturing mind is to learn from foolish mistakes. We will make mistakes. We will act foolishly. But if we are maturing, we will learn from them and become wiser.

The fool not only doesn't learn from his folly, he does not catch on that he is committing folly. What disgusts everyone else, he thinks is funny or clever. He doesn't even catch on how others feel about him.

And so man appears before God. In his great intellect and sophistication he grovels before images that have no reality; he values and praises the ridiculous. He mocks the truly wise. He scoffs at God. He even kills God when he appears. He looks back at God Incarnate and belittles him or turns him into an image that man can be comfortable with. And he thinks he is wise to do so. How does God view such a person? Re-read the proverb.

The Proud "Wise"

Proverbs 26:12

Do you see a man who is wise in his own eyes?
  There is more hope for a fool than for him.

The very sign of wisdom is knowing how little one knows. A person cannot attain wisdom until he recognizes how small he is in the universe. Thus, there are many persons with high IQs and with great knowledge but are as fools. They mistake their small amount of knowledge for wisdom.

There is more hope for fools because some fools do know they are lacking in mental ability and through discipline can be trained to curb their folly. But the person wise in his own eyes cannot receive correction. He doesn't believe he needs it. The idea is repugnant to him. It is not intelligence that keeps him from correction and certainly not wisdom, for the wise person seeks knowledge and correction. No, it is pride that prevents him from humbly receiving

453

needed correction. And pride is the most difficult barrier to break down, far more difficult than folly.

Remember this. However much people may protest that intellectual honesty keeps them from acknowledging God and his truth, the ultimate problem is pride. Until a person is willing to bow the knee before a Being who has absolute authority over him, he cannot attain wisdom. Until he is willing to acknowledge his utter dependence upon another for forgiveness and removal of sin, he cannot exercise wisdom. He may have a measure of discernment that compares favorably with the rest of mankind. God does give a measure of truth through general revelation. But without the humility to receive the truth of the gospel, that very measure of discernment will keep the individual from acknowledging the Truth. He will think he is on the right path, when he is as far away as the most foolish fool.

> Trust in the LORD with all your heart,
>   and do not lean on your own understanding.
> In all your ways acknowledge him,
>   and he will make straight your paths.
> Be not wise in your own eyes (Prov. 3:5-7a).

Lion in the Streets

Proverbs 26:13

The sluggard says, "There is a lion in the road!
*   There is a lion in the streets!"*

And so he stays home instead of going to work. And so the excuses never end.

"The weather looks bad; I might catch cold."
"I'm not feeling well; I should save my energy."
"The traffic is too bad to go out in."
"I might miss a phone call for a better job."
"I think there is a terrorist alert."

And the number one remark: "I'll start tomorrow."

The difference between the good worker and the sluggard has nothing to do with circumstances and everything to do with attitude. The good worker will overcome obstacles to get to work; the sluggard will use any excuse for an obstacle. The good worker applies himself to whatever is the task; the sluggard is always looking for the "right fit." The good worker makes the most of his circumstances; the sluggard is always complaining of bad luck. The good worker works his way up to better positions; the sluggard seems to always have supervisors who show favoritism to other workers. The good worker is thankful for the work he has; the sluggard is never thankful. The good worker takes pride in the work he does; the sluggard takes pride only in getting paid for little work.

In truth, the "lion in the streets" is very real for the sluggard. The "lion" is a job.

The Sluggard's Instinct

Proverbs 26:14

As a door turns on its hinges,
  so does a sluggard on his bed.

There is one form of action a sluggard does well; he turns his body smoothly to the other side in bed. He has got sleeping down pat. Indeed, sleeping is the one activity that he does not have to be cajoled to do. It is his instinct, in his blood.

That instinct is in all of us and is a good instinct. It is sleep that rejuvenates our body for activity. Many people do not get enough sleep through too much activity. Sleep is good, but like with most things too much of a good thing is bad for us.

The problem of the sluggard is that he is an extremist. He does not practice moderation. He is no different from the alcoholic or workaholic or anyone else obsessed with one activity. His happens to be sleeping. And he must discipline himself like everyone else to practice moderation. Everyone who over engages in an activity does so because he likes it. It is a pleasure he cannot control even when it brings bad consequences. Sleeping can be addictive; so can lying on the couch watching TV; so can any form of goofing off. Taking a break is an activity to control.

How disciplined are you? Do you get enough sleep but not too much sleep? Do you work hard but take the necessary breaks (though not too many) to rejuvenate your body? Self-discipline is needed to keep a healthy balance. What do you need to be disciplined about?

No Motivation

Proverbs 26:15

The sluggard buries his hand in the dish;
  it wears him out to bring it back to his mouth.

The sluggard finds it wearisome to do the most basic of tasks that nourish him. He is "so tired." His problem is not depression, nor is it a physiological illness, both of which can plague any of us. What the sluggard lacks is motivation. Nothing inspires him; nothing brings pleasure except sleep. The most creative thing he is able to do is come up with excuses for why he does nothing.

In the previous proverb we spoke of his lacking discipline, of giving in to an extreme – in that case, sleeping. He has the same problem of the workaholic – unable to discipline himself to keep a balance. Another way of looking at his problem is his unwillingness to "make an effort." Each day we must make the effort to go about our daily tasks. We make the effort because we are motivated to accomplish something. Our primary motivation is to provide for ourselves. We eat, ultimately, to live. We work to buy what we eat. We think it necessary for survival to have family and friends. Thus, we cultivate relationships and work to provide for our family. The list can go on and become quite complex, but the bottom line is that we must be motivated for whatever we do. The sluggard lacks basic motivation.

We must be careful not to fall into the same rut. The higher and worthier our motivation, the greater work we will do and the greater pleasure we will experience. As life falls into a routine in which we forget our reasons for doing what we do, we slide almost imperceptibly into the life of a sluggard. And the day comes when the most basic of tasks become a burden.

Do not forget the one motivation that is to guide every day of your life. It is wrapped up in why you exist. It is to glorify God. And every small, routine task serves that purpose if you remember why you exist and take delight in that purpose of glorifying God. You can only delight in that purpose if you delight in the God you are to glorify. The sluggard has no love. If you are growing weary of living each day, check if you have not forgotten the love of God that first gave you joy and meaning.

The "Wise" Sluggard

Proverbs 26:16

The sluggard is wiser in his own eyes
than seven men who can answer sensibly.

Oh so true! The sluggard is not lazy because he lacks instruction but because he will not receive it. And he does not argue that he refuses to be instructed but that no one understands him. He would be happy to listen to someone who understands him. Of course, by understanding he means accepts his own view of himself. He can receive the same counsel by seven different persons at different times and still not see or agree with them.

This is the "catch-22" of helping the sluggard and the fool. They will listen only to those who accept their view of the world and of themselves. Therefore, reasoning has little value. What is required is discipline, of which a number of proverbs have already spoken.

And so the pattern to deal with the sluggard and the fool is to first try reasoning, then move to discipline. Do not frustrate yourself trying to reason over and over. Do not create more trouble by giving him chance after chance to reform himself. Speak the truth in love; give reasoning the first try; then move to consistent discipline. And do not

457

give in until his behavior actually changes. Such an approach to the sluggard is the best hope for him. Until he bears consequences for his actions, he will not change his perspective; and until he changes his perspective, he will not change his behavior.

Ear Grabbing

Proverbs 26:17

Whoever meddles in a quarrel not his own
 is like one who takes a passing dog by the ears.

As a dog will turn on and snap at whoever tries such a move, so will the quarrelers turn on whoever tries to "help." Helping is what we think we are doing when we involve ourselves. Isn't that what Christians are to do, especially when other Christians are quarrelling? Are we not to be peacemakers?

To be peacemakers, we must exercise wisdom. And the first step in wisdom is to discern when and when not to get involved. We need to discern when our involvement is true help or being meddlesome. Often our involvement only stirs the pot for a number of reasons. For one thing, we step into the middle without understanding. We don't understand the real cause of the argument, mistaking what they are fighting about as being the real issue, when it is much deeper. We get involved often when we have heard only one side of the story, not knowing that it is distorted. We get involved without being asked and thus earning resentment from both parties. Until they are ready for intercession, any attempt – especially any blundering attempt – will only aggravate them more.

We get involved for the wrong reasons. We overestimate our own ability, meddling in a matter that is beyond our skill. We tell ourselves we want to help, when we really want to be acknowledged for our help. Then we get offended when our help is not welcomed or acknowledged. We get involved with arrogance, believing that we know better than the quarrelers, that they are foolish or at least know less than we. Such arrogance and naivety is quickly seen and rejected.

When then do we get involved? Pray for wisdom and for the right opportunity. The Lord will lead. We can ask if our help is wanted and do not be offended if it is turned down. The key is to pray and to observe well, biding our time.

No Joke

Proverbs 26:18-19

Like a madman who throws firebrands, arrows, and death
is the man who deceives his neighbor
and says, "I am only joking!"

"It was just a joke." And so we excuse all manner of mean-spirited behavior and speech. We ridicule a person, and then when it is found out and he takes offense, we reply, "I was only joking." We play a prank that humiliates its victim, and when his feelings are hurt we reply, "It was just a joke. Through the "joke" we say all manner of denigrating words and play demeaning tricks, but because it was a joke, then we are excused.

There may be a place for practical jokes and facetious humor, but we should be careful of using denigrating humor. And what we need to be careful of is not so much that the person receiving it can handle it, but our real motive in using it. Many a "joking" remark is made from deep-seated resentment or from arrogance. Many a practical joke has the very real intent of humiliating the victim or at least shows a lack of regard for him.

We use the joke to hide behind real intent, oftentimes hiding from ourselves our intent. And so we need to ask before we quickly play the joke, what is our purpose. Is it to produce merriment for everyone including the recipient, or is it to merely get a laugh for ourselves at someone's expense? We too easily claim the former not admitting even to ourselves the latter. But the result typically reveals the motive. When the result is that of a firebrand being hurled, our motive needs to be examined. Either we did want to hurt or shame, or we are guilty of lacking regard for the victim.

The Power of Doing Nothing

Proverbs 26:20

For lack of wood the fire goes out,
and where there is no whisperer, quarreling ceases.

There is great power in talk. It only takes a few words to create a fire. A few words can enrage, humiliate, scandalize, create dissension. A few words can break up friendships and loyalties, cast suspicion on people of integrity. A few words can spread trouble like winds spreading a wildfire.

In like manner, there is great power in silence. The spark that needs the wind to turn into flames dies out. The fire that has begun burns itself out. All you have to do is not spread the words. Such inaction is effective, not only because you are not a conduit but because you set the tone for others to follow. The whisperer loses his boldness when you do not respond. The excitement of gossip loses its energy when you do not join in.

There is a thrill to spreading gossip that needs others to join in. Refuse to join and you ruin the "fun" of the other gossipers. Don't become a whisperer. Your very inaction will make you a powerful firefighter.

The Quarrelsome Man

Proverbs 26:21

As charcoal to hot embers and wood to fire,
so is a quarrelsome man for kindling strife.

It is the quarreling spirit that kindles the fire. Tempers flare guaranteeing that trouble, not peace or understanding, will be the result.

"All I said was..."

"I don't know why he should be so bothered..."
"All I wanted to know was..."

These are the words of the person supposedly baffled as to why others are taking offense. He considers superficially his words but not his tone of voice, his facial expressions, and whatever other signals that he is giving about his anger.

"I was caught off guard."
"I was upset at the time."
"I didn't know he would take it that way."
"If you knew what he had said to me."

These are the superficial excuses of the offender. And they are the excuses that reveal his heart. He does not grieve over the mischief and harm he has caused but rather over the grief he is receiving.

And so the years go on without him ever learning, continually stirring the pot, and wondering why everybody else overreacts to him. Meanwhile, others leave the ministry he is engaged in or the small group he attends; meanwhile, peace in the church is troubled because of the things he has said and the division over what to do about him. So is the sad and mischievous life of the quarrelsome person.

Watch your own heart. It is easier than one thinks to fall into such a pattern through disappointments and bitterness. Being quarrelsome is easy to do; it is the simple matter of letting one's guard down. It is being a person of peace that requires diligence, that requires attention to the peace of God given in Christ. The error of the quarrelsome person is that he is attentive to his perceived offenses rather than to the grace of God.

Delicious Gossip

Proverbs 26:22

The words of a whisperer are like delicious morsels;
they go down into the inner parts of the body.

Simply put, we enjoy gossip. That is the reason it spreads easily and quickly. We enjoy receiving it, and we enjoy passing it on. When we receive news that excites us, our natural inclination is to share the excitement. News about someone else's discomfort somehow arouses our interest to hear and "share." As Christians, we mask our sinful interest by telling ourselves we are interested out of Christian concern.

The whispering of gossip, notwithstanding "Christian concern," typically adds to the pain of the person or trouble to the situation that is being whispered about. Word gets back to the person, filling them with shame and stirring up anger. More "solutions" are offered to the problem situation, creating more complexity to deal with.

What is the solution to whispering gossip? Proverb 26:20 has already given it. Stop whispering. Don't go on a diet of whispering. Go on a fast. It may be difficult at first. But as the person discovers, who seriously cuts out foods that seem sweet but are harmful, the very denial opens up the taste buds to more natural, enjoyable tastes.

Fervency

Proverbs 26:23

Like the glaze covering an earthen vessel
  are fervent lips with an evil heart.

In a way, the glaze hides what is underneath while giving the appearance of revealing its inner makeup. We can see the clay, but the glaze covers over the imperfections and causes the clay to have a shine that it really does not possess of itself. In the same way, we may use our lips to deceive what is underneath.

Some speak fervently with the intention of covering up their evil. Others speak fervently merely out of their nature. In both cases, the fervency does not measure the sincerity of their hearts. It is not speech that ultimately reveals the heart. It is the long-term obedience in both speech and action that provide the best test. And that

462

obedience is not a mere performance of duty but one that bears the fruit of the Spirit – love, joy, peace, patience, kindness, goodness, faithfulness, gentleness, and self-control.

Look at their fruit – the fruit born in them and the fruit of their lives, that is, the impact on others around them. Fervency is not bad; just don't use it to measure the heart.

The Disguise of Hate

Proverbs 26:24-26

Whoever hates disguises himself with his lips
*   and harbors deceit in his heart;*
when he speaks graciously, believe him not,
*   for there are seven abominations in his heart;*
though his hatred be covered with deception,
*   his wickedness will be exposed in the assembly.*

Let's follow the train of thought. There is the type of person who, though he in truth is hateful, he covers it up by speaking graciously. He is the illustration of verse 23's "the glaze covering an earthen vessel." This phenomenon is seen on all levels: the entertainer who tells his audience he loves them while he actually despises them; the politician who speaks admiringly of his constituents whom he regards as fools; the hired worker or salesperson who behaves respectfully to the one controlling his paycheck and yet is filled with envy; the "friend" who wants to be considered "one of the guys" but can barely tolerate those same guys.

We are not to believe him because of the condition of his heart. It is the heart that must be dealt with. Knowing how to speak graciously does not signify a good heart. It signifies merely cleverness. Indeed, to speak graciously to those whom one hates signifies a wickedness that goes deeper than that of the man who does not hide his hate.

The third point is that a person's hatred will be revealed. Hatred will come out. Indeed, if one gives time to observation a hateful heart is detectable. Like a movie set of a town made up of facades that shake or fall when buffeted by wind, so the "gracious" facade of the hateful heart is shaken and revealed. It takes effort to keep up appearances, and even then it is difficult to coordinate the artificial words with the artificial mannerisms. The hateful person is merely reading lines.

What then are we to do? Be on our guard. Don't be taken in. But all the more befriend such a person. Most persons like that believe they are doing what everyone else is doing. They do not believe in a true loving heart. Perhaps you will be the one to prove that not all is a disguise.

The Pit and the Stone

Proverbs 26:27

Whoever digs a pit will fall into it,
and a stone will come back on him who starts it rolling.

He who starts trouble will get caught up in his own making. Typically he underestimates the response of others. He expects them to cower when they instead get angry. He expects them to get upset when instead they remain cool. He may be good at pit digging or stone rolling, but he is poor in calculating the human heart. He may anticipate the initial reaction, but he does not think further. He does not anticipate how the victim will eventually retaliate.

Nor does he consider the One who is watching his every step and who will see that justice is done. Understand that, however large the pit may be that the wicked digs, there is a greater, more terrible pit that awaits him. However large the stone may be that he sends rolling, there is a greater stone that will crush him. For his own good, he will hopefully fall into his own pit and be hurt by his own stone so that he might be brought to his senses.

Pray for the wicked to now say, "What have I done?" Pray for the wicked to come now to his senses, look beyond his little pit, and see how his mischief will engulf himself. Pray now for the wicked to repent as we have done for our own wickedness.

The Revealing Liar

Proverbs 26:28

A lying tongue hates its victims,
and a flattering mouth works ruin.

The lying tongue and the flattering mouth – weapons of deception – are the true revealers of the heart. The liar may consciously despise his victim or regard the victim indifferently; so the flatterer. He has one aim – his advancement. He may want money or power or pleasure. Whatever the case, he will lie and flatter for that one goal. He is single-minded.

And he is a hater whose real love is to ruin others. Deny as he might, his very lying reveals his heart as a hater. He hates his neighbor. Most of all, he hates God. Like his father Satan, his character is expressed through his deception.

Such a person cannot be happy with mere advancement of his own situation. He must see that others experience disappointment. He delights not only in their being deceived, but by their misery over the deception. Ruin – the ruin of others – is what satisfies their inner craving.

How comforting it is to know the intent and the power of our Father who is Truth, who intends on building us up even to glory, and who will not fail. The world is filled with lying tongues, but it is also under the sovereign control of our God who cannot be deceived, who is advancing his kingdom, who is turning liars into truth-bearers, even us. There is one who seeks our ruin; but there is a greater One within us who seeks our victory and will attain it.

Tomorrow

Proverbs 27:1

Do not boast about tomorrow,
for you do not know what a day may bring.

James provides a good commentary for this proverb:

> Come now, you who say, "Today or tomorrow we will go into such and such a town and spend a year there and trade and make a profit"— yet you do not know what tomorrow will bring. What is your life? For you are a mist that appears for a little time and then vanishes. Instead you ought to say, "If the Lord wills, we will live and do this or that." As it is, you boast in your arrogance. All such boasting is evil (Jas. 4:13-16).

The sooner we grasp how little control we have of the future, then the better prepared we will be for it. We become flustered and lose our temper because our plans are interrupted. If we know that tomorrow is in God's hands and not ours, we will then be better prepared for what will actually take place, whether or not it goes according to our plans.

It is good to make plans; but understand that our plans are nothing more than that – plans. We are not God whose plans are fixed. Nor do we want them to be, for we lack God's knowledge and his goodness. Do not boast about tomorrow. It is the humble attitude to take, as well as a wise attitude that will lead to contentment and to true readiness.

Self-Praise

Proverbs 27:2

Let another praise you, and not your own mouth;
  a stranger, and not your own lips.

"See what I have done!" That is a cute phrase from a young child. We smile and respond how impressed we are. But as the same person grows older, the cute phrase becomes increasingly irritating to hear. We judge the speaker to be immature at best or egotistical. When the self-praise is patently off base, we consider the speaker to be delusional, and he is scorned as a fool. When the self-praise actually

466

has merit, then all the more that praise is resented as being prideful and arrogant. Whatever may be the case, self-praise reveals a character that is self-centered.

But the same praise, when it is spoken by others, not only is acceptable but regarded as the right thing to do. "See what he has done!" That is an apt phrase from an objective outsider. We don't merely concur with the words; we find them pleasing to be spoken. We want to join in on the praise. We will even urge the recipient of the phrase not to be modest.

But what if the praise does not come? That is the egotist's real worry. What if others do not notice his accomplishments? Or perhaps they do notice, but are not the type to give praise? How then will others take notice? How will he get his due acclaim?

That very line of thinking reveals the small-mindedness and self-centeredness of the thinker. It reveals that his accomplishments are little more than attention getters. He has not strived to achieve great things but to achieve greatness. He has not performed for love of the game or love of the deed or love for others but for the acknowledgement of others. The irony is that his very attempt at gaining praise through his self-praise causes him to lose the admiration he would have likely received. His very zeal to make himself admired destroys his goal.

Christians, of all people, should have little concern about being praised, not because praise is bad, but because of what lies before us – "an eternal weight of glory beyond all comparison" (2 Cor. 4:17). Is that not enough to satisfy?

Heavy Weight

Proverbs 27:3

A stone is heavy, and sand is weighty,
*   but a fool's provocation is heavier than both.*

It is odd how much a fool's provocation weighs upon us. We may

467

exhaust ourselves carrying stone or moving sand, but we may put either down whenever we desire; we can then rest and recoup. But the provocation of a fool weighs upon us and we cannot lay it down. Indeed, the weight only seems to grow.

Perhaps someone has taunted us; perhaps has teased us; perhaps has simply acted foolish in front of us. We cannot get it out of our minds. We keep thinking about it. We begin to fume about it. Perhaps something was said that has an element of truth, and we argue in our minds about it. Perhaps we were embarrassed. The problem is that we cannot get it out of our minds.

How do we get rid of such a weight? The simple answer is to turn it over to God. But how is that done? Through prayer of course, but specifically through scripture-informed prayer. To get the words of the fool out of our minds, we need to fill our minds with the words of God. All scripture is good to read, but especially effective is to read that which speaks of the character and works of God. If we turn our minds to the praise of God, then there is not room to carry the provocation of a fool.

Jealousy

Proverbs 27:4

Wrath is cruel, anger is overwhelming,
  but who can stand before jealousy?

A person can be jealous toward us. He is jealous of our good fortune – the money we earn, our popularity, whatever it is that he perceives we have and he wants. In that jealousy, he becomes our enemy, or, rather, makes us the enemy. We have what he does not, and he will act, not merely to attain what we have, but to take it from us. Indeed, more important than getting what we have is to see that we lose it. He wants us to feel the loss that he feels.

A person can also be jealous for us. He wants us, and he does not want to share. He is resentful of the attention others show us. Nor does he want us sharing. He cannot abide us being friendly towards others. He certainly cannot abide us loving others. He would rather us feel his pain than be happy with others.

How dangerous then is such a person. An angry man loses his anger when his attention is diverted to other things. Cruel wrath often is not personal. We experience harm while we are in its way, but it will pass. The jealous man, though, is obsessed with the person about whom or for whom he is jealous. His happiness is tied up in the fortune of the person with whom he is obsessed.

We are in danger of becoming that jealous person if our joy is not found in God alone. For as much as we love God, then as much will we rejoice in the fortune of others, especially in their standing with our Lord. Because the love of God is so satisfying, we cannot be jealous of what others have. Jealousy, the lack of it, is a good measure of our satisfaction with God.

Hidden Love

Proverbs 27:5

Better is open rebuke
  than hidden love.

Open rebuke is painful and shameful. It is difficult enough to receive rebuke well, but to receive such in the presence of others naturally leads to shame. We then want to defend ourselves and especially prove the rebuker wrong. Whether we are able to or not, we no longer trust him or regard him as a friend.

But as painful as such an incident may be, even worse is to withhold love, to keep it hidden. Hidden love does not shame or offend; it discourages. It does not shock; it quietly demoralizes. Open rebuke, as painful as it may be to receive, can awaken us to what has been lacking or offensive in us. It can spur us to change that is good. Hidden love reinforces our faults because it is love that motivates us to good. Hidden love is offensive, for it is a lie. To love someone and keep that love hidden is deception.

How then does one display love? God gives the model. He showed his love by sending his Son to be an atoning sacrifice for us. Christ showed his love to the Father by willingly obeying. Jesus has told us that we show love to him by obeying his commandments. We know that the Father delights in our worship. And so then, we learn to show our love to one another – when we gladly make sacrifices for one another; when we listen to one another, do what matters for the other; and when we praise one another. And even when we rebuke (privately) each other for the other's good. Love is to be displayed, as God displays his love to and for us.

Faithful Wounds

Proverbs 27:6

Faithful are the wounds of a friend;
  profuse are the kisses of an enemy.

A friend cares about our good. Thus, as a doctor who will inflict some pain to heal, so a friend is willing to do the difficult task of "wounding" for our good. He will tell us hard truth; he will not flatter us about what is false. He will not cater to our vanity. He will speak the truth in love, and he will be there for us when we fall, even if he must let us fall to awaken us to our senses.

The enemy is only too happy to greet us with kisses, to spill out flattery, whatever it takes to stoke our vanity and lead us astray. As a friend is single-minded in desiring our good, so an enemy is single-minded in our destruction.

"Why would he lie?" "Why did he pretend to be my friend?" Because he hates you.

"Why did my friend not speak as well of me?" "Why did he say things that would hurt my feelings?" Because he loves you.

Both act in keeping with their motive. What we need to do is exercise discernment to understand which is easier to do than we admit. The only reason we are not discerning is when we let our vanity cloud our thinking. We are blind to what others easily see because of our pride. But if we love our friends, we will listen to them and consider carefully what they see. If we desire honoring God, we will be cautious of flattery and kisses from strangers or those who have not proven their friendship.

Extremes

Proverbs 27:7

One who is full loathes honey,
  but to one who is hungry everything bitter is sweet.

In the extremes of life, everything we experience takes on an extreme flavor. When we are full, we despise what we normally enjoy; when we are hungry, we relish what we typically would reject as bitter. The need dictates the experience.

The one who is full has no one to blame but himself. He makes himself full by giving into his impulses. Because he cannot resist the honey, he satiates himself until he loathes the honey he craved. The one who is hungry finds sweetness in what normally is bitter because his body craves nourishment. His taste buds acclimate to the bitter in order to satisfy the hunger.

Neither state is good. Though the satiated person has only himself to blame and the hungry person perhaps has circumstances to fault, neither are in good positions. It is better that the hungry person obtains nourishing food, and it is good to be able to enjoy honey. And it is better not to be overly stimulated and satiated with rich food. What is most desirable is disciplined enjoyment of what one earns. It is best to work for one's food and obtain the sweet, and then to enjoy it in a measured manner that keeps the sweet from turning bitter.

Thus, the proverb cautions against the philosophy of eat, drink, and be merry that leads to bitterness, and that of the sluggard whose laziness leaves him ever hungry.

Straying

Proverbs 27:8

Like a bird that strays from its nest
  is a man who strays from his home.

The bird that strays is alone; he is lost and in danger. So is the person who strays from his spiritual home and often his physical home. He is alone. At home he had the support of family and trusted friends. Now he is alone, trying to learn whom to trust. Now he is lost, trying to get a sense of direction. He is in danger, no longer living to be fulfilled but merely to survive.

There may come a time for a person to leave his home, to make his way into the world. But that is different from straying. To move forward is the result of having matured, becoming well grounded, so that he in a sense takes home with him. He keeps his faith; he keeps in good communication with his family and trusted friends.

Straying is moving with no direction. It is the result of getting diverted, of losing focus, of forgetting home. Where are you now? You could be hundreds of miles from your physical home but have "home" with you in the faith and values you have kept. You could be living at home but have in truth strayed, forgetting and rejecting that faith. Do you need to come back home? Don't know what you will find? The story of the prodigal son should clue you in.

Sweet Counsel

Proverbs 27:9

Oil and perfume make the heart glad,
  and the sweetness of a friend comes from his earnest counsel.

There seems no solution to your problem. You stay awake with worry. Life could not be worse. Then a friend appears. You share your trouble. He provides insight into the problem that you had not seen. Yes, that's it! How wonderful is his counsel!

You are embarking on a new venture. It seems a bit risky, but you are excited about the potential. Everything seems to be falling into place. You share your plans with your friend. She reminds you of a weakness you have that would lead to trouble. It is hard to receive but as you consider what she says, you realize that she has saved you from disaster. How good it is to have such a friend.

The scenarios vary, but the lesson is the same. The counsel of a friend who is wise and truly loves you, of a friend who is godly, is real pleasure. The counsel itself is good because it is true, but receiving it from a friend who gives it out of earnestness, because he feels love for you – that gives the counsel its sweet aroma. For you leave not only wiser but having felt loved. That is good friendship.

The Nearby Friend

Proverbs 27:10

Do not forsake your friend and your father's friend,
and do not go to your brother's house in the day of your calamity.
Better is a neighbor who is near
than a brother who is far away.

This proverb is not denigrating the value of family relations, but it is promoting the value of friendship, especially of friends who are with us. How guilty are we of bemoaning that we are far from family or old friends, all the while ignoring or discounting the friends God has placed around us? How guilty are we of keeping our neighbors at a distance?

When immediate needs arise, when a calamity occurs, we will find it so much better to have a friend who is next door to aid us, than to depend upon a relative or friend who is far away. Let those who are near to you physically become those who are near to you relationally. Develop those friendships. Assume that God has placed you where you are to be a friend to those who are near. Perhaps your neighbor needs a good friend.

The Wise Son

Proverbs 27:11

Be wise, my son, and make my heart glad,
  that I may answer him who reproaches me.

This proverb may be regarded as a transitional verse. Similar ones appear throughout the book indicating a change in subject. But taken by itself, it impresses upon us that our acting in wisdom or in folly impacts more than ourselves. The parent does, and must, care about the behavior of the child regardless of age. The teacher should care whether his teaching is making a difference in the lives of his students, and so the mentor for his disciple, the craftsman for his apprentice. Solomon is not writing and collecting proverbs as a hobby. He intends for them "to give prudence to the simple, knowledge and discretion to the youth" (1:4). It matters, then, if youth do learn knowledge and discretion.

Think of a case in which God was questioned about the behavior of a "son" – that of Job. Satan "reproached" God, saying that Job only lived a righteous life because of the good he received. God allowed Job to be put to the test in order to answer Satan.

How well Job handled the test can be questioned, but there is a better story, the story of God's Only Begotten Son. He also was put to the test. He proved himself wise through his complete obedience so that God was able to say, "With you I am well pleased." Let us be thankful for this son who was and is wise, and who will be able to answer for us on the Day of Judgment when our accuser comes with his reproaches.

A Time to Hide

Proverbs 27:12

The prudent sees danger and hides himself,
  but the simple go on and suffer for it.

What may be taken as bravado or perseverance may in truth be mere folly. God may call us to risk danger; he may call us to persevere through trial. But that is far different from entering into dangerous trials out of our own folly. Many, if not most, of our trials are brought on because of our own doing.

We may be lazy and not prepare properly for the task before us. We may be simple and not discern the consequences of what we do. We may be wicked and let our desires overrule what is proper. We may be prideful and prefer suffering if we think we keep our independence and pride. We walk into danger unnecessarily and wrongfully. We ought to suffer for such foolishness.

The truth is that hiding is sometimes the appropriate response to danger. We should hide from temptation when possible. We should hide from whatever temptation strikes us at our weakness – be it pornography or alcohol or whatever we easily are addicted to. We should hide from needless confrontations that draw out our anger. We should count the cost of venturing forth in a risky venture. It is not shameful to admit our limits and our weaknesses.

The shame comes in acting as a Peter and boasting of bravery that we do not have. There is no shame in confessing our frailty and casting our security on God to provide, which includes turning to others to accomplish what we cannot. Hiding from responsibility is shameful; hiding so that we can carry out our responsibility is honorable. There is a time to hide and a time to step forward into danger. It takes godly discernment to know what is needed. Seek such discernment.

Cautious Loans

Proverbs 27:13

Take a man's garment when he has put up security for a stranger,
and hold it in pledge when he puts up security for an adulteress.

The simple message here is to be cautious in loaning money or costly resources. It is one thing to give generously; it is another to freely loan or make risky agreements. To do the latter is to create troubling situations for everyone involved. Consider the three parties above (considering "adulteress" as synonymous with "stranger").

You have loaned money that you need back and now must depend upon your neighbor to be true to his word and pay up if the stranger (whom you do not know and cannot trust) does not come through on his end. If that stranger does not come through, the neighbor must somehow come up with money he evidently does not have (thus the reason he has approached you). Your neighbor is caught in the middle, having made his own risk. He has vouched for someone you have reason to suspect will not come through. Thus anxiety is created for at least you and your neighbor, and possibly hard feelings if the stranger does not pay up, which will only magnify if the neighbor then must come through and is unable. Even if the neighbor does cover the stranger, there will some difficult feelings between you and him.

How does taking your neighbor's garment as security help? First, if you are uncomfortable asking for such a security, then don't make the loan at all. You are doing no one a favor by making loans that you cannot afford nor freely give as a gift. But asking for a security of some kind does have the effect of making clear at the outset to the neighbor and the stranger the seriousness of asking for the loan. People will glibly promise to pay back, thinking all the while that the lender really doesn't care or at least can afford not to recoup the money. Asking for security impresses upon the receiver how seriously you take his paying you back. This is especially important for the neighbor, as it will cause him to count the cost of the risk he is taking. It can be too easy to say, "I'll vouch for him." To make him prove his confidence in the stranger will motivate him to be surer of what he is doing.

It is good to be generous with what we have; it is also good to be wise. Indeed, it is only because we are wise with our money that we can afford to be generous. Give freely; loan cautiously.

The Cursed Blessing

Proverbs 27:14

Whoever blesses his neighbor with a loud voice,
rising early in the morning,
will be counted as cursing.

There is the "friend" whom we wish would not be so friendly. He may think that he is sincere in his friendliness, but it is evident that he acts either out of neediness or of self-promotion. He does not think of what we truly need but of what he wants to do. In this case, he blesses loudly early in the morning, disturbing us and our neighbors. If rebuked, he replies that he only wants to bless us.

And so, out of this "desire" to bless, this friend will impose himself upon us at all times of the day and night and in all sorts of manner. He will embarrass us and inconvenience us out of his perceived motive of love. A true friend loves by taking the time to observe us and know what pleases us and does not please us. A true friend thinks through what is a true blessing. In brief, a true friend is respectful of his friend.

We can think of such persons who fit this description of the self-absorbed friend. Are we able to examine ourselves for such traits? It is difficult to separate acting for the good of a neighbor and acting to fulfill our own neediness. The key element is taking the time to observe our friend or neighbor before we act. It is taking the time to observe his body language, to listen to the tone of his voice, and to hear from him first how he is doing. The true friend, the good neighbor, observes first, then acts accordingly so that his blessing does not become counted as a cursing.

Bad Shelter

Proverbs 27:15-16

A continual dripping on a rainy day
and a quarrelsome wife are alike;
to restrain her is to restrain the wind
or to grasp oil in one's right hand.

One purpose of a home is to find shelter from the storm. To enter a home on a rainy day and find the roof leaking is discouraging at best. Being powerless to stop that leak during the storm stirs feelings of frustration. So it is to come home to a spouse who is quick to complain. There is no rest. But of particular frustration is the impotent feeling of being unable to stop the complaining. To restrain her is like restraining the wind. Imagine standing in a strong wind with arms out trying to make the wind stop. Or imagine holding on to oil being poured into your hand. It can't be done, and it is particularly frustrating to watch precious oil, meant to be a soothing balm, slip through your fingers and fall wasteful on the ground.

The home is meant to be a place of rest. A marriage is meant to be a place to build up one another, to shelter one another. All the more reason then that tempers explode and patience is broken when storms enter into the home. All the more reason then to do whatever is necessary for yourself. If you cannot restrain the wind, then you need to think how to find the shelter you need.

God's Word tells us what that shelter is to be:
> He who dwells in the shelter of the Most High
> will abide in the shadow of the Almighty.
> I will say to the Lord, "My refuge and my fortress,
> my God, in whom I trust" (Ps. 91:1-2).

Our complaining and our frustration say more about our failure to find the real Shelter than it does about the terribleness of the storm. A quarrelsome wife is a woman who does not find contentment in her Lord. A husband who retaliates does not turn to the Lord for his shelter and strength.

Do what is necessary – that is, do what the Lord gives instruction about finding your peace, your shelter in him, so that you will be a wife who is a true helpmeet to her husband, and be a husband who is a true head sheltering his wife.

Iron Sharpening

Proverbs 27:17

Iron sharpens iron,
  and one man sharpens another.

The image is that of a sword or some tool being sharpened by a whetting iron. Unlike the neighbor of verse 14 who shouts out shallow blessings or the quarrelsome wife of verses 15-16, the "iron" friend is one who listens and then has the good hardness to give constructive counsel, even if it needs to be critical.

The iron friend's goal is to sharpen his friend, to make him a useful tool for service or a good weapon for battle. He himself must be hard, not in the sense of being uncaring but of having strong enough character in a couple of ways. One is to be strong enough to care more about telling his friend what the friend needs to hear, rather than saying only what the friend wants to hear. He must be one made strong from having going through his own difficult struggles, so that he has good counsel to give.

Do you have such a friend? Are you such a friend? It is not easy. Iron hitting iron can produce sparks and at the least be grating. But that is what friends are for: to be there for one another, supporting and sharpening one another.

Reward

Proverbs 27:18

Whoever tends a fig tree will eat its fruit,
  and he who guards his master will be honored.

There is reward that comes with conscientious, faithful service. The farmer giving such care to his fig tree will eat of its delicious, nourishing fruit; the servant protecting his master will receive honor.

Does it not seem so for you? Perhaps you have been conscientious for a while but need to be patience with time. Perhaps you have labored long in your mind, but the quality of your service in truth has been sporadic. You have allowed disappointments impact your work. In your mind you are working hard, but others hear your complaints and observe weaknesses that you will not allow yourself to see.

Perhaps the fruit you seek is not the fruit God has prepared, which will be sweeter than you know. It may be the unexpected fruit that comes when you become content with what you have. It may be the fruit that comes from other labor that you have not given much thought to, such as befriending someone in a time of need, of being an encouragement to others, or other acts that you do by second nature and therefore do not consider the reward that results. Perhaps the fruit will be the consequence of feeling barren and even stripped of fruit, such as our Lord experienced, and who because he did was rewarded with honor and many "offspring."

Remember what is promised to those who belong to Christ – the weight of glory (2 Cor. 4:17). Every other earthly reward should pale in comparison. No matter what we receive here, it will pass and we will be forgotten. Remember where our true hope lies – in the return of our Lord and in the inheritance that cannot be lost, nor can we lose it because we ourselves our guarded by our Master (1 Pet. 1:3-5).

Reflection

Proverbs 27:19

As in water face reflects face,
so the heart of man reflects the man.

This seems simple enough. To know ourselves we merely need to look at our heart. But peering into a still pool of water to see one's face is much easier than looking into one's heart. Indeed, looking into the heart is the most difficult task for anyone. Why?

The heart, of course, is a figure of speech and difficult to define. Is the heart what I intend or what I do? Many times I do the opposite of what I intend to do. I discourage when I mean to encourage. I take when I intend to share. I want to do good but end up doing wrong.

In my mind I have a good heart; it's just that my behavior distorts the heart's true reflection.

Or the actions may be reversed. What many see as reflecting kindness is really an attempt to earn advantage for myself. If people only knew the *real* reason for the good things they see, they would be appalled. I know my behavior is covering my heart's true reflection.

As one whose face has been scarred loathes to look into the mirror at his reflection, so we all have an aversion of looking fully into our own hearts. It is not overly complicated to see our true reflection, which can be seen in both behavior and thought-life; rather, it is painful to see, and we lack the will to stare into the heart-mirror.

And the only way we can possess the will is to first possess the grace that allows us see both the scars and the beauty of being remade in Christ. We are afraid to get below the skin and see a wicked heart; but if you are in Christ, there is yet another level deeper that reveals true beauty – the beauty of our Lord which is growing within us through the activity of the Holy Spirit. Look into the mirror to the sin and then through it to the beauty of Christ Jesus in you.

Craving Eyes

Proverbs 27:20

Sheol and Abaddon are never satisfied,
and never satisfied are the eyes of man.

The grave is never satisfied. No matter how many bodies it receives, it is always craving for more. So are the eyes of man, as advertisers know well. No matter what a person may have, when he sees something desirable, he craves it and will spend himself into deep debt or turn to wicked ways to obtain it. He cannot be satisfied.

Tolstoy illustrates this truth well in his short story, "How Much Land Does a Man Need?" The peasant Pahom keeps moving, keeps acquiring more land, until it leads to his death. "If I had..." drives him to acquire and acquire, never being satisfied.

It is a fine balance between desiring to improve our lot and obtaining contentment. Because our eyes see what we could obtain if we labor diligently, we work hard and produce good fruit. But it is easier than we realize to step off that fine line and become gluttoness. Balance is what we need, and it is what we cannot attain as long as we are not contented in the love of Christ. That seems a cliché but it is a profound truth that few have known.

The Apostle Paul knew it and learned to be content in every circumstance (cf. Phil. 4:12). Oddly enough, his very contentment in Christ led him to be extremely ambitious in his life's service. Is there a connection between contentment in what is of true value and motivation to achieve? That may be a good thought to contemplate today. In what are you contented? What motivates you? How do they relate? Knowing that answer may be the difference between restless craving and true fulfillment.

Of Praise and Testing

Proverbs 27:21

The crucible is for silver, and the furnace is for gold,
 and a man is tested by his praise.

The crucible and the furnace serve to both test and purify their metals. If there are impurities, they will surface and be removed. If there are none, then their purity will be proved. Either way, the fiery process produces good character.

So praise works in similar ways. Typically, a person will not receive public praise without proving himself through some sort of trial. Oftentimes the very praise will invite scrutiny to see if there are impurities. Many a praised idol has been brought down through the scrutiny brought on in the light of attention.

But another test for a person's quality is the quality of the praise. We can test a person's quality by who gives him the praise and by what he is praised for. Thus, the praise of one's peers is valued more than that of those who know him little or understand the work he has done. The praise of persons known for their integrity and wisdom reveals more than that of the fool who "blesses his neighbor with a loud voice" (v. 14). To be praised by fools and the wicked reveals troubling impurities.

The proverb may also be speaking of testing the person by what he praises. This certainly is a good test. What does he value? Of what and of whom does he speak highly? He who praises a fool is likely to be a fool; likewise, he who praises the wicked reveals the wickedness of his own heart.

Whom do you admire? For what reasons? Answer the question truthfully and you may discover more about yourself.

The Fool

Proverbs 27:22

Crush a fool in a mortar with a pestle
 along with crushed grain,
 yet his folly will not depart from him.

It is difficult to change a fool. Try explanation. The fool nods as though understanding; he then acts as if he had received none. Try reasoning with a fool. He argues irrationally so that you become befuddled. Try education. He will take in little, and what he does take in, he will misapply. Try discipline. He may behave better, but still without understanding and likely with resentment.

A likeable fool will at least try to please others and even acknowledge his deficiency (thus being wiser than many a "wise" man). But especially troublesome is the fool who is angry with everyone else for getting it wrong. He goes his whole life offending others and bothered by the reaction of everyone else.

Like a disease that cannot be cured but instead managed, so one must accept the same for the fool. We will only frustrate ourselves in attempting to change his way of thinking and behavior. We need to

483

think, rather, in terms of setting boundaries so as to restrain his offending behavior and to protect him from his own folly.

And then pray. For though we cannot change a fool, it is the specialty of the Holy Spirit to do just that. After all, consider what he has done in us. Without the Spirit, we also are fools easily going the way of the world. It took the "folly" of the cross to make us wise in Christ.

Keeping Vigilant

Proverbs 27:23-27

Know well the condition of your flocks,
    and give attention to your herds,
for riches do not last forever;
    and does a crown endure to all generations?
When the grass is gone and the new growth appears
    and the vegetation of the mountains is gathered,
the lambs will provide your clothing,
    and the goats the price of a field.
There will be enough goats' milk for your food,
    for the food of your household
    and maintenance for your girls.

Do not rest on your present riches or your present success. You must continue to be vigilant with maintaining how you receive your income and be caring of those who serve you. Verse 24 indicates that this proverb is to be applied to the shepherd-king. He is to regard his people as his flock, tending to their needs. Through such care he is actually assuring his own prosperity.

Two lessons we can learn. One, we are to be always vigilant. Many a successful entrepreneur has lost what he earned because he thought he had "made it" and could now rest. It is true that one can alter his work, but he cannot rest from work. He must be diligent in looking over his enterprise, even if he turns it over to trustworthy stewards.

For – the second lesson – if he does not give proper care to his stewards, and they do not give it to the workers, then the system will break down. Just as the farmer must provide nourishment to his flock to assure that they produce, so an employer or manager must nurture his workers. It is through nurturing, not through threats, that employees do their best work and remain loyal.

One other lesson is to remember our Shepherd-King who keeps watch over us, who feeds us with his Word, who nourishes us in the gospel. Here is one who gave up riches to make us rich. And as a result his crown will endure to all generations.

Boldness

Proverbs 28:1

The wicked flee when no one pursues,
  but the righteous are bold as a lion.

The wicked flee when they believe the odds are against them. Much of their bravado lies in the unfair advantage they exploit. They lie; they cheat; they strike behind the back; they rely on greater numbers and greater strength to fight their battles. Thus, because their confidence lies in what they can see and exploit, when they are alone or cannot see clearly, when they perceive they have no unfair advantage over their enemy, they run away.

David, a man known for courage, expressed well in his psalms the reasons for why the righteous may be bold. Psalm 18 is a prime example. Consider the first three verses:

I love you, O Lord, my strength.
The Lord is my rock and my fortress and my deliverer,
    my God, my rock, in whom I take refuge,
    my shield, and the horn of my salvation, my stronghold.
I call upon the Lord, who is worthy to be praised,
    and I am saved from my enemies.

The righteous may be bold because their confidence rests in the Lord. David understood this and tested it. Under such confidence he killed Goliath. Listen to his words before battling his foe.

485

For who is this uncircumcised Philistine, that he should defy the armies of the living God?... Your servant has struck down both lions and bears, and this uncircumcised Philistine shall be like one of them, for he has defied the armies of the living God. The Lord who delivered me from the paw of the lion and from the paw of the bear will deliver me from the hand of this Philistine (1 Sam. 17:26, 36-37).

Where does your confidence lie – in your ability to calculate the odds or in your faith in the "living God"? Only in the latter will you find a steady peace that weathers the trials of life and keeps you even keeled. Only in the latter will you find wisdom to know what to do when faced with dilemmas. For much of our quandaries about how to live are not based on lack of knowledge, but lack of faith. When we peacefully trust the Lord to be our stronghold, then we are free to focus on doing what is honorable.

Stability

Proverbs 28:2

When a land transgresses, it has many rulers,
but with a man of understanding and knowledge,
its stability will long continue.

Interestingly the proverb notes that it is when a land transgresses – not a ruler – that it will experience the rule of many rulers. The people are difficult to manage, and so many rulers are required to keep order. These rulers may be local chiefs taking advantage of a weak central ruler to form their own little rival kingdoms. They may be government agents using their positions to oppress the people under their authority. Under such conditions the rulers inevitably battle with each other trying to undermine one another to gain more power. Thus, there are not only many rulers, but many have reigns cut short through violence and intrigue.

What is needed is a person of understanding and knowledge, a person of integrity who understands people and how to govern them

486

for the welfare of the land. He needs to understand how to deal with his enemies so as not to be undermined. He must be fair, but not naive. He must have ideals, but works towards them in a practical way. He must be aware of the temptations of power and keep his integrity.

The task is difficult, but if he succeeds in maintaining his rule and is patient with the process of establishing just conditions, then he will bring stability to his land. Are you willing to weather the course in your position of leadership? Are you willing to go through the arduous task of patiently observing and then acting with understanding and knowledge?

Let us be thankful for our King who faithfully remains on his throne and rules us. Even though we are guilty of transgression, he remains our ruler, keeping stability throughout his kingdom until the day he returns in his glory.

Beating Rain

Proverbs 28:3

A poor man who oppresses the poor
  is a beating rain that leaves no food.

The first line is a bit unclear. It may be as the translation reads or be translated as "a poor man and an oppressor of the poor." Either way, the primary message is the effect of oppression, whoever commits it.

We look to rain to nourish the ground and to provide water to drink. Rain is welcomed, especially in an arid country such as the Middle East, and especially to the poor who need the rain for crops and quench their thirst. All the more disheartening, then, that when the rain does come, it comes with such force as to actually destroy the crops. It seems cruel to receive destruction by the very element intended to bring life.

So it is with the oppressor who is in position to help, whether he be a neighbor who can provide mutual support or the person of power and wealth who could use those same resources to strengthen the needy. To turn around and use those resources to oppress is cruel.

Are we using what we possess, however great or small, for the good of our neighbor? Do we leave "food" for our neighbor when he is with us or do we leave nothing? Apply this to the great wealth that we do have – the Word of God, the gospel of Christ. Do we use the Word and the gospel to produce fruit or do we use those very same resources to beat down with the law? Do we use the gospel in our hearts to show grace or do we withhold it, so that our neighbor receives no food from the very people who have the Bread of Life?

What will you do with your wealth today?

Forsaking vs. Keeping

Proverbs 28:4

Those who forsake the law praise the wicked,
  but those who keep the law strive against them.

The heroes of the wicked are the wicked. Lawbreakers admire successful lawbreakers. They think their fellow transgressors are clever and brave. To them the wicked follow their passions, which is what gives real fulfillment in life. They are those who truly follow their heart. And they are realistic about life: they understand their fellow man – that he is not to be trusted and that the fool deserves his treatment.

Law-keepers do not merely disapprove of the wicked; they strive against them. They work to foil the efforts of the wicked to break the law. They recognize such transgressors for what they are – selfish to the point of being cruel, heartless, and reckless. They know that real fulfillment does not lie in trampling the weak and disrupting order. They know the difference between cleverness and ruthlessness, between bravery and defiance of the good. They also understand their fellow man and so bind the wicked and protect the weak and the foolish.

Society tries to blur the line between the two, but Scripture is clear. On which side do we stand? If on the side of the law-keepers, take note that we are not merely to shake our heads at lawbreakers but strive against them. We are to work for justice; we are to be our brothers' keepers. We are not to turn our gaze from the evil about us but strive against it.

Justice

Proverbs 28:5

Evil men do not understand justice,
   but those who seek the Lord understand it completely.

The wicked don't get it about justice. They despise the weak who in their minds deserve their fate of being oppressed. They despise the righteous who must be either hypocritical or repressive. They follow the logic of natural evolution – we are animals controlled by animal instincts for self-protection and self-satisfaction, and the cleverer and stronger animals will dominate the weaker. To them, justice is a man-made idea (enforced by religious hypocrites) that has the semblance of protecting the weak, but in reality is another way for those in power to stay that way.

The righteous who seek the Lord understand justice as the law of God springing from his character. Justice is good because it comes from the God who is good. Justice is needed to control the animal instincts that have been corrupted by the fall. If the fall had not occurred, justice would not be a means of enforcement but the very nature of the universe. It is justice not fallen animal instinct that is eternal. The righteous understand further that justice is not so much about bridling passion, as it is directing passion to what is good – to delighting in what is honorable, pure, and loving. The righteous delight in justice, and it is a truer delight than that of the wicked who delight in their base desires; for it is a delight that will only grow into eternity, while that of the wicked will only lead to their destruction.

Better a Poor Man

Proverbs 28:6

Better is a poor man who walks in his integrity
than a rich man who is crooked in his ways.

This is a concept that the evil men of the previous proverb would not understand. To them and to most people, being rich is what matters. The wicked are blatant about this and thus will commit crime with impunity to get money. Most will do whatever is within "reasonable" bounds to attain wealth. What happens is that their greed inevitably corrupts them.

The blessing of the poor man who walks in his integrity is the very integrity itself. It provides him with peace of mind. It protects him from the anxiety of having to hold onto his riches or to keep up with his neighbor. It allows him to focus on real pleasures, such as enjoying good relationships. He has clearer perspective about what matters. Most importantly, he is in good standing with his Maker and gains eternal riches (understanding that walking in integrity is walking in Christ).

The crooked rich man has only momentary pleasure in his riches, which he has to continually protect. He cannot be sure of his friends nor can they trust him. It is difficult for him to see what is truly good. He is blind to his need for God. When he dies, he loses all. Pray for the crooked rich who are the poorest on earth.

Of Law-keepers and Gluttony

Proverbs 28:7

The one who keeps the law is a son with understanding,
but a companion of gluttons shames his father.

Here is a contrast of two sons – the one who keeps the law and the one who is gluttonous. Note, though, the descriptions of the law keeper and the glutton. The former has understanding; the latter is a companion of gluttons, that is, he is swayed easily by his worthless companions. This understanding, or lack of it, is at the heart of the father's pride in one and shame in the other as can be seen in Jesus' parable of the prodigal son (Luke 15:11-32).

The younger son was reckless and squandered his money in gluttonous living. He eventually "came to himself," that is, he came to his senses. He acquired understanding, which led him back to his father. The older son was a law keeper yet also without understanding. He kept the law out of duty. That is better than breaking the law, but what the father really desired was a son who kept the law out of desire to please him; who kept the law because he understood how good the law was in blessing his life.

Keep the law but with understanding. Understand that the law is summarized by the commandments to love God and to love one's neighbor. Understand that the law is good and that by keeping it you are blessing yourself. Then you will give your heavenly Father delight. Then he will not be shamed by either your hypocritical law-keeping or your gluttony.

Exploitation

Proverbs 28:8

Whoever multiplies his wealth by interest and profit
  gathers it for him who is generous to the poor.

The first line depicts the individual who charges interest to his poor neighbor who is in need. The neighbor perhaps needs money to buy seed for his crop or to purchase food. He is in a difficult circumstance and needs help for the moment to get by. The rich individual exploits that opportunity to increase his own wealth and charges his neighbor in the same way a commercial institution would charge clients.

The intent of such a person will be thwarted, so that he ends up supporting the wealth of another – the person who is generous to the poor. Compare this proverb with 11:24: "One gives freely, yet grows all the richer; another withholds what he should give, and only suffers want."

God blesses generosity to the poor. He disapproves of the miser who withholds blessing to others and punishes the oppressor who uses his wealth to exploit the poor. We can apply this to ourselves literally in how we use our money, which we should examine closely.

Furthermore, apply this principle to how we use all that we possess – our time, our friendship, the gospel, etc. Is our focus on protecting what we have or being as generous as we can be? And if our focus is on self-protection, do we not easily cross the line into exploitation? We do favors expecting favors in return. We give expecting to receive back. We calculate the investment we will receive in whatever we do.

There is only one investment that should be on our minds – investing in the pleasure of God. Seek first the kingdom, and whatever else we may need will be provided.

Prayer as Abomination

Proverbs 28:9

If one turns away his ear from hearing the law,
even his prayer is an abomination.

This lesson is taught elsewhere. Consider Isaiah 1:15-17:
When you spread out your hands,
I will hide my eyes from you;
even though you make many prayers, I will not listen;
your hands are full of blood.
Wash yourselves; make yourselves clean;
remove the evil of your deeds from before my eyes;
cease to do evil,
learn to do good; seek justice,
correct oppression;
bring justice to the fatherless,
plead the widow's cause.

Consider 1 Peter 3:7:

> Likewise, husbands, live with your wives in an
> understanding way, showing honor to the woman as
> the weaker vessel, since they are heirs with you of the
> grace of life, so that your prayers may not be
> hindered.

To break God's law, to ignore God's law and then to presume that he
will hear our prayers is an abomination to him. Yes, we are always
guilty of some sin when we pray. But this proverb addresses the
attitude that one can consciously sin and then expect God to listen to
one's prayer as though no wrong had been done. It is good to pray
aware of God's mercy; it is an abomination to pray presumptuous
that God will excuse our sin.

The Inheritance

Proverbs 28:10

Whoever misleads the upright into an evil way
  will fall into his own pit,
  but the blameless will have a goodly inheritance.

Consider the consequences of our actions. This is where the wicked
miscalculates. He digs his pit and cleverly leads the upright to fall in
it. Perhaps he does so through temptation, causing the upright to
walk off the righteous path; perhaps the concealment of the pit
causes the upright to fall in even as he is walking in obedience. Either
way, the upright who possesses the righteousness of Christ will be
delivered, and the wicked will find himself trapped in the very pit he
prepared.

The blameless in Christ will receive his goodly inheritance. It is an
inheritance "that is imperishable, undefiled, and unfading, kept in
heaven for [him]" (1 Pet. 1:4). But can he be waylaid from receiving
that inheritance by the pit dug by the wicked? No, for he is "by

God's power guarded through faith for a salvation ready to be revealed in the last time" (1 Pet. 1:5).

Can he stumble and fall into a pit? Yes. For he can be led into temptation. He can rest from being alert to the "adversary the devil [who] prowls around like a roaring lion" (1 Pet. 5:8). And so he needs to be delivered out of sin and trouble. Thank God that receiving the promised inheritance lies in the strength and faithfulness of our Savior to carry us through.

All the more then, we are to strive to walk in obedience to our Lord, looking to him each day to guide us, protect us, and deliver us from evil. Let us be thankful to the "God of all grace, who has called [us] to his eternal glory in Christ [and who] will himself restore, confirm, strengthen, and establish [us]. To him be the dominion forever and ever. Amen" (1 Pet. 5:10-11).

Found Out

Proverbs 28:11

A rich man is wise in his own eyes,
   but a poor man who has understanding will find him out.

Wealth can deceive the one who possesses it. Because he has money, he thinks he is wise, especially if he earned his wealth. His success with money gives him the illusion that he is wise in general. Thus, he may very well lose a case brought against him by a poor man. It does not occur to him that one who is poor could be clever enough to win.

It also does not occur to him that one who is poor could understand him. He thinks his wealth defines him. He thinks his wealth conveys that he is wise and happy. As Proverbs 14:24 says, "The wealth of the wise is their crown." Therefore, he concludes he must be wise. Wealth can be bestowed upon the wise, but wealth can also come to the fool who then is ruined by his very wealth. Wealth can be earned by the wicked who likewise will come to destruction.

It is not wealth itself that measures a person's wisdom or his happiness. It is the fruit of his life – the blessing that he is to others – that provides a more accurate measurement. It is the joy in that fruit that measures his wisdom and his happiness.

Glorious Triumph

Proverbs 28:12

When the righteous triumph, there is great glory,
but when the wicked rise, people hide themselves.

When the righteous triumph, it results in good being accomplished for others. A righteous ruler is a good ruler who blesses his people. Contrariwise, when the wicked rise to leadership, then trouble goes forth. The wicked ruler uses his power to oppress, to take advantage of others for his own gain.

As Jesus said, a person is known by his fruit. This is all the more evident in a leader. The less power, the less harm one does. But as a person rises in power, so the consequences of his actions – both good and bad – have a wider effect on others.

So we see this played out spiritually. Satan, the Prince of the World, has a deadly reign, bringing despair and death through his rule. And yet, we glory in the triumph of our King Jesus Christ who has triumphed over him, over sin, and over death. What glory, what joy flows from the triumph of our righteous King.

Obtaining Mercy

Proverbs 28:13

Whoever conceals his transgressions will not prosper,
but he who confesses and forsakes them will obtain mercy.

Consider this proverb in light of Psalm 32:1-5:
Blessed is the one whose transgression is forgiven,

495

whose sin is covered.
Blessed is the man against whom the Lord counts no
iniquity,
    and in whose spirit there is no deceit.
For when I kept silent, my bones wasted away
    through my groaning all day long.
For day and night your hand was heavy upon me;
    my strength was dried up as by the heat of
    summer.

I acknowledged my sin to you,
    and I did not cover my iniquity;
I said, "I will confess my transgressions to the Lord,"
    and you forgave the iniquity of my sin.

What can we expect of God when we confess our sin before him? Mercy. Why? Why not rebuke? Unlike us, God already knows the sin. He has already been dealing with it before we confess it. That is why we experience heaviness of heart and guilt. That is why we experience the discipline of trials and consequences. He is bringing us to repentance. Our confession is the result of his loving discipline. His forgiveness is the result of the work he has already done in stirring our hearts.

If we are in Christ, we can know that all discipline – including the grieving of our hearts – is done out of God's mercy so that we may experience God's mercy all the more.

Blessed Fear

Proverbs 28:14

Blessed is the one who fears the Lord always,
    but whoever hardens his heart will fall into calamity.

The one who fears the Lord is blessed because he has the true perspective on reality and because God will bless him for his faithfulness. Fear of the Lord is not about living in terror of the Lord, but about knowing God for who he is – Creator, King, and

Redeemer. To fear God is to understand (as much as a human is able) God's attributes – his holiness, his eternal nature, his power, his mercy, etc. It is to understand that one's purpose is to glorify him. As one grows in understanding, so his fear of the Lord enriches his relationship with his Lord so that he is filled with awe and filled with love.

To harden one's heart so as to reject God, or to think of limiting who God is, will lead to calamity because of a skewed view of reality and because God will withhold his blessing. God will not be mocked. He is jealous for his glory, and the one who refuses to live for God's glory will inevitably stumble into the pit of destruction. He cannot escape it, for God will accomplish his purposes.

And hardening one's heart will be the verdict for all who do not embrace his redemption, specifically the Redeemer he has provided. Whatever protests anyone may give, whatever excuses they may offer, the verdict will be the same – hardening one's heart. There are only two options – to fear the Lord or to harden one's heart.

Lions and Bears

Proverbs 28:15

Like a roaring lion or a charging bear
is a wicked ruler over a poor people.

The ruthlessness of a wicked man can be measured by the amount of his power. A wicked ruler's evil is more devastating than that of the wicked person with no or little power. The wickedness of a ruler over a poor nation is greater than that over a wealthy nation precisely because there are fewer rivals capable of standing up against him. Like a school yard bully, he is more ruthless when all the kids on the playground are smaller than he, than he would be if there were a number of strong kids standing about.

It is being among the weak and the poor that the nature of a ruler is tested. Does he use his position to nurture his people or to take advantage of them? Does he act in their best interest when they are not a threat to him or unable to reward him? Or does he squeeze what he can from them?

A system of checks and balances are needed in the government and the workplace to help those in power curb their tendency to abuse power. And all of us have such a tendency because we are sinners. We desire power so that we may do good, but once we receive it, once we obtain our position, we then face temptations we have not faced before – the temptation to use our position for our own advantage, and the temptation to use our power to exploit those under us and to act out of our frustrations. A poor people can be just as difficult to rule or manage as those who are wealthy and strong. All the more tempting then for us to use our power in sinful ways to "help" them become more manageable. It is easier to become a "roaring lion" than we may think.

Prolonged Days

Proverbs 28:16

A ruler who lacks understanding is a cruel oppressor,
  but he who hates unjust gain will prolong his days.

The contrast here is between lacking understanding and hating unjust gain. What the ruler lacks understanding about is the privilege of rule. He regards power primarily as a means to advance his interests. And so he uses his position to gain more wealth and power by oppressing those unable to stand up against him. The righteous ruler understands that the position of ruler is one of privilege, granted to him to advance the interests of his people. He is measured by how well he protects and promotes the welfare of those under his rule.

It is such righteous rule that is blessed by the Lord who rules over life and death, and thus possesses the power to prolong or shorten our days. From human experience, such rule often does result in a prolonged reign, because the ruler wins the support of his people who in turn protect him and willingly serve him, thus promoting his welfare.

Perhaps this is the fundamental misunderstanding of the wicked ruler. He believes the key to staying in power is to ruthlessly grab more and just as ruthlessly protect it. Thus, he is always creating enemies and forfeits the support of his people. There is a reason why it is common for ruthless rulers is to be violently removed from their position.

The same holds true in the workplace. It is common for the leader who operates out of self-interest to find himself being pushed out by others with the same desire. To seek any position for the sake of wielding power and grabbing more wealth is likely to lead to a shortening of days. But to use one's position to promote the good of the company and the welfare of the employees is likely to lead to a prolonging of days.

No Interference

Proverbs 28:17

If one is burdened with the blood of another,
he will be a fugitive until death;
let no one help him.

Let no one interfere with the hand of God in bringing just retribution to a murderer. As we are told to leave vengeance to the Lord, so we are not to interfere with his vengeance. The burden placed on the murderer is from God and used by God to drive him to "the pit," translated here as death. Such an end may very well be his sentence, though it could include any form of retribution, whether it be in this life or afterwards. The point is that he must bear the consequence of taking innocent life. Justice cannot be denied.

And if there is to be any hope for the murderer, justice must be rendered. It is in facing the consequences of one's wickedness that the wicked is most likely to come to grips with his sin, and if he does not, then all the more reason justice needs to be fulfilled.

This is a sobering proverb, especially because of the last line. How can we not help a fugitive? We can exercise such restraint when we learn to trust God more than ourselves. Too often our help is nothing more than interference. We interfere with justice, even with grace; for grace shines best when justice is rendered. When a sinner bears consequence for his sin, when he accepts the consequence, it is then he sees clearly the grace that is shown him. No man turns to Christ while he feels no conviction for sin. It is conviction and consequence that will drive him to his knees. It is experiencing the pit of punishment and despair that is likely to turn him from the eternal pit.

Of Integrity and Crookedness

Proverbs 28:18

Whoever walks in integrity will be delivered,
but he who is crooked in his ways will suddenly fall.

This is a common lesson in proverbs. Walking in righteous integrity carries with it the protection of the Lord who watches over those who fear him. The crooked will fall suddenly, disastrously because the Lord will bring judgment.

More often than not, this is played out in one's lifetime. The wicked are setting their own traps because of creating enemies, associating with like-minded evil-doers who are quick to turn against their own, raising the opposition of the righteous who will bring justice, being blinded by pride and greed, and so on. The righteous, on the other hand, create friends, associate with like-minded individuals who respect one another, win the support of the community, and grow in wisdom.

But the main matter is as previously stated – the righteous who walk in integrity have the blessing of the Lord; the wicked who are crooked in their ways have his wrath. Whatever one receives in this lifetime, what really matters is the life after where one receives either eternal blessing or an eternal curse. The latter is a sudden fall that never ends.

Worthless Pursuits

Proverbs 28:19

Whoever works his land will have plenty of bread,
but he who follows worthless pursuits
* will have plenty of poverty.*

Whoever goes to work each day and labors diligently will see the produce from his labors. Whether he be the farmer who works his land or the office worker who manages his projects, if he works conscientiously he can expect fruit from his labor.

What of the one who "follows worthless pursuits"? He also may expect a return for his labor – poverty. Why? The primary reason is that he has shifted his energies from productive work to fruitless labor. The hours that could have been devoted to productivity are wasted in the other pursuit. Furthermore, what he pursues is likely to cause him to lose what he has. He invests money in pursuits that not only fail but create greater debt.

What are these worthless pursuits? They are pursuits that seem worthwhile. They may be get-rich schemes that promise quick returns. They typically promise good income with minimal labor. They promise to be fail-proof. They promise to work for anyone. They make the same pitch that Satan made to Jesus – gain the world without the cross. Gain wealth without the labor.

Jesus did not distain the world. Indeed, he did gain the world but did so the right way. He labored, even suffered, to gain his rule. Likewise, the proverbs do not distain wealth, just the means by which we go for it, such as through worthless pursuits or unjust means. Wealth should be the byproduct of a productive life, not the goal for which we live. Or we should have a broader understanding of wealth, which rests not so much in possessions as in quality of life – a life blessed with a good name, that is respected and experiences love, that blesses others. That is true wealth which can only be gained by worthwhile pursuits.

Faithfulness vs. Get-Rich-Quick

Proverbs 28:20

A faithful man will abound with blessings,
  but whoever hastens to be rich will not go unpunished.

The contrast between the character of the faithful man and the get-rich man lies in integrity. The faithful person's priority is to carry out his responsibility well. Whatever the task before him, his concern is to complete it and to finish well. Thus, he is one to be trusted to keep his word, trusted to act ethically and do quality work.

The get-rich person has one over-riding desire – to get rich. That desire controls his mind and heart. Thus, it clouds his thinking, pushing him to move from one get-rich-quick scheme to another. It clouds his moral judgment so that he resorts to lying, scheming, manipulating, even stealing to accomplish his purposes.

It is easy enough then to see how blessings come to the faithful person. He is well thought of by his neighbors. His supervisors and those whom he supervises praise him. His faithful work will overflow into blessing others and thus result in blessings returning to him. Because he has remained faithful, he is likely to see monetary reward from his labors. He earns respect as a worker; he nurtures his business through the difficult times into prosperity.

The get-rich-quick person may experience quick riches but is just as likely to quickly lose them. He is more likely never to achieve his dreams because he lacks staying power. He lacks the necessary discipline to carry his labors through to harvest. He earns distrust from his neighbors; indeed, he is likely to earn their enmity so that they work against him. They desire his downfall.

Two persons with the same abilities – one possesses integrity; the other does not. So then their destinies are set.

Partiality and Bribes

Proverbs 28:21

To show partiality is not good,
but for a piece of bread a man will do wrong.

This proverb is speaking against the taking of bribes. The second line points to the triviality of the bribe. A dishonest person is willing to take anything. His one motive is his own gain. He has no interest in fairness. Indeed, justice is a game to him. Like the board game of Life, his object is to finish with the most money.

This mindset is particularly appalling because it denies human dignity. There is no sense of giving to another his "fair due." Even the wicked at times will acknowledge a person earning a reward, even respect. But the bribe taker cynically reduces everyone to an economic pawn used to serve his end. Whether he ruthlessly demands from the poor or bows before the rich, he treats everyone as mere means to his own ends. The bribe taker respects no one.

He even reduces himself to a calculating machine. His one skill is knowing when, where, and how much to extract from others. Everyone has something to give and everything has a measure of value, even a piece of bread. All he has to do is calculate whose gift has the higher value.

We should be careful lest we fall into a similar mindset, calculating whose favor is more advantageous to us. It is easier to do than we suspect and usually we fall into such a mindset before we realize we have.

Hastening after Poverty

A stingy man hastens after wealth
and does not know that poverty will come upon him.

The Hebrew reads "a man whose eye is evil." Such is the eye of the person who treats wealth as the all-consuming goal and thus withholds generosity.

Stinginess from the fear of poverty can hasten a person to the realization of that very fear. For he loses the friends who will care for him. He will create enemies who will take advantage of him when possible.

Dicken's Ebenezer Scrooge depicts this person and captures the real impoverishment. His passion for wealth leads to a miserly life bereft of compassion for his fellow man, especially for the poor. It is not financial poverty that awaits him but, rather, poverty of the heart that overtook him long ago. Hastening after wealth indeed is hastening after poverty.

Rebuke and Flattery

Proverbs 28:23

Whoever rebukes a man will afterward find more favor
  than he who flatters with his tongue.

The contrast here is between rebuking and flattering. That is essential to note, for one may think that the proverb is exalting the person who is quick to rebuke as opposed to being an encourager. The flatterer is essentially a liar; his motive is his own advantage. He flatters to win favor or to appease anger. He is thinking of himself. The rebuker's motive is to advance the cause of truth and justice, as well as to save his neighbor from calamity. The very reason he will find favor is that his motive is pure and eventually becomes recognized as such.

The rebuke may be gentle; it may need to be harsh. The one who rebukes well gives thought to the occasion. Consider Jesus who at times is gentle as a lamb in the correction he gives and at other times is like a roaring lion. He speaks with discernment – discerning the occasion and the person to whom he speaks.

Again, the motive is essential and it is what controls the tongue. Just as flatterers may confuse their fair words with encouragement, deceiving themselves about their motives, so arrogant rebukers may confuse their harshness with honest admonition. "I am only speaking the truth." "I am only saying what needs to be said." And then they leave a trail of the wounded, blaming the results on the persons they have wounded.

Better to rebuke than to flatter. But use rebuke for what flattery pretends to do – to help, to build up, to save a person from downfall.

Parent Robbers

Proverbs 28:24

Whoever robs his father or his mother
and says, "That is no transgression,"
is a companion to a man who destroys.

How would such a person justify robbing his parents? One way is to justify his motivation. His parents are unfair to withhold support, he claims; he justifies that he is taking what they owe him. His parents are unjust in the way they treat him; he argues that he is giving back the same mistreatment they give him.

He minimizes his crime. He is taking only a small amount of what his parents have. They will never notice. They are not using it anyhow.

Another way is to redefine his robbing. He is borrowing and intends to return what he has taken. He is borrowing against his inheritance. He is investing for his parents, using their money and belongings to invest for greater gain.

And then, he fails to recognize the broader definition of robbing. What Jesus said to the Pharisees about how they break the commandment of honoring one's father and mother is true of breaking the commandment to not steal.

> You have a fine way of rejecting the commandment of God in order to establish your tradition! For Moses said, "Honor your father and your mother"; and, "Whoever reviles father or mother must surely die." But you say, "If a man tells his father or his mother, Whatever you would have gained from me is Corban"

(that is, given to God) – then you no longer permit him to do anything for his father or mother, thus making void the word of God by your tradition that you have handed down (Mark 7:9-13).

Likewise, we rob our parents when we fail to support them when they need us and when we rob them of the honor due them. And so, we are partners with those who destroy.

Greediness vs. Trust

Proverbs 28:25

A greedy man stirs up strife,
  but the one who trusts in the Lord will be enriched.

Note the contrast – greediness versus trusting in the Lord. The greedy man lacks trust. He does not trust God to provide, but more to the point, he does not trust God to give him everything he desires. Perhaps God does provide the necessities, but he wants more. He feels he is entitled to more. And he wants it now. He is impatient with the teaching that wealth should be accumulated by patient hard work and steady saving.

So what does he do? He acts rashly and foolishly. He goes after wild schemes. He resorts to unethical means to obtain his ends. He lies, he steals. He imposes on others. He mistrusts others, seeing his neighbor as a competitor or obstacles to his quest after more things and money. Thus, he stirs up strife.

But the one who trusts in the Lord to provide what he needs *and* what is good for him so as to be happy and content, such a person will be enriched. He will be patient and content in his labor, thus over time enriching himself financially. He will win friends since he is free to think of their welfare and not be competing against them. He will receive the blessing of the Lord who shows favor to those who glorify him by trusting in him.

Of Trust and Wisdom

Proverbs 28:26

Whoever trusts in his own mind is a fool,
  but he who walks in wisdom will be delivered.

The proverb does not equate trusting in one's own mind with wisdom. Then in whom or what should we trust? Are we not to think for ourselves? We are to develop the ability to do our own thinking, but that very skill entails listening to others and knowing who to trust. The wise person listens to the counsel of others, especially those whom he knows to be knowledgeable and discerning. He has to make his own decision, but he does so in the context of having listened well. More to the point for Christians is that the wise person will listen carefully to God's Word. It is scripture that he trusts foremost.

This is all in direct contrast to the modern perspective that one ought to follow one's heart regardless of what others are saying or is acceptable teaching passed down. Such a perspective is foolish for it leads a person to trust in his small knowledge and in his feelings, both of which are insufficient and even dangerous.

Wisdom begins with the fear of the Lord, trusting God to know what is best. It grows with reliance on one's fellow man, both past and present, to share knowledge and wisdom. Trusting God and cooperating with one's neighbor will provide deliverance through the trials and challenges of life. To trust only in one's self is the way of folly that leads to downfall.

Giving to the Poor

Proverbs 28:27

Whoever gives to the poor will not want,
  but he who hides his eyes will get many a curse.

Giving to the poor seems a bad investment if your concern is to grow wealth or maintain your present financial status. The poor cannot return money with interest, and indeed are likely not to return money at all. They have no influence with powerful or wealthy men who could befriend you because of your generosity. The money given to them or for them does not return. And so it seems preferable to avoid noticing them. Let others help.

But this proverb makes a guarantee – provision for the giver and curses for the miser. On what basis can this be made? On the basis of the guarantee of God. It is God who watches over the poor; God who provides. Indeed, it is God who provides for everyone – both rich and poor. This is what the "haves" fail to recognize. We have money because our Father has provided for us, not because we were clever enough or hard-working enough to obtain it. Unforeseen circumstances have ruined the fortune of many gifted persons; likewise, such circumstances have made the fortune of many.

It is true that wisdom and hard work will typically lead to security, and that folly and idleness to poverty. But it is also true that circumstances play a critical role. God is in charge of those circumstances. And it is he who gives wisdom, who gives strength and the gifts to do well. As he gives, so he can take back. Understand that of ourselves we are all poor. We have what we have because God gives to us; he can just as easily "hide his eyes" toward us, leaving us destitute and without hope. He wants us, though, to have his spirit of generosity and to leave the business of worrying about our future to him. Seek first the kingdom, which is about the generosity of the gospel, and everything you need will be added. Trust your heavenly Father. That is what giving to the poor is really about – trusting your Father and loving with the heart by which he loves.

The Wicked vs. the Righteous Reign

Proverbs 28:28

When the wicked rise, people hide themselves,
but when they perish, the righteous increase.

When the wicked rise to power, people think in terms of protecting themselves. They hide; they take cover; they try not to draw attention to themselves, for they know that the wicked delight in mischief. The wicked think first if a person will benefit them; if not, then the wicked will be entertained by hurting that person. The wicked also are obsessed with looking for rivals. Anyone who gives the impression of being a rival is destroyed.

Interestingly, the proverb does not then give an exact comparison of what happens when the wicked perish. Instead of saying that people come out of hiding, it speaks of the righteous increasing. The argument is thus: Either the wicked or the righteous take power. As one rises, so the other must decrease. They cannot exist together. As the wicked perish, so the righteous increase, and so the people do come back out and flourish. They know that the righteous think first about the welfare of others. They know that the entertainment of the righteous is to see others happy. The righteous are obsessed with seeing that justice takes place.

What a difference in the atmosphere by which one lives. Under the wicked the atmosphere is that of fear and distrust. Under the righteous it is of peace and harmony. All the reason then to work for the rule of the righteous and to oppose the wicked, whether this be in the arena of government or business or other. All the reason then to give glory to our righteous King who reigns over us. All the reason to remember the hope we have of living in his everlasting kingdom to come.

The Stiffened Neck

Proverbs 29:1

He who is often reproved, yet stiffens his neck,
  will suddenly be broken beyond healing.

It is the stiffening that produces the break. As painful as reproof may be, it should make the person stronger; it should condition the spirit and train the mind, molding the individual to be a person of perseverance and wisdom. If received properly, reproof will shape a mind that is foolish and give that mind discernment; it will turn a rebellious spirit into one that blesses and builds up others. Reproof is healing.

Stiffening – resisting reproof – is destructive. Like the arm that stiffens and refuses the healing medicine of a doctor's syringe, so the stiffening person of reproof denies what is for his good. Like the neck that stiffens against pressure, it will suddenly break. The very reproof intended to heal can be made destructive. Or more likely, the rebellious spirit learns to become deaf to it and to deny its healing intention. He trains himself so well to be deaf that he misses the warnings leading to his sudden calamity.

Reproof is never pleasant to receive. But if we will learn to learn from it, however painful it may be to take, then it will have the effect that God intends. For he does intend for every experience, every reproof – regardless of how it comes and from whom – to make us stronger, to make us wiser, to sanctify us for godliness. Will we bend and receive such reproof or will we stiffen?

Righteous Joy

Proverbs 29:2

When the righteous increase, the people rejoice,
  but when the wicked rule, the people groan.

This proverb makes clear the impact of the righteous when they increase. It brings rejoicing. People may rejoice in the concept of righteousness and justice, but what brings out the rejoicing here is their own freedom from oppression. The wicked, in advancing their own pleasure, exact money and labor from the people. To protect their wicked endeavors, they repress any attempt to exert freedom or vindication or even to be left alone. The wicked have one goal – their own happiness – and will do whatever is needed to obtain it.

The righteous also have the goal of happiness. The difference is what makes up that happiness. For the righteous, having a people who are happy and contented makes them all the more contented. To see people who are fulfilled makes them feel fulfilled. And the righteous are most righteous according to how much they share in the joy of their heavenly righteous Father. So we see this in the Son whose greatest delight is to delight his Father. And so he brings forth justice at the greatest of cost, knowing that an even greater joy awaits in what his work will produce – joy to his Father and the re-making of sinners into righteous children.

And so he has established a kingdom in which the righteous increase and the people who belong to it rejoice. And so that joy will be made complete when the King returns and consummates his kingdom, bringing a day in which there will be no more groaning.

Loving Wisdom

Proverbs 29:3

He who loves wisdom makes his father glad,
but a companion of prostitutes squanders his wealth.

One is led to think of the parable of the prodigal son. He took his father's inheritance and "squandered his property in reckless living" (Luke 15:11ff). He would have thought he was spending his money to enjoy life, to experience pleasure. But his problem was not that he loved pleasure too much but that his love was misguided.

Not so the one who makes his father glad. He is not described as being a stoic, one who chooses wisdom over enjoyment. He is one who *loves* wisdom. Wisdom is not a discipline to endure in order to keep secure. Wisdom itself is pleasurable. Recall Proverbs 1:13-18:
> Blessed is the one who finds wisdom,
>   and the one who gets understanding,
> for the gain from her is better than gain from silver
>   and her profit better than gold.
> She is more precious than jewels,
>   and nothing you desire can compare with her.
> Long life is in her right hand;
>   in her left hand are riches and honor.
> Her ways are ways of pleasantness,
>   and all her paths are peace.

> She is a tree of life to those who lay hold of her;
>   those who hold her fast are called blessed.

The double bonus of loving wisdom is experiencing the joy of one's father, but even more so, one's heavenly Father. Because his Son exercised perfect wisdom, the Father delighted in him. And if we follow along the same path, choosing wisdom over sinful pleasures, we also shall know the blessing of delighting our Father.

By Justice

Proverbs 29:4

> *By justice a king builds up the land,*
>   *but he who exacts gifts tears it down.*

The "gifts" could be bribes or, as suggested in one translation, heavy taxes. The point is that such a ruler is unjust. Furthermore, his very injustice tears down the land by which he is sustained. This is a principle that the unjust somehow cannot understand. By exercising justice, a ruler builds up the land so that his people prosper. Because they prosper, they are able and more willing to support the ruler. If the ruler would seek first the welfare of the kingdom, everything else would be provided for him.

Does that sound familiar? "But seek first the kingdom of God and his righteousness, and all these things will be added to you" (Matt. 6:33). The context is somewhat different in which Jesus spoke these words, but the essential truth remains. If a ruler concentrates on what really matters – belonging to and serving the kingdom of God, seeking and promoting righteousness – then he is likely to find many of the things he worries about falling into place. He is more likely to find his physical needs met.

God blesses the ruler who is just, and he has in his providential care seen that the very work of justice produces good fruit. See what the King he sent was able to accomplish with his justice.

Flattery

Proverbs 29:5

A man who flatters his neighbor
  spreads a net for his feet.

Flattery, as used here, is a tool by which to deceive. It is the tool by which to earn favor or to hide real intentions. In this case, an unscrupulous neighbor uses flattery to set up the downfall of his unsuspecting neighbor.

The proverb raises the matter of how seemingly good words can be used maliciously. Praise, which should be a means of showing due honor and encouragement, is twisted into shallow, even devious speech. Words intended to build up others are used to either make fools of them or tear them down.

The further harm of flattery is that it spurs its opposite to take place – rudeness. If flattery lays nets, then should we not avoid praise altogether? Should not our greater concern be to tell the truth? Truth does matter, but we are commanded to speak the truth in love (Eph. 4:15). We are commanded to build up one another. The Apostle Paul, who clearly did not avoid speaking what needed to be heard, also took the time to praise the very people he corrected.

The cure for flattery is not rude "truth-telling," but speaking the truth in love. It is looking for what is truly good to praise in a person. The protection against flattery is to find one's value in the love of God, not in the praises of neighbors, even if the praises are true and sincere.

To Sing and Rejoice

Proverbs 29:6

An evil man is ensnared in his transgression,
  but a righteous man sings and rejoices.

The wicked create their own trouble. Because they deceive, steal, and

513

commit violence, they expose themselves to the same troubles. They create enemies. Even the traps they lay for others often end up being their undoing.

But the righteous are often free of what plagues the wicked. They typically do not make enemies. There may be enemies, but such foes exist because of their own wickedness, not because the righteous had done them wrong. The righteous have friends and the just arm of the law on their side providing further protection. They do not worry about what the law will do to them.

Their greater reason for being able to sing and rejoice without fear is the peace of their conscience. They do not wake up in the morning worried about the repercussions of their actions from the night before. They do not worry about what friend has turned into an enemy. Indeed, their singing and rejoicing is done in the presence of their many friends.

The greatest reason for the singing and rejoicing is the status the righteous have before God. For righteousness is not ultimately about keeping all the rules but of walking with one's Lord; and to know him, to walk under his blessing, is to be blessed indeed. Do you have a song to sing today?

Getting It

Proverbs 29:7

A righteous man knows the rights of the poor;
  a wicked man does not understand such knowledge.

The wicked man just doesn't get it. His brain does not comprehend the concept of justice. To him, the winnings go to the rich and the powerful. Life is about getting to the top and staying on top. To him, this is the ways things are. Indeed, it is his code. He does not complain about not being treated mercifully. He doesn't expect anything to be given him. He doesn't assert his rights. Instead, he tries to play the system of beating rivals. He might get angry if he loses, but he doesn't think of appealing to justice.

The righteous man knows there is a code determined divinely under which all creatures are to live – great and small, rich and poor. The "rights of the poor" are divinely instituted. Furthermore, he understands that in relation to God everyone is poor. There is no strong man who can assert himself above anyone else and certainly not God. To respect the rights of the poor is a concession that God is the one who sets the code and that we are all under obligation to obey him. "Rights" are not about asserting what we have coming to us, but of asserting that there is such a thing as justice that does not bend to anyone's power or position.

The righteous man gets it; the wicked man does not. The result is seen in the way they live and treat others. One will bear good fruit as a result; the other will bear sour fruit. One will inherit the kingdom of God; the other will go to his destruction. Such are the stakes for "getting it."

Dousing Scoffers

Proverbs 29:8

Scoffers set a city aflame,
but the wise turn away wrath.

Like a pyromaniac, scoffers like to stir up trouble. They get their kicks out of causing a commotion. It is fun to them to see a city aflame with angry words, gossip, and slander. Somehow their ego is stroked to think that they started it all. They are the perverted image of the artist and the builder who delight in what they construct. Scoffers delight in what they destroy.

The answer to the scoffers is the wise person. The wise think through carefully how to bring the scoffers' flames under control. They use discernment rather than anger to guide their actions. They are able to use discernment because they keep their goal before them, which is to bring peace.

Do you let scoffers set you aflame? Are you frustrated by your inability to "turn away wrath" or to put a scoffer in his place? Remember the goal of the wise – to bring peace. Turn to discernment rather than anger. You will be surprised at how easily discernment can come if you remember your goal.

Foolish Argument

Proverbs 29:9

If a wise man has an argument with a fool,
  the fool only rages and laughs, and there is no quiet.

The fool has no interest in wisdom. He may enjoy words, but only as toys in which to enjoy foolishness. When a person tries to reason with him, the fool treats the effort as nothing more than a game of words which he believes he always wins. And he does. For if the purpose of an argument is to win over the other, the man of reason always loses against the fool. The fool is not only unconverted but believes he has out-done the wise man, for it is the wise man who always gives up first.

That is why other proverbs recommend discipline as the only effective means in controlling the folly of a fool. Corrective discipline, rather than corrective reasoning, is what can quiet the fool. And that is at least one credit for the fool. Unlike the wicked, his heart is not bent on evil. He is merely foolish in his thinking, and if he cannot comprehend what is reasonable, at least he will avoid what is painful.

Wisdom understands this principle. The wise man may first try argument, that is, use rational thought with the fool. But when the raging and laughing come, the wise man will turn away if he has no authority in the matter or use appropriate discipline. In a similar manner, God so uses reason or discipline with us. As much as we like to think we are rational, the truth is that corrective discipline is needed to deal with our foolish ways.

Bloodthirsty Men

Proverbs 29:10

Bloodthirsty men hate one who is blameless
  and seek the life of the upright.

Why such hatred? Because the blameless reveal the depravity of the wicked's souls. Simeon said of Jesus that he would be a "sign that is opposed…so that thoughts from many hearts may be revealed" (Luke 2:34-5). This is why the bloodthirsty men of Jesus' day put him to death. He exposed and pronounced judgment against their hypocrisy and cruelty. His own blameless life shamed their pretensions. His purposeful life showed up their fruitless lives. They hated him for being what they were not.

They hate because hatred is in their nature passed down from their father, the devil. Listen to what could be considered Jesus' commentary on this verse:

> "If God were your Father, you would love me, for I came from God and I am here. I came not of my own accord, but he sent me. Why do you not understand what I say? It is because you cannot bear to hear my word. You are of your father the devil, and your will is to do your father's desires. He was a murderer from the beginning and has nothing to do with the truth, because there is no truth in him. When he lies, he speaks out of his own character, for he is a liar and the father of lies. But because I tell the truth, you do not believe me. Which one of you convicts me of sin? If I tell the truth, why do you not believe me? Whoever is of God hears the words of God. The reason why you do not hear them is that you are not of God" (John 8:42-47).

Venting

Proverbs 29:11

A fool gives full vent to his spirit,
  but a wise man quietly holds it back.

517

This is not a distinction between being demonstrative and reserved, as though the one who expresses emotions is foolish and the one who expresses little is wise. Rather it is a distinction between one who does not exercise discernment and the one who does.

The characteristic trait of the fool is that he does not think; he merely reacts to his circumstances like a knee-jerk response to the tap of a hammer. He is like the infant who laughs when happy and cries when discomforted with no thought given to anyone else. Unlike the infant, the fool when questioned will reflect that his reactions are quite appropriate. How so? Because he is expressing what he truly feels.

The wise man quietly holds back his inner feeling as he assesses the situation. He knows there is a time for everything, including giving full vent to his spirit, but the key is in understanding the time. Jesus, at times, gave full vent to his spirit, including anger (overturning tables at the temple), grief (before Lazarus' tomb), and even fear (in Gethsemane). But as a wise man, he discerned the right time.

Are you a knee-jerk reactor who gives full vent to your spirit at anytime, or are you a discerner who holds back and give full vent according to the appropriate time?

The Ruler's Responsibility

Proverbs 29:12

If a ruler listens to falsehood,
*   all his officials will be wicked.*

If a ruler listens to falsehood, then he is listening to wicked counselors. And if he cannot distinguish the false from the true, then the wicked will rise and multiply. Much depends on the ruler's ability to discern.

Much also rests on the ruler's commitment to the truth. He should not be willing to listen to falsehood. It is one thing to listen to opposing points of view; it is another to listen to those who are wicked and who lie. A ruler should not test himself against such persons. He should ban them from his presence. Much also rests on the ruler's righteousness. His discernment will only be as great as his inner integrity. Likewise, he will be as committed to the truth according to how much he is committed to righteousness.

Much rests on a ruler. As he goes, so does the sphere that is under his control. If he becomes corrupt, so will those who serve him. If he is negligent, even though he may desire righteousness, it will be injustice that prevails through those serving under him. To whom much is given, much is expected because much rests on his shoulders.

Using Light

Proverbs 29:13

The poor man and the oppressor meet together;
  the Lord gives light to the eyes of both.

This may be the case of a debtor meeting with his creditor. Whatever the case, one person has control over the other. The oppressor or creditor "owns" the poor man who is under his power. It is the prerogative of the oppressor to extend or withhold mercy.

But now comes the reminder. Both men are under the Lord, and it is the Lord who is the Giver, who has the prerogative to extend or withhold mercy. It is the Lord who gives light to the eyes of both and who may, if he desires, cast both into darkness. Jesus said, "For [God] makes his sun rise on the evil and on the good, and sends rain on the just and on the unjust" (Matt. 5:45). In that context, he is instructing us to love our enemies. But it is a further reminder that it is God who controls our fortune.

This proverb reminds the poor man what he does have and in what sense he is as rich as the oppressor. It reminds him of the same advantages he holds. God has also given him light. Indeed, perhaps the poor man would fare better if he made better use of that light instead of bemoaning what he does not have.

It is a warning to the oppressor that nothing he possesses is of his own making. God may easily remove his very sight. It is a warning of the misuse of his light. Using light to see how to take advantage of the poor will result ultimately in being cast into the outer darkness. Nor will he be without excuse for not seeing with a right perspective. God has given him light; if he does not see God and God's justice, he has no one but himself to explain.

Whatever our present lot in life, let us use that light which is common to all to see our God at work and follow him.

The Poor and Security

Proverbs 29:14

If a king faithfully judges the poor,
his throne will be established forever.

There is a consistent message throughout the Bible that the measure of a person's integrity, of his faith even, is found in the way he treats the poor. God hates the oppression of the poor; indeed, he is their defender against oppressors. The righteous person is one who gives to the poor and, as noted here, a righteous king is one who treats the poor with justice.

How are we to measure those in authority? Consider their attitude towards the poor. How are we to measure ourselves? What is our attitude? Are we concerned that the poor receive justice? Are we desirous to extend mercy?

Note the result of faithfully judging the poor. The king's throne is made all the more secure. This seems to go against logic. For every ruler and politician knows that it is by giving attention to the rich and the powerful that a position is made secure. Rocking the boat by being attentive to the poor places one in a precarious position. But the proverb is not considering how to secure favor with the affluent but with God. For it is God who secures a throne, God who raises and brings down princes. It is God who gives life and takes it away.

Follow the heart of God who cares for the poor. Only then can one know eternal security.

The Rod and Reproof

Proverbs 29:15

The rod and reproof give wisdom,
but a child left to himself brings shame to his mother.

It would seem that reasoning and instruction would give wisdom to a child. Such things do give wisdom when the heart is inclined to learn. But a child is not so inclined because he is born with the malady of being a sinner. As such, his heart is inclined to do as he pleases, which leads to rebellion and/or folly. Children are born with varying dispositions. Some show strong self-will, while others have an even temperament and are ready to please others. Whatever the disposition, they act according to what pleases themselves, and they will carry their dispositions to sinful extremes.

Thus, they need early on to receive appropriate discipline, which includes punishment for wrong-doing coupled with expressions of disapproval. Parents must be careful not to be harsh, fathers in particular because they are more likely to be so. But there is equal danger in harming the child by not providing appropriate discipline. A child left to his own devices will bring shame because he will act shamefully. He will not learn how to discipline himself. He will not learn how to set appropriate boundaries for his behavior. He will fail to learn how to discern the character of friends and associates. With no consequences to check his behavior, he will lead himself astray.

Wisdom is a trait that must be desired; it must be chosen. But if one has not learned discipline, he will choose the way of folly because folly appeals to his surface desires. It is the way of what seems pleasant at the moment. By its very nature, it keeps the individual from looking to the future, even the near future, and discerning consequences. No child naturally discerns future consequences. All he understands is immediate consequence. That is where discipline comes in – giving the child an immediate consequence by which he learns to discern what is good and bad for him. Over time, he develops discernment and learns to discipline himself for his good. But it all begins with the discipline rendered in the home.

When the Wicked Increase

Proverbs 29:16

When the wicked increase, transgression increases,
  but the righteous will look upon their downfall.

When the wicked increase in number and power, transgression increases. As the wicked rise, they are more emboldened to sin, as well as having the liberty to sin. Furthermore, their transgression encourages others to sin who had felt restricted under the rule of the righteous. Their transgression leads others astray who follow their example because of their being the leaders and because they seem to demonstrate that their transgression will go unpunished. Indeed, not only does the transgression seem to go unpunished, but the wicked seem to prosper precisely because of their transgression. Others fall into sin by fighting against the wicked in an unrighteous manner. They lie and cheat, claiming the ends justify the means.

But the downfall of the wicked will come. God will not be mocked. He will not allow wickedness to go unpunished. Then, those who did not give into sin will look upon the wicked's downfall.

Will you, then, persevere through the reign of the wicked? Such a reign may take place in your community, in your workplace, even in your home. Will you refrain from taking on the traits of the wicked? Will you refrain from unrighteous retaliation? Will you wait patiently for the vindication and the salvation of the Lord according to his timetable and his measure of justice? Will you remain among the ranks of the righteous who will see justice prevail?

Of Discipline

Proverbs 29:17

Discipline your son, and he will give you rest;
  he will give delight to your heart.

The purpose of discipline is not to keep your child under control, but to give him opportunity to develop the good character that he is capable of. He is born in sin. If left to his own devices, he will develop selfishness, rebellion, meanness, and other such traits. Discipline is the means to correct these tendencies and to help him to find the blessing of virtuous traits.

According to the child, discipline will vary. Some children are more self-willed than others. Each child has peculiar tendencies. Some are fearless in their behavior, while others are fearful. The wise parent will take time to understand each child and discipline accordingly.

Oftentimes parents will avoid discipline for the sake of avoiding conflict or avoiding making their child sad. But this shows a lack of discipline in the parent, who looks only to the moment and does not consider the long-term future. It also shows selfishness, as the parent cares more for his or her own feelings at the moment than what is best for the child. The irony is that such a parent is working against himself. He is setting up his child to be a source of contention and anguish over the years. If he truly values rest and wants to delight in his child, he will discipline himself to exercise fair, consistent discipline with his child.

Prophetic Vision

Proverbs 29:18

Where there is no prophetic vision the people cast off restraint,
  but blessed is he who keeps the law.

The prophetic vision is the word of the Lord given to instruct people what God requires of them, as well as giving knowledge about himself and his promises. When there is no such word, people will naturally do what is "right in their own eyes." There are no warnings by which to restrain their behavior. There are no promises to motivate them to do what is right. There is no instruction to give them understanding as to what is right and wrong.

To give such a word was the role of the prophet – from Moses to Nathan to Elisha. But it was also the role of Aaron the priest, of David the king, and of Ezra the scribe. They exercised their role not in receiving new revelation, but by carrying out, enforcing, and teaching the prophetic word, which once given became the law.

As this proverb points out, a people need prophetic vision. They need revelation from God to know him and to obey him. But they also need the will to obey. And so they need prophet to reveal the vision, priest to enact the vision, ruler to enforce the vision, and teacher to instruct on its full implications. And they need to become the keepers of that law. Such a people will be blessed.

We are such a people in Christ. For Jesus Christ is the Word revealed; he is the prophet who presented the vision; he is the priest who carried out his own visionary sacrifice; he is the king who now enforces his word; and he is the teacher who explained his visionary work. Now he calls on us to be a people who keep his commandments. Let us do so today.

Necessary Discipline

Proverbs 29:19

By mere words a servant is not disciplined,
  for though he understands, he will not respond.

There are those with a slave mentality who take opportunity to slouch on the job and steal from their employers and fellow workers. Such persons do not respond to instruction or to reasoning. Rebuking them has no effect. Their problem is not a lack of understanding or the need for more training. Their problem is that they are lazy and self-serving. Then, to defend their behavior, they complain about too hard of work given, bad conditions, and unfair treatment. Teachers see this in certain students, as well.

Again, to reason with them will not suffice, for they do not want to work. Thus, discipline is needed. They cannot be reasoned with nor motivated positively. Because they are self-centered, they will at least avoid the negative consequences of punishment.

Wisdom is then required to discern what is effective with different persons. We are a society of second and third and fourth chances. It is good to keep trying with individuals who are troubled, but we must be careful not to harm them by withholding discipline. A lazy person is headed for disaster if he is never allowed to be disciplined or receive consequences for his behavior. If we keep giving chance after chance to change without consequences, we reinforce in his mind that he deserves his good opportunities that come without having to work.

Hasty in Speech

Proverbs 29:20

Do you see a man who is hasty in his words?
  There is more hope for a fool than for him.

This is a harsh indictment against a person "hasty in his words," considering the low opinion the proverbs have for the fool. What is it that is so terrible about such a person?

He stirs up trouble. When a fool acts up, he mostly is holding himself up for derision. The person who speaks hastily stirs the water, causing others to become troubled. He makes a smart-aleck remark that cuts. He throws out an opinion that embarrasses. He draws a quick, false conclusion that slanders. He pretends to have knowledge that in truth is false and misleading. He is hasty with harsh words that wound and offend.

Thus, he continually offends and stirs up trouble. At least a fool is seen for a fool, and his behavior has limiting impact. The hasty speaker will likely be spotted for a fool but only after the trouble he has caused. And even when his reputation is established, his words remain offensive.

There is little hope for him because he does not connect the trouble with his tongue. He blames others for misunderstanding him, for being overly sensitive, for being judgmental and biased. Even if he does acknowledge the connection, he still does not curb himself. He accepts that he causes misunderstanding, but he "can't help himself." What he really wishes is to be accepted for who he is.

Meanwhile, he talks and talks and talks...

Fair Play

Proverbs 29:21

Whoever pampers his servant from childhood
will in the end find him his heir.

The final word of this proverb is difficult to translate. But the common understanding of all translators is that the pampering of a servant leads that servant to become spoiled. Instead of growing in devotion to his master, he becomes insolent. Indeed, the roles become reversed; the servant expects special treatment from the master. This is especially true if there are other servants who are not pampered. But then, there is the opposite problem of masters who are harsh with their servants, who in the end find such servants to be rebellious and surly.

What then is the answer? (And this applies, by the way, to all relationships in which one person is in a position of authority over another.) Paul gives the answer in Col. 4:1: "Masters, treat your slaves justly and fairly, knowing that you also have a Master in heaven."

The person in authority makes his mistake by either acting as though there is no leader-subordinate relationship and thus tries to be a mere friend, or he accentuates the leader-subordinate relationship, emphasizing the exercise of authority. His focus needs to be on justice and fairness. Each – the one in authority and the subordinate

– has a role to play and job to do. Ignoring the distinction between the two will only create misunderstanding as expectations are not met. One works under and for the other. That needs to be understood.

But all the more important, then, for the one in authority to treat the subordinate fairly by not being harsh, by giving clear direction, by making expectations understood, by rewarding in a fair manner good work, as well as disciplining in a fair manner. Fairness is the key concept here. You can harm the subordinate by being too harsh and by being indulgent. What is needed is fair play.

Man of Wrath

Proverbs 29:22

A man of wrath stirs up strife,
and one given to anger causes much transgression.

Anger is a particularly difficult vice to have because of its impact on others. People may laugh at or sympathize with a person struggling with various vices and sins, but they are offended by anger. In anger a person will lash out at others; he will say hurtful words or even physically strike. In anger he will scheme against others. In anger he will seek vengeance; he will intentionally stir up strife.

In anger he will commit other transgressions – lying, slandering, stealing, etc. Anger causes him to lose his ability to think straight. In anger he throws caution to the wind; he does not consider the consequences of his actions. In anger he harms the very persons he loves.

If you have a temper problem, make it your priority to deal with it. Seek the counsel of others. Get friends to hold you accountable. Examine your heart. Do whatever is necessary. It is the one sin you cannot hide, the one sin that will nullify all your good works and intentions. It is the sin that will plague you with broken relationships and hurt feelings that will cause others to mistrust you and to hold grievances against you.

Seek help.

High and Low

Proverbs 29:23

One's pride will bring him low,
  but he who is lowly in spirit will obtain honor.

The person of pride seeks to be exalted. He desires honor. He wants to be on top. That very desire which spurs him on is what will bring him low. The more we seek to exalt ourselves, the more likely we will be humbled.

There is the person who does not think of himself but rather seeks to promote the welfare of others and the glory of God. He thinks not about how he will be exalted but the good that he can accomplish. That very desire which spurs him on is what will lead to honor.

It is the same principle that Jesus expressed: "For whoever would save his life will lose it, but whoever loses his life for my sake and the gospel's will save it" (Mark 8:35). If we focus on ourselves – our pleasures, our pride, our security – we will lose the very things we crave, for nothing of this world is permanent or secure. If we focus on God – glorifying him, living for him and for his kingdom – we will obtain what is permanent, for what belongs of God is eternal and secure.

Seek first the kingdom of God, and whatever else is needed for your happiness and welfare will be provided by God, who is the only one who can carry through on his promises, and the only one whose regard truly matters.

The Cursed Life

Proverbs 29:24

The partner of a thief hates his own life;

528

he hears the curse, but discloses nothing.

The curse is possibly a legal pronouncement made in general against unknown lawbreakers or against witnesses who will not reveal the truth. Here is a person who has joined up with a thief as an accomplice of some kind. Either he has helped to commit the crime or knows about the crime. In either case, he keeps silent, allowing the criminal to go unpunished and the crime to be unresolved, even after a curse is invoked.

Does he think he will escape with impunity? Does he think to mock God, who is called upon by the invoker of the curse to bring about justice? If so, then he in truth acts as one who hates his own life, for he is condemning himself to judgment. He will live under the fear of being found out. If he has a conscience, it will plague him. And what awaits him after death is the final judgment that will expose all crimes and deliver perfect justice.

Perhaps this person joined up with the thief because he thought the thief to be clever. Perhaps he joined in out of fear of the thief. Perhaps he had in a moment of folly committed himself and feels that he cannot break his word. Whatever the case, he shows that he fears man more than God. The day will come when he will rue such a mix-up in whom to fear.

Fear of Man

Proverbs 29:25

The fear of man lays a snare,
but whoever trusts in the Lord is safe.

One would think that by fearing man, he could avoid the snares of man. But this proverb says that such fear actually lays a snare. How so? Isn't man dangerous? Does he not possess evil intention? It would seem prudent to have a healthy fear of those who can do harm.

The second line helps put the first into perspective. Yes, we should be wary of man, but that very caution should then turn us to the Lord to be our safeguard. But more to the point, we are to find our safety in living for the Lord and according to his commands for us. We often lose our focus on living for the Lord because of the fear of man – fear of what man thinks of us, fear of what man may do to us. We often swerve off the path of God's commands because of the same fear, not trusting God to safe-keep us. Keeping the commands of God and living for him is the prudent way of keeping safe.

Jesus' comments in Luke 12:4-7 serve as a commentary of this proverb:

> I tell you, my friends, do not fear those who kill the body, and after that have nothing more that they can do. But I will warn you whom to fear: fear him who, after he has killed, has authority to cast into hell. Yes, I tell you, fear him! Are not five sparrows sold for two pennies? And not one of them is forgotten before God. Why, even the hairs of your head are all numbered. Fear not; you are of more value than many sparrows.

The Face of the Ruler

Proverbs 29:26

Many seek the face of a ruler,
but it is from the LORD that a man gets justice.

We seek the help and favor of "rulers," those in position to see that we receive justice and favor, who will protect us from the wicked and the oppressor. We look for those who "have connections," who know those who can do something. Such connections can help and much depends on the favor of those in authority with means to help.

But remember, whatever such persons possess, they have received those things from the Lord to do his will. Even their hearts are under the power of the Lord. It is God who caused Pharaoh to show favor to Moses and to harden his heart against Moses, as well. It is God who creates the "connections," God who determines if the ruler will be in a good mood or poor one. It is God who controls the timing and even the "chance" circumstances. And it is God who gives you the words to say to the "ruler," who gives you discernment, who guides your very manner before the ruler so that he listens to you and grants your petition.

So, if you want justice, then go to the top and submit your petitions to the Lord who raises and brings down rulers, who alone carries out his will, who is your Father and cares for you. Seek the face of this Ruler.

Of Abomination and Abomination

Proverbs 29:27

An unjust man is an abomination to the righteous,
   but one whose way is straight is an abomination to the wicked.

We understand the first line. The unjust, who deceive, scheme, cheat, steal, and murder – of course they are an abomination. A whole justice system is set up to punish them. And certainly the righteous – those who follow the moral, straight path, who believe in fair play and who are bent on doing what is good and right – surely they would be antagonistic against the wicked.

But we fail to understand the very real antagonism that the unjust feel against the righteous. They are not so much angry that the righteous oppose them, but rather, they really do despise the ways of the righteous whom they regard as hypocrites. The unjust do have a code by which the strong and the clever exercise control over the weak and simple. They recognize that all humans have natural desires for power, for wealth, and to indulge their physical desires. They, thus, despise the righteous, who, in their minds, either are weak persons deluding themselves or practicing outright hypocrisy, using the public righteousness to hide their inner cravings and activities.

The unjust see themselves as bold men who are willing to take risks and endure the spite of others in order to indulge in their natural ambition for power and for pleasure. They see the righteous as rigid and frigid weaklings who oppose them out of secret envy or smallness of mind.

The unjust do not understand persons who delight in righteousness, who protect others against the unjust because they actually love their neighbors, who understand and value an inner code that exalts fair play and kindness. The unjust do not understand a self-denial that produces deeper and long-lasting reward. And the unjust certainly do not understand the freedom of a humble spirit that allows the righteous to promote the welfare of others, even to seek the reform of the unjust.

What Do We Know?

Proverbs 30:1-4

The words of Agur son of Jakeh. The oracle.

The man declares, I am weary, O God;
  I am weary, O God, and worn out.
Surely I am too stupid to be a man.
  I have not the understanding of a man.
I have not learned wisdom,
  nor have I knowledge of the Holy One.
Who has ascended to heaven and come down?
  Who has gathered the wind in his fists?
Who has wrapped up the waters in a garment?
  Who has established all the ends of the earth?
What is his name, and what is his son's name?
  Surely you know!

We enter into a new section of Proverbs, the last two chapters being the words of other sages. Chapter 30 presents the observations of Agur, son of Jakeh. He begins with an observation about man's ability (and himself) to uncover the secret knowledge of God. Compare his thoughts with those in Job 38:1-7.

> Then the LORD answered Job out of the whirlwind
> and said:

"Who is this that darkens counsel by words without knowledge?
Dress for action like a man;
　I will question you, and you make it known to me.

"Where were you when I laid the foundation of the earth?
　Tell me, if you have understanding.
Who determined its measurements—surely you know!
　Or who stretched the line upon it?
On what were its bases sunk,
　or who laid its cornerstone,
when the morning stars sang together
　and all the sons of God shouted for joy?

In brief, man cannot by reason nor by exploration know God truly. He can, through natural revelation, deduce some basic traits of God, but he cannot delve into the great mysteries. For that, divine revelation is needed. Without such revelation who could have begun to think of the Trinity? Who could have thought through his omniscience, omnipresence, and omnipotence? His eternal nature, his immutability? Who could have explored with depth his holiness, his justice, and his mercy? Who could have grasped grace?

And who could have anticipated and understood such love by which the divine Father sent the divine Son to die for his enemies, and then to adopt such enemies to be his children and be united with them through the divine Holy Spirit?

What divine revelation reveals is enough to overwhelm our powers of reason. What more is left out because we could not handle such mystery? What is given is enough for us to spend all our lives – even in eternity – contemplating and then living in response to. And let us begin by giving the answer to the last question of verse 4. It is God the Father and his son's name is Jesus Christ, our Lord and Savior. Give praise that our God has revealed such wondrous knowledge to us!

Every Word True

Proverbs 30:5-6

Every word of God proves true;
*   he is a shield to those who take refuge in him.*
Do not add to his words,
*   lest he rebuke you and you be found a liar.*

Every word proves true – every promise, every warning, every instruction. What we are commanded to do is to study every word in his Word. Because every word is true, we need to systematically study the Scriptures, not skipping over the portions that seem uninteresting and with no application. Because every word is true, our one intent is to understand what the words are teaching. We are to let the words determine what we are to learn; for if we do not, we will become guilty of adding to his words.

Such guilt works like this: I have a topic I am interested in, so I "search" the Scriptures finding verses that may have a word I am looking for or seem to speak to my topic. I then pull those verses out of their context and make them say what they do not actually mean. Thus one "health and wealth" preacher twisted 1 Corinthians 2:9 – "What no eye has seen, nor ear heard, nor the heart of man imagined, what God has prepared for those who love him" – to mean that God intends physical prosperity for those who love him. In its real context, the verse is a rebuke to those who prefer the wisdom of the world over the wisdom of the cross.

Or to take another example of a preacher who took the story of a sinful woman washing Jesus' feet (Luke 7ff), which teaches the mercy of God towards those who repent, to be a lesson that it is okay to cry. Or yet another example of a preacher taking the story of the paralytic being lowered through a roof to speak disapprovingly of people who damage other people's property.

Such addition to God's words will result in rebuke and the verdict that the speaker is a liar. For perverting God's Word – whether it be to contract scripture or misapply or misinterpret – is to add what is not true. We undoubtedly will make our mistakes in understanding, but let it not be because we will not submit ourselves to hearing whatever it is that God wants us to hear, and all because we have our own agenda.

Two Requests

Proverbs 30:7-9

Two things I ask of you;
deny them not to me before I die:
Remove far from me falsehood and lying;
give me neither poverty nor riches;
feed me with the food that is needful for me,
lest I be full and deny you
and say, "Who is the Lord?"
or lest I be poor and steal
and profane the name of my God.

If you were given two wishes to be granted, would these be the two you would choose – to be kept from committing falsehood and to be given only what is needed so that you would not be tempted to sin?

Truly this is a request coming out of wisdom; for it is the wise person who recognizes his moral frailty and dependence upon God to sanctify him and to "deliver me from evil." The best of us are prone to falsehood, and the one we are most likely to deceive is ourselves. The best of us have our prejudices and fears that keep us from hearing and accepting the whole truth, whether it be about God, ourselves, or others. To paraphrase the movie line: "[We] can't handle the truth."

Then there is the recognition of our susceptibility to temptation. If we have an abundance, we tend to take what we have for granted and to credit ourselves for what we have. Our religious fervor declines or we become like the Pharisee who turns religious faith into an opportunity for self-exaltation. If we are poor, we are likely to lose confidence in God and trust to our own means – even unethical means – to provide for ourselves. The real crime, then, becomes the disgrace we lend to God's name, because of being known as believing in him.

Recognition of such dangers as expressed here is not meant to lead us to be fearful, but, rather to turn to the Lord who alone can save us, preserve us, and lead us along his righteous path. It is meant to keep us from pride and false confidence in ourselves. It is meant to lead us to glorify God and to give him the due honor that is his alone.

Slander

Proverbs 30:10

Do not slander a servant to his master,
  lest he curse you and you be held guilty.

This is a warning to us not to be quick to get someone in trouble. We can slander by fabricating a lie; we can slander by exaggerating a supposed offense; we can slander by accurately telling what happened without considering the circumstances. We can be quick to slander when we ourselves are in a bad mood and are unforgiving; we can be quick to slander if our pride has been wounded; and we can be quick to slander to cover up our own guilt.

We can be quick to slander a "servant" because he is in a vulnerable position. He cannot get even; he has less standing, and his job security is on the line. By complaining to the "master," we have an easy means of attack without endangering ourselves. We let the master carry out our vengeance for us.

But let us be wary of the servant's curse. The proverb does not mean simply angry or profane words. Rather, the servant is calling upon God to bring justice against his offender. He may not have recourse to earthly justice, but he does have the ear of the Judge who sees all and weighs the human heart. No one gets away with anything. Let us remember that before we are quick to slander. If we have been ill-used, remember that God will provide justice, and, thus, we do not need to take sinful actions to get satisfaction. Don't be in position where another person must call upon God to get satisfaction against us.

There Are Those

Proverbs 30:11-14

There are those who curse their fathers
  and do not bless their mothers.
There are those who are clean in their own eyes
  but are not washed of their filth.
There are those—how lofty are their eyes,
  how high their eyelids lift!
There are those whose teeth are swords,
  whose fangs are knives,
to devour the poor from off the earth,
  the needy from among mankind.

We are given four observations of probably one type of person or generation. It is of the arrogant whose pride and self-absorption lead to spite and self-deceit. They despise their parents (and others in rightful authority) whom they regard as fools. They regard themselves as being clean, that is, without fault, while in truth they are most defiled. They look down upon everyone, whom they regard as lesser beings and fools. And they are especially severe with the poor and needy, which they despise precisely because of their poor position.

They only admire the powerful who are also ruthless, for they believe sincerely in the law of survival of the fittest. They despise their parents because of their parents' attempt to instill a moral code, which they regard as oppressive and unrealistic. Like the fool, they think they have life figured out, indeed, that they are among the few who understand the ruthlessness of life and the rules that one must play to survive and succeed.

And what is required to deal with them is a righteous use of discipline. For their problem is not a lack of education but a lack of goodness. We cannot change another's heart. We can curb the behavior, and we can point in the right direction, using reason and a charitable spirit. But what is truly needed is the work of the Holy Spirit. Therefore, pray for those whom you know following the path of arrogance. Pray for their being brought low, that they might recognize their poverty and folly, rise through humility, wash off their filth by the blood of Christ, and bless their fathers and mothers and everyone who persevered in pointing them along the path of God.

Craving

Proverbs 30:15-16

The leech has two daughters;
"Give" and "Give," they cry.
Three things are never satisfied;
four never say, "Enough":
Sheol, the barren womb,
the land never satisfied with water,
and the fire that never says, "Enough."

We are given vivid imagery of the spirit which is never satisfied. The impression being made is that such a spirit feels a true hunger that cannot be satiated, not so much out of greed but out of an inability to receive or maintain nourishment. This is made clear in the last three examples – the barren womb (that feels the emptiness of no child), the barren land (which would be the common condition in the Middle-east), and fire (which ceases to exist the moment its fuel runs out). They crave to receive, like the leech and his family that must have "blood" to survive. And so Sheol is represented. No matter how many dead it receives, it has an unending appetite for more. Again, their problem is not being greedy but being unable to benefit for long in what they receive.

The owner of such a spirit is pitiable. He craves for fulfillment but cannot attain it. Like the Teacher of Ecclesiastes, he explores the different ways to find it – in work, in pleasure, in entertainment, in riches. He may seek it by exploring philosophies and religions. He may try to find it in noble and sacrificial work. And at times he seems fulfilled, but then the craving comes again, only stronger. "Give, give," he cries.

The saddest position is when he cannot profit even from hearing the gospel. His heart does not possess the proper soil, because in his pursuit to find fulfillment through other means he has left his heart hardened and incapable of receiving the seed of the gospel. Like hardened barren land which cannot profit from the rain, so is his heart to the gospel.

Let us pray for our neighbors who are in such a state. Who crave for fulfillment and, yet, by the very means they seek to satisfy their cravings, they are hardening their hearts to make it all the more difficult to attain. Pray for them, that the Spirit will touch their spirits and satisfy them with the blessing of the gospel.

Dishonoring Parents

Proverbs 30:17

The eye that mocks a father
*   and scorns a mother*
will be picked out by the ravens of the valley
*   and eaten by the vultures.*

Disrespect of one's parents clearly is not a modern phenomenon. This is the second time in chapter 30 that the matter has been raised (see v. 11). There is the tendency of youth and, perhaps more so, of adult children to denigrate their parents. Among youth there is the natural tendency to assert independence, and that often comes through questioning one's parents. Nor is it unusual for youth to resist what they feel are restraints on their instincts for pleasure and acceptance among their peers.

It is the adult child, having never grown out of that youthful attitude, who is most troubling. As he grows into adulthood, he should be learning the trials and temptations that have beset his parents, thus making him more understanding of whatever defects they possess. He should be learning from his own failures the frailty of the human spirit and so identifying with his parents as fellow sinners needing grace.

Bless your parents; honor them by doing whatever is for their good. Act according to the principle of grace and not out of your hurts. Perhaps you cannot help them (though you have more of a chance to do so than if you act out of resentment and pride). But what is really at stake is your heart. Do not let it be filled with pride; do not let scorn come to life in it.

The Way

Proverbs 30:18-20

Three things are too wonderful for me;
    four I do not understand:
the way of an eagle in the sky,
    the way of a serpent on a rock,
the way of a ship on the high seas,
    and the way of man with a virgin.

This is the way of an adulteress:
    she eats and wipes her mouth
    and says, "I have done no wrong."

The proverb contemplates the mystery and grace of "ways." There is the graceful flight of the eagle in the sky, moving its way through the air and the winds seemingly with ease. There is the serpent without legs sliding along easily over rock. There is the way of the small ship navigating over high waves. And then there is the way of the "man with a virgin" – the way of a man wooing a maiden or a husband intimate with his new bride, a picture of the mystery of love that brings physical intimacy.

These "ways" have sacredness about them as one contemplates the physics and the beauty about them. How repugnant, then, it shows the way of an adulteress, who treats sex as nothing more than having a meal. The eagle is nothing more than a bird flapping its wings, the snake a wiggly creature, the ship but a boat floating on water, and the man with a maiden – well, that is nothing more than a man giving way to lust. There is no mystery, no beauty, no sacredness; there is just creatures getting around and carrying out their instinct. Nothing is good, nothing is bad; the "ways" are simply creatures going through the motion.

The adulteress can make a decent living with such an attitude. So can anyone doing what they do merely for the profit. But what they lose is their soul, their ability to see mystery, to sense the sacred, and ultimately to know real joy.

Trembling Occasions

Proverbs 30:21-23

Under three things the earth trembles;
*   under four it cannot bear up:*
a slave when he becomes king,
*   and a fool when he is filled with food;*
an unloved woman when she gets a husband,
*   and a maidservant when she displaces her mistress.*

In our modern democratic age, we might take issue with this proverb. Our stories of success are the very things held up here as troubling. We admire the slave who overcomes his circumstances to become king. We may not admire the fool but at least appreciate the wit he uses to get his food. Is not the story of an unloved woman finding a husband who loves her romantic? And as for the maidservant, we think of the servant girl mistreated by the arrogant mistress who lives out a Cinderella story and displaces the mean mistress. Indeed, we regard all these instances as Cinderella stories.

But here is what the proverb is speaking about. It looks at the slave who by devious means obtains the throne, which his ignoble spirit demeans. The fool should be receiving what he needs – discipline, and yet through the folly of life gets rewarded for his foolish behavior. The unloved woman is not one who has found a husband to love her; rather, she is unloved because of her own critical, unloving ways, and woe to the man who is forced or beguiled into marrying her. And as to the maidservant, like the slave she has used deceit and probably her sexual prowess to displace her mistress.

Cinderella stories are nice, and it is good to see those who are good and who possess noble spirits rise above their circumstances. But for all such stories, there are many others in which the wicked and the ignoble have used evil means to displace those who are in rightful places of authority and circumstances that befit their character. Such ignoble persons turn noble positions into opportunity to bully. The slave bullies all those for whom he holds perceived offenses, raising the wicked to power and humbling the noble. The unloved woman turns the role of help-meet into opportunity to bully her husband. The handmaiden as mistress struts arrogantly before the household. And the fool feels like a clever man because his stomach is full.

Small and Yet...

Proverbs 30:24-28

Four things on earth are small,
*   but they are exceedingly wise:*
the ants are a people not strong,
*   yet they provide their food in the summer;*
the rock badgers are a people not mighty,
*   yet they make their homes in the cliffs;*
the locusts have no king,
*   yet all of them march in rank;*
the lizard you can take in your hands,
*   yet it is in kings' palaces.*

Observe nature and learn. We are quick to blame our failure to succeed on a defect that gives us decided disadvantage. "I am too small to go against big opponents." "I am not strong enough for the work." "I am not smart enough; I don't have the education needed."

The examples given from nature in this proverb all have disadvantages. They are small and thus could not survive a fight with a larger opponent. They are weak and could not lift heavy objects. But where they are small in comparison to other creatures and weak in comparison to the task required, they are nevertheless wise to overcome their supposed weakness, even to turn their weakness into their strength.

The ant and the locust are wise enough to work as a group so that the ant more than provides for himself, and the locust becomes even a fearful adversary. The rock badger, as small as he may be, uses his size and ability to dwell in impregnable fortresses in the cliffs. The tiny lizard, which is regarded as common and unclean, is able to live in palaces precisely because of his size.

Even in sports, where talent is matched against talent, the less talented athlete often emerges as victor because he uses his wits to outsmart his competitor, even to make the competitor's greater talent a liability.

The battle belongs not so much to the strong but to the wise and to the great of heart. Determination, matched with wit, is powerful in both the large and the small. Do not let your "small defect" determine what you can and cannot do. Do not be quick to give in to your weakness. Turn, rather, to the strengths you have. You do not know what they are? Then use your wit to find out. You have more wisdom than you know. All you need to do is observe. Observe nature; observe what goes on about you; observe yourself. It will not be long before you learn and profit from what you see.

The Noble

Proverbs 30:29-31

Three things are stately in their tread;
four are stately in their stride:
the lion, which is mightiest among beasts
and does not turn back before any;
the strutting rooster, ☐ the he-goat,
and a king whose army is with him.

They feel a sense of nobility who feel confident in their position. The lion by virtue of his strength and size; the rooster who protects his hens; the he-goat who heads the rest of the flock; and the king who possesses might – each of these carry with them an air of nobleness which comes from their sense of confidence or security. And that noble bearing has the added effect of increasing their courage so that when a threat comes upon them, they will defend the den, territory, or home for which they are responsible.

These examples before us are not viewed for their aggressiveness. Even the lion is not depicted as an aggressor but as one who will "not turn back from any" who threatens. He is king wherever he walks, not fearing an attack. Likewise a king with his army: he need not fear. Rather, he and the lion and the rooster and the he-goat may be attentive to their responsibility to watch over and protect those under them.

Thus, they do not walk about in a hulking manner trying to intimidate anyone they meet. They are not bullies who feel that they have something to prove or who are mean-spirited. They are strong but strong with the knowledge of their responsibility. That is what makes them noble even if they are no more than a rooster or a goat.

And you? Does responsibility ennoble you or debilitate you? Does power fill you with a sense of responsibility to exercise it wisely and for good purpose, or does it lessen your sense to care for the weak and any under your authority? Whether you are a mighty lion or a strutting rooster, a king with an army or a he-goat with a flock, it is the spirit of your inner being that ultimately determines whether your outward bearing is noble or ignoble.

Pressing Anger

Proverbs 30:32-33

If you have been foolish, exalting yourself,
or if you have been devising evil,
put your hand on your mouth.
For pressing milk produces curds,
pressing the nose produces blood,
and pressing anger produces strife.

The surest mark of a fool is his boasting. He betrays his folly and his ego through exalting himself – exaggerating his deeds, putting himself above others, drawing attention to himself, delighting in the abasement of others. Such is folly and evil. The remedy for such boorish behavior is to stop speaking. It is better to be silent than to reveal one's foolishness; it is better to hold one's tongue than to use it to produce strife, which is the point of verse 33.

The effect of such speech is compared to the act of physical pressing. Such pressure on an object forces it into another mode. Pressing milk through a strainer produces curds. We may think such pressure, then, to be good, but the image of pressing the nose reminds us of the negative point.

Walk into a room where there is already some tension. Begin to boast. The result will be anger pressed into outward strife. There will be anger expressed against you, anger against others in the room, anger against whatever seems to be a cause for grievance.

In life, there is always an element of tension, however happy the occasion may be. We are sinners, and so there is always in us a readiness to be angry. Sin is all about us and has impacted us, and so there is always a cause to get angry. Anyone can mar a happy occasion, and the easiest manner is to exalt oneself as the expense of another. Someone will get offended. Someone will make a remark or express a facial disapproval. The boasting will press inner anger so that it comes out in strife. All the reason then to control one's tongue. It is better not to be thought of at all than to receive such attention that produces strife.

The Role of a Ruler

Proverbs 31:1-9

The words of King Lemuel. An oracle that his mother taught him:

What are you doing, my son? What are you doing, son of my womb?
What are you doing, son of my vows?
Do not give your strength to women,

your ways to those who destroy kings.
It is not for kings, O Lemuel,
  it is not for kings to drink wine,
  or for rulers to take strong drink,
lest they drink and forget what has been decreed
  and pervert the rights of all the afflicted.
Give strong drink to the one who is perishing,
  and wine to those in bitter distress;
let them drink and forget their poverty
  and remember their misery no more.
Open your mouth for the mute,
  for the rights of all who are destitute.
Open your mouth, judge righteously,
  defend the rights of the poor and needy.

A ruler is placed in his position for the purpose of serving those under him, judging righteously, and defending the rights of everyone, especially those who are vulnerable to oppression. As such, he is to see his advantageous position of power and wealth as a responsibility to all the more act soberly and maintain integrity, both of which these very possessions dangerously tempt him to lose.

Power corrupts. It leads to arrogance. It takes the powerful man and breaks him so that he has no power to control his sin and folly. The same is true with wealth. It also corrupts him, weakening his moral resolve. It attracts leeches who gather around to suck his money and favor. And when the two are combined in the life of a ruler, the results can be devastating for himself and for all who are under him.

Note the two likely temptations – drink and sex. The ruler not only has to restrain his own lusts, but he has to resist those who would try to foist these things upon him, for they desire to see him give way because of the advantages they receive – namely, to get his money and his favors.

The ruler – and the ruler may be a government official or a boss or some other kind of leader – must keep before him the high responsibility of his position. It is for doing good not for gaining personal advantage. The one who understands his purpose and keeps to it is one who obtains nobility. The one who gives into the lusts his position can afford becomes a slave to others and a tyrant over those whom he should be serving.

Give thanks for our Ruler Jesus Christ who resisted all temptation and kept his eyes on the purpose of his calling.

An Excellent Model

Proverbs 31:10-12

An excellent wife who can find?
  She is far more precious than jewels.
The heart of her husband trusts in her,
  and he will have no lack of gain.
She does him good, and not harm,
  all the days of her life.

Proverbs, which presents lesson after lesson about the way of wisdom and righteousness, closes by presenting the example of a wife living such a way. She embodies the attributes of wisdom, also depicted as a woman in chapters 3, 8, and 9. As wisdom is declared to be more precious than jewels in 3:15, so is an excellent wife. As a man may trust in wisdom and profit from her, knowing that good comes from her, so a husband may trust the wise and righteous wife.

Many women are praised for their appearance, and, indeed, many men choose wives for that reason alone. But it is the inner spirit that she possesses which is of true worth, as this chapter will show. And the excellent wife serves as a model for us all – male or female, married or single. For it is God's purpose that we all be "excellent." We all should be such persons who can be trusted, who do good all our days.

May there be those who know us who can say, "an excellent wife/husband/parent/ friend/boss/teacher/coach" – whatever our status – may we be praised because we have taken the proverbs we have read and applied them to our lives.

Productive Work

Proverbs 31:13-19

She seeks wool and flax,
  and works with willing hands.
She is like the ships of the merchant;
  she brings her food from afar.
She rises while it is yet night
  and provides food for her household
  and portions for her maidens.
She considers a field and buys it;
  with the fruit of her hands she plants a vineyard.
She dresses herself☐ with strength
  and makes her arms strong
She perceives that her merchandise is profitable.
  Her lamp does not go out at night.
She puts her hands to the distaff,
  and her hands hold the spindle.

What is the excellent wife like? She is industrious. She works with willing hands, making good use of her time to provide food and be productive. How different she is from the sloth who declares, "There is a lion in the street!" and so does not get out of bed.

And so she is a model for us. How do you use your time? Are you productive? Are you able at the end of the day to look back with satisfaction at the work you have done? For work – productive work – is good. The work will be based on your circumstances. You may be delivering products or making products. You may be teaching or doing manual labor. You may be raising children or being a student. Whatever the case, you are using your time wisely so as to be productive.

Again, your circumstances affect what productivity may mean for you. If your health is poor, if you are limited with a disability, if restrictions have been placed around you, you may not be able to accomplish what you could otherwise. But still, you cannot avoid the question of whether you have used what you have to be productive, even if that productivity is doing what you can to heal or to maintain your strength.

What about rest? There is a place for rest and for recreation. However, unlike the pop philosophy of today which says that we work in order to rest and "have fun," the wisdom of the proverbs teaches that rest and recreation are meant to restore us to work productively. Productive work itself is pleasurable. Productive work is what gives a person a true sense of being valuable, of having a purpose. And it is feeling that the work one does has a purpose, which gives the person joy in living even through the most difficult circumstances.

Good Purpose

Proverbs 31:20-27

She opens her hand to the poor
and reaches out her hands to the needy.
She is not afraid of snow for her household,
for all her household are clothed in scarlet.
She makes bed coverings for herself;
her clothing is fine linen and purple.
Her husband is known in the gates
when he sits among the elders of the land.
She makes linen garments and sells them;
she delivers sashes to the merchant.
Strength and dignity are her clothing,
and she laughs at the time to come.
She opens her mouth with wisdom,
and the teaching of kindness is on her tongue.
She looks well to the ways of her household
and does not eat the bread of idleness.

The woman of wisdom engages in productive work for good purposes. Many people are productive so that they may enjoy wealth for themselves. Many work hard so that they can attain fame, wealth, and power for themselves. The wise woman works that she may help the poor and needy; that she may provide for her household. She is a blessing to her husband. Furthermore, her good work is not limited to the ability of her hands, but she teaches with wisdom; she teaches others what she has learned, what it is to be kind; she teaches the joy of doing good for others.

Do you work with the right motivation? Do you work so that you might bless others through your productivity? Are you kind? Do those who work with you or for you attest to the good spirit in which you work and treat them? Is your family blessed by your work – both in benefitting from your productivity and in being touched by the spirit in which you labor for them? Can your family trust you to provide, whether that provision be income or managing the home? Can people who depend on you know that you will come through for them, and that you will do so with a kind spirit? Such is the model that the excellent wife presents for us.

The Fear of the Lord

Proverbs 31:28-31

Her children rise up and call her blessed;
*   her husband also, and he praises her:*
"Many women have done excellently,
*   but you surpass them all."*
Charm is deceitful, and beauty is vain,
*   but a woman who fears the LORD is to be praised.*
Give her of the fruit of her hands,
*   and let her works praise her in the gates.*

In the praise of the wife by her husband and children, we learn the real source of her virtues. She is a person "who fears the Lord." And so the end of Proverbs leads us back to the beginning: "The fear of the Lord is the beginning of knowledge" (1:7).

Do you desire to possess the wisdom of Proverbs? Then fear the Lord. You may study philosophy; you may gain much experience; you may learn from many wise people. But if you do not fear the Lord, you remain a common fool.

For the Lord is your Maker. You exist and continue to be sustained in life by him. He has made you for himself – to glorify him. To live without this knowledge is to live in ignorance and without purpose.

And the Lord is the one Redeemer. Others may save you from foolish choices and from wicked people, but only the Lord can save you from your sinfulness. To live "wisely" in this world and yet die in your sinful state is the greatest folly of all. Only the Lord Jesus Christ can save you from such a fate.

As we have learned from Proverbs, the Lord will judge the wicked. Because he is righteous and just, he will not let sin go unpunished. As we have learned, he sees everyone and everything. Fear the Lord.

Fear the Lord and know the joy of that fear. For it brings blessing. It lifts one's eyes to the glories of God; it puts our lives in true perspective so that we see God's holiness and majesty which humbles us. It then fills us with the wonder of God's mercy and love. And so we are then moved and enabled to live wisely as this excellent wife. And so we are to know even the more amazing praise that will be given us from the Lord whom we fear on the Day of his return – "Well done, good and faithful servant... Enter into the joy of your Master" (Matt. 25:21).

Author Information

D. Marion Clark is a pastor in the Presbyterian Church in America. Sermons and writings may be accessed at www.dmcresources.com. He may be contacted at mg79clark@yahoo.com.

Made in the USA
Charleston, SC
13 March 2017